EDWARD SAID

EDWARD SAID

Criticism and Society

———————◆———————

ABDIRAHMAN A. HUSSEIN

VERSO
London · New York

First published by Verso 2002
© Abdirahman A. Hussein 2002

1 3 5 7 9 10 8 6 4 2

Verso
UK: 6 Meard Street, London WIF 0EG
USA: 180 Varick Street, New York, NY 10014-4606
www.versobooks.com

Verso is the imprint of New Left Books

ISBN 1-85984-670-X

British Library Cataloguing in Publication Data
A catalogue record for this book is available from the British Library

Library of Congress Cataloging-in-Publication Data
A catalog record for this book is available from the Library of Congress

Typeset in Garamond 10/12 by YHT Ltd, London
Printed and bound in Great Britain
by Biddles Ltd, Guildford and King's Lynn
www.biddles.co.uk

Contents

Acknowledgments

This study was completed with generous financial help from the A. M. Qattan Foundation. The grant was originally meant to cover my expenses in the United States during what was to have been a one-year sabbatical (1997–98) from Kuwait University but instead turned out to be a much longer hiatus. I am profoundly grateful to Abdul Mohsen Al Qattan, the founder of the foundation, both for the financial support and for the understanding he showed as the project fell behind schedule. I also wish to express my gratitude to Ismail el-Zabri and Mohamed K. Mohamed for their unwavering commitment to the project over the years. At a time when it seemed to me almost impossible to take the project off the ground, Ismail and Mohamed came to the rescue, assuring me that it could – and had to – be done. That initial encouragement tremendously boosted my morale – as did the support they gave (and the confidence they had in) me in subsequent years, as the project dragged on for what seemed like an eternity. I am particularly appreciative of the fact that both of them helped me secure this grant.

I have also incurred debts to a large number of other people, including friends ready with help and encouragement, and scholars who suggested ways of improving the study. The project began in the early 1990s as my PhD dissertation in the English Department of the University of Tennessee. To the original members of the dissertation committee – George Hutchinson, Ron Baxter Miller, and Christine Holmlund – I offer my sincere thanks. Over the years, other faculty members and graduate students have commented on various drafts of the study: John Zomchick, Charlie Biggs, Mary Moss, James Gill, and Thomas Heffernan provided valuable suggestions that no doubt saved me from embarrassing mistakes. My warmest thanks to all of them.

Outside the University of Tennessee, Christopher Norris and Barbara Harlow greatly energized me with their encouragement when I inflicted several chapters of the old dissertation on them.

And then there is Allen Dunn, the director of the dissertation. Allen is one of those rare individuals who have the capacity to combine erudition, rigor, modesty, and caring in equal measure. I have been extremely fortunate to have benefited from all of these qualities – first as a student and advisee of Allen's, later as a resident research scholar. Without his constant guidance and insight, this project might never have amounted to anything. I am also fortunate to count Allen as a member of a small number of valued friends whose generosity I can hardly find words to express: Allen, Mary Papke, Mary Moss, Charlie Biggs, Laura Howes, John Hodges, Abe Kuhang, and Allen Carroll (in Knoxville), and Linda Sue (in Kuwait) – these wonderful friends have, over the past several years, extended unstinting moral and material support at a time when I needed it most. But for them, this study would not have been completed. I owe them more than I can ever repay in word or deed.

I also extend my sincere thanks to Professor Edward Said for his interest and encouragement. I corresponded with Professor Said several times over the years, and each time he (or his secretary) promptly sent me the bibliographical and other material that I requested. The telephone conversations have also been wonderfully exhilarating.

Finally, I am profoundly obliged to Mrs Jan McGuire, who has typed and retyped what must have seemed to her countless drafts of this study. Her great patience and wonderful sense of humor helped her survive both my inscrutable handwriting and my incurable addiction to revisions. Hats off to her!

Introduction

> My background is a series of displacements and expatriations which cannot be recuperated. The sense of being between cultures has been very, very strong for me. I would say that's the single strongest strand running through my life: the fact that I'm always in and out of things, and never really of anything for long.
>
> — Edward Said, Interview with Imre Salusinszky

One of the most challenging problems to be confronted by interpreters of Edward Said's large, seemingly disparate body of writing concerns the issue of methodology. Any commentator on him is bound to pose questions like these to himself or herself: how does one approach a critic whose interest ranges from intellectual history to current affairs, from philosophical to journalistic discourse? Granted that Said (on his own admission) thrives on creative, often strategically selective eclecticism, is it possible – or even desirable – to demarcate the different, sometimes incompatible tributaries of modern thought that have contributed to forming his ideas? Can one isolate the phenomenological moment from the poststructuralist moment or tell the Vichian insight from the Foucauldian? Exactly how does one come to terms, between the covers of a single study, with all the topics – large and small – that Said has addressed in his various texts? Is it possible to discover a common denominator between, for example, the rarefied, literary-philosophical themes treated in *Beginnings*, on the one hand, and the public, hotly contested political issues discussed in *The Question of Palestine*, on the other? Is there a non-episodic, theoretically cogent way of relating these two texts (or any others for that matter) – a way of explicating them so that they illuminate each other while each maintains its own integrity? How does one adjudicate between the different levels of generality or between the divergent rhetorical modes? Given that Said often conjoins in the same sentence or paragraph – and examples of this type of critical practice can be found in any one of his texts – epistemological with ethical concerns, materialist constructions with speculative leaps, or existentialist self-definitions with broad socio-political matters, given this lack of respect for traditional boundaries between genres, modes of inquiry, and areas of intellectual combat, what grid or criterion does one use and to what specific interpretive end?

Apropos of all these problematics, how does one engage the large number of (often seemingly unrelated) debates that Said's works have generated – or at least considerably intensified – over the past two decades? Is it possible to revisit directly all the debates about culture and identity; about canon-formation and exclusionary knowledge; about intellectuals and collusion with power; or about critical consciousness, methodology, and hegemony – and revisit them in such a way that a neat synthesis or resolution can be effected? Given Said's well-known aversion to resolutions or syntheses, should these be considered as desired goals at all?

In considering these and similar questions, most critics have found it necessary to use the notion of boundary or in-betweenness as an almost self-evident point of purchase from which to draw various implications. Hence in discussions of Said's oeuvre – by, for example, Bruce Robbins, James Clifford, and Abdul R. JanMohamed – it is not uncommon to come across words like "ambivalence," "vacillation," "neutrality," "contradiction," "paradox." Sometimes this Saidian strategy is glossed in positive ways – as a sign of subtlety, reflexivity, self-transcendence, or impatience with received dogmas. In his important article, "Homelessness and Worldliness," Robbins – though not entirely uncritical – interprets what he calls Said's (Foucault-inspired?) "amoralism," off-centeredness, and neutrality as being generally commendable critical attitudes.[1] Daniel O'Hara is less reserved in his praise for what he considers to be Said's mediating, insightful capacity and his commitment to the most positive values that literary and cultural criticism can offer.[2] Other critics – for example, JanMohamed – consider this fascination with in-between zones an indication of passivity and self-limitation.[3] Oftentimes, the criticism becomes much sharper – as when James Clifford characterizes Said's "ambivalence" about what constitutes Orientalism as a "confusion" between several incompatible designations.[4] One of Said's severest critics, Aijaz Ahmad, has gone so far as to claim that Said's (tendentious?) eclecticism leads to various species of inflation, conflation, and misconstruction.[5] A similar line of attack has been adopted by Mahdi Amil.[6]

A fairly common interpretation of Said's ability to go "in and out of things" (to use his own phrase) turns on the theme of exile. Even though Said himself implicitly acknowledges that he has been more fortunate than the vast majority of Palestinians,[7] who have been made either literal camp-dwelling refugees or strangers in their own homeland, there is no doubting the enormous impact the flight from Palestine in the late 1940s had on him. The state of being in exile (*ghurba* or *manfa* in Arabic) – the loss of home and hearth, of a nurturing tradition, of the cultural horizons associated with continuity and rootedness – this state of dispossession and banishment to which an entire people has been condemned, together with the remarkable resourcefulness summoned by this deracination, this acute awareness of ferociously enforced "displacements and expatriations which cannot be recuperated," has invited Said's attention with unusual though understandable urgency. It has occasioned some of the most memorable passages to be found anywhere in his varied writing – such as this one from *After the Last Sky*:

> Since our history is forbidden, narratives are rare; the story of origins, of home, of nation is underground. When it appears it is broken, often wayward and meandering in the extreme, always coded, usually in outrageous forms – mock-epics, satires, sardonic parables, absurd rituals – that make little sense to an outsider. Thus Palestinian life is scattered, discontinuous, marked by the artificial and imposed arrangements of interrupted or confined space, by the dislocations and unsynchronized rhythms of disturbed time.[8]

Said's ongoing, variously nuanced reflections on the Palestinian diaspora, in which his own dispersed family participated, are therefore in a literal sense an exercise in the denial of denial, an attempt to transmute decreed silence into, as he puts it, "permission to narrate."[9] It is for this reason that a fairly large number of commentators – among them Bruce Robbins, Mustapha Ben T. Marrouchi, Asha Varadharajan, and Ella Shohat[10] – have ascribed Said's remarkable ability to transmute ideas or cross boundaries to that enormously wrenching experience. Indeed a recent book-length study of Said's postcolonial writings, Bill Ashcroft's and Pal Ahluwalia's *Edward Said: The Paradox of Identity*,[11] is largely premised on Said's alleged need to construct an identity of sorts in the unavoidable reality of exile.

A Technique of Trouble: Dialectical Subversion and Archaeo-genealogy

My own study unfolds over an intellectual space cleared by all these scholars, as well as others too numerous to name here. As such, it is intended as both an expansion and a refinement of some of their insights. It is, however, also proposed as a substantial corrective to some of the more extravagant claims made about Said's career. More specifically, I want to suggest a broad methodological reconception of Said's career as a whole – a reconception without which it would be difficult not only to make insightful statements about the issue of borders but also to appreciate the full range and complexity of his thought. My thesis is that, at its metacritical or infrastructural level, Said's intellectual project is guided, often explicitly but sometimes as a presumed backcloth, by what could best be described as "a technique of trouble" (to use Said's own Blackmurrian metaphor for Michel Foucault's methodology).[12] Marked by both eccentricity and difficulty, this technique of extremes involves an activated confrontation between agonistic dialectic and archaeology/genealogy. By "eccentricity" and "difficulty" I mean that Said is deliberately countering what he considers to be normalized methodological attitudes and frames by de-defining, derailing, and dismantling their conceptual armor and by generally challenging the ideologically enhanced values derived from them; another way of formulating this point is to say that he subjects received wisdom both to left-handed theoretical and historical insight and to what might be called the controlled anarchism of critical consciousness. At a broad level, therefore, his "methodology" is manifestly dramatic, immanent, and open-ended; but it is also carefully – one might say choreographically – maneuvered through the concrete realities of contested knowledge systems and historical topographies.

At a more specific level, the dialectical and archaeo-genealogical "moments" each add a distinctive flavor and inflection to the methodological drama: with respect to the former, Said often directly reflects on the implications of an extreme double-bind, which he sometimes calls an "either/or" transaction;[13] the unusually persistent, though by no means easy, pendular swings of this dialectic throw into sharp relief (without, however, resolving) the multiple dilemmas of modern critical consciousness as he sees it. That is to say, for example, the tensive transactions between a given writer and his/her imaginative universe, between the mnemonic and the volitional dimensions of the mind, between methodology and critical intelligence, between the autonomous self and its socio-cultural horizons, between one historical moment and another, between the material preponderance of written language and humanity's desire for transcendence: these and similar aspects of dialectical reflection have been utilized by Said both as occasions for eccentric interpretation and as unstated but important presuppositions.

But precisely because the either/or transaction is conflictual and therefore involves an extraordinarily difficult negotiation, it instantiates a multiplicity of disjunctions, torsions, and oppositions that have the capacity to induce a state of vertiginal intellection. In other words, the "form" or "shape" assumed by this double-bind – the vectors of its movement; the contours of its topography; the points of contact or intersection, of limitation or pressure; the nodes of growth, depreciation, or transformation, etc. – does not manifest itself as a relatively smooth, predictable, and straightforward sublation, à la Hegel or Marx. To phrase the point differently, the agonism of this dialectic should be understood not just in existential terms but also (and this is ultimately of far greater import for Said's critical project as a whole) in logical, epistemological, historical, and ethico-political terms. The implication is that if (in Said's own lights) "a critical consciousness worthy of its name"[14] meditates on the expansive freedoms and enormous burdens brought in the wake of modernity, it will find dialectical reflection as such at once impossible and unavoidable – giving rise as much to an intense awareness of crisis as to an (almost) irresolvable paradox: the onset of dialectical thinking itself also locks into place a mechanism of resistance that neutralizes any possibility of synthesis or resolution. It should also be immediately clear that, as a result of the high premium Said places on dramatic confrontation, the idea of socio-historical totality (an idea central to both Hegelian and Marxian conceptions of dialectic) is altogether ruled out. Instead Said draws attention to multiple processes, rifts, tensions, and juxtapositions.

The most cogent summational statement in Said's oeuvre on this dialectical agonism that I know of can be found in the final paragraph of "Travelling Theory Reconsidered," a late revisionary article:

[W]hen Adorno uses Lukacs to understand Schoenberg's place in the history of music, or when Fanon dramatized the colonial struggle in the language of the manifestly European subject–object dialectic, we don't think of them simply coming after Lukacs, using him at a belated second degree, so to speak, but rather as pulling him from one sphere or region into another. This movement suggests the possibility of actively different locales, sites, situations for theory, without facile universalism or over-general totalizing. One would not, could not, want to assimilate Viennese twelve-tone music to the Algerian resistance to French Colonialism: the disparities are too grotesque even to articulate. But in both situations, each so profoundly and concretely felt by Adorno and Fanon respectively, is the fascinating Lukacsian figure, present both as travelling theory and as intransigent practice. To speak here only of borrowing and adaptation is not adequate. There is in particular an intellectual, and perhaps moral, community of a remarkable kind, *affiliation* in the deepest and most interesting sense of the word. As a way of getting seriously past the weightlessness of one theory after another, the remorseless indignations of orthodoxy, and the expressions of tired advocacy to which we are often submitted, the exercise involved in figuring out where the theory went and how in getting there its fiery core was reignited is invigorating – and is also another voyage, one that is central to intellectual life in the late twentieth century.[15]

The passage is imbued with what Said has elsewhere characterized (in reference especially to Adorno) as the style of lateness – a given thinker's meditation on the fact that a productive career is in its absolutely final, terminal stage.[16] As the title makes clear, Said is in a manner of speaking rereading one of his earlier articles, "Traveling Theory," more than ten years after its publication. Both the important original article (more about which in the fourth chapter of my study) and its later reconsideration respond to this question: what happens to a radical theory (in this case Lukacs's theory of bourgeois reification and the opposing revolutionary consciousness of the proletariat) when it travels from its place of birth to very different times and places? My citing of the passage here is intended, not only to show that Said – in keeping with his crucial concepts of beginning and repetition – often revists and radicalizes his own earlier critical positions, but also to illustrate the extent to which dialectical agonism has served as a powerful theoretical engine throughout his career. With the exception of a few perceptive critics (among them Daniel O'Hara and Asha Varadharajan), Said's many interlocutors have virtually ignored the dialectical dimension of his writing. Yet, as I try do demonstrate throughout my analysis, his interest in dialectical agonism lies behind studies of such conservative writers as Conrad, Swift, and Eliot, as well as radical thinkers like Lukacs, Williams, Gramsci, and Adorno. It should be stressed at this point that Said almost always associates the assimilative, synthesizing version of dialectical thinking with the consolidations of ideology – for example, in the context of imperialism or of critical system-building.

On the other hand, Said activates the agonistic dialectic in conjunction with that other conception of history, mind, and language – associated mostly with Nietzsche and Foucault but also adumbrated by Vico – which I have placed under the awkward compound rubric of archaeology/genealogy. His distinctive appropriation of this methodological complex can be summarized as follows: it involves the excavation of mental, textual, and other cultural archives which have hitherto been considered sacrosanct or otherwise simply taken for granted. This demythologization of the Ur-substance (truth or origins in Said's phrasing) and of received wisdom in general exposes the extent to which what has been labeled as "normal," "ideal," "natural," or "commonsensical" in a given cultural or historical conjuncture has achieved that privileged status in virtue of the vast amount of concerted effort invested in its behalf by individuals, institutions, and indeed entire societies; in Said's judgement, these collective energies, which have been channeled so that the power made available by knowledge systems is strategically combined with cultural capital – or value – can (and often do) have enormously destructive consequences; in contradistinction to traditional historians, who have on the whole tended to be collusive, the archival/genetic historian gives us critical insight into the specific agencies, mechanisms, and operations that have made this great ideological feat possible: he or she (a) unmasks the concepts, strategies, and modalities fashioned in order to construct, fortify, and validate fundamentalist thought forms and institutions; (b) illustrates the different ways in which the indigestible, aberrant element – what is usually referred to as the other – has been co-opted (if possible), suppressed, or destroyed outright in the course of the above enactments; (c) demonstrates how the concealed forensic evidence that bespeaks guilt can be rediscovered and put on display.

The difficult transactions performed by the typical Saidian technique are indicated, if only in the most general terms, in this passage (from "The World, the Text, and the Critic") in which Said grapples with textual agency and the worldly responsibilities of the critic: the idea of agonistic dialectic is processed through Foucauldian and Derridean lenses:

> Everything I tried earlier [in the article] to say about a text – its dialectic of engagement in time and the senses, the paradoxes in a text by which discourse is shown to be immutable and yet contingent, as fraught and politically intransigent as the struggle between dominant and dominated – all this was an implicit rejection of the secondary role usually assigned to criticism. For if we assume that texts make up what Foucault calls archival facts, the archive

being defined as the text's social discursive presence in the world, then criticism too is another aspect of that present. In other words, rather than being defined by the silent past, commanded by it to speak in the present, criticism, no less than any text, is the present in the course of its articulation, its struggle for definition. We must not forget that the critic cannot speak without the mediation of writing, that ambivalent *pharmakon* so suggestively portrayed by Derrida as the constituted milieu where the oppositions are opposed: this is where the interplay occurs that brings the oppositions into direct contact with each other, that overturns oppositions and transforms one pole into another, soul and body, good and evil, inside and outside, memory and oblivion, speech and writing.[17]

Dismantling Ideological Walls

The idea of the boundary or in-between zone that I referred to earlier should be considered in the context of this broad, complex metacritical infrastructure. The notion of boundary is, of course, not unique to Said's criticism: discussions of marginality, migration, and border sites are fairly common in contemporary thought, especially with respect to the causes and consequences of postmodernity and post-coloniality; what is particularly interesting about Said's use of this notion – which was of vital importance to his career right from the outset – is that, in addition to its originally geographical and political designations, it is intended to convey subtler connotations – cultural, historical, epistemological, perhaps even ontological. Equally relevant, in all these designations, the idea of boundary is not merely an end in itself, but is further deployed as an instrument of ideology critique. It is therefore particularly apposite to note that, in my view, the notion of the in-between zone, as it is rendered in Said's writing, is far more than a studied ambivalence – a kind of equipoised (and ultimately aesthetic) contemplation of difference; nor is it an indication of ambiguity in the semantic or formalist senses; nor finally is it a state of neutrality and passivity, a symptom of confusion and lack of rigor, or a species of nomadic restlessness embarked upon for its own sake. Rather, it must be conceived both as an active field of engagement – and hence an experiential gestalt or space – and as a multi-vectored process, that is, an awareness of transformation in a temporal dimension. On the one hand, the emphasis falls on aleatory intellectual events *taking place* rather than on a contemplative attitude; on the other, these events are consciously guided in specific ways all of which are intended either to sharpen the critique of ideology as such or to confront specific ideologies.

The following passage from "Opponents, Audiences, Constituencies, and Community" captures what I am getting at with
remarkable clarity and brevity (once again the idea of dialectic is used
by Said as an indispensable point of purchase):

> [T]he politics of interpretation demands a dialectical response from a critical
> consciousness worthy of its name. Instead of noninterference and specializa-
> tion, there must be *interference*, a crossing of borders and obstacles, a deter-
> mined attempt to generalize exactly at those points where generalizations
> seem impossible to make. One of the first interferences to be ventured, then, is
> a crossing from literature, which is supposed to be subjective and powerless,
> into those exactly parallel realms, now covered by journalism and the pro-
> duction of information, that employ representation but are supposed to be
> objective and powerful ... [F]or the most part, such consumer items as "the
> news" – a euphemism for ideological images of the world's population – hold
> forth, untouched by interfering secular and critical minds, who for all sorts of
> obvious reasons are not hooked into the systems of power ... [W]e need to
> think about breaking out of the disciplinary ghettos in which as intellectuals
> we have been confined, to reopen the blocked social processes ceding objective
> representation (hence power) of the world to a small coterie of experts and
> their clients, to consider that the audience for literacy is not a closed circle of
> three thousand professional critics but the community of human beings living
> in society, and to regard social reality in a secular rather than a mystical mode,
> despite all the protestations about realism and objectivity.[18]

The emphasis in this starkly prescriptive passage falls primarily on
political (and beyond that epistemological) contestations, but even in
his less overtly interventionist moments, Said actively engages multiple borders in the manner I have outlined. In his various studies, all
the different, sometimes contrastive connotations of the boundary
zone or condition are suggested: an indication of mediation, transition, or mutation; a road map between a point of departure and a
destination; a demarcation line to be straddled, crossed, recrossed, or
erased; a rupture or mark of separation – to be repaired, acknowledged, denied, or smoothed over as the case might be; a threshold of
emergence into consciousness or onto an external cultural site (discursive or otherwise) – these and similar features, including various
contours of multiple arrangement (such as repetitions, parallelizations, and lateral connections) can be identified in Said's work. They
include constraints as well as pressure points and instantiations of
freedom; often what at first looks like a gap or a loose end on closer
examination turns out to be a strategic enactment constitutive of the
structural and thematic logic of a specific argument or a broad program of action. However different their specific locales, arrangements,

and orientations, all these boundary zones and conditions have one thing in common: in the final instance, they are intended to dramatize the deployment of critical knowledge against ideological phenomena.

Debating with Knowledge, Wrestling with History

Said's multi-vectored methodology – a technique sharpened for profound suspicion (or radical skepticism about received wisdom) – makes it possible for him to clear a viable space for an extremely eccentric version of historicity. It is primed both to bypass what he considers to be the untenable dichotomies associated with empiricist and idealist conceptions of history and to provide a far more accurate accounting of what the actualities of history have wrought in the lives of millions over the past three hundred years or so. As I will demonstrate in various contexts, Said's dissatisfaction with idealism and empiricism stems from his conviction that, separately and together, these two modes of intellection (and, by extension, the two broad philosophical-cultural traditions deriving from them) have repeatedly collaborated with ideological coercions and mystifications. The co-activation of agonistic dialectic and archaeology/genealogy is intended as a philosophical meditation with a sharp critical edge to it, but it is also an attempt to turn history inside out.

A slightly different way of putting this point is to say that the critical mind must debate with knowledge and wrestle with history – and, paradoxically, undertake both challenges immanently. This is to say, on the one hand, it becomes necessary to present historical reconstruction, not teleologically, "objectively," antiseptically, or assimilatively, but existentially (or at any rate phenomenologically) and materially; such an approach acknowledges the presence of what Vico calls conatus (or appetite, as distinct from the so-called dispassionate light of "reason") and comes to terms with socio-cultural practices. But on the other hand, the mind cannot arrogate to itself originary, totalistic, or teleological powers beyond its reach: it cannot be allowed to obviate, absorb, undermine, or otherwise disregard the indubitable positivity – the brute, material thereness, if you will – of the object domain given to it: that is, intentionality, understood individually and/or collectively, comes to terms with the spatial and temporal circumstances (whether remote or close at hand) that constitute humanity's cultural and natural environment in a manner that demonstrates how this environment both empowers and constrains us.

In effect, the mind interrogatively engages the world but does not subsume it altogether. On this view, Said's various historical studies – despite their considerable thematic disparity – can be seen as attempts to render as cogently as possible the anthropomorphic geneses, deracinations, dispersions, and transformations of modernist consciousness since the eighteenth century. His critical approach, therefore, shares a great deal with the two closely related methodologies which have come to be known as cultural materialism and new historicism – with the important difference that he is both far more eclectic and far more conscious of the present ideological realities than most of the critics (among them Steven Greenblatt, Catherine Gallagher, Alan Sinfield, and Catherine Belsey) who are associated with these critical attitudes.

As I will be pointing out throughout this study, of central importance to Said's "technique of trouble" are several interrelated assumptions which can be syllogistically ferreted out from the historical studies and critical interventions. (1) In the unfolding of modernity, unmediated or complete truth – whether philosophical, divine, or scientific – is decidedly unavailable; the anti-metaphysical promptings of the past two to three centuries attest to this loss of foundations, a condition which has brought both anxiety and freedom in its wake. (2) The ideas and ideals brought into being by modernity, which in turn have determined the way modern societies have fashioned themselves, inevitably reconcile us to the pervasive, enveloping materiality and contingency of thought and action; rational congnition, that is to say, is immanent, "earthbound" (Said's term), and saturated with passion. (3) It follows that all forms of knowledge are the products of interpretation and judgement, that "normative" conclusions based on (or derived from) this knowledge are necessarily provisional and tentative, that "certainty" – wherever and whenever it is loudly proclaimed – is more often than not a camouflage for both dogmatism and imperialism (in Said's writing, the will to truth and the will to power are almost always directly implicated in each other). (4) Secular criticism – as that form of knowledge which configures (or ought to configure), at various historical-cultural conjunctures, maximum skepticism about received dogma with maximum utopianism – furnishes tools which, used properly, can enable us to distinguish ideological illusions from what Said has on occasion called "life-enhancing" ideas, ideals, and modes of thinking.

These are of course not new species of value dreamt up by Said – on the contrary, as he reminds us untiringly, they are age-old imperatives (such as justice and equality) which have traditionally been considered as vital to non-coercive visions of human community. Rather, his point is that these imperatives have been, on the hand, used selectively and duplicitously and, on the other, aligned with more sinister promptings (e.g., racialism and imperial dogma) in such a way that extremely unjust, tremendously destructive historical consolidations have been made (often in the name of these very principles) over the past three centuries. Hence, Said's diagnostic writings light up the disconnection or "discrepancy" (to use his term) between what has historically come to pass and what could have been, might have been, or might yet be. It should be added that the assumptions in the syllogism outlined above – which could be more accurately described as flexible, revolving interpretive principles rather than programmatic, "explanatory" the-ories – are meant to offset the deleterious consequences of what Said has characterized (in *Beginnings*) as a form of "rationalism based on dry-as-dust traditionalism, memory, and scholastic rigidity."[19] This, as we shall see, is a reference to empiricism and idealism.

The Myth of "Postcolonial" Theory: Intellectuals, Collusion, and Opposition

A subthesis implicit in my argument is that there is a widespread misrecognition of Said's writings, which is due at least in part to a strangely lopsided reception of his oeuvre and the theoretical mis-conceptions that reception has nurtured. Whereas the early work, including *Beginnings* (a study of great theoretical importance for Said's entire career), has attracted barely any attention beyond the initial reviews at the time of publication, a good deal of commentary has been generated by the later, more politically explicit writings. And of the latter, *Orientalism* stands out in virtue of the visceral reaction it prompted from the very moment of its publication in 1978 – a phenomenon that testifies to the raw political and academic nerves touched by the text. Since those early responses, a vast, inter-disciplinary palimpsest has mushroomed around the book; one could go so far as to argue that, for good or ill, *Orientalism* has given rise to an entirely new discourse – one which goes far beyond what is known as postcolonial theory. "The result of all this," Said remarked recently, with obvious ambivalence if not outright discomfort, "is that *Orientalism*, almost in a Borgesian way, has become several different books" – adding that this fascination with the book has led to "misreadings and, in a few cases, willful misinterpretations."[20] However chary we may be about taking complaints like these at face value (after all, all authors tend to be a little partial to their work and do not always welcome negative observations made about it), there is little doubt that, besides being embraced by a large number of thinkers as an unusually empowering text, *Orientalism* has also been the object of severe criticisms, some of which cannot be easily dismissed on grounds of mere polemicism or political partisanship.

Yet, by virtue of its very provocativeness (in positive or negative senses), *Orientalism* may have occasioned a rather unintended (and perhaps unfortunate) consequence; in my opinion, the contentious response to the text has helped cast a distorting – not to say inhibiting – sort of light on Said's work as a whole. In spite of what I have been calling an infrastructural consistency in his oeuvre, the publication of *Orientalism* has been made to effect – sometimes consciously but more often by default – a major discontinuity in his career.

This rather misleading interpretive attitude manifests itself in two complementary ways: on the one hand, the study is usually treated, implicitly or explicitly, as the theoretical watermark for all of Said's writing – the text where he has delivered his final, once-and-for-all say on the matter of theory. On the other hand, the book is for all practical purposes sealed off from the works that both preceded and succeeded it (although it is occasionally briefly related to the odd text or two). One particular consequence of this cock-eyed reception is the repeated claim that *Orientalism* (and by implication Said's criticism as a whole) is Foucauldian in conception. The long Foucauldian shadow which has been cast around *Orientalism* has obscured a great deal of non-Foucauldian (and in some cases anti-Foucauldian) reflections – both in *Orientalism* and in Said's other writings. Even those critics (among them Bové and Clifford)[21] who cite his dissatisfaction with – or departure from – some aspects of Foucault's analytics use it as evidence to support the claim that Said is inconsistent and self-contradictory, failing to note (except in the form of cursory allusions) Said's strong affinities with Vico, Lukacs, Williams, Gramsci, or Fanon – all of them thinkers whose views on history, society, politics, culture, language, and critical consciousness have been examined (and often directly invoked) in Said's writings, both before and after the publication of *Orientalism*.

My argument is that the strategic reconception which I have proposed will give us a more insightful understanding of *Orientalism*'s place in Said's critical project as a whole. As it relates specifically to *Orientalism*, this shift in interpretation can be sketched out as follows. First, it would be a mistake to impute any theoretical exclusivity to

Orientalism; the book does not bear an irreplaceable theoretical signature or trademark – something identifiable as a permanently held
position or doctrine; nor does it project an overarching, formulaic
principle which can be examined totalistically, swallowed whole, and
recycled formalistically. In fact everything that Said says about the
matter of theory as such – or more precisely about the interplay
between theory and critical consciousness – militates against this kind
of restorative interpretation.

Second, its actual theoretical insight is as much Gramscian as
Foucauldian. That is to say, in addition to discursive power, with its
associated baggage of anonymity, determinism, and (potential?) tot-
alism, we must remember such things as hegemonic control, together
with the possibility of counter-hegemony, residual and emergent
authority, historical/cultural blocks, civil and political knowledge,
and so on. We must also remember the vital role assigned by Gramsci
– as by Said – to intellectuals (be they traditional, organic, or both at
once), a role deliberately de-emphasized by Foucault. Above all, we
must remember the extent to which Said's criticism, in *Orientalism*
and elsewhere, is rooted (unlike Foucault's and very much like
Gramsci's) in a dialectical tradition which affords considerable latitude to individual agency. When we add to this Said's early interest in
existentialism, as well as the phenomenological underpinnings of his
conception of intentionality throughout his career, we can see how
reductive the Foucauldian ascription of *Orientalism* really is.

Finally, *Orientalism* does not mark a discontinuity in Said's career – if
by "discontinuity"one means a methodological or thematic parting of
the ways, something analogous either to a rupture or to a watershed.
Rather it is part of an *affiliation* (a very important concept in Said's
thought) of texts which together dispose of multiple topics all of which
will be carefully examined in the course of my study. This affiliation
designates what I have been calling the unfolding of modernity, with all
its gains and losses, over the past three centuries or so – that is, the
cognitive and affective contours of modernist consciousness as a historical, epistemological, cultural, and ethico-political problematic. Seen in
this light, the so-called postcolonial debate supposedly inaugurated by
Orientalism is not so much a rancorous disputation between an arrogant
West and its various others as it is a dialogue about demystification of
culture, in which "culture" is to be understood both locally and globally;
more specifically, Said's criticism as a whole involves an attempt to
describe (and pass judgement on) the intellectuals' variable positionality
vis-à-vis the powerful ideologies which have shaped the modern world.

All of this explains the relatively limited attention I have given to "postcolonial" themes (only the final chapter deals with them directly) and the enormous importance I attach to *Beginnings*. If it were possible to identify one single study in which Said confronts theoretical problems at the philosophical level, that text – I argue – would have to be *Beginnings*; it is a compendious, extremely subversive meditation on modern intellectual history which is meant, successfully or otherwise, to grasp the problem of ethical, epistemological, and cultural norms at the level of foundations. In this respect, it is comparable to Foucault's *Archaeology of Knowledge* and Derrida's *Of Grammatology* (to name two influential texts of the last several decades) but is far more sensitive than the former to individual agency and far more historically conscious than the latter. In *Beginnings*, Said grapples with the consequences of modern rationality, as both boon and bane, in a manner that foregrounds its primordial well-springs, its expansive desires, its refractive multiplications and its self-deflating ironies; hence, of course, his choice of terminology (origin, beginning, intentional structure, repetition, dispersion, reversal, etc.).

Beginnings, therefore, clears a theoretical space for all of Said's later writings – a fact which is indeed recognized (but not sufficiently illuminated) by Tim Brennan, Rashmi Bhatnagar, and James Clifford, among others.[22] The adumbrative contours of this theoretical space are initially mapped out in Said's first book, *Joseph Conrad and the Fiction of Autobiography*. Hence there is a direct methodological link between these two early books. *The World, the Text, and the Critic*, to which I have devoted my fourth chapter, is a more polemical text partaking of the spirit which animates Said's later, move overtly political works. It is, however, in some important respects analogous to *Beginnings* in its complexity, erudition, and subtlety; it brings to the ethico-political plane the implications of the multiple historical-epistemological insights of *Beginnings*, but it also radicalizes and modulates these implications in significant ways. The two concepts of worldliness and affiliations are particularly crucial in this regard; but the text also sheds a great deal of light on such slippery notions as culture, hegemony, system, and critical consciousness. For all these reasons, the first four chapters of my study, which may at first seem a bit overwritten, are intended to bring about a strategic rethinking of Said's entire career at the most basic theoretical level. Only after this reconception has been made will his indictments of collusive intellectuals of various persuasions become clearer.

Determining the worldly responsibilities of the intellectual calls for an examination of the tensive transactions that take place between individual agency and the multiple collectivities in which that agency is embedded; that critical task constitutes a considerable dimension of the boundary conditions which I outlined above; it is, of course, never an easy task because it directly concerns the vexed issue of identity formation. As such, it responds to the following historically and culturally specific questions: how have various thinkers helped construct, subvert, maintain or otherwise come to grips with the specific identities and alterities (say "Englishmen," "Orientals," the "West," or "natives") that have been made available to them at given conjunctures in the context of modernity? And a corollary: what have been the actual historical consequences of these intellectual enactments? What particularly animates Said's various studies is the proposition that most intellectuals – including those involved in constructing and sustaining Orientalism, high imperialism, and American hegemonism, as well as Zionist political philosophy and practice – have not only failed in subverting but on the contrary contributed to the creation of hierarchist, supremacist versions of identitarianism. In other words, these intellectuals have helped install the doctrine that (a) there are such things as pure, unadulterated, national, racial, religious, or cultural identities and that (b) they themselves (as individuals and collectivities) embody the highest, noblest forms of identity to be found in all of humanity.

Most of my study consists of an explication of Said's direct and indirect critique of such an identitarian vision and the normative authority that has sustained it over the past three centuries or so. It would be misleading, however, to conclude from all this that Said is intent on resurrecting a species of simple-minded nativism, a claim which is directly or indirectly made when the facts of his exilic life, his critique of Orientalism, and his struggle on behalf of the Palestinian people are strategically foregrounded. On the contrary, he has often been critical of those "third world" intellectuals who – sometimes taking his own "postcolonial" writings as a point of purchase – have helped create false dichotomies inimical to the nurturing of a non-coercive human community. In the following passage, for example, Said alerts us to the multiple post-independence pathologies that have cropped up in the past several decades. Notice how his chiding of the nativists is filtered through (and strengthened by) insights appropriated from Fanon, the critic of imperialism *par excellence*:

Fanon is scathing on the abuses of the postindependence nationalist party: on, for instance, the cult of the Grand Panjandrum (or maximum leader), or the centralization of the capital city, which Fanon said flatly needed to be deconsecrated, or most importantly, the hijacking of common sense and popular participation by bureaucrats, technical experts, and jargon-wielding obfuscators. Well before V. S. Naipaul [whose almost mindless endorsement of Orientalist stereotypes in the West is severely criticized by Said elsewhere[23]], Fanon was arguing against the politics of mimicry and separatism that produced the Mobutus, Idi Amins, and Saddams, as well as the grotesqueries and pathologies of power that gave rise to tyrannical states and praetorian guards while obstructing democratic freedoms in so many countries of the third world. Fanon also prophesied the continuing dependence of numerous postcolonial governments and philosophies, all of which preached the sovereignty of the newly independent people of one or another new third world state and, having failed to make the transition from nationalism to true liberation, were in fact condemned to practice the politics, and the economics, of a new oppression as pernicious as the old one. At bottom, what Fanon offers most compellingly is a critique of the separatism and mock autonomy achieved by a pure politics of identity that has lasted too long and been made to serve in situations where it has become simply inadequate. What invariably happens at the level of knowledge is that signs and symbols of freedom and status are taken for the reality: You want to be named and considered for the sake of being named and considered. In effect this really means that just to be an independent postcolonial Arab, or black, or Indonesian is not a program, nor a process, nor a vision. It is no more than a convenient starting point from which the real work, the hard work, might begin.[24]

Is an Affiliated Human Community Possible?

Said's own proposed non-identitarian conception of human community, which has been inspired as much by Vichian thought as by the later (largely socialist) tradition of critical humanism, can broadly be characterized as an interrelated plurality of cultures. A careful, comprehensive examination of his writing reveals that, beyond the polemically charged, anti-imperialist indictments which he is best known for, there is an abiding commitment to (one might say a dogged, even desperate belief in) a common humanity engaged in a collective but variegated enterprise. Advanced as a radical vision – one which at once intersects with and interrogates the traditional ideals of humanism as these were articulated by Enlightenment theorists and their heirs (from the philosophes to Kant, Marx, Habermas, and beyond) – Said's invocation of humanity's collective destiny is designed to fuse together (and transvaluate) two important themes in modern thought which are normally dissociated from, and sometimes even opposed to, each other: plurality and universality. On Said's view, difference or distance – whether in time, place, mode of thinking, or societal organization – ought not to be used as a license to build exclusionary walls but as a testament to the rich diversity of human cultural forms. The dramatic interactions and affinities of this rich heritage in turn should be affirmed in a complementary fashion: they should become occasions, not to create a false universality that conceals ideological investments, but to recognize interconnections among autonomous cultures conceived as being equal to one another. Articulated in *Beginnings* at its most rarefied – and hence most purely "theoretical" – level and in its most politically explicit (and hence most worldly) form in *Culture and Imperialism*, this radical vision of *sensus communis* underlies all of Said's writings, from his first book on Conrad to the latest editorial reflections on the peace process in the Middle East.

A propaedeutic sketch can therefore be drawn quickly at this early stage of my discussion: Said must be seen, not (or not merely) as a postcolonial critic, but as a radical historian (of ideas, practices, and institutions) and as a critic of ideology qua ideology. In all these roles, he radicalizes (through extensions, departures, modifications, and complementations) the responsibilities assigned to intellectuals in traditional left criticism. His technique of extremes is therefore designed to achieve several goals at once: as a heuristic of historical retrieval, it helps him recover an alternative account of modernity, bringing to life the counter-memory of privileged narratives and normalized consolidations – thus activating the resistance of the historical, cultural, and psychic alterities which have been suppressed (or co-opted) by dominant ideologies. As an instrument of critical intervention, this technique empowers him to combine the intellectual equivalent of guerrilla combat with the probing techniques of the investigative reporter. And as a compass for pointing to a better future for *all* humanity, it serves as a non-totalizing but nevertheless utopian thought experiment. Needless to say, in all these enactments Said's own process of self-understanding – the creation and interpretation (in the most exacting sense of modernist intentionality) of an emerging, at once integrated and dynamic self – is taking place, with its own specific challenges assuming existential, historico-cultural, and ethico-epistemic forms that must perforce coexist. My analysis will attempt to shed light on all these aspects of his criticism.

1

Reflexivity and Self-creation in Said and Conrad

Said's preoccupation with Conrad's life and writing career has endured over the decades. Conrad happens to be the only writer – literary or otherwise – to whom Said has devoted an entire monograph, namely, *Joseph Conrad and the Fiction of Autobiography*.[1] Moreover, in many of Said's other major texts – among them *Beginnings*; *The World, the Text, and the Critic*; and *Culture and Imperialism* – there are extended reflections on aspects of Conrad's career. Finally, one comes across the "occasional" odd article which at least partially deals with Conrad.[2] Given that Said, on his own admission, is temperamentally averse to certain types of intellectual fixations; given the fact that he tends to move "in and out of things" and rarely ever remains with "anything for long,"[3] one may be justified in asking: why all this attention to Conrad? If his own view (as expressed in *The World*, for example) of the calling of secular intellectuals in general and of literary critics in particular is that precious little is to be gained (and, on the contrary, a great deal can be lost) by the creation of personality cults around specific thinkers – say, a Derrida or a Foucault[4] – whose works are credited, often for the wrong reasons, to have provided the terminal cure for long-standing intellectual headaches: if all this, then how does Said account for his prolonged interest in Conrad? In the absence of a direct response from Said, we may be permitted to combine a certain amount of speculation with a close examination of his texts on Conrad in order to explain this apparent inconsistency.

One plausible way of answering the above question is to note the biographical similarities between Said and Conrad – and then tease some possible implications out of them. That is to say, inasmuch as the Polish exile's existential and artistic development prefigures in an uncanny sort of way the career of the Palestinian exile, Said's meditations on Conrad can be seen as a way of paying homage to a political and intellectual fellow traveler; an acknowledgment of affinities with a thinker who, exposed to similar dislocations, made virtue out of necessity and, in the process, earned the right to create himself out of the only materials made available to him under difficult historical circumstances. In both, the loss of cultural roots manifests itself not only in the registration of the old – that is, the familiar but absent – world, as well as the new, potentially disorienting one, but also in a continual process of willed self-suturing. To resist the sheer dispersal of psychic energy, the displaced intellectual must steel himself the better to resist powerful centrifugal forces that have already wrought havoc on his own paterfamilial community; the self must also intend the freedom to inscribe a bricoler personal history into the large writ of the adopted tradition. Thus emerges a refracted personal identity – a series of subject positions that maintain their own inner consistency in the form of a tortuous career trajectory. On this view (one could argue) the gyrations, discontinuities, and transformations of Conrad's literary career could be seen, if not as an instantiation of a directly replicable model, then perhaps as a broad analogue that, in Said's own lights, might have merited serious study.

This interpretation is undoubtedly an appealing, and on the face of it valid, one: after all, the crises that shaped Conrad's consciousness from early on – crises which to a large extent determined his belated literary career – are no less (indeed are in some respects more) harrowing than Said's: Conrad had to leave at an early age a hapless Poland which at the time seemed fated to remain indefinitely under the repressive heel of Czarist Russia, a Poland which had just added his own parents to a long list of apparently futile martyrs. And like Said, Conrad was forced to hone a highly idiosyncratic personal style – an idiolect, if you will – out of the uninviting vocabulary of an alien language. If, for the time being, we set aside some important ideological differences between these two thinkers, it is obvious that Conrad and Said have a good deal in common.

Yet there are two minor problems with this neat parallelism. First, although Said has extensively reflected on exile as a *theme*, usually in contexts involving the Palestinian experience, neither his analysis of this topic itself nor his extensions and transformations thereof easily cohere with his treatment of Conradian themes. A slightly different way of phrasing this point is to say that there is indeed a sense in which Said's writing on Conrad, especially *Joseph Conrad and the Fiction of Autobiography*, is meant to illustrate *partially* or *indirectly* the different ways in which Conrad, like Said, registered and transmuted the reality of homelessness – what Said at one point calls the Polish exile's "dream-nightmare"[5] about his homeland. Conrad's implacable hatred of Russia; his 1914 visit to Poland as an established author, after a decades-long absence from it; as well as his recollections of usually unpleasant childhood experiences in Poland: these and similar Conradian enactments are cited by Said to indicate Conrad's pre-occupation with Poland. It is also the case that Conrad does – at his most exacting and rigorous – embody what Said has characterized (in *Beginnings*, for example) as a metaphysical state of homelessness, a condition resulting from the ferocious skepticism of modernist consciousness over the past two to three centuries. On the whole, however, exile as such is rarely ever explicitly thematized by Said in his discussions of Conradian dilemmas, and if it is occasionally mentioned, it is never foregrounded. Second, Said has over the years examined different ways in which other thinkers (among them Swift, Auerbach, and Massignon) came to terms either with actual exile or with circumstances analogous to it. And yet his standard treatment of these writers has usually assumed the form of the occasional article or two rather than copious meditations involving a multiplicity of texts. What, then, is it about Conrad that Said finds so interesting?

An appropriate response to this question could begin with the following two passages from Conrad's *Heart of Darkness*.

> Now when I was a little chap I had a passion for maps. I would look for hours at South America, or Africa, or Australia, and lose myself in all the glories of exploration. At that time there were many blank spaces on the earth, and when I saw one that looked particularly inviting on a map (but they all look that) I would put my finger on it and say, When I grow up I will go there.

> The conquest of the earth, which mostly means the taking away of it from those who have a different complexion or slightly flatter noses than ourselves, is not a pretty thing when you look into it too much. What redeems it is the idea only. An idea at the back of it; not a sentimental preference but an idea; an unselfish belief in the idea – something you can sacrifice to.

The two passages, both of which are spoken by Marlow, Conrad's most garrulous narrator, are cited by Said.[6] Juxtaposing them here enables us to illuminate with unusual clarity the ways, both very similar and vastly dissimilar, in which Said and Conrad confronted another shared concern – one which is every bit as symptomatic as, but nevertheless far broader in scope and far more consequential for humanity at large than, the personal matter of exile: that is, the phenomenon of modern

European imperialism (aptly christened "the Great Game" by Rud-
yard Kipling). What must be immediately noted – at risk of saying
the obvious – is that Conrad and Said are in a fundamental sense
approaching this phenomenon from diametrically opposing perspectives. Writing as a European – and for a European audience – in a
historical context in which Europeans directly or indirectly controlled
more than eighty per cent of the world's landmass, Conrad, the Polish
nationalist cum Victorian gentleman, was only too aware of the
superior position he occupied vis-à-vis the natives. The pre-eminent
discourse of his time, both in its daily accents and in its overarching
long-term projections, exuded the enormous self-confidence of high
European imperialism. Said, on the other hand, is writing, or more
precisely writing *back* (as that famously palimpsestic title reminds us),
as a native in an era which, though putatively known as "postcolonial," has nevertheless witnessed the recrudescence of virile
imperialism in a highly technologized world loaded with weapons
capable of wiping out all life in a matter of days.

Despite these differences between Said and Conrad, the two passages from *Heart of Darkness* draw attention to certain features in
Conrad's writing which Said has found useful in buttressing his
continuing indictment of imperial culture. But that is not all. For
there are other features, all of them testifying to Conrad's capacity for
extreme self-reflexivity, which Said has made use of in several other
related areas of great concern to him: critiquing ideology in general
(and not just the specific ideology of imperialism); mapping the
difficult unfolding of modernity – that is to say, rendering as cogently
as possible the potentially liberating, and yet profoundly disorienting,
challenges confronted by modernist consciousness over the past three
centuries; and finally coming to terms in a very personal way with the
ethical, epistemological, and aesthetic consequences of these dilemmas. Said's fascination with Conrad, then, involves a multiplicity of
agendas: the homeless citizen of the world; the postcolonial critic of
Eurocentrism and Western imperialism; the corrosive genealogist –
that profoundly suspicious historian of ideas and their interconnections with the material realities of bodies, institutions, artifacts, and
societies; the interpreter-historian of literary culture; the demystifier
of ideological epiphenomena – all of these different Saidian personas
can find specifically appropriate points of departure in Conrad's large
body of writing. The two passages cited above enable us to isolate –
and recombine – a few of the strands that form this variously
embroidered Conradian tissue of themes and techniques.

The first passage, arguably one of the two or three most famous paragraphs in *Heart of Darkness*, encapsulates that aspect of the imperialist impulse which is closely implicated (though not entirely coextensive) with the grand narrative often fondly described as "the Enlightenment": the urge, even compulsion, to find out what lies "out there" – the desire, that is, to claw one's way up jagged, lonely, snowcapped peaks; to traverse forbidding deserts; to brave steamy jungles; to sail across vast, turbulent oceans: in short, to "explore" the world, to use the unselfconsciously euphemistic terminology of Marlow. Marlow's thirst as "a little chap" is in effect the thirst of European man ever since Vasco da Gama and Columbus. By the turn of the nineteenth century, this thirst had matured into a grand ideology, which was overtly and covertly buttressed by the positivistic self-confidence of the period: the dark – or blank – places (the difference hardly matters here) of "South America, or Africa, or Australia" are all "inviting" in an almost metaphysical sense; like ancient mysteries that must divulge their inner secrets, they solicit attention again and again – pleading, as it were, to be exposed to the light of day. In the end, rationally generated knowledge "disenchants" the world, as Weber would have put it (though in a somewhat different context).

But if Marlow's (and behind him Conrad's) awareness of the interaction between knowledge and world were limited to this vector alone; if the matter of enlightenment involved only the straightforward – and hence commendable – endeavor of dispensing pure, disinterested knowledge about value-free facts, then it is highly unlikely that Said would find Conrad's writing so suggestive. For, as the wonderfully nuanced verbal echoes make abundantly clear, the Cult of Reason has also bequeathed to us "rationales" – that is, alibis, screens, justifications, camouflages, and various other species of orchestrated make-believe which make highly attractive something which, "when you look into it too much," will turn out to be quite otherwise. The chameleonic duplicities of "Reason" have of course been scrutinized far more thoroughly – and more explicitly – by thinkers other than Conrad. Even if we put aside the great reactionaries, such as Burke and Maistre, and the Romantic rebellion of an earlier period, we can still find modern and contemporary leftists and other demystifiers (prominent among them Horkheimer, Adorno, Habermas, and Foucault – as well as Weber before them) who have used their immense combined talent and erudition to think rigorously through the legacy of the Enlightenment and evaluate judiciously its dual consequences *for European humanity*.

Conrad's importance for Said lies in a sphere where none of these thinkers have ever turned their attention seriously: the connection between rationality and imperium. It is this particular capacity of Conrad's – the ability to reflect intensely and repeatedly on the dubious ethical and political implications of imperialism – that, in Said's view, sets him apart not only from the critics of the Enlightenment but also from nearly all the other European writers of his time (among them Kipling) who also meditated on the theme of empire-building. Conrad, in other words, was unusually conscious of the way in which what I would like to call the intellectual laundering of unseemly practices outside Europe was enacted – practices such as "the taking away of [land] from those who have a different complexion or slightly flatter noses than" Europeans. One transmutes these practices into "an idea"; one decontaminates this idea, cleanses it of anything crude, lowly, quotidian. In the course of this antiseptic elevation, an almost religious experience takes place; one commits oneself to "an unselfish belief in" the innate superiority of that idea – and then bows down before it, makes sacrificial offerings to it, protects it from heretical defilement. And yet one knows all along that this idol, as Bacon phrased it long before high imperialism came along, is essentially a creature of one's own imagination.

It is particularly this aspect of Conrad's work – this double awareness – that, in my view, Said finds most fascinating and, ultimately, most symptomatic. It instantiates Conrad's deep ambivalence towards Europe's imperial project. On the one hand, this schizoid mentality harbors something – call it a moral sentiment, intuition, or judgement – that, if Said is right, has manifested itself only rarely and fitfully in Western cultural life with respect to the West's dealings with the rest of the world: a *critical view from within*, that is, an acute interrogation – even indictment – of the way in which culture as a whole, and more specifically high culture, has been used to conceal the operations of power in the most self-serving fashion. Said's affinity with Conrad as a *fellow intellectual* is therefore very strong at this point. Conrad the critic of imperialism belongs to the ranks of distinguished thinkers – among them Swift, Fanon, and Chomsky, to name a few – each of whom has been singled out by Said as being, in his own inimitable way, an exemplar of intellectual responsibility in his opposition to brutality and dehumanization. On the other hand, Conrad's honesty and perspicacity about the horrendous cost of imperialism are deeply compromised precisely because he is either unable or unwilling to see the victims of imperialism as anything *but* natives – with all that this famous solecism designates or implies. Conrad, observes Said (in *Culture and Imperialism*),[7] can never foresee the day when the natives will run their own affairs – even if, through his numerous hedgings, elisions and hesitations, he suggests an "outside" which lies beyond the Arnoldian sweetness and light of the knowing (read Western) subject – and hence beyond the imperial hold: to Conrad, the civilized, civilizing Westerner is condemned to rule, rob, destroy. In Conrad, therefore, unusually illuminating critical insight resides in the vicinity of a powerfully reactionary strain of dogmatism – just as identitarian thinking of the most essentializing variety is closely imbricated with a version of non-identity which is deposited below the bar of acceptability.

This strangely bifurcated vision that Said detects in Conrad's consciousness is not particularly restricted to the latter's understanding of imperial culture. For, to paraphrase Said's description of T. E. Lawrence (another European who also related ambivalently to empire), there is a sense in which Conrad was an embattled soul for most of his life, a man engaged in an almost permanent civil war with himself.[8] Hence Conrad's predilection for extreme situations; his indifference, even hostility, to various political doctrines whose claims must nevertheless be unflinchingly examined (in *Nostromo*, for example), if only to be modulated for ambiguous conclusions; his recurring tendency to articulate collective guilt and suffering through the perversions and aberrations of the individual (witness Jim and Kurtz, to take two famous examples); his fascination with half-illuminated "secrets" and unnameable crimes; his utilization of multiple narrative voices that skew and distort as much meaning as they reveal – all of these traits add up to the protean, self-doubting (even self-torturing), and yet in his own way undoubtedly doctrinaire Conrad whose writing has invited the scrutiny of critics for generations. His conflicting attitudes towards the European colonial project, whose victims he can neither muster sympathy for nor simply dismiss, is part of this powerful Conradian psychodrama.

In the end, this, I think, should be understood as Conrad's way of negotiating his own multiple boundaries, his own way of laying the ghosts of yesteryear to rest – and coming to grips with the pressure-laden realities of his day. Said's repeated interpretive confrontations with Conrad – as well as his occasional defense of Conrad against charges of racism[9] – constitute an attempt to work through all these facets of Conrad's career, the career of a "distinguished" mind (Said's phrasing) struggling with the burdens of two powerful cultural currents, one inherited, the other adopted: an aristocratic (but repressive and moribund) East European legacy, and a liberal but thoroughly imperialized West European tradition still bent on a grand civilizational mission.

My own analysis of Said's writings on Conrad will be highly selective, henceforth concentrating on *Joseph Conrad and the Fiction of Autobiography*.[10] Admittedly, some of Said's most illuminating passages can be found elsewhere. In *Beginnings*, for example, the long chapter about the genealogical evolution of the modern novel, from its earliest mimetic awakenings in the eighteenth century to its mutation into the mode of high modernism in the early twentieth century, contains a nearly forty-page explication of *Nostromo*, Conrad's most ambitious novel. In *The World, the Text, and the Critic*, there is a brilliant article in which Said tells us that Conrad "was misled by language even as he led language into a dramatization no other author really approached." He adds:

> For what Conrad discovered was that the chasm between words saying and words meaning was widened, not lessened, by talent for words written. To have chosen to write, then, is to have chosen in a particular way neither to say directly nor to mean exactly in the way he had hoped to say or to mean.[11]

The multiple ironies of such a passage occurring in a book which is emphatically *meant* to demonstrate the interconnections between word and world are obvious, and we will have occasion to reflect on this aspect of Said's own critical agenda both in this and in subsequent chapters.

In this chapter, however, my intention is to show through a careful, comprehensive explication that Said's very first monograph is an interpretive tour de force – opening up, in ways I have already suggested, possible new frontiers for students of Conrad – but also serves as a remarkably appropriate inaugural point for Said's own career. By this I mean that, if it were possible to identify a single, unified study – major or minor – in which Said has brought together (though in some cases adumbratively) not only all the Conradian themes sketched above but also all (or nearly all) the other more generally Saidian concerns to which I have thus far alluded, that text would undoubtedly be *Joseph Conrad and the Fiction of Autobiography*. The study is primarily about (Conrad's) difficult self-definition, but it is also about ideas in general (a theme central to *Beginnings* as well); about the operations of the human mind in the circumstances of space and time; about intellectuals and responsibility; about the interconnections of the will to truth and the will to power. It is also emphatically about Eurocentric vision, European imperialism, and the *sensus communis* implied in these two related consolidations. Finally, the methodological drama which I have characterized as a co-activation of archaeology/genealogy and an agonistic dialectic is far more explicitly thematized in this text than in any of Said's major texts with the possible exception of *Beginnings* and *Culture and Imperialism* – though, as we shall see, my employment of the archaeology/genealogy notion in this chapter will require some explanation. In my exposition, I will examine all these concerns as carefully as possible.

The Artistic Self in Conditions of Extremity

A phenomenological–existentialist examination of Conrad's letters and short fiction, *The Fiction of Autobiography* is a study written against the grain of realist, formalist, and psychoanalytic approaches to Conrad's work, approaches which had gained wide currency in the years preceding the publication of Said's study. Written at a time when both existentialist philosophy (particularly Sartre's version) and the criticism of the Geneva School (particularly Poulet's) were making significant headway in American academia, Said's book was part of a broad critical front, one of whose major goals was to rejuvenate literary theory and practice by asserting the centrality to any serious intellectual work of a category which had been all but banished by the New Critics: namely, human consciousness. Besides Said himself, the early J. Hillis Miller, Geoffrey Hartman, and Ihab Hassan (among others) all contributed to that revisionary current, even though Said's scathing reviews of *Beyond Formalism* and *The Dismemberment of Orpheus* throw into bold relief the differences among these critics rather than their shared phenomenological assumptions.[12]

At a more specific level, Said's book is an inquiry aimed at searching out the extreme limits and pressure points of the artistic self's will to freedom and – ultimately – to mastery. The study is an attempt to understand the way in which Conrad fashioned, and refashioned, a series of images of himself through what was to him a painful, purgative process of artistic and intellectual development. According to Said, these images approximated the author's personal and cultural identity at various points in his career. What Said detects in this slow, fissured development of Conrad's self-reflection is a strange marriage of irony and heroism, of egoism and self-transcendence: in the torsions of an "either/or" dialectic, the artist experiences intense self-abnegation in order to win authenticity, a dialectic that for Conrad attains its final synthesis through a complete identification with European humanity and civilization in the last stage of his career. In the end also ratifying, if only implicitly, European imperialism, this self-transformation is, according to Said, realized at an exorbitant moral and aesthetic price. The spirit – or perhaps the demon, to be more precise – that attends this difficult process of self-fashioning is a deep strain of pessimism, which accounts for Conrad's grim stoicism. Said traces the twisted trajectory of Conrad's unfolding career in the context of the author's personal crisis and the historical crises of European society in the late nineteenth and early twentieth centuries. Both the specific tragedy of Conrad's own family and the unhappy fate of Poland form an important backdrop to this drama, as I have already pointed out. However, it is Conrad's own struggle with himself in the course of his literary career that is foregrounded by Said. This struggle takes place in tandem with the violent destruction of an old European order which had long presided over the worldwide acquisition of overseas empires: these are the raw materials reprocessed, and defamiliarized, in Conrad's art.

Said's thesis is that the multiple tensions in Conrad's career will not be fully understood unless the latter's stories are studied in conjunction with the great number of letters he wrote about himself and his views on writing, and unless the complementary relationship between the two modes is recognized. Such a study will reveal the therapeutic, existential nature of Conrad's artistic endeavors. The strengths and oft-criticized "weaknesses" of Conrad's fiction will then be reappraised in an entirely new light: fundamentally psychic rather than formal, the shifting contours unveiled by such a critical approach will instantiate the spiritual history of a powerful, alienated mind in the process of painful self-understanding. Unable to derive any sustenance from established normative categories, Conrad found himself repeatedly confronting the "whole mechanism of existence" in an attempt to position himself authentically vis-à-vis an outside world that often seemed fearful and opaque:

> Conrad's absorption, as I understand it, was that he consciously felt a large measure of unrestful submission to the complexities of life, on the one hand, and, on the other, that he remained interested in the submission not as a *fait accompli* but as a constantly renewed act of living, as a *condition humanisée* and not as a *condition humaine*. "The whole mechanism of existence" further explains Conrad's preoccupations by allowing him the assumption that life

was a series of particular occurrences [which] were connected and informed by a mechanical and perverse inevitability.[13]

Elaborating the frightening implications of this dialectic, in which the possibility of "cosmic optimism" is ruled out by the strict determinism of a self-perpetuating process, Said sets out to trace the various "economies" that Conrad used in successive stages of his artistic evolution.

Said identifies three phases, two of which are crucial and the third transitional. The first (from the late 1880s to 1912) covers the most productive and experientially most enervating period of Conrad's writing career. After the tentativeness of the apprenticeship years, during which he wrote his first two novels, Conrad produced the great works of the mature artist. Such novels as Lord Jim, The Nigger of the "Narcissus," Heart of Darkness, and Nostromo, as well as his most important short stories, were all written during this period. The second phase, described by Said as an "interlude," is ushered in with the emergence of the glib, partially manufactured public image of the celebrated "author," but during the rest of this six-year period Conrad is preoccupied with the terrible carnage of the First World War. A strange ambiguity can be discerned in his reaction to the conflict. On the one hand, he witnesses the trauma of his hitherto private – and hence ontologically suspect – nightmare reflected in, and confirmed by, the gigantic conflagration, a feeling which erupts into a "perpetual crisis" in his mind. On the other, he hints for the first time in his artistic career at the possibility of some kind of resolution. In the meantime, the transformation enables him to recast issues of concern to the broad plane of European destiny. During the last six years of his life (from 1918 to 1924), a serene Conrad transsubjectively "looks over" a devastated European homeland, searching for ways of sweeping away the rubble of the "Old Order" and inaugurating a new era. It is with these successive, progressively refractive transformations in mind that Said deploys phenomenological insights honed to come to grips with the ethical crises and epistemological problems thrown up – and in his view misrecognized – by formalistic, naturalistic, and psychoanalytical approaches to Conrad (more about these three stages later).

Even though Husserl is not even mentioned in the book, the broad parameters and the terminology which Said employs in it are derived from Husserl's ground-breaking inquiries in phenomenology. Husserl initiated his radical project in order to go beyond what he considered to be the naive realism of the scientific method and the reductive solipsism of idealism. He also wanted to heal the rift between the subject and the object, a rift bequeathed to philosophy by Descartes' privileging of the cogito. Husserl argued that philosophical inquiry should be directed at the conscious process of human intentionality as it animates, and is in turn molded by, the external world present to it. Briefly stated, this method, which Husserl believed would dissolve the given and disclose the mind's dynamic transactions as it structures reality, involves a number of interrelated steps each of which is intended to extend the cogency of the one preceding it: (a) suspending the natural, commonsensical attitude and adopting a critical or pre-suppositionless posture; (b) activating the subjective pole, or noesis, of the act of consciousness and sharpening it in its encounter with the noema, or the objective pole, and hence transforming them both into an active dialectic; (c) initiating, from the outset, a series of eidetic and apodictic "reductions" – or, in Husserlian parlance, enacting an *epoche*: that is, bracketing off and neutrally putting on hold successive layers of the spatio-temporal dimension of reality in order to uncover the essential structures of lived experience intersubjectively. The ultimate seat of authority in this investigation is what Husserl calls the "transcendental ego," a problematical concept that suggests a prereflexive unity of experience and yet serves as the constitutive guarantor of authenticity.

It is on the broad intellectual space cleared by these Husserlian insights that Said's argument unfolds, an interpretive maneuver designed to advance beyond literary formalism and naturalism, and to interrogate them both at the meta-critical level. Said is therefore at one with Husserl on the latter's insistence that any form of inquiry (scientific, philosophical, artistic, or whatever) involves a radical transaction between human agency and its world, that human experience does not consist of atomized units but constitutes a unified spatio-temporal gestalt brought into being by a dynamic encounter between subject and object.

It should be clear by now, however, that some aspects of Husserl's transcendental phenomenology would be viewed with some reservation by Said. The co-presence of several interpretive imperatives, both in Said's critical project as a whole and in this early text, would make Husserl's theses only partially useful to him: the need to uncover the agonistic (and not just assimilative) labors of an individual thinker's self-fashioning, as well as to account for the socio-historical processes, forces, strategies, and institutions that both empower and constrain the intellectual (a dimension in which Husserl was woefully deficient, despite his talk of what he called the "lifeworld"); and the desire to demystify personal and cultural norms for purposes of ideology critique – these Saidian concerns, which I have already outlined in preceding sections of this chapter, call for the use of critical tools which are far more incisive than the largely restorative insights furnished by Husserl. Also, quite aside from the claim – made by Paul Ricoeur,[14] for example – that Husserl has not advanced beyond idealism, there is little doubt that Husserl's unabashed scientism would be particularly inhospitable to Said's critical project. To the extent that Husserl was intent on establishing science as an ultimate epistemological ideal; to the extent that his efforts were aimed not only at determining the sound minimal conditions for acquiring any kind of knowledge but also at putting in place an air-tight veridical criterion – that is, a strong theory of truth – which would guarantee the absolute validity of putative decisions made about scientific knowledge, to that extent Husserl's objectives are quite different from (and in some respects opposed to) Said's immediate aim of overturning a normativity which has in his view been infected by an ideological virus. It is not surprising, then, that Said was obliged to turn to Sartre's existentialist phenomenology, which was emphatically meant to turn transcendental phenomenology inside out.

Existentialism was of course a loose, multifaceted philosophical movement contributed to by thinkers with different orientations and agendas. And although he has elsewhere written appreciatively of Maurice Merleau-Ponty, Sartre's contemporary and one-time associate, existentialism as such has not been of great concern to Said.[15] The appeal of Sartre's version to the early Said appears to lie in the fact that it both evolved out of and critiqued Husserlian phenomenology: that is, Sartre (like Heidegger before him) retained Husserl's stress on consciousness but at the same time deeply problematized it. Briefly stated, Sartre's broad argument was that there is no essence prior to existence; that the transcendental ego is a Husserlian fiction; that human consciousness is conscious of nothing except itself – since it cannot grasp the objective pole, the in-itself, and is therefore forced to shrug off the noematic content; that humanity is condemned to an imaginatively creative yet painful freedom; that meaning and value in an absurd universe must be reconstructed from this free activity of the human agent. This argument is crucial for Said's study of Conrad, although it is not explicitly articulated. What is directly woven into the argument of *The Fiction*, as we shall see later on, is Sartre's anti-

Freudian psychology. There is another thinker who, though predating both phenomenology and existentialism proper, is nevertheless central to Said's argument: Schopenhauer, the arch-pessimist of German idealism, whose philosophy (Said suggests) may indeed have directly influenced Conrad.[16] This is how Said formulates the Schopenhauerian dimensions of Conrad's experience:

> It is important to distinguish the dominant mode of Conrad's structures of experience: quite simply, it can be called their radical either/or posture. By this I mean a habitual view of experience that allows *either* a surrender to chaos *or* a comparably frightful surrender to egoistic order. There is no middle way, and there is no other method of putting the issues. Either one allows that meaningless chaos is the hopeless restriction upon human behavior, or one must admit that order and significance depend only upon man's will to live at all costs. This, of course, is the Schopenhauerian dilemma.[17]

The dilemma that Said alludes to is Schopenhauer's opposition between a world which is ontologically alien to human agency, on the one hand, and a willfully created but ultimately false "idea" of that world in the human mind, on the other. In later stages of my discussion, I will provide a more detailed exposition of Said's critique of epistemology, concentrating on the way in which he deploys these Sartrean and Schopenhauerian insights to overturn naturalist and idealist conceptions of truth, an interpretive step which coheres with the imperatives of what I have been calling the archaeological/genealogical dimension of Said's method. I will also reflect on the long-term implications of this inaugural suspicion – on the fact that, for example, while neither existentialism nor will philosophy features to any significant extent in Said's later studies, their skeptical "spirit" in a sense does persist throughout his career: more about all these thematic concerns later. At this point, however, I would like to draw greater attention to one aspect of Said's complex methodology which I have accorded paramount importance, namely dialectical modes of reflection.

Dialectical Agonism in Conrad and Said: The "Either/Or" Imperative

I have argued that, despite the fact that it is rarely ever acknowledged by the vast majority of Said's interlocutors, this methodology – and more specifically an agonistic version of it – constitutes an indispensable strand that runs through his entire career. Apropos of this methodological project, the illustrative value of Said's first book can hardly be overestimated. *The Fiction of Autobiography* affords far greater insight into Said's utilization of agonistic dialectic than most of his other works. By this I mean that, as the last passage I cited indicates, the entire argument of this early study hinges on the *explicit thematization* (not just implicit assumption) of the double-bind that Said ascribes to Conrad. That is to say, the enervating pendular swings of the "either/or posture" are used directly by Said in order to account for Conrad's harrowing dilemmas. This move enables Said to give an existential cast to the "content" engaged by the dialectical transaction, at least insofar as that content constitutes the psyche of an individuated self – whether Conrad himself or any of his numerous characters – as that self confronts the socio-cultural realities surrounding it. In its vectors, intersections, and transformations, the Conradian dialectic does not bring about syntheses (at least until the last years of Conrad's career) but only irresolvable conflicts which manifest themselves as psychic pain, logical paradoxes, and epistemological negativities.

At this point an important question arises: to what extent is this dialectical double-bind Conradian or Saidian in its origins? That is to say, is it something inherent in – perhaps even constitutive of – Conrad's work, or is it a methodological preference that gives us an early indication about the direction Said's critical project is likely to take in the years to come? Since the investigation is phenomenological in character, and since in this particular case the primary textual material embodies an enormous amount of existential investment on the author's (i.e. Conrad's) part, it would seem that the specific operations of the double-bind are taking place wholly in the author's consciousness – and by extension in his characters' – with critical intentionality using these operations to lodge interpretive signposts strategically. In other words, Said's approach in this early study might at first appear to involve not so much a strong critical method as an interpretive attitude or, more precisely, an attitude of reception: hence to say that one is interpreting an author's oeuvre phenomenologically is to affirm, with Poulet, that one is engaged in a sympathetic co-meditation with that author. Strictly speaking, the critic is not imposing a schema on the material he is examining; rather he is discovering patterns already present in the author's work, patterns which he then proceeds to illuminate by using a descriptive mode of analysis. If that were the case, then a natural conclusion would almost automatically follow from this assumption: that the either/or dialectic discerned by Said is incidental to his critical project as a whole; that while it may be employed unusually fruitfully on some occasions (say, with respect to a Conrad), its value is more local than global.

And yet it is precisely this kind of interpretive enactment – namely, the extreme either/or and the double-bind which it brings into play – that we encounter in one form or another throughout Said's large corpus of writing. This, despite the fact that none of the texts he has written since *The Fiction* incorporate existentialist themes, and none are exclusively phenomenological in methodology. The point I want to insist on, then, is this: whether explicitly stated (as in *The Fiction*) or simply assumed, there is a sense in which Said's entire critical project is predicated on the very idea of a radicalized dialectical engagement – an engagement between an author and his work, between critical consciousness and the material (textual or otherwise) under its scrutiny, between the intellectual and the category of culture (whether broadly or narrowly conceived) that empowers and constrains him or her, and so on. In short, in Said's understanding dialectic is constitutive of our very cultural reality, and none of us can negotiate out of it. There is a corollary to this: the smoother this dialectical transaction, the more assimilative its movements, the greater its ideological pressure.

It is precisely this ideological pressure (whose actual mechanics or "economy" will be the subject of a later section) that all of Said's works – major or minor – are emphatically meant to resist, accounting for the presence of what I have been describing as dynamic boundary conditions or in-between zones: the often-noted ambiguities, gaps, elisions, contradictions, and loose ends are part of that methodological enactment which is sharpened above all as an instrument for the subversion of received dogma. It is also precisely this ideological pressure that, in Said's view, has not been sufficiently resisted by the large number of thinkers and opinion-makers who have come in for direct criticism in his studies, among whom are most Orientalists, Zionists and their fellow travelers, most contemporary journalists, and the army of "experts" who are mobilized by the powers that be whenever a new crisis erupts. It should also be noted immediately that, according to Said, the vast majority of intellectuals in the Arab-Islamic world have been as collusive with the powers of state as their counterparts in the West. Finally, it is this kind of ideological pressure that Conrad in turns tenaciously resisted and actively endorsed during his long literary career; in Said's estimation, Conrad maintained this extremely painful but enormously productive either/

or rhythm until the last six years of his life, a period of final synthesis and consolidation.

Said's elucidation of the Conradian dialectic delivers meaning along several axes all of which are designed to accentuate specific aspects of the noetic-noematic interaction. Considered as a struggle over the contents of the psyche, the dialectic assumes the form of a tug of war between the claims of immediate perception – apprehension of the manifold; spontaneous activity; the profuse, often searing flow of experience, etc. – and those of reconstruction, evaluation, and order. Characterized by Said as alternating periodic tensions and relaxations, these transactions gradually lead to a process of separation and sedi-mentation: the psychic materials gravitate towards different poles, forming their own raisons d'êtres and eventually fortifying their prerogatives into the powerful forces of memory and will respectively. (Said's utilization of Sartrean and Schopenhauerian insights is parti-cularly evident in his emphasis on these two modes of mental life.) It is this inevitable bipolar oscillation between two modes of awareness that, according to Said, accounts for Conrad's endorsement of often conflicting views on the nature of his self-rescue at various stages of his career. Especially in the early years of his career, Conrad in turns ratifies vital emotional claims (what he calls the "full heart") and the steely coldness of reason, the former because of their cornucopic completeness, the latter because of its communicative clarity and disinterestedness.

In Said's view, Conrad's inability to arrest the pendular motion highlights the severity of the contradictions involved in his attempt at self-definition: despite their sincerity and authenticity, emotional commitments leave no room for intellectual grasp, proportionality, or sound judgement. Conversely, the kind of lucidity encouraged by reason – the meaning fashioned in accordance with some schema or system – is achieved in Conrad only by deploying a severe form of skepticism; in other words, discrimination, transparency, and cogency are the products of a critical, even transgressive enactment of the will. One is left in the end with the nagging suspicion that the embraced "certainty" is nothing more than "a web of illusions."[18] This tortuous double-bind is further illustrated by Conrad's insistence on the "consistency" of personality on one occasion and on the validity of the eccentric particles of experience on another. The psychosomatic symptoms Conrad complained about throughout his entire career, as well as the waxing and waning of his artistic capabilities, should be understood as the consequence of this double-bind. To the extent that the poignancy and difficulty of self-understanding are accentuated, Conrad's work gains in complexity and suggestiveness. His best writing, according to Said, is the product of extended periods of crisis.

The axes of this difficult dialectic can also be shifted slightly to take account of what could broadly be called loss and gain. What is implied in this long process of artistic and spiritual self-fashioning is both a certain progression and a definite slippage. If writing *per se* is understood as an activity of self-rescue, then the trajectory of Conrad's three-stage career can be conceived in terms of a fulfillment – of artistic promise, of ideas about personal and cultural identity, of psychic recovery, and so on. But because Conrad achieves this self-liberation through a particularly concentrated exertion of the will, an effort that progressively desensitizes him to the subtler aspects of experience and imposes order on its own terms, a certain exhaustion is also implied in this process of completion. That exhaustion, suggests Said, is both artistic and ethical. A passing gloss on two metaphors utilized by Conrad in his letters illustrates the nature of the transformation. In the late 1880s and early 1890s, during the most difficult years of the first phase, an anguished Conrad complains that he feels as though he were trapped in a deep, dark hole with steep, forbidding walls, a hopeless situation from which it is impossible to escape. Years later, during the third phase of his career, this frightening incarceration has given way to confidence; Conrad compares his experience as a writer to the wide noose of a rope, one designed to facilitate both a process of in-gathering and the deftness of control. Unwilling to re-enact psychic dislocation – the kind of inner struggle that in the past enabled him to create such self-lacerating characters as Jim, Kurtz, and Arsat – this later Conrad is able to content himself with books like *The Rover* and *The Shadow Line*, whose protagonists represent complete stability, full emergence, and ideological explicitness.

Said's treatment of the Conradian either/or dialectic – it should be clear by now – implies a certain conception of space and time (or more precisely space-time, since the two notions are always fused together in Said's understanding of them) as both a radicalized condition of possibility and an almost insurmountable constraint. That is to say, the very character of intentionality is such that it is an *event*, that it takes place, in a manner of speaking. On the one hand, it is a cognitive-affective subjectivity involving a corporeal human agency (not a disembodied, disinfected reason) inserted in a socio-cultural horizon or field. Said's insistence, throughout his career, that thought is always profoundly motivational is a direct consequence of this basic assumption about intentionality. But on the other hand, human consciousness itself is not something static or continuous in identity – if these adjectives are meant to designate an essentialized, unchanging "human nature." On the contrary, "identity" is never at one with itself: it is constantly exposed to the tensive workings of historical circumstance. Considered in this light, intentionality assumes the form of a refracted series of enactments marked by discontinuities, repetitions, and transformations. Said's conception of space-time, then, considerably radicalizes traditional historicism, departing in important ways from approaches to historical reconstruction based on empiricism and idealism.

Normativity as Negativity

But before offering a more detailed analysis of Said's conception of space-time and its implications for both his critical project as a whole and his treatment of Conrad, I would like to reflect on a problematic which I have already touched upon briefly: the logic of epistemology entailed by his appropriation of Sartrean existentialism and Schopenhauer's will philosophy. Two related questions present themselves immediately: first, in what specific ways does Said effect his critique of epistemology, and what ethico-political implications can be derived from that critique? Second, exactly what constitutes the ultimate ground of validity in Said's inquiry, the criterion or grid that demarcates what is to be counted, in his own lights, as true or right from what is indubitably false or wrong? As we shall see both here and in later chapters of my study, a consideration of these questions brings us to the heart of Said's critique of what he calls rationalism, and more specifically of idealist-empiricist conceptions of knowledge. By this I mean that the questions address the extremely complex and, for that very reason, often unrecognized transaction between ideas, ideals, and ideologies in the context of modernity, a transaction, Said suggests, which calls for maximum alertness on the part of intellectuals. In other words, we have brought the discussion to a point where we can examine the way in which critique confronts the ultimate Ur-substance – the province of ontology or the repository of truth. What will become clear is that, even in this early text, Said's technique of suspicion, though not directly inspired by either Vico, Foucault, or Nietzsche (as in the later studies), nevertheless comes very close, both in its operations and in its effect, to the archaeological/genealogical methodology which he has used so fruitfully in *Beginnings*, *Orientalism*, *The Question of Palestine*, and other major texts of the later period.

Said's investigation into this matrix starts, as I have been implying all along, with a radical claim: that the determination of indubitable truth is well nigh impossible. This, of course, is neither particularly new nor unique to Said. An inevitable consequence of modernity, the belief that truth is (at least partially) inaccessible to insight has been part of the intellectual landscape of the last two centuries. That such a sobering conclusion can be arrived at through a Kantian route almost as easily as through a Nietzschean one is a measure of how persistent the spirit of radical skepticism has been in modern thought. If the alliance seems a bit contrived (after all, what should the austere systematization of the Königsberg sage have in common with the declared intellectual terrorism of the arch-perspectivalist?), let us not forget that it was Kant whose critique of what he considered metaphysical hubris first severely limited the province of theoretical reason and then extended it in a different (that is, anthropocentric) direction. There has been an extended concatenation – a genealogy, if you will – of pronouncements stressing, in different ways, the incommensurability of meaning and medium: this is a lesson that we have learned from such widely diverging traditions as psychoanalysis, literary modernism, postcolonial discourse, and postpositivist philosophy (to name only a few of the various strands of modern and contemporary thought).

And yet, if Said is right, there is a sense in which the twin legacies of empiricism and idealism – primarily to be understood as modes of reflection but also by implication as broad philosophico-cultural traditions – suggest that the process of arriving at true self-knowledge and true knowledge about the external world is not a particularly difficult problem, with the proviso that truth in this case is to be understood in postmetaphysical terms. Although Said's studies are never "philosophical" in the narrow and sometimes privileged sense in which this term is used in the analytical tradition, there is little doubt that his direct assaults on the mimetic tradition in literature (exemplified by the realist novel), critical formalism (which, he often implies, is a species of cultural idealism), Orientalism, Zionism, and journalistic discourse – as well as allusions he makes to positivist social science – are ultimately intended as metacritical enactments: that is, they are meant to offer – successfully or otherwise – challenges at ground zero equally to the objectivist claims of empiricism and to the claim that unsullied ideas have primacy over mere matter. In other words, that challenge is made at the level where theoretical evaluation assumes a philosophical (rather than a literary, sociological, or scientific) form. As we shall see in the next two chapters, Said's critique of normativity at the philosophical level reaches its highest point in *Beginnings*.

Said's invocation of Sartrean existentialism and Schopenhauerian will philosophy in *The Fiction* fulfills that metacritical requirement. His immediate aim is to show that genuine truth is ungraspable – that it is an opacity, a lacuna, or a blind spot which thought cannot break through or make a positive purchase on. Once this negative insight is delivered, it becomes possible to argue that error is not something necessarily external (or opposed) to our "true beliefs" but rather is constitutive of, or at least directly implicated in, our very ideas and ideals. Conrad's importance to Said, I think, manifests itself at this point more clearly than at any other: the Polish exile's entire career instantiates a long struggle with the implications of that insight.

Said argues that Conrad's artistic techniques can best be understood, not in terms of unconscious drives and impulses which (however pre-eminent their causative power) cannot be made logically comprehensible, but in terms of the demands, frustrations, and maturation of the conscious ego. The consequences of this process should be examined under the light of Sartre's "analytic psychology of recollection"[19] and in terms of "Schopenhauer's distinction of the intelligible, the empirical, and the acquired character."[20] In *The Emotions: Outline of a Theory*, Sartre argues that human consciousness normally finds external reality impenetrable or ungraspable as it is; therefore, it tends to shrug that opaque object off and deny its existence. This sour-grapes attitude amounts to a magical transformation that permits us to "make sense" of the world, even if that world refuses to yield to us. The noetic thrust of intentionality, which of necessity engages what is external and present to it, discovers that it cannot possess its "noematical correlative."[21] But because consciousness is an active agent, it must pronounce judgement on what it lacks the capacity to understand. Hence a magical negation takes place – precisely because only through this enactment of the will can the emotional structure achieve its equilibrium. The point to be stressed here is that, despite this emotional equilibrium, no epistemological insight has been delivered about objective reality: because of the fundamental split in the heart of being (i.e., being in-itself and being for-itself), consciousness confronts an absence, a void (Sartre's idea of nothingness), and is therefore left to its own existential devices. Strictly speaking, the magical transformation is an alibi, a suasive ruse.

Said's invocation of Schopenhauerian psychology at this point is particularly important: besides serving as a broad analogue to Sartre's existentialist conception of the ego, it is meant to draw special attention to the social dimension of agency: "We have a sense of ourselves within us (intelligible); when put into practice (empirical) this sense is modified; and when put within the framework of the society in which we live, it becomes further modified (acquired). As a result of the interplay between the individual and the world, we endow ourselves with a sense of ethical and psychological self-location ... which in most cases stays with us all our lives."[22] According to Said, Conrad's experience was such that this process of acculturation and socialization very often failed as a result of "a shocking unsettlement that disrupts the continuity of our hold on life,"[23] an unsettlement that could assume any conceivable form – for example, an unpleasant situation which must be faced, a particularly difficult problem that calls for an impossible solution, or a potentiality which cannot be realized. Stated in Sartrean terms, this means that there is a point beyond which the magical negation of the noematic content – the normalization of the world – is no longer possible, and affective neutrality or equilibrium is recaptured at the price of accepting total defeat. Similarly, the Schopenhauerian distinctions necessary for self-location in society are erased.

The result, as Hervey (the betrayed husband in "The Return") discovers, is an undifferentiated, nightmarishly frightening darkness which also paradoxically serves as the repository of authenticity:

> In sheer physical terms, the weight of experience has made of [Hervey] a new world of totally isolated "symbolic" density. Living previously as a hollow man of conventionality in a complex world, Hervey has possessed the world in a successive series of noetic acts that obliterate the distinctions between truth and illusion, time and space, himself and the darkness. To his hyperenlarged vision, the world itself is mere representation, a sham: he himself is far richer in meaning – and he has an apprehension of the immense darkness to which he has finally penetrated. Past and present thus both become actual, and equally impossible, in his own mind. He sees the great night of the world breaking through the discreet reserve of walls, of closed doors, of curtained windows.[24]

This negative plenitude – which Said equates with Sartre's universal gloom and solitude as well as Schopenhauer's pure, unobjectified will – is none other than truth itself as Conrad understood it: "dark, sinister and fugitive,"[25] truth is the equivalent of both the total absence of thought (and hence of knowledge) and an equally total internalization of experience. That is to say, it is on the one hand imageless, silent, and passive but on the other hand deep, concentrated, and "almost mystic[al]."[26] What particular consequences follow from this negative valuation of truth? What does this at once opaque and cornucopic self-subsistence entail for our conceptions of self, society, value, indeed reality itself? Before considering these and similar questions in detail, I would like to make some further observations about Said's understanding of truth in this early work.

First, a close examination of what constitutes truth reveals a certain ambiguity in its content at a primary, perceptual level. At times, it would seem, what is labelled as "truth" refers to a set of past events which are almost impossible to reconstruct but also nevertheless appear to be tantalizingly close. Said suggests that the best, though by no means the only, example of truth as silent but insistent gloom is the primal pall that hangs over everything in *Heart of Darkness*; reading the story, one instinctively gets the uncanny suspicion that the same originary darkness cocoons together the small group of men listening to Marlow on the Thames and the frightening events on the Congo – even though they are separated in time and space. Elsewhere in Said's analysis, the notion of truth is actually bodied forth in concrete but incomprehensible representation. Hence the lake in "The Lagoon," the unfaithful wife in "The Return," the sea in many of Conrad's adventure tales, the sick black sailor in *The Nigger of the "Narcissus,"* and especially the physical presence of Africa in *Heart of Darkness* – all of these are in their own different ways symbolic "manifestations" of what Said characterizes as truth. Since there is no ontological (as opposed to existential) substance that brings into being true entities susceptible of understanding, what "defines" truth as such is the grip that the noema has on the mind: to the extent that *something* enigmatic – some person, object, or lack – intrigues consciousness (the author's, the narrator's, the protagonist's, etc.) by soliciting attention because of its weirdness, its promise, its power, or its malevolence, that *something* serves as the absent cause, the ultimate category of determination which is also emphatically negative. "Truth," then, assumes the characteristics of irrational worries and fears, of secret fantasies and obsessions, of hidden guilt and shame – in short, an approximation of what in Freudian terms would be called the unconscious, even though – as I pointed out earlier – Said steers clear of psychoanalysis.

Apropos of these conceptualizations, Said appears to be, at least to some extent, taking Conrad's treatment of the noematic content at face value, leading to perhaps unintended interpretive consequences. I say "appears" because, as we shall see presently, Said is fully aware that the noematic content, at least in some of its forms, is nothing more than a representation (in the sense of both concealment and construction) of what is sometimes called the Other of (Western) subjectivity – aware, in other words, that "truth" furnishes the ideological "difference" necessary for self-fortification and self-valorization: it constitutes the point of slippage, the supposedly inarticulable but useful "mystery" in contradistinction to which a Conradian personal and cultural will to mastery comes into self-identity. Nevertheless, there is a sense in which Said fails to cut through the rhetorical ruses that enable Conrad to create these asymmetrical dichotomies. The essentialized, seemingly inchoate and imageless negativity that Said nominalistically labels as "truth" could actually be further differentiated (as he himself does in his later writings). My point is this: the "heart of darkness" in Africa, the symbolic blackness of James Wait (in *The Nigger of the "Narcissus"*), the mysterious silence of the East (in "Youth" and elsewhere), as well as the various suggestive, often repellent traits of "truth" in Conrad's oeuvre, do not, from Said's analysis, come through to us as primarily ideological investments conferred on an at least partially manufactured "object," whose humanity is seriously questioned if not completely annihilated. Rather, these characteristics are by and large presented by Said – as by Conrad – in the form of natural predications that fit their substance perfectly. This collaboration of language and silence is especially assailed by critics like Achebe and Bhabha.[27]

It may be concluded, perhaps with some justification, that my comments on Said's treatment of truth in the Conradian context are meant to shed light on interpretive blind spots in Said's own work. Yet to leave the matter there would be to lose sight of the fact that Said has a broader critical agenda, an agenda in which this "blind spot" itself is being transformed into a critical insight of far-reaching implications. Said, in other words, consciously or otherwise fails to take Conrad the Eurocentrist to task for the simple reason that Conrad's dark conception of truth enables Said to position himself at a cuspidated point from which he can launch critiques of epistemology, ideology, and imperialism all at once. This claim will sound paradoxical only if we forget that Said thrives on ambiguity or, as I have insisted from the outset, uses the notion of the boundary in creative ways.

A specific in-between zone that needs consideration here is the grey area between the intellectual and the community with which he or she identifies. In this regard, *The Fiction of Autobiography* is remarkable for its ambivalent equipoise between an emergent assault on institutionalized privilege, on the one hand, and a recognition of (even commitment to) individual autonomy, on the other. Said's analysis hovers between a qualified endorsement of the suffering, self-defining artist and a back-handed indictment of the untenable cultural baggage he is carrying. In other words, if the polemical Said of *Orientalism* or *Culture and Imperialism* is known for his assertions about Eurocentric thought and Western imperialism, the early Said only hints at these issues, concentrating instead on his reconstruction of Conrad's artistic and spiritual journey. What is, nevertheless, beyond any doubt is that Said is using Conrad's suspicion of ideas and ideals in general not only to overturn ethical and epistemic norms in the manner of radical critique of ideology as such but also to X-ray the subterranean transactions that enabled a specific ideology – that is, high European imperialism – to consolidate itself in the late nineteenth and early twentieth century. This critique is possible because, thanks to his difficult reflexivity, Conrad's version of truth – namely, authenticity as an occluded meaning, as a logical aporia, or as a cause manqué – constitutes one of the two poles of what I have been characterizing as an either/or dialectic in one of its forms.

Conrad and the Imperialism of Ideas

And this brings us to another in-between zone – or, to be more precise, a process of mutation: the construction of what Said describes (after Newman) as "economies" of (self-) creation out of the potentially infinite forms of experience. That is to say, as a direct consequence of the pendular swings discussed earlier, it is inevitable that, sooner or later, truth be made by human agency, whether individually or collectively, to give birth to conceptual knowledge, and knowledge – in the Conradian universe as well as in Said's appropriation of it – is intimately connected not only with error but also with power. The following passage, which must be quoted at length to deliver its full significance, illustrates what I mean; its point of departure, already encountered here, is that genuine truth is a deep shadow:

> So sufficient is this all-enveloping shadow that one can rest entirely within it, away from any of the common rational forms of human hope or regret. Lodged

within the obliterating shadow of truth, a man feels indifferent to everything outside. After a time, the self begins to exercise a kind of brutish vindication of itself, probably out of a surfeit of rational inactivity and emotional pride. When one boasts of being safely alone in the embrace of truth, it becomes impossible to avoid the inception of thought: the thoughtless repetition of a subrational sentiment inspires, no matter how empty the sentiment, some *idea of himself* in the mind of the person who has the sentiment. Now thought, under the sway of the ego, systematizes "truth" simply into an image of the self in possession of truth. As soon as this egoistic image is formed, then the individual begins to think that the world must be organized according to the image. To Conrad "thought" apparently designated the process whereby a human self-image is elevated into an idea of truth that inevitably seeks perpetuation. Beneath its rational articulation, however, the idea is only a man's desire for protection from the impinging confusions of the world. Immediately after the intellectual organization of the world according to an idea, there comes the expedient of devotion to the idea, which in turn breeds conquest according to the idea. But the moment a man begins to examine the idea itself, he slowly begins to negate the distinctions he had organized for viewing the world: encircled by its own work, the intellect has no positive, objective criterion for evaluation. All the structures of its differentiated organization of the world disappear, and the cycle begins again.[28]

The importance of this passage for an understanding of Said's critical project as a whole can hardly be overestimated. For what is etched out behind the immediate, foregrounded appraisal of Conrad's dilemmas is a notion that underlies, in one form or another, all of Said's subsequent studies: that human intentionality is a truncated yet highly ambitious affair.

The inaugural imperative of this thesis, which imparts its skeptical hue to the ethical and epistemological dimensions of experience alike, is that any form of intellection whatsoever – any enactment which activates the operations of thought and its powers of discrimination – involves both the embrace of illusion and the exercise of coercion. To put the matter bluntly, all knowledge and the claims that are used to vouch for its validity are the products of the will, where "will" is to be understood as an individual and/or cultural agency that intends sense and intelligibility; acts and reacts; resists, overcomes, and masters; pronounces binding judgements – and executes all these undertakings, not in accordance with transcendent ordinances or value-neutral laws inherent in the nature of things, but at the bidding of that agency's immanent directives. In later chapters, we will see how Said buttresses this mythopoetic thesis by adapting insights from a large number of modern thinkers – prominent among them Vico and Foucault – but in this early text it is Schopenhauer's principle of differentiation (*principium individuationis*) that is deployed by Said to describe the process by virtue of which explicit images and ideas are teased out of the silence and opacity of truth.

In *The World as Will and Idea*, Schopenhauer argues that, before the awakening of intellectual faculties, man subsists in the grey, undifferentiated shadow of pure will; that as soon as the process of thinking is initiated, man (in Said's paraphrase) "asserts his ego and becomes objectified will"; that civilized man – by virtue of the fact that he has sharpened his intellectual skills to the highest degree – has attained the "highest form of objectified will."[29] The end product of this self-induced awakening is an enormously narcissistic ruse of self-persuasion: "the world is my idea."[30] This, according to Said, is the principle underpinning Conrad's vision of reality (though he does detect a slight difference between Schopenhauer and Conrad): the slumbering self possessing the "truth" vindicates itself by creating *an idea* of itself; then, by further systematization, the self fashions an *"image* of the self possessing the truth;" next, that "self-image" is translated into the higher idea of unsullied truth; once this elevation has been effected, the self begins to pay homage to its creation as one would to a divine being; finally, a project of conquest according to that idea of truth is launched. "But the moment a man begins to examine the idea itself," the moment the intellect further meditates on the concepts, strategies, and modalities which it has deployed to forge that idea, the entire edifice collapses – leaving its author with nothing except the grey originary void or opacity that furnished the "raw materials" for the idea in the first place.

The immediate epistemological implications of this sobering, post-Enlightenment vision should be obvious enough. Conrad, in a quasi-Nietzschean frame of mind (an affinity which Said pointedly remarks elsewhere),[31] seems to be saying this: in order to shield itself "from the impinging confusions of the world," human agency, whether embodied in the individual self or in the community at large, constructs self-ratifying monuments out of the ensemble of fictions available to it at specific historical and cultural conjunctures. In other words, every foundationalist logic that has ever been employed in the construction of ideas and institutions is being (indirectly) described as a strategy of containment, an instrument of control, or a chimeral imago fashioned under a false light. From Said's analysis, Conrad, then, comes through to us as a thinker who has confronted the deracinative conditions of modernity head-on; as a writer, that is, who has thoroughly internalized what Said characterizes (in *Beginnings*) as the almost mind-bending "oppositions" of modernist consciousness.

The consequences of this profound "disenchantment" (and here I am radicalizing Weber's notion somewhat) for Conrad are as grim as they are perdurable. Conrad, believes Said, early on in his career arrives at a dystopian conclusion about the meaning and quality of human life, a conclusion that, for him (though not for Said), precludes the luxury of nurturing any lasting universalist ideals. We are all chained prisoners, Conrad moans in a letter to his aunt, Marguerite Poradowska; the few who, like Conrad himself, have attained a heightened sense of awareness are at once the "elect[ed]" and the "convict[ed]"; the rest are mere idiots.[32] In another letter – this one to Robert Cunninghame Graham – Conrad argues that the universe has been tailored by a gigantic, particularly efficient knitting machine – an indifferent, uncontrollable monster which "is thinner than air and as evanescent as lightning."[33] In numerous other letters, he complains about aches, nightmares, and inertia. Said notes that Conrad's ethical impulse is pervaded by this stubborn strain of pessimism almost throughout his career. Man, decides Conrad, must come down from the tall "stilts of principles"[34] and accept the grimness of his situation. What, in the end, humanity is left with is nothing more than a "refuge," a "set of rules" for an unpleasant game, an idea that demands fidelity.[35] That idea, Said suggests, is partially furnished by Conrad's ability to create and recreate himself through his writing, both fictional and non-fictional.

There is something else implicit in the long passage I quoted above: Said's view on European imperialism. In its foreground, the passage is an attempt to de-transcendentalize "true" ideas and ideals by tracing them back to their anthropomorphic genesis. By laying bare the techniques and strategies that normalize ideologies in general into transparent truths, Said is counteracting the occlusive mystifications of empiricist and idealist historians, thus implicating ideas as such with their material moorings: the psychological, historical, and cultural phenomena which give rise to ideas and determine their further unfolding in the circumstances of time and space. The passage therefore serves as a metacritical, ground-clearing exercise in a broad theoretical sense. However, it is clear that, even in this early text, one of Said's goals is to make a specific political statement by drawing attention to the link between what he calls the "imperialism of ideas" and the "imperialism of nations":

The trouble with unrestrained egoism as Conrad saw it was that it becomes an imperialism of ideas, which easily converts itself into the imperialism of nations. In spite of the obvious injustice done to those upon whom one's idea can be imposed, it is important to understand that the reason an individual imposes his idea is that he believes he is serving the truth.[36]

The full implication of the two passages from *Heart of Darkness* which I cited early on in this chapter now emerges: according to Said, Conrad was unusually conscious of the fact that European imperialism was ultimately indefensible precisely because the "ethical" and "epistemological" principles which were used to support it were themselves little more than manifestations of the will to truth and the will to power. Here is Marlow once again, this time quoting some of the last fragmentary phrases fetched by Kurtz before he gives his final gasp: " 'My ivory.' Oh yes, I heard him. 'My Intended [i.e., his fian-ceé], my ivory, my station, my river, my' – everything belonged to him."[37] Let us juxtapose this enormously hubristic bit of self-endowment with the last sentence (again cited by Marlow) of the little report Kurtz had compiled for the International [read European] Society for the Suppression of Savage Customs: "Exterminate all the brutes!"[38] The "brutes" are the Africans. This theme – Euro-America's ability to conjoin "right" and "might" in the most self-serving fashion in order to carry out the most extreme measures against "inferior races" who also happen to own valuable resources coveted by the West – has solicited Said's attention repeatedly. It lies at the heart of his indictment of Orientalism, Zionism, high European imperialism, and American postcolonial hegemonism. It also indirectly sheds light on his profound disappointment – articulated most clearly in *The World, the Text, and the Critic* and *Representations of the Intellectual* – with contemporary "critical" intellectuals in the West.

At this point, Said could well be open to the charge that his "critique" is dogmatic; that, in his zeal to expose the common foundations of knowledge, ideology, and power, he may have cut the ground from under his own feet; that, because of an inability on his part to distinguish genuinely utopian ideals and intersubjectively shareable knowledge from rationalized mystifications and instrumentalized knowledge, he has deprived himself of any viable justificative space. This charge has considerable force to it, especially with respect to this early work. Said's suspicion of empiricism and idealism in the manner I have been discussing almost automatically obviates certain types of ethical and epistemic comforts – for example, those offered by so-called theories of reference based on correspondence or coherence: meaning and value are equally inexplicable in any terms other than those of a constructivism entailing socio-historical localisms and specificities.

Complaints like these have been registered about a large number of contemporary thinkers, including such "Nietzscheans" as Foucault and Derrida, cultural materialists, and postmodernists of various hues. Yet such an interpretation of Said's views on the matter is only partially valid. For, as I have pointed out repeatedly, Said's criticism is a multifaceted and multivalenced undertaking – the very consistency of his basic "technique of trouble" implies strategic nomadism. In its most comprehensively articulated form, this nomadic eclecticism has taken a historical route – indeed, I have insisted, the best way to approach Said's various studies, particularly the major texts, is to view them not just as eccentric works of literary analysis but also as postnarrative histories of ideas and institutions. And through a careful study of Said's historical vision, we can arrive at a reasonably informed conclusion about what seems to be his ultimate "ground" – a locus where, as we shall see in the next chapter, a clear-cut distinction is made between ideological constructions, on the one hand, and what could be called critical knowledge, on the other. In this final section of the first chapter, I would like to examine Said's radical historicism more closely. What becomes clear is that his conception of space-time is as much a result of agonistic dialectic as it is of archaeology/genealogy: it involves the conflictual, multivectored sublation of the former and the discontinuities, sedimentations, and mutations of the latter – this despite the fact that Said's analysis in this early study is neither "Marxian" nor "Foucauldian" in the strict senses of these terms.

The Ego Historicized: Space-Time as Sedimented Gestalts

The problem of space-time is treated by Said in two complementary ways: in terms of critical moments of dynamic situatedness and in terms of broad, discontinuous cycles which he describes as phases. Said analyzes the first conception primarily as it is illustrated in the narrative structure and characterization of Conrad's fiction rather than in the letters. What happens at such tense, pregnant moments is that a mutual co-activation of spatio-temporal poles takes place as a result of the major character's desire for equilibrium. The ghosts of yesteryear (usually hitherto carefully hidden, shameful secrets) demand to be laid to rest, but this invasion of past events often triggers prolonged soul-searching and agony in the character instead of bringing the much-needed relief. Especially in Conrad's earliest stories (including his best), this struggle ends in defeat or death. The past short-circuits the present and abolishes the future. In most of the later stories, characters achieve a Pyrrhic victory. The idea of space-time which Said presents here reflects human facticity, with all its precariousness and transi-toriness; the embeddedness (of the author or character) in a hostile environment is measured synchronically as moments of painful sen-tience and difficult reflection, wherein authenticity resides. To adopt the other alternative is to surrender to the will – at the risk of losing that authenticity. If this isolation of the dialectical moment accent-uates the situatedness of the self in specific horizons, the second view of space-time articulated in Said's analysis relates to the three trans-posed phases of Conrad's career.

At first glance, Said's employment of the notion of phase seems disarmingly familiar: after all, the various empiricist or idealist models used in traditional literary and intellectual history – the kinds of narrativist or formalist presentations that dwell on zeitgeist, sources and influences, formative touchstones, etc. – imply, often explicitly state, certain assumptions of progression or evolution in stages. However, it should be clear by now that Said's conception of historical change is meant to de-domesticate what he would almost undoubt-edly consider the easy psychologism and naive syncretism of such approaches: "phase," here as elsewhere in his works, is intended not only to capture biographical and literary evolution but also to throw into relief the distinct interruptions and cross-sections of that movement; not only to give a sense of linearity and continuity but also to come to terms with the grey areas that I have been describing as in-between zones – that is, to mark the points where the inevitable hiccoughs, punctuations, mutations, and transpositions take place.

In the context of Said's first book, the Conradian self pauses peri-odically, makes a general survey of the territories it has traversed, and recognizes the need to shift gears. The resulting fields of meaning and value constitute neither "extrinsic" or "objective" narratives nor "intrinsic" histories composed of "clear and distinct ideas" but dia-lectically created, unified gestalts of lived experience understood phenomenologically and existentially. The evolution of the artistic career takes the form of ever-widening contours which are sedimented on top of each other. Caught up in what of necessity acquires the properties of both process, rupture, transformation, and stability,

Conrad's attempt at self-understanding is found to travel along ret-
rospective, proleptic, and vertical vectors – all at one and the same
time. The change of valence is therefore a complex affair: it is at once
exponential, recursive, and repressive, the three Conradian phases
being registered as both growth and loss, along different (even
opposing) vectors. The ego increases its strength by raising itself to
the second power, in the process recouping valuable, progressively
larger chunks of reality. The lacunae of the past become occasions for
new totalizations as well as new points of departure. But at the same
time, a mechanism of censorship is at work right from the outset,
gradually sharpening itself in the service of a hubristic, Faustian
impulse. It is with this complex process in mind that Said examines
the three Conradian phases.

Said argues that the first phase of Conrad's career is a period of
groping and moral struggle; that the letters and stories of this period
act as registers of pain and anguish; that the tortuous plots, multi-
layered themes, and ambiguous conclusions of the early stories
instantiate the near-impossibility of self-rescue; that the cause of the
ennui – as much in the author as in the important characters of a
given story – is a shameful lump of memory that disturbs the present
but resists all attempts to dissolve it; that, therefore, Conrad's writing
from the late 1880s to about 1912 exudes a cloud of pessimism and
despair.

In contrast, the second phase (a six-year interlude during which
Conrad comes to grips with the horrors of the war) is a prolonged
implosion that nevertheless oversees the birth of a Baudelairean
"homo duplex" in him. Said detects several different impulses in the
Conrad of this phase. First, a duplicitous dissociation of aesthetic
sensibility and ethical imperatives enables Conrad to institute an
artful, efficient principle of selectivity. In effect, the raw materials of
experience are screened carefully at the threshold of pen and paper,
and undesirable details are duly suppressed. Henceforth, dubious,
sanitized "biographies" are authorized and foisted on the world,
despite the protest of close personal friends. These manipulative
tactics of the mature writer, Said suggests, are not hypocritical,
deliberately misleading gimmicks so much as they are ruses of self-
persuasion. In the absence of truth, the writer must install "belief" by
fiat. Conrad carries this hoodwinking into the world of his fiction: he
creates a series of protagonists each one of whom leads a double life
with a public façade and a closely guarded secret (consider the
unnamed captain in "The Secret Sharer" and the murderer he harbors

on board). Second, in part necessitated by the demands of a growing public audience, this separation of private and public domains obliges Conrad to shrug off, at least for a while, the searing pessimism of the first phase. What replaces the nightmarishness of those earlier stories is a relatively positive but contrived resolution. Finally, apparently because of the terrible cost of the war, Conrad once again yields to an intensified version of despair. "The Planter of Malatta," the last story to come out of the second phase, is – according to Said – the most pessimistic tale Conrad ever wrote.

The key terms of the third phase (from 1918 to 1924) are "mastery" and "conquest," with their attendant associations of stability and calmness, perspicacity and self-assurance, not to say dogmatism and arrogance. The end of the war brings out a state of completeness, which, because of the dialectical nature of Conrad's experience, delivers meaning in two different but complementary directions. In the most obvious sense, completion signifies the end of a process: extending to its logical conclusion the already valorized interactive evolution between his own identity and that of European civilization, Conrad concludes that an entire historical and biographical era has passed away. Just as the old political order of the continent has been reduced to rubble, so also an entire inner dimension of his own personal experience has been brought to an end. But at the same time new transmutations have occurred; because a consummation has taken place, a new plane of maturity and fullness has been consolidated. The ego has achieved both complete autonomy and complete control. It is as though, because of the process of externalization, Conrad's psyche has been emptied of its burden of anxiety, terror, and instability, now enjoying a state of transsubjective serenity and clarity. Conversely, as a result of the concomitant centripetality, the new state of mind is also pregnant with a highly idealized sense of a pan-European identity – even at the same time that Conrad "looks out upon"[39] an actual Europe which has become a wasteland. The two related preoccupations of Conrad during the last six years of his life, argues Said, are celebration of the freedom announced by the birth of a new era and the burial of the dead.

Said's analysis exposes in no uncertain terms the megalomaniacal self that is born in the last phase of Conrad's career. What emerges is a strange paradox. On the one hand, Conrad never loses his sensitivity to the purgative nature of experience and its value at the level of the individual human being; but on the other hand, he can barely conceal his contempt for those who arouse his ire, an odd assortment that includes politicians, the masses, Germans, and Russians, among others. He condemns "bloodless" abstractions, as well as such "infernal" political doctrines as socialism. Conrad's pontifications about European destiny; his argument that this idealized sense of Europe required the sacrifice of a worthy individual who is intimated to be none other than himself; his trenchant attacks on the newly created Soviet Union; his cavalier dismissal of such ideas as peace and the creation of the League of Nations – all of these pronouncements suggest more than a touch of intolerance and egomania. Adequately illustrated in the letters of the last phase, this self-satisfied equilibrium is, according to Said, fully articulated in a novella Conrad wrote shortly before the war: *The Shadow Line*. The young protagonist, a patriotic English captain, has his dreams realized in the most propitious manner: he achieves "[i]deal completeness, self-fulfillment, permanence."[40]

In spite of the ideologically valenced self-confidence in Conrad's final years, Said's judgement of him is on the whole a positive one. Indeed, his concentration on the existentialist cast of Conrad's experience is itself an act of empathy between two displaced intellectuals who – at least in part because of that displacement – share a great deal of inaugural suspicion. Let me conclude with a passage from the final pages of *The Fiction*, a passage which sheds almost as much light on Said as it does on Conrad:

> Conrad's achievement is that he ordered the chaos of his existence into a highly patterned art that accurately reflected and controlled the realities with which it dealt. His experience, as both man and writer, is unique in English literature: no expatriation was as complete or as complex as his, no literary production as profoundly strange and creative. *Because he*, like so many of his characters, *lived life at the extreme, he was more acutely conscious of community even if, most of the time, his was a negative or critical view. He dramatized the plight of man divorced from and yet still incriminated by the past, the man committed to but paralyzed by society.* Driven back on his individuality, he accepted its burdens and its uncompromisingly pessimistic vision of reality. [italics added][41]

2

Beginnings and Authority: Ideology, Critique, and Community (I)

A Theoretical Intervention

Commenting on the peripeties and transformations in Georges Poulet's critical techniques, Paul de Man observes that, despite the thread of continuity, "the various critical narratives are organized in terms of a series of dramatic events: reversals, repetitions, about-faces, and resolutions."[1] At various points of his discussion, de Man describes these events as "points of departure," "apogees," "moments de passages," or "instants de passages," and tells us that Poulet deployed them in studies on Julien Green, Benjamin Constance, Marcel Proust, and others. They constitute a radical form of dissonance, de Man notes, adding that they cannot be "explained," because they represent "the very essence of discontinuity." Paradoxically enough, however, the typical point of mutation at once serves as a "source" and as a "center." That is, these points of discontinuity ratify both stability and evolution. Predicated on an extremely sensitive brand of sympathy between critic and author, the kind of interpretation practiced by Poulet – an intellectual and emotional engagement in which the boundaries of literary language and its interpretation are all but erased – sustains itself precisely because the self repeatedly runs the risk of annihilation: "Poulet can reach the quality of genuine subjectivity because ... he is willing to undermine the stability of the subject and because he refuses to borrow stability for the subject from outside sources."[2]

Some aspects of this brief discussion have a certain ring of familiarity to them. Idiosyncrasies aside, Said's reading of Conrad, as we have seen, unfolds within a cognitive-affective field whose contours

and transformations are largely determined by the triumphs and
failures of an overburdened literary consciousness. Conrad fashioned
his artistic career – Said has told us – in the course of a particularly
tortuous dialectic involving an individual self and its cultural world.
In confronting the existential and logical implications of that difficult
dialectic, the author (to adapt de Man's apt phrasing) was able to
"reach the quality of genuine subjectivity" precisely to the extent that
he was "willing to undermine the stability of" that same subjectivity.
There is, then, an obvious sense in which Said's first book, *Joseph
Conrad and the Fiction of Autobiography*, occupies an intellectual space
that Poulet would have recognized instantaneously. That common
space, as we have noted already, is phenomenological both in its broad
assumptions and in its idiom. What might not be so obvious – and
this is more immediately relevant for this second chapter of my study
– is that de Man's appraisal of Poulet and other modern critics, which
appears in his seminal work, *Blindness and Insight*, constitutes, like
Said's second major study, both an important critical "event" and an
interpretive "re-enactment": that is, like de Man's book, *Beginnings*
was intended both as a radical break with and as an ambitious reappropriation of a disciplinary prehistory within the compass of a new
methodological horizon.

From the privileged perspective of the early twenty-first century, it
may seem a bit disingenuous on my part to lump together two critics
who have in important respects come to be seen – at least since the
publication of Said's *The World, the Text, and the Critic* – as adversaries.
And yet consider the implications of the following passage from the
first chapter of *Beginnings*:

> Now it is Paul de Man's thesis that in criticism the very blindness of a theory
> with regard to certain aspects of literature makes possible the discovery of the
> most valuable insights ... Intention, then, in my sense of the term, is the
> interplay between such blindness and such insight. In other words, intention
> is the link between idiosyncratic view and the communal concern.[3]

This short passage invites commentary in terms of several configurations and on several levels, all of which are germane both to the
specific project of *Beginnings* in itself and to the strategic place it
occupies in Said's career as a whole. First, as is evident from Said's
invocation of de Man, it lights up the methodological – if not
necessarily ideological – affinities between *Beginnings* and the work of
other contemporary theorists. Like de Man's then influential writings
and those of other critics who have come to be known as the practi-

tioners of "uncanny" criticism (among them J. Hillis Miller, Harold Bloom, Geoffrey Hartman, and de Man himself), Said's study was designed to effect the subversion of literary tenets that had increasingly come to be seen as rigid dogmas. *Beginnings* emerged out of the insurrectionary Sixties and early Seventies, a period during which a young generation of critical intellectuals was devising ways of severing what it considered to be the hobbles of New Criticism. Like *Beyond Formalism*, *Blindness and Insight*, and *Anxiety of Influence*, *Beginnings* was intended to enact a major critical intervention. Hence, the brief passage places Said's study in its immediate intellectual milieu.

But Said, of course, fields his own personal agenda – an agenda whose provocativeness is announced in the very title of his study: his choice of topic – namely, the nature of a beginning as a methodological problematic – acts as an unusual, even oxymoronic trope; it serves at once as a point of rupture, seed, and recovery. As a notion that marks both a break with orthodoxy and an identification of (and with) novelty – that is, a point of inauguration for an alternative conception of a given subject matter – a beginning records both loss and liberation. But precisely because it is transgressive and is therefore dogged by anxiety, a beginning also constitutes the site of profound reflection on anteriority, a slippery yet deliberately stabilized site where the authority of silenced Origins is registered, scrutinized, pondered, dismantled, de-defined, recovered, projected, and refined in various ways for purposes of self-legitimation. Said's study – pointedly subtitled *Intention and Method* – is an attempt to come to grips with all these often contradictory implications of the idea of beginning as an intellectual enactment – whether that enactment involves a specific project (say, a book or an article), an entire career, or even a broader disciplinary (or discursive) transformation. The brief passage I cited above can be used as a point of engaging these historical and methodological problematics at a relatively broad level.

A closer examination of the passage enables us to revisit – and transform – a set of more focused (primarily though not exclusively epistemological) topics which we have already reflected on. "Intention," Said tells us, to him signifies "an interplay between" "blindness" and "insight." Although the specifically predicative terminology (as distinct from the central idea of intention) is inflected in a way that does not immediately and unproblematically cohere with either existentialism or will philosophy, it should nevertheless be clear enough that Said is making an encapsulated restatement (rather

than a reinterpretation) of certain claims which he has previously
made in *The Fiction*: claims about the perceptual opacity of truth;
about the way in which ideas and ideals almost inevitably merge into
ideological doctrines; about human agency's co-activation of the will
to truth and the will to power – all these concerns, which we have
encountered in the study of Conrad, are addressed in *Beginnings* too.
Like the problematical notion of either/or, the paradoxical trope
which Said appropriates from de Man – namely, that real critical
insight can be achieved only at the risk of accepting (perhaps even
embracing) theoretical blindness at a fundamental level – is intended
to reaffirm in the new study critical positions which have already been
staked out in *The Fiction*. And yet it should be equally clear that the
introduction of the new terminology is at least in part meant to signal
an important conceptual transformation. Said, in other words, has
made what could broadly be called a linguistic turn in his career –
even if, from the central place occupied by the idea of intention, we
can surmise how crucial phenomenological hermeneutics continues to
be in his career. Although, as we shall see later, Said's linguistic turn
is a very complex, multifaceted affair (it is never restricted to the
narrowly rhetorical dimension suggested by his adaptation of de
Man's metaphor), there is an important sense in which *Beginnings* is as
much a confrontation with textuality (and intertextuality) as it is a
reconceptualization of intentionality. In fact, it could be argued that
the entire study constitutes, at its most fundamental level, a co-
activation of both of these two dimensions of intellectual life,
accounting for the deep tension that weaves through the entire text.

But this is not the only tension manifested in *Beginnings*; for, as the
passage once again reminds us, part of Said's objective is to investigate
the different ways in which intentions determine "the link between
idiosyncratic view and the communal concern." In my first chapter, I
hinted at the enormous importance which Said attaches to the connection (or boundary) between autonomous agency, especially as it is
embodied in the intellectual, and the multiple communities in which
that agency is embedded. It is apposite at this point to note the
various nuances that the idea of "community" acquires in Said's work
from here on, particularly in *Beginnings*, but also in the more overtly
political writings that came in its wake. The term at times suggests an
interpretive community (in the sense popularized by Stanley Fish)[4] to
which a scholar is "affiliated," as Said would later phrase it in *The
World, the Text, and the Critic*.[5] It is also obviously to be understood as
denoting an existential or political community, large or small (it

could be called a tribe or a nation; it could also designate a larger cultural construct – for example, the "West" or the "Orient"), to which an individual belongs by birth, training, or both. (The idea of "filiation" – dynastic, linear, traditionary – approximates this sense of community.) Finally, the idea as Said uses it incorporates the human community in its entirety, a community conceived as a plurality of interrelated cultures.

Although the specific inflection in the passage quoted above draws attention primarily to the methodological tensions between the lone intellectual and his or her interpretive community, *Beginnings* ultimately constitutes an attempt to account for all the three aspects outlined here. A slightly different way of formulating this point is to say that the idea of culture, an extremely important but in its own way slippery concept, assumes a far more differentiated, theoretically reflexive form in *Beginnings* than it did in *The Fiction*. Investigating the shifting border regions "between idiosyncratic view and the communal concern" in a manner of speaking therefore turns on the response to this vital question: in the unfolding of modernity, exactly what has the category of culture entailed epistemologically, aesthetically, historically, and (ultimately) politically? Although in such later texts as *The World, the Text, and the Critic* and *Culture and Imperialism* the notion of culture takes on neo-Marxist inflections, in *Beginnings* Said's response to the above question, especially at the metacritical level, partakes greatly of Foucauldian and (especially) Vichian insights.

I have ferreted a seemingly disparate tassel of strands out of what is after all a very brief passage in order to indicate from the outset both the enormous theoretical importance of *Beginnings* for Said's entire critical effort and the considerable difficulties entailed in interpreting it. This dual challenge, it should be immediately added, is part of a deliberate strategy – a strategy built into the very structure of the text – rather than the result of an oversight. The study incorporates a number of features – both thematic and methodological – which contribute to this challenge, features which are perhaps best understood as an interrelated series of dramatized dissonances, confrontations, or even contradictions. A brief (but representative) example can be offered here: on the one hand, Said insists that critical intervention is ultimately a matter of both self-invention and self-positioning – a willed act of personal freedom; but on the other hand, a considerable part of his argument is an attempt to demonstrate that, in the context of modernity, both suprapersonal theoretical postulations (say, Marx's class and capital or Foucault's episteme) and the primordial material presence of language itself have acted as powerfully constraining forces that operate behind (and below) the feeble enactments of the historically situated human being – even as these same forces empower him or her in obvious ways. Later on in the chapter, I will investigate in somewhat greater detail some of the localized consequences of these dramatized confrontations. At this point, however, I would like to draw attention to the way in which Said's strategy manifests itself at the global level, the level where it matters most for propaedeutic purposes.

One of the most fascinating aspects of *Beginnings* is that its sheer compendiousness is directly pitted against its highly unconventional methodology. Unlike *The Fiction of Autobiography*, a relatively streamlined study focusing on a single author, his oeuvre, and his immediate socio-cultural world, *Beginnings* is an ambitious omnivore covering a large number of thinkers, a multiplicity of genres and traditions, and a varied range of socio-historical contexts. Yet there is a deliberate and sustained effort on Said's part to subvert the triadic, Aristotelian organization common in academic scholarship – the kind of presentation which is at one and the same time designed to respect the continuity of history or tradition, to vouch for logical consistency, and to account for any level of complexity in subject matter. Said's own idiosyncratic methodology is what he has called "a meditation." It enables him, he suggests, to negotiate between rationalist formalism and analogical flexibility, and to avail himself of the strengths of both while avoiding the constrictiveness of the former as well as the laxity of the latter. His argument weaves back and forth, sometimes taking giant leaps, creating in the process a multiplicity of conjunctions, breaks, configurations, and transpositions. His copious reflections wend their way from seventeenth-century Protestant literature in England to twentieth-century Continental thought; oblique connections are established between, say, the realistic novel and psychoanalysis, or between modernist literature and structuralism. A whole host of eccentric thinkers – among them Sterne, Kierkegaard, and Nietzsche – are considered in conjunction with more orthodox writers, such as Wordsworth, Dickens, and Auerbach. Often the profoundly revolutionary impulse is closely implicated with the unabashedly conservative – sometimes in the writing of the same thinker. Said's aim in all of this, it would seem, is to combine maximum resilience with maximum rigor; more precisely, the argument of the book is intended as an exercise in demystification and reappropriation. At once grand and adventurous, it is putatively catholic in some respects but disorientingly speculative in others. *Beginnings*, then, is clearly an academic text designed to subvert the very protocols of academic scholarship.

It is therefore not particularly surprising that the early reception of *Beginnings* ranged from praise to bemusement. What *is* surprising is this: in the years since its publication in 1975, the study has provoked very little further discussion – the kind of serious discussion one would expect in response to such a high-caliber text. This relative neglect is all the more difficult to explain given the unusually animated, astonishingly varied commentary generated in the wake of *Orientalism*. *Beginnings* was indeed recognized as a major intellectual event when it first came out: it was accorded the special honor of being the first book to win the Lionel Trilling Memorial Award, and *Diacritics* devoted an entire issue to it and its author (the journal conducted a long interview with Said). The reviewers who contributed to that issue – among them such major critics as Hayden White and J. Hillis Miller – are on the whole sympathetic to Said's general project in *Beginnings*; nevertheless, they express reservations about what they perceive as shortcomings in the study.

White, for example, draws attention to the theoretical difficulties entailed in Said's argument. Noting Said's departure from conventional methodology, he observes that the author of *Beginnings* "wishes to make valid statements about a host of entities, problems, movements, ideas, and above all texts that exist beyond the confines of his discourse." That is to say, Said disallows both logic and analogy as primary guiding principles for his argument and yet wants to illuminate a large complex of phenomena. White pointedly (if somewhat misleadingly) asks, "how can a discourse which denies the authority of logic to guide arguments and of analogy to suggest striking connections between ideas claim validity for its own assertions?"[6] White concludes that *Beginnings* is not methodologically convincing: the two introductory chapters, he insists, do not provide a "metacritical" framework for the rest of the book. He believes that the only way to make sense of the book is to see it as a veiled political manifesto – a shrewd (though not entirely accurate) suggestion, since Said's major political works still lay in the future. He considers it especially significant that Said speaks Arabic and is acquainted with certain kinds of questions – about language, intention, etc. – that may have been raised in the Arab-Islamic tradition.

J. Hillis Miller puts the matter somewhat differently but also highlights the ambiguities of *Beginnings*. He argues that the book, like its Palestinian author, "resists pigeonholing."[7] Like Said, whose commitment to Marxism does not prevent him from appreciating the writings of deeply conservative intellectuals, *Beginnings* draws insights from various genres none of which it can belong to. Said's project, Miller believes, is an attempt to theorize what cannot be said:

> What "cannot be said" in *Beginnings*, without making the production of the book impossible, is just those latent aporias about the self and its intentions, about history, and about beginnings, out of which the book constantly goes on producing itself, like a mushroom out of its mycelium. *Beginnings* constantly recognizes these contradictions, without quite recognizing them, in passages which are like slips of the tongue or of the pen or scarcely visible geological faults in the strata of thought making up the book, traces almost but not quite covered over, evidences that something has been repressed which is nevertheless explicitly revealed.[8]

Miller's article elucidates the various ways in which *Beginnings* authorizes itself out of these tropes of contradiction. Joseph Riddel sees Said's "meditation as a method recuperated on the other side of deconstruction."[9] In its uncanny collapsing of Foucauldian and Vichian methodologies, the book creates a productive tissue of contradictions. Riddel especially contrasts Said's affirmation of a problematized version of historical thinking as the triumph of the modern with Derrida's deconstruction.

Despite the differences in individual styles and modes of presentation, these early reviewers are in general agreement on one point: *Beginnings* is a complex, fluid, highly ambiguous study shot through with tensions, incongruities, elisions, occlusions, gaps, and loose ends. A broader implication can also be teased out of these early evaluations of the text: Said's unconventional methodology is as much an act of self-empowerment as it is an instrument of (unintended) self-subversion.

One of the few commentators on *Beginnings* in more recent times is Abdul R. JanMohamed, who offers a brief but nuanced interpretation of the book. JanMohamed presents his remarks on the study as part of a wide-ranging discussion of Said's career as a whole – a discussion which is pointedly structured around Said's place in a typology of what JanMohamed describes as border intellectuals; JanMohamed, it should be noted in passing, provides some of the most illuminating insights into what I have been calling the "in-between zone" – although his focus is largely restricted to cultural and political designations of the term. He reflects, for example, on the subtle dis-

tinctions between exiles and immigrants and between colonial functionaries and anthropologists – all of whom have in their own different ways crossed cultural borders. JanMohamed's general thesis is
that one way of making sense of the multiple aporias in Said's oeuvre
is to consider him in his capacity as a doubly alienated intellectual
(since he is unwilling or unable to identify wholeheartedly either with
Western culture or with its Arab-Islamic counterpart); that, unlike
some other border intellectuals (among them Wole Soyinka and
Salman Rushdie) who have been able to fuse syncretically elements of
the old and the adopted cultures, Said has deliberately fashioned "an
intersticial cultural space," a vantage point from which he can subject
"the [different] cultures to analytic scrutiny rather than combining
them";[10] that his fascination with exiles in general and intellectual
exiles in particular is as much an attempt to come to terms with the
existential realities of being a dispossessed Palestinian as it is an
acknowledgment that, as an identity-transcending agency, he belongs
precisely to the border as such.

That is, Said and like-minded minority intellectuals (among whom
are W. E. B. DuBois, Richard Wright, and Zora Neale Hurston) are
neither "organic" nor "traditional" – to use Gramscian terminology.
Rather "they are forced *to constitute themselves as the border*, to coalesce
around it as a point of infinite regression"[11] (italics in the original). A
slightly different way of formulating this point is to say that Said
continually crosses and re-crosses borders – which is to say that he
doesn't quite cross them at all. JanMohamed's main point in all of this
is that Said's insistence on the "worldliness" of criticism is belied by
the very practice he undertakes as a critic – by the fact that, in
(politically?) substantive terms, Said is a detached observer rather than
an active combatant. In other words, Said's labors define him, not as a
truly engaged intellectual, but as a "specular border intellectual" par
excellence.[12]

The Lacanian inflection of JanMohamed's metaphor is not to be
underestimated. The implication of specularity is that Said's intellectual position, in contradistinction to that of a truly committed
anti-imperialist activist, is fundamentally neutral, passively mirroring
(rather than resisting or contributing to) the cultural realities surrounding him. It is particularly these notions of neutrality, self-
restriction, and passive contemplation that predominate JanMohamed's evaluation of *Beginnings*. He insists that, despite the unusual
stress Said lays on the idea of intentionality, and more specifically on
the forms assumed by beginning intentions, the entire project of

Beginnings strikes the reader as a highly impersonal exercise: "the agency of the writer is almost totally repressed, and the writing subject is implicitly split between the active scribe and the passive meditator. Indeed the meditating mind turns itself into a reflective mirror."[13] *Beginnings*, according to JanMohamed, is precariously poised between what Said calls "intransitive" and "transitive" beginnings:

> One might reasonably expect a scholarly meditation on beginnings to scrutinize its own beginnings and intentionality, and one might assume that, for it to be rigorous and hence productive, such an endeavor would ultimately have to be either intransitive, thereby pushing the beginning of *Beginnings* to its fundamental epistemological and ontological ground, or specifically transitive, thereby providing a concrete socio-political and biographical account of the origin and *telos* of the task. Said not only avoids each alternative, he also evades biographical reflexivity about his project. Instead, he provides us with the most passive and impersonal account of the book's genesis.[14]

JanMohamed finds it symptomatic that Said on the one hand characterizes "beginning intentions" as totalizing appetites – that is, as appetites which conceive culture in its entirety *from the beginning* – but on the other hand refuses to provide "a thorough scrutiny of beginnings [which] necessarily involves an analysis of economic, political, social, ideological, and psychological relations."[15] Instead, Said has "construct[ed] an analytic mirror that reflects and refracts the structures of the host [i.e., Western] culture."[16] JanMohamed's conclusion is that, if *Beginnings* was intended – as Said would have us believe – to activate the empowering mandate of transitivity (as opposed to the aporetic regressiveness of intransitivity), then the book has succeeded only in limited ways: Said's "specular meditation produces a transitive phenomenology of beginnings that is not particularly goal-oriented."[17] In other words, Said has locked himself in the ahistorical, apolitical horizons of a contemplative mind meditating on beginnings qua beginnings – a critique which, we might add, Said himself makes of such writers as Husserl and Heidegger.

JanMohamed's article on Said has some of the merits of hindsight. Published in the early Nineties (that is, in the wake of most of Said's major political writings) as part of a multi-author collection of articles on Said's criticism to date, it is informed by a subtle awareness of the complicated relationships that obtain between the seemingly disparate topics addressed by Said in the various texts. JanMohamed is also clearly aware of the enormous controversy unleashed by *Orientalism*.

Yet there is a sense in which his commentary on *Beginnings* does not advance much beyond that of the earliest reviewers, some of whom he cites approvingly. That is to say, after reading his analysis we are not much closer to a theoretically more cogent understanding of Said's critical project as a whole. Nor does he give us a clearer insight into *Beginnings* in itself, or a fuller appreciation of just how crucial this early study is to the rest of Said's oeuvre. I do not want my remarks to be misconstrued. I am not suggesting that either the evaluations of the early commentators or JanMohamed's more recent reflections are somehow distorted or flawed. I am insisting, however, that they are all in different ways *partial* appropriations of the text and as such have contributed to what I have been describing as a serious mis-apprehension of Said's career as a whole. In my two-chapter explica-tion of the book, I intend to provide a corrective to that misapprehension, which has resulted as much from the uneven reception of Said's oeuvre as from an insufficient attention to the theoretical dimension of his criticism.

Formulated broadly, my argument is that, despite its enormous disciplinary complexity, *Beginnings* is *primarily* a philosophical exer-cise: it brings to a methodological high point the philosophical (as distinct from the purely literary, existential, or political) concerns inaugurated in *The Fiction of Autobiography*. That is, the study is not just a revisionary investigation into literary history or theory along the lines, say, of Hartman's *Beyond Formalism* or de Man's *Blindness and Insight*, although much of its analysis obviously takes the form of literary interpretation; nor is it meant as a critique sharpened for direct political intervention in the manner of *Orientalism* or *The Question of Palestine*. Rather, the argument of *Beginnings* is in the main concerned with ideas in general – their history (or histories); their variously conceived formations, deformations, and transformations; the contexts of their inception, appropriation, and disappropriation; their close imbrications with words, texts, minds, and bodies; the conflicts and cohabitations that obtain among them; their suffused presence in the very texture of human cultural life. The important double-bladed notion of border or in-between zone, which in Jan-Mohamed's hands acquires nuances of passivity and neutrality, is itself caught up in this complex, dynamic understanding of how, in Said's own lights, ideas operate in circumstances of space and time.

I specifically foreground these matters because – in my estimation – therein lies the crucial importance of *Beginnings* for Said's entire career. Like the book on Conrad, it is intended as a ground-clearing exercise, a theoretical cleaning of the slate which fuses together – and activates – a highly idiosyncratic history of modern ideas and an obliquely directed but far-reaching critique of ideology. Unlike the earlier text, however, it lights up a vast discursive/intentional stage designed to display the panoramic sweeps, spectacular ruptures, and radical transformations of modernity conceived as a (differentiated but) shared intellectual space rather than as the anguished struggles of a single self. To phrase the point differently, Said is renewing, expanding, strengthening, and refining his earlier critique of empiricism and idealism, two varieties of "rationalism" (Said's term) whose socio-political consequences have, in his view, been at best ambiguous. *Beginnings* is, therefore, more purely philosophical than any of Said's major texts (including *The Fiction*) – with the important clarification that "philosophical" in this context is being used, not in the narrowly formalistic, almost technical sense of the mainstream Anglo-American tradition, but in the broader, subtler, more comprehensive sense of Continental thought.

Hence, despite JanMohamed's suggestion to the contrary, the argument of *Beginnings* directly confronts epistemological and ontological problems, but undertakes this confrontation in a way that (Said would insist) permits the irreducible historicity – the situatedness, nomadism, mutability, etc. – of modern thought to emerge. A proper accounting of that historicity, suggests Said, will also enable us to appreciate other aspects of reason which are usually unacknowledged or systematically suppressed: the unthought (or unthinkable) background or originary void, which in a manner of speaking "gives rise" to consciousness itself; the appetitive force (what Vico calls conatus) of reason, its power as sheer motivation; and the fugitive, surreptitious element in it – the accidental, incidental, oblique, or roguish impulse that always finds a way to scuttle the self-totalizations of reason. These constitutive quirks and contaminations illustrate the extent to which postmetaphysical rationality has been transformed into an "earthbound" (Said's characterization) – and therefore thoroughly anthropomorphic – but highly ambitious affair. *Beginnings* is an attempt to think through the consequences of modernity conceived in these terms for normativity in the realm of ideas, ideals, and (always closely hugging both of them) ideologies. As we shall see later on in my discussion, of immediate relevance to this conception of rationality are the reflections of such maverick thinkers as Nietzsche, Foucault, and Vico.

To be successful, an intellectual project of this nature needs to undertake two seemingly opposed but complementary enactments: on the one hand, it operates at the level of the lowest common denominators between thought, expression, and occasion – the zero point where the mind, language, and spatio-temporal circumstance engage one another in primal conditions, *in the beginning*, as it were. The various historical, linguistic, and psychological repetitions and transformations of these inaugural "moments" are in turn registered in such a fashion that they also orient themselves to these archaic or Ur-conditions – even if there is always a distanciation between what constitutes "a beginning" and the effort of "beginning again." It is primarily in this respect that *Beginnings* comes across as a highly abstract, rarefied text: it has less to do with the quotidian, "worldly" concerns of common humanity than with the careers of major thinkers in the last three centuries as they perform radical thought experiments. It is also in virtue of this rarity and abstractness that *Beginnings*, although never "disinterested" in the manner decried by JanMohamed, nevertheless rises above the kind of partisanship sometimes attributed to Said's more politically explicit works. In fact, the study is remarkably egalitarian and global in its vision, another reason why (I believe) it is vital to Said's entire career: humanity assumes the dimensions of a variegated collectivity – an autodidactic brotherhood, as Vico would have phrased it.

On the other, however, the text is intended, not just as a descriptive reconstruction of modernity, but also as a sharp critique. This claim might sound a little odd at first glance. After all, it is quite clear that *Beginnings* is not "polemical" in the same sense as *The World, the Text, and the Critic*, for example. One doesn't find in *Beginnings* provocative verbal sparrings, a combative tone, a prescriptive idiom, or extended reflections on the perceived shortcomings of contemporary criticism – all of them techniques Said has used with a vengeance in the later text. Nor is *Beginnings* organized around an explosive public topic – such as, for example, the link between Orientalism and imperialism, or the duplicitous agenda of Zionism – about which one is obliged to make decisions with immediate ethico-political implications. Hence, *Beginnings* manifests none of the spirit of urgency, even indignation, that surges through Said's more overtly political writings. Nevertheless, it has, in my opinion, a far greater interventionary potential than any of Said's other works: it serves as a philosophical (rather than, say, political) "call to arms." Echoing – and radicalizing – Kant, we could say that the primary aim of the book is to rouse critical intellectuals out of their philosophical slumber.

By this I mean that, like Said's other texts, *Beginnings* is indeed a suspicious, even transgressive (as opposed to restorative, celebratory, or redemptive) investigation. However, to the extent that its inter-rogation is directed not so much at the commonplaces of the socio-political world but rather at the *authority* that stands behind, and gives ideological sustenance to, these commonplaces, to that extent the study has a primacy all its own. As such, it should be interpreted as a propaedeutic for radical action in the political arena. Its argument responds to the question: "What are the minimum conditions necessary for critical thinkers, no matter where they hail from cul-turally, to intervene directly in the worldly affairs of the socio-poli-tical sphere?" It would appear, then, that – in Said's own lights – the philosophical-critical "moment" licenses the political-critical "moment," and that therefore the former has strategic precedence over the latter: for a study like *Orientalism* to make a compelling case in its argument, an inquiry into the foundations, or "beginnings," of cul-ture as a whole has *to have taken place already*. In short, *Beginnings* consolidates a theoretical plane but also marks a threshold by virtue of which a viable horizon for effective praxis can be opened up.

Finally, in light of these broad philosophical aims of the book, the question of methodology in *Beginnings* should be afforded much greater attention than it has been thus far. To be more precise, my contention is that what I have characterized as Said's own "technique of trouble," a Blackmurrian metaphor intended to evoke both sub-version and difficulty, fully comes into its own in *Beginnings*. This, in effect, is what Said means by "meditation." It is an attempt to raise the dramatic co-activation of agonistic dialectic and archaeology/genealogy both to a higher level of intensity and to a greater degree of articulation and complexity. It should be mentioned at this point that, despite his abiding interest in human consciousness and its interaction with the world – an interest that manifests itself in one form or another in all of his writings, from the most academic to the most journalistic – Said no longer directly invokes, in *Beginnings* or elsewhere in his later writings, either existentialism or will philoso-phy, both of them crucial to the argument of his first monograph. In fact, after *The Fiction of Autobiography*, Schopenhauer almost com-pletely drops out of sight – along with the metaphor of the either/or alternation – and Sartre reappears only briefly and fitfully. Yet I have been insisting that, however varied the specific formulations and terminologies may be, there is a fundamental constancy to Said's methodology, a form of constancy recognizable by its characteristic configurations, the directions of its movement, the kinds of ruptures and transformations it effects, and so on. My employment of agonistic dialectic and archaeology/genealogy, together with the tension between them, is aimed at approximating this consistency.

In *Beginnings*, although it is not always as narrowly focused or as explicitly thematized as in *The Fiction*, this methodological drama is theoretically at its most cogent. On the one hand, the dilemmas of modernity assume the logical (and by extension epistemological) guise of an extremely unyielding, almost mind-bending double-bind. To put the matter briefly and bluntly, truth – or more precisely its equivalent, presented here as originary normativity – remains as elusive, as inaccessible, and as mute as it ever was in *The Fiction*. Conversely, however, the demands and pressures of that normativity – its solicitations for attention – acquire a more metaphysical inflection than was the case in *The Fiction*. Whereas in Conrad's oeuvre "truth" was often directly apprehended as an objectified but impenetrable opacity or otherwise took the form of a shameful, irrecoverable moment of the past, in *Beginnings* – where a large number of thinkers are considered – the entire category of truth and normativity is deposited outside the compass of experience; but at the same time, precisely by virtue of its assumed transcendence or primacy, it activates a vastly expansive desire – an obsessive search – in human consciousness. Humanity is condemned to an ontological orphanhood but cannot quite dispense with what it cannot have.

The immediate epistemological (and ultimately ethical) implications of this paradox should be clear enough: a whole battery of empiricist and idealist assumptions – about the nature of intelligibility and referentiality, about the self-evident validity of putative knowledge, about the proper criteria for judging what *is* and is not the case, etc. – assumptions which usually fall within the broad domains of so-called coherence and correspondence theories of knowledge or truth, become practically useless. A further point needs to be stressed: although it is not articulated exactly in these terms by Said, the extremely difficult dialectic of negation, a version of which we have already encountered in *The Fiction*, is also in full operation in *Beginnings* – with the important difference that, in the later text, it is primarily honed for more purely epistemological purposes than in the book on Conrad. This extreme double-bind constitutes one dimension of Said's "meditation."

But on the other hand, it is in *Beginnings*, rather than *The Fiction*, that Said first develops the oblique technique of historical retrieval which he is best known for – namely, archaeology/genealogy – into a fully fledged methodology. Said's deployment of this methodology has enabled him to demonstrate how (in his view) the thinkers of modernity were obliged to provide radically historicist solutions to the logico-epistemological problem represented by the above double-bind. That is to say, in the absence of definitive, metaphysically (or theologically) sanctioned normativity, modern thinkers have been obliged to invent it anyway: they have found ways of casting an aura of legitimacy around what they know to be mythopoetic fictions created by human agency in historically contingent circumstances. As will become clear in later stages of my discussion, the fulcrum of the study – the notion of beginnings (as distinct from origins) – is closely implicated in these strategies of willed freedom, constructivity, and fictionality. One could say that "truth" is repeatedly performed rather than revealed once and for all, whereby performativity is meant to suggest both idiosyncrasy and theatricality.

Bringing to light these local geneses and further refractions of modern ideas calls for a reconceptualization of what was traditionally known as history in general and more particularly the history of ideas. History is no longer a unitary narrative – a vertical line of trans-mission and progress chronicling the grand story of civilization as it beautifully transforms everything in its path, hurtling unpro-blematically towards its chosen telos. Rather, it has to be conceived as a post-originary, anti-dynastic, anti-conceptual plurality. More spe-cifically, it becomes a dispersed, variously arranged series of cultural archives sedimented on top of each other, somewhat in the manner of a gigantic palimpsest. The historian of ideas is therefore obliged to at once excavate and dramatize this constellation of archival sites. Besides configuring the logico-epistemological double-bind which I outlined earlier, the meditational structure of *Beginnings* is intended by Said to approximate this archival/genetic conception of historicity – history of ideas as an ensemble of *tableaux vivants* each one of which has the features of the library, the museum, the stage, and the archaeological field all rolled into one. An important element in my thesis is that the theoretical challenge posed by *Beginnings* will not be fully appreciated unless we pay close attention to the way Said uses the meditational structure to create a logic of multiplicity, com-plementarity, and contiguity – all of them implicit both in the logico-epistemological predicament and in the spatialization of his-tory.

A further more vital implication needs to be noted. By virtue of the complex meditation, Said is able to make extreme demarcations of both negation and affirmation – demarcations which I would like to describe respectively as being Foucauldian and Vichian in inspiration. By this I mean that, in its boundaries and in-between zones – its extreme limits and pressure points, its nodes of mutation and intersection, its lateral arrangements and parallelizations, etc. – the meditational method is characterized by both "negative" and "affirmative" saliences; the former registers pure critique in the manner of Foucault's negative valuation of modernity; the latter, which provides pointers and signposts for a utopian transformation of human community, is derived primarily from Vichian insights. This utopian vision can best be described as the coexistence of unity and diversity. It is therefore worth noting at this point that the theoretical seeds of such important notions as "affiliations," "contrapuntality," and "structures of attitudes and references" – all of them utilized by Said in the later writings – are to be found in *Beginnings*. Although none of them is reducible to a "meditation" as instantiated by *Beginnings*, each of them can be seen as a further working out (as spin-offs, refinements, intensifications, etc.) of the implications of the meditational structure as such. Equally important, each can be used as a double-edged blade: it can become in turns the instrument of pure negation and the topos of a utopian thought form. In my explication of *Beginnings*, I will try to shed light on all these aspects of the texts.

A quick synopsis of Said's broad argument will be followed by a fairly detailed examination of such interpretive devices as silent origins, transitive and intransitive beginnings, intentionality, and textuality. A major objective of my analysis in these early sections will be to determine the extent to which Said's deployment of these notions is intended to effect a critique of rationality in the context of modernity. It is out of this cluster of important notions that his distinction between ideological mystifications and critical knowledge emerges – the former closely linked to intransitivity, the latter to transitivity. In the next chapter, I will provide detailed discussions of Said's reflections on the novel, modernism, and structuralism in that order. What will become clear is that he is highly critical both of the novel's realist epistemology – which, in his view, has led this genre to a conservative, even constrictively tragic vision – and of structuralism, which is condemned as much for its anti-humanism as for its lack of a serious critical bite. Modernist literature, on the other hand, stands out by virtue of the fact that its four "oppositions" instantiate the confrontation between agonistic dialectic and archaeology/genealogy

in its most intensely personal form. The final sections of my explication will be devoted to an exposition of Said's appreciative evaluations of Foucault and Vico – two thinkers whose speculations (about
the power of language; about the nature of historical understanding;
about rationality, knowledge, and truth, etc.) are crucial to the entire
project of *Beginnings*.

The Paradox of Modernity

Synoptically presented, Said's broad thesis can be stated as follows:
First, since the eighteenth century a persistent habit of mind has
gradually established itself in various fields of writing, one that has
adopted a progressively anti-dynastic, anti-mimetic, and anti-conceptual stance. This mode of thinking has created an alternative order
of textuality in which irregularity, obliqueness, and performativity
predominate. That valorization of aberration and eccentricity can be
seen in such early classics as *Tristram Shandy* or *A Tale of a Tub*, but it
intensifies from the late nineteenth century onwards. Familiar
examples of this tendency can be found in philosophy – witness
Nietzsche's or Kierkegaard's interrogation of system-building – as
well as in psychology (Freud's psychoanalytical theories come to
mind). But the turn-of-the-century literary movement known as
modernism, whose exponents include Conrad, Hopkins, Eliot, and
Joyce among others, incarnates the most self-conscious version of this
mindset.

Second, the progressive symptomatization of writing is ultimately
to be explained in terms of a growing crisis in the notion of authority.
To the extent that the modern thinker has found it difficult to believe
in the validity, meaningfulness, and relevance of a unified vision of
reality (that is, unity of divine purposiveness, of tradition, of filiative
descent, etc.), he has willy-nilly been obliged to intend the point of
departure for his career in a manner that empowers him to invent
himself. But precisely because of the violence and transgressiveness of
this move (one must metaphorically kill off one's paterfamilias), the
new authority sows the seeds of its own negation. Modern writing is
thus often pervaded by doubt and anxiety; its meaning tends to be
dispersed, refracted, contingent; it is haunted by a spirit of secon-
dariness, inferiority, even ineptness.

Third, it is inevitable, then, that the idea of beginning ceases to be
a relatively straightforward decision; the question of where, when, or

how to start a career or a specific project acquires an enormous amount
of symbolism for thinkers. That writers as different as Marx, Sterne,
Wordsworth, and Husserl obsessively meditate on – or parody – the
notion of beginning illustrates that the issue has become both a
problematic to be investigated and a position, an intellectual space to
be staked out and appropriated. Typically, making a beginning
requires an a posteriori reflection, and as such has less to do with an
actual beginning than with one's own need for a beginning. Ultimately, it is nothing more than "a necessary fiction" manufactured in
the wake of historical understanding. Similar enactments can be
discerned at the broad level of disciplinary changes – say, the inauguration of psychoanalysis or structuralism. Methodological delimi-
tations involve decisions arrived at by fiat – after the fact.

Fourth, it follows, therefore, that the moment of beginning implies
a moment of repetition, of beginning-again – with a difference – and
univocality gives way to multiplicity and self-distanciation. Subjectivity (whether as individual self or as cultural superego) is never at
one with itself: it is strung out in time and space. What results from
this entropement of finiteness and dispersion in modern writing is a
certain nomadism and restlessness: the modern philosopher, artist, or
literary scholar has to come to grips with continual reversals, mutations, and sedimentations. The result is the following double-bind.

On the one hand, the modern artist, historian, literary critic, or
philosopher "does not possess a manageable existential category for
writing – whether that of an 'author,' a 'mind,' or a 'zeitgeist' – strong
enough on the basis of what happened or existed before the present
writing to explain what is happening in the present writing or where
to begin."[18] That is to say, the modern writer finds it necessary to
dispense with, disengage from, or write ironically against such stabilizing notions as the classical canon, traditional genres, historical
continuity, or empirical evidence, yet is at the same time impelled by
an aboriginal human need to hark back to, or mark, a beginning. On
the other hand, the writer is initiated into the vast, impersonal
domain of textuality – an independent, self-contained cosmos whose
different entities endlessly echo, allude to, quote from, and merge into
one another, practically obviating any self-evident, precursively
definable point of departure. Beginning is inevitably found to be
already under way in a fundamental sense. Despite the writer's
rejection of origin and self-evident knowledge of beginning, the
profuse details of data available in various knowledge-systems at any
one time, as well as the individual thinker's desire to effect his own

autonomy within the compass of his own experience, necessitate that he must at once dream his own dream and impose his own sense of order on the vast wealth of materials available to him.

In *Beginnings*, then, Said undertakes the task of examining the historico-philosophical consequences of this double-bind. The extraordinary significance that Said confers on the idea of beginning itself shows the extent to which the determination of initial conditions has – in his view – become both a necessity and a near-impossibility.

The Destruction of Foundations: Beginnings in the Absence of Origins

One of the challenges presented by *Beginnings* relates to the manner in which the very question under investigation – namely, the "object domain" of beginnings as a methodological problematic – is broached by Said. The notion of beginnings as it is used in the study is fairly unusual: it is meant not only to de-define traditional conceptions of initial determination but also to fuse together – and dramatize – both the most practical and the most theoretical understandings of the notion of beginnings. Normally, the beginning of (or beginning) an intellectual project refers to, or at least implies, a relatively straightforward matter which critics, philosophers, or historians of ideas have not found themselves unduly compelled to take seriously. It would suffice to say of a specific thinker whose works were being studied that, for example, he or she had begun such and such a book (or article, or series of projects, etc.) in this or that year; or that his or her career had begun with the publication of this or that text. Beyond this type of beginning, which would be directly relevant to the author's career, biographical "beginnings" (for example, the year and place of birth, early education, etc.) would also sometimes be mentioned as a matter of course. Generally speaking, analogous approaches would normally be adopted with respect to the inauguration of intellectual movements going beyond – and subsuming – individual thinkers. Setting aside differences in style (and sometimes in broader modes of presentation) between individual investigators, the questions which would have to be answered would be similar to the following. When did modernism (or the realistic novel, or the romantic movement, or whatever) come into being? Who is the real father of psychoanalysis (in contradistinction to actual or potential pretenders)? What was the cultural climate – or zeitgeist – which gave rise to or propitiated the ideas of the early philosophes, ideas which in time bloomed into the Enlightenment? And so on.

Conceived in such terms, the specific beginning of the investigator's own project (or even his career as a scholar) would likewise be merely a chronological problem that could in principle be ascertained without much difficulty. In all these formulations the idea of beginning would be either a relatively minor detail at issue only to the extent that a point of historical reference or biographical accuracy needed to be disposed of (after which presumably more important matters would be attended to) or, if not that, then the historical or biographical record was considered crucial evidence that would establish (positivistically or psychoanalytically, for example) an explanatory or causal connection between beginnings and what subsequently transpired in a given project, career, or movement. This straightforward understanding of beginning (and what follows it) is profoundly problematized in Said's study. In Said's view, the issue of beginning – as a practical matter – becomes an extremely serious challenge in the context of modernity.

But the question arises: why this challenge? Answering this question requires a preliminary reflection on what Said suggests to be a fundamental confusion in modern thought. Early on in the first chapter of *Beginnings*, he notes the large number of "words, and ideas in current thought and writing [that] hover about the concept of 'beginnings': *innovation, novelty, originality, revolution, change, convention, tradition, period, authority, influence*, to name but a few. Altogether they describe the rather broad field in which the present study is located ... I am centrally concerned, however, with what takes place when one consciously sets out to experience or define what a beginning entails, especially with regard to the meaning produced as a result of a given beginning."[19] This, I think, brings us to the heart of the matter: beginning as a theoretical, not just practical, problem. Both the constellation of "words and ideas" that hover around beginnings and the intellectual's conscious decision to mark a beginning for himself or herself are being subjected to close examination in a highly transactive idiom that brings to mind both interrogation and affirmation.

The diverse meanings and nuances of the cluster of terms listed by Said are especially instructive. They include words which normally signify continuity, consensus, or stability (e.g. "convention," "tradition," "period," etc.) as well as others which denote process, discontinuity, or transformation (i.e. "change," "innovation,"

"revolution," etc.). But what is particularly noteworthy is the extent
to which two words – "originality" and "authority" – each suggest a
multiplicity of meanings, some of which are decidedly opposed to
each other. Equally important, they are closely implicated in each
other – although that nexus is not obvious from the above passage.
"Originality" is of course etymologically related to the idea of origin,
of which it is a morphological inflection; in that sense, it brings to
mind uniqueness, primacy, source – a sort of profundity, plenitude,
and priority not enjoyed by its issue, who are judged to be mere copies
of it. On the other hand, however, the word "originality" itself is
often used to express innovation or novelty of a special kind. An
"original genius," then, is someone who is purported to be unique,
gifted, set apart from the common run of humanity by virtue of his or
her intellectual or artistic prowess. And yet, of course, there is a sense
in which this privileged novelty is meant to echo or recapture the
primordial newness of the origin. To be "original" in a manner of
speaking means "to be at one with the origin" – a temporal and
spatial impossibility. Closely caught up in this tissue of inflections is
the notion of authority, a term which carries a great deal of significance in the context of *Beginnings*: Said tells us that, in matters
related to writing, authority, or "rules of pertinence" as he also calls
it, can be used "both in the sense of explicit law and guiding force . . .
and in the sense of that implicit power to generate another word that
will belong to the writing as a whole."[20] Elsewhere in the text, Said
unpacks this cryptic definition of authority:

> *Authority* suggests to me a constellation of linked meanings: not only, as the
> OED tells us, "a power to enforce obedience," or "a derived or delegated
> power," or a "power to influence action," or "a power to inspire belief," or "a
> person whose opinion is accepted"; not only those, but a connection as well
> with *author* – that is a person who originates or gives existence to something, a
> begetter, beginner, father, or ancestor, a person also who sets forth written
> statements. There is still another cluster of meanings: *author* is tied to the past
> participle *auctus* of the verb *augere*; therefore *author*, according to Eric Par-
> tridge, is literally an increaser and thus a founder. *Auctoritas* is production,
> invention, cause, in addition to meaning a right of possession. Finally, it
> means continuance, or a causing to continue. Taken together these meanings
> are all grounded in the following notions: (1) that of the power of an indi-
> vidual to initiate, institute, establish – in short, to begin; (2) that this power
> and its product are an increase over what had been there previously; (3) that
> the individual wielding this power controls its issue and what is derived
> therefrom; (4) that authority maintains the continuity of its course.[21]

We have now arrived at a broad understanding of Said's ultimate objective. *Beginnings* is an investigation into the fundamental – or foundational – dimension of modern thought. Conceived in this manner, the idea of beginning is less about methodology narrowly understood as a practical matter than it is about the very nature of self-definition in all the senses traditionally conveyed by the idea of origins (or origination), the normative weight (or authority) reserved for that idea, and the continuous transmission of that authority through history and society. In other words, it relates to individual thinkers' conceptions of the entirety of cultural life – that is, of meaning and value, of self and society, of autonomy and responsibility, of freedom and constraint, of the very idea of what it means to be a human being understood both locally and globally. More precisely, the study is an attempt to answer the following questions as cogently as possible: How, in the course of the past three centuries, have various thinkers come to terms, not just with the matter of settling on propitious inaugural moments for various discrete projects, but also with the far more difficult problem of *grounding* (i.e., justifying ethically, aesthetically, or epistemologically) their own work as intellectuals embedded in multiple communities? How have philosophers, historians of ideas, literary-critical thinkers, and linguists, among others, responded to the recognition that origins and their authority – the transcendent warrants of meaning and value – are no longer either attractive or even available? What conditions of possibility have obtained for the creation of novelty without a priori criteria – the creation, that is, of new identities, new knowledge systems, or new horizons and destinations without the sanction of truth? What kinds of judgements have had to be made about areas of inquiry; about adequate techniques; about when, where, how, or even why to begin?

Said responds to these questions by drawing an initial demarcation line between origins and beginnings.

A major thesis of this book is that beginning is a consciously intentional, productive activity, and that, moreover, it is activity whose circumstances include a sense of loss. Furthermore, as Vico's *New Science* demonstrates, the activity of beginning follows a sort of historical dialectic that changes its character and meaning during the processes of writing and intellectual production. Thus beginning has influences upon what follows from it: in the paradoxical manner, then, according to which beginnings as events are not necessarily confined to the beginning, we realize that a major shift in perspective and knowledge has taken place. The state of mind that is concerned with origins is ... theological. By contrast, and this is the shift, beginnings are eminently secular, or gentile, continuing activities. Another difference ...

[is that] a beginning intends meaning, but the continuities and methods developing from it are generally *orders of dispersion*, of *adjacency*, and of *complementarity*. A different way of putting this is to say that whereas an origin *centrally* dominates what derives from it, the beginning (especially the modern beginning) encourages nonlinear development, a logic giving rise to the sort of multileveled coherence of dispersion we find in Freud's texts, in the texts of modern writers, or in Foucault's archeological investigations.[22]

What Said calls origin is meant to convey a complex of notions which, though different in their philosophical or theological formulations and directions of development, have always signified the idea of foundation. At a broad level origin as Said is using it seems to suggest ontological notions like center, being, essence, first principle, or any such concept that may have traditionally ratified modes of inquiry which built philosophical systems on the logic of origination and derivation, or on the existence of a primal, one-of-a-kind agency and various echoes, memories, approximations, and transumptions of it. Concepts like these, Said suggests, have been used to explain natural processes and phenomena (say, biological succession and the view of imitation implicit in it). Even more important for the present context, they have often been allegorized to serve as essentialized normative instruments; that is to say, the unity of tradition, historical evolution and other narrativist notions, the autonomy of the self: these and similarly restorative formulas that have been used to validate human institutions and ideas are all in one form or another traceable to that fundamentalist vision. And so are utopian and chiliastic visions – those gigantic, eschatological leaps of faith which serve both as destructions and as totalizations of history and historicity. All these once influential conceptions of reality, among which would be Plato's ideal forms, Descartes' cogito, and Hegel's Geist (to take a few familiar examples), have been, according to Said, decidedly superseded since the eighteenth century – and in some cases as early as the seventeenth. For self-conscious modern writers, these assumptions have been so thoroughly eroded that they have been rendered virtually irrelevant.

It is especially noteworthy that Said explicitly includes in this class of defunct concepts visions of divine authority as the latter has normally been portrayed in various religious doctrines. Hence, even though Said does not provide a *sustained*, variously illustrated analysis of origins (in contradistinction to, for example, beginnings – which do get a great deal of attention from him), it is clear that origin designates everything that would traditionally fall not only under the rubric of metaphysics but also under that of theology. The following assessment of Milton's *Paradise Lost*, whose "theme is loss, or absence," gives us an insight into how – in Said's view – anthropomorphic "ideas" conceived in the context of modernity have overwhelmed those once-privileged origins:

> Milton's theme is loss, or absence, and his whole poem represents and commemorates the loss at the most literal level. Thus Milton's anthropology is based on the very writing of his poem, for only because man has lost does he write about it, must he write about it, can he only write about it – "it" here being what he cannot really name except with the radical qualification that "it" is *only* a name, a word. To read *Paradise Lost* is to be convinced, in Ruskin's phrase, of the idea of power: by its sheer duration and presence, and by its capacity for making sense despite the absence at its center, Milton's verse seems to have overpowered the void within his epic. Only when one questions the writing literally does the obvious disjunction between words and reality become troublesome. Words are endless analogies for one another, although the analogies themselves are for the most part orderly ones. Outside the monotonous sequence of analogies, we presume, is a primeval Origin, but that, like Paradise, is lost forever. Language is one of the actions that succeeds [*sic*] the lost Origin: language *begins* after the Fall. Human discourse, like *Paradise Lost*, lives with the memory of origins long since violently cut off from it: having begun, discourse can never recover its origins in the unity and unspoken Word of God's Being. This, we know, is the human paradigm incarnated in *Paradise Lost*.[23]

Even a mighty epic which is emphatically meant to record sacred history falls far short of its goal. "The Truth," Said tells us, "is about five removes from the reader" of *Paradise Lost*; he adds: "Words stand for words which stand for other words, and so on. Whatever sense we make of Milton is provided by our use of accepted conventions, or codes, of meaning that allow us to sort out the words into coherent significance."[24] In short, privileged origins and the normativity they once mandated are now consigned to a silent dimension which cannot be accessed by human consciousness, language, or action. Hence these origins cannot be given currency or translation; they cannot "take place" in the spatio-temporal circumstances in which modernity unfolds.

These metaphysical and theological notions have been displaced by a radically transgressive mode of reflection that has effected a disengagement and taken upon itself the responsibilities of both parent and offspring. That impulse sometimes manifests itself as corrosive irony deflating hubris through satire (Swift's assault on human folly is a good example); it is often enormously ambitious (witness Milton's and

Marx's grand reconstructions of history, sacred and profane); at times it takes the form of a dramatically polemical declaration of independence (Said cites Wordsworth's critique of an ossified poetics). Also, however, that mode of thinking consciously or unconsciously holds within itself the cause of its own unraveling: that tropes of doubt, contradiction, and self-abnegation are inscribed in almost every text written by such artists as Conrad, Eliot, Joyce, and Hopkins attests to the persistence of loss, disorientation, and homelessness in modern thought. Most important, the disengagement initiated by this new habit of mind is instantiated in the obsession with the proper conditions of beginning a project, a career, or a mode of inquiry.

Found in almost every discipline, this obsession is impelled by a desire to recapture a sense of plenitude – call it a golden age, an Edenic experience, or the genius of a founding father – that is always ascribed to anteriority. More specifically, the quest typically hankers after an original state of simplicity and purity. But precisely because the transcendent authority that had once been regarded as the repository or source of that salubrity has now been nullified by the prevailing mood of skepticism, the quest inevitably entropes a contradiction. Another way of phrasing this point is to say that origin, the object of this search, is something that lies outside the horizons of historical experience, something that cannot be conceived within the compass of language. (It should be noted as a matter of course that the typically Saidian double-bind, which I have referred to repeatedly, manifests itself most explicitly at this point; although not characterized as such in *Beginnings*, its configuration describes precisely an "either/or" transaction remarkably similar to the difficult Conradian dialectic which we examined in my first chapter. Whether implicit or explicit, this agonistic dialectic is crucial to all of Said's writings, complementing in interesting ways the archaeo-genealogical component in his methodological infrastructure.)

It follows, therefore, that the primacy reserved for first-comers (say, an Abraham, a Marx, or a Freud) is the product of historical reflection, a decision reached after their influence on succeeding generations has firmly established itself as a result of continual selection, propagation, codification, and saturation. In other words, inasmuch as they have had an impact on the ideas and institutions that have shaped human culture, inaugural acts and agents are already implicated in a web of circumstance quite different from the assumed simplicity and purity. "Beginnings," in effect, take place *in medias res*, and the widely held belief that they are otherwise, the belief that they are substantively different from or superior to what follows – or flows out of – them, is nothing more than a "necessary fiction" invented by the human mind-in-language. A beginning is a purposive, intentional act that presides over a "created *inclusiveness*," a new totality.[25] A beginning in the course of modernity, therefore, is not so much an empirically recognizable event as it is an appetite, which takes the form of "either [a] *type* or [a] *force*"[26] and thereby launches an imperative of development, one which exhausts itself through the very process of articulation and elaboration. Hence, the inevitability of reversals and repetitions. But Said also makes another distinction, this one within the category of beginning itself, between "transitive" and "intransitive" beginnings.

The distinction is inherent in the crisis that the idea of beginning creates in the mind and in the two contradictory – or at least divergent – solutions that this crisis has necessitated. On the one hand there are thinkers, like Heidegger and Husserl, who vigorously pursue the "essence" of beginnings centripetally, thereby pushing interpretation "further and further forward" in order to transform "the point of departure" into "philosophy itself." These writers trap themselves in a self-parodic gesture – a lunging grasp at complete mastery of what is assumed to be the absolute beginning, with all its presumed purity and simplicity intact. Such an enactment is premised on a radical tautology and is therefore bound to miss its target: "Husserl tries to seize the beginning proposing itself *to* the beginning *as* a beginning *in* the beginning."[27] This, concludes Said, is a self-defeating, intransitive exercise: it is a pure "sentiment of beginning purged of any doubt . . . yet from the standpoint of lay knowledge [it is] thoroughly aloof, because always at a distance, and thus almost incomprehensible."[28] Elsewhere in the study, Said glosses this type of beginning in this way:

> [This] archetypal unknown is the beginning, which is also the certification of what we presently do. Newman called such a beginning an economy of God, and Vaihinger called it a summational fiction. We might call it radical inauthenticity, or, looking as far back as Husserl and Stevens did, the tautology at the end of the mind, or with Freud, the primal word, literally, with an antithetical meaning: the beginning that is not *the* one. Such a beginning is the partially unknown event that makes us – and with us, our world – possible as a vessel of significance.[29]

The implication is that, whatever its ultimate ontological status or causative power, an intransitive beginning amounts to an epistemological mystification, an "unknown" – and ultimately unknowable – "event" which cannot be operationalized *inside* history. It is for all practical purposes indistinguishable from silent origins. Whether formulated ontologically (as in Heidegger's thought), epistemologically (as in Husserl's), or psychoanalytically (as in Freud's), intransitive beginnings are self-subsistent, self-referring, closed in upon themselves.

On the other hand, there are those thinkers – Milton, Marx, or Auerbach, for example – who have opted for "a problem- or project-directed"[30] vision of beginnings, who have aimed at a more enabling, "transitive" point of departure – transitive because it is "temporal [and] foresees a continuity that flows from it. This kind of beginning is suited for work, for polemic, for discovery. It is what . . . allows us to initiate, to direct, to measure time, to construct work, to discover, to produce knowledge."[31] It is this pragmatic type of beginning that Said's book is primarily concerned with. Not always obsessed with anteriority but nevertheless empowering, this heuristic figure of thought underlies these largely anonymous, revolutionary concepts: Marx's "class and capital," Kuhn's "scientific paradigms," Darwin's "natural selection," Nietzsche's "Dionysus," Freud's "unconscious," and Foucault's "episteme." None of them are verifiable entities open to direct, actual, unmediated scrutiny, but each has exerted a powerful influence on modern thought. "These beginnings perform the task of differentiating material *at the start*: they are principles of differentiation which make possible the same characteristic histories, structures, and knowledges they intend."[32] The irreducible arbitrariness and resilience of these constructs, suggests Said, illustrate not only the extent to which the imagination is involved in the creation of "knowledge" but also the unabashed transgressiveness of the modernist impulse: each of these constructs is contingent on the simultaneous suppression and recovery of "authority," whereby authority is endowed with all the nuances which we have already examined above.

It should now be clear that Said's object domain is a vastly expanded, variously articulated version of a topic which we have already examined in my first chapter – namely, the way in which modernist intentionality has engaged its socio-cultural world in order to generate conceptual knowledge. What was characterized in *The Fiction* as economies forged by consciousness for the solicitation of ideas and images (of oneself, one's society, otherness, etc.) out of mystical, opaque truth is now subjected to far greater scrutiny and extended to a much larger historical context. Beyond this expansion and differentiation (whose implications for ideology and critical knowledge will be examined in a later section), Said has shifted the emphasis from ideas as mechanisms of awakening (and self-persuasion) to what might be called "moments" of initial determination and the way in which they bestow both shape and substance on the knowledge systems that flow out of them. One could therefore argue that, whereas *The Fiction* was concerned with the existential psychology of knowledge in the writings of one modernist writer, *Beginnings* is in a fundamental sense a historico-philosophical inquiry into the sociology of knowledge in the context of modernity as such. Another way of formulating this point is to say that Said's foregrounding of beginnings as a tissue of problems and potentialities is above all designed to answer this question: what is Enlightenment modernity, and how have various thinkers appropriated or disappropriated it?

Rationality and Its Discontents: The Case Against Idealism and Empiricism

This particular problematic has exercised the energies of thinkers as diverse as Habermas, the pre-eminent theorist of the Enlightenment; Lyotard, one of whose books (*The Postmodern Condition*) is usually cited as the text which energized the postmodernist project more than any other; and Foucault, whose implication of power and discourse in the course of modernity uncovers what he considers to be the manipulative technology of Enlightenment rationality. The vastly complex discourse of this debate, directly contributed to by a large number of thinkers trained in various disciplines, is largely outside the narrow confines of my study. Nevertheless, one can say with some confidence that there is a set of broad concerns that have invited the attention of the participants in the debate. Questions like the following are either explicitly raised or suggested in oblique ways: Just exactly what has modernity as theorized by Enlightenment thinkers and their heirs entailed? What have been the consequences of such programs of action as the liberation of humanity from religious dogma and other superstitions; the rationalization of thought (and hence the institution of rationalized conceptions of self, society, etc.); the propagation of "disinterested" scientific knowledge; the embrace of technological know-how for the purpose of engineering socioeconomic constructions; and the insinuation of "progress" into the domain of temporality? After the experiences of the past two hundred years or so — which have included enormously destructive wars, the most expansive projection of imperial power the world has ever witnessed, and the

most massive genocides in history – what is the existential, epistemological, and moral status of the "rational" subject of modernity?
That is to say, in what different ways is the self-transparent, self-
possessing, punctual subject of modernity (as autonomous selfhood or
as supersubject) exposed to be a myth constructed by philosophers,
historians, novelists, and others intent on reinventing man as self-
declared lord and as master of himself and of nature? To what extent,
for example, has the "discovery" (or, more precisely, theorization) of
the psychic, historical, or cultural unconscious given the lie to the
claim made by various thinkers – from Descartes to Marx, Habermas,
and beyond – that rational subjects can have access to truth?

Apropos of this whole constellation, just exactly what constitutes
truth, reason, or conscious thinking? Can one talk blithely about these
things after Kierkegaard, Nietzsche, or Freud? Can one speak about
truth, for example, without implicating it with various mythologies
and fictions or with the various rhetorical techniques employed in its
construction and normalization? Can reason or consciousness rise
above, suppress, or otherwise dispose of its Other without contamination? What is the relationship between, on the one hand,
reason, and, on the other, such modes of mentation as will, fantasy,
memory, and dream? To approach this whole matter from a slightly
different perspective, in what ways have theorists of language – from
Vico, Saussure, Wittgenstein, to Derrida and beyond – problematized
commonsense conceptions of meaning, intention, and communication? Rather than a transparent medium, which either makes possible
intersubjective communication or affords neutral access to an objective world "out there," isn't language more like a recalcitrant tool
which is only imperfectly understood or utilized? Or, if not that, then
a culturally and historically relative mechanism of encodement?
Aren't conceptions of "reality" in the end made-up versions of human
cultural production and reproduction – a process in which language,
mind, and historical circumstance are all actively engaged?

Such questions can be greatly multiplied, but the important thing
is that the modernity debate – even in its least immediately political
moments – has called into question Enlightenment commonplaces.
Certain ideas – about historical evolution and the progress it implies;
about the unity, autonomy, or self-presence of the rational subject;
about rational organization, human emancipation, and the good life;
about the very nature of civilization itself – these and similar ideas,
which have had an enormous impact on the West (and on the rest of
the world by virtue of Western imperial outreach) have been opened

up for re-examination over the past several decades. The answers to these questions have been variously inflected. The advocates of modernity as an ongoing, but as yet uncompleted, process have generally tried to shore up the rationalist project of the Enlightenment and the idea of normativity it implies (Habermas, McCarthy, Norris among others are in this camp). Poststructuralists, on the other hand, have in different ways tried to undercut the viability of the subject, reason, and humanism even if they do not envision the possibility of liberation from these chimeras (Derrida, Foucault, and Lacan are the best-known members of this group). Postmodernists and neopragmatists (among them Lyotard, Baudrillard, Rorty, and others) have generally tended to view the death of the grand narratives and totalizing conceptions of modernity as a welcome development. In lieu of these "mythologies," these thinkers propose various post-Enlightenment celebratory moods of plurality in which sublime ineffability, hybridity, Bakhtinian carnivalism, mass culture, and counter-culture all figure in different combinations. Lyotard's (Wittgenstenian) idea of language games and Rorty's conversation of mankind are examples of this type. Said's study is caught up in this ongoing debate, though in a highly oblique, eccentric fashion attested to by the fact that he cannot be placed neatly in any one of these camps – although some commentators have tried to do just that.[33]

The reason for this ambiguity is that, both in *Beginnings* and elsewhere, Said seems determined to dethrone conventionalized forms of rationality and yet at the same time (re)install the authority of reason – or at least an enhanced version of it. This is a particularly tricky business to discuss because nowhere in his entire oeuvre does Said confront the problem of rationality as a delimited topic head-on – say, in the historical manner in which Weber, the Frankfurt social theorists, Habermas, or Foucault have. Nor has he ever discussed extensively the issue of rationality, skepticism, and relativism as a problem concerning normativity – something that has persistently come up in recent debates among philosophers (mostly Anglo-Americans, but also Continental theorists like Habermas). Nevertheless, to the extent that Said's critical effort constitutes an indirect engagement of the Enlightenment and its consequences – an engagement which involves both a thorough critique of its totalitarianism and an acknowledgment of its importance for a humanistic conception of culture – to that extent, both *Beginnings* and Said's other works can be seen as a running debate with rationality. More specifically, both in *Beginnings* and in the other major texts, one finds brief

but revealing passages which focus on the idea of reason or rationality
as a category. The most explicit (and in some respects most important)
of these passages occurs in "A Meditation on Beginnings," the theoretical fulcrum of *Beginnings*. Using Nietzsche's metaphorization of
truth as a lever, Said confers a cluster of both catholic and eccentric
nuances on the idea of reason:

> Nietzsche must not be interpreted, here or elsewhere, as a puerile, naysaying
> nihilist. On the contrary, his interest ... includes, and appropriates, the
> *subjective underside*, or the *charlatanry*, of reason ... those faculties of reason
> that remind us how earthbound are even its highest flights. Earthbound, but
> rational. Such considerations are forced upon the contemporary mind by the
> wish to grasp fully whether one's activity has either begun or will begin ...
> Attempting such a grasp always compels the mind into a rational severity and
> asceticism ... I intend first to draw attention to – perhaps even to exacerbate,
> as Nietzsche does – the problem we face when we begin an intellectual task
> ... Second, I should like to arrive at an understanding, however tentative, of
> what sorts of beginnings really exist. The word *beginning* itself is and will
> remain a general term covering a large variety of scattered occasions; like a
> pronoun, it has specific roles to play, at different points in the discourse ...
> These roles, however, are as much in the control of reasonable convention and
> rule as they are in the control of reasonable assertion. I should like to examine
> all this as it bears on the possible kinds of beginnings available to us. Lastly, I
> should like to record a part of the rational activity generated within us in the
> act of dealing with a beginning (where "rational activity," it will become
> clear, includes rational sentiment, passion, and urgency).[34]

The passage invites commentary both in terms of the way in which
"beginnings" and "reason" hold purchase on each other and in terms
of what, in Said's view, constitutes "rationality" as such. At least three
different clusters of nuances (around both "beginnings" and "reason"
or around "reason" alone) can be isolated. One cluster, which is
presented as a passing gloss, is not particularly startling or unnerving.
Said tells us that the idea of beginning as he is treating it cannot be
placed beyond "the control of reasonable convention and rule" and
comes to terms with the claims "of reasonable assertion." That is to
say, the putative protocols of intellectual work as these are understood
conventionally – among which would be knowledge of, or careful
research into, the area of inquiry; logical cohesion, rigor, and consistency; sincerity and truthfulness; awareness of the audience's needs,
etc. – would have to be attended to. Beyond these "academic" concerns, the idea of beginning must also be adequate to what an
intelligent, educated adult embedded in a broad community would
acknowledge as a "reasonable assertion" – an assertion which in

principle could be verified, falsified, or modified in one way or another by subsequent experience.

On these two related views, "reason" would seem to cohere with the common sense, naturalist, and various other models of realism and quasi-realism advocated by most mainstream Anglo-American thinkers. The latitude within which "reason" operates here would seem to accommodate empiricism broadly understood, American pragmatism, and the inductivism of the natural sciences. The same broadly positivist philosophical assumptions lie behind much of what has traditionally been known as the social sciences, historiography, and the realist novel. This conception of rationality would not be entirely incompatible with idealism either. Although the province of philosophical idealism (for example, the unabashedly speculative German brand and its English off-shoots) has been severely limited in Anglo-American circles since the assault on it by Moore and Russell, there is a sense in which fairly common varieties of formalism (prominent among which is literary-critical formalism), as well as essentialist, generally linear species of intellectual history also cohere with idealism. Interpretive labors of this sort have, of course, come to be known as cultural idealism in recent years. All these nuances appear to fall within the domain of "reasonable convention and rule" and "reasonable assertion." The methodological desiderata associated with these attitudes are generally those of objectivity, verifiability (or falsifiability), coherence, lucidity, precision, and so on. Both careful analysis and precise description are expected to shed light on a potentially vast arena where logic, narrative, and "data" can interact. Said's use of the word "reasonable" twice here is not incidental: catholicity, consensus-building, the weight and authority of tradition – these constitute the ultimate court of appeal.

But it is clear from the passage that Said, though along the way making use of insights made available by this conception of reason, has in mind a much further destination. Seriously thinking about beginnings, he contends, "always compels the mind into a rational severity and asceticism." He adds: "My view is that an intensified, even irritated awareness of what really goes on when we begin – that is, when we are conscious of beginning – actually projects the [intellectual] task in a particular way."[35] This, I think, means that in the context of modernity serious thinkers have been obliged, willy-nilly, to impose extreme discipline on themselves, to search out (and test) extreme limits, and to cope with extreme self-consciousness all at once. These extraordinarily severe enactments, it would seem, are the

very conditions necessary for the inauguration of intellectual work in
the post-lapsarian world of modernity. The mind ferrets out normally
disregarded connections, confronts potentially overwhelming difficulties, and delineates multiple – often contrastive – vectors of
engagement. Conceptualized in these terms, "reason" can be described
as a heightened form of awareness, an intense reflection on both the
enablement and the constraint entailed in being human – that is,
being "earthbound but rational." That this is indeed the case is made
abundantly clear in the very next paragraph, whose centrality for
Said's entire critical project can hardly be exaggerated:

> The best descriptive characterization of these enlivened ideas of rational
> activity that I know of is found in Bachelard's 1936 essay "Le Surrationa-
> lisme" (which also happens to be an indirect commentary on Bachelard's own
> rationalism). The essay rejects a rationalism based on dry-as-dust tradition-
> alism, memory, and scholastic rigidity. Bachelard says: *"One must return to
> human rationality its function as a force for turbulence and aggression.* In this way
> surrationalism (*un surrationalisme*) will be established, and this will multiply
> the occasions for thought." ... To use reason as a means of setting tasks, to
> generate thought in order to activate itself beyond the bounds and limits set
> by the mere historical conventions of reason – this experimental type of reason
> is to reality what for Tristan Tzara, the experimental surrealist, dream was to
> poetic liberty.[36]

I have provided these rather lengthy citations not only because they
shed light with unusual clarity on the methodology of *Beginnings* but
also because they help us understand Said's indictment, in *Beginnings*
and elsewhere, of the foundationalist epistemology that mandates
both empiricism and idealism, two modes of reflection (and by
extension two broad intellectual traditions) which come across in
Said's analysis as two sides of the same fraudulent coin.

   In the two passages quoted above, Said is appealing (it can be
inferred) to a distinction between two conceptions not just of epistemology but of rationality in general: one of them is dualistic and is
therefore oriented towards abstraction, distillation, and representation; the other is phenomenological and materialist, thereby
acknowledging (even embracing) its complete enmeshedness in socio-
historical circumstance. What Said identifies as "a rationalism based
on dry-as-dust traditionalism, memory, and scholastic rigidity" does
not neatly coincide with the thought of the great seventeenth-century
system-builders (i.e., Descartes, Spinoza, and Leibniz), with whom
"rationalism" is normally associated. In fact, with the exception of
Descartes, some of whose methods of inquiry are briefly examined in

Beginnings, these thinkers are hardly ever mentioned anywhere in Said's corpus of writing.[37] Nor are his critical remarks here directed at the medieval "schoolmen" who dominated European (as well as Arab-Islamic) thought at a time when religious dogma reigned supreme. Rather he is deliberately pressing into service such terms as "rationalism" and "scholastic" in order to implicate certain aspects of modern thought with the rigidity, pedantry, and aridity sometimes ascribed to pre-Enlightenment thought. Elsewhere in *Beginnings*, Said makes his antipathy towards this type of rationality more explicit: "mimetic representation," he tells us, has been "discredit[ed]," and it is no longer viable to claim that "history" (his term) can be "referred back docilely to an idea that stands above it and explains it." In other words, one can no longer posit a pure, self-subsistent, atemporal origin out of which flow the temporality and concreteness of history as an incomplete realization and imitation. Likewise, it is not possible to argue that – by virtue of such an originary, transcendent sanction – history is unified, evolutionary, or teleological. Said also insists that in interpreting "reality," "literature," or "history," we should "avoid such dualities as 'the original versus the derivative,' or 'the idea and its realization,' or 'model/paradigm versus example.'" These "dualities," which are sometimes blamed on Descartes' split between the conscious ego and the material world (including the body), are of course pervasive in modern thought – the distinctions between "thought and expression," "reality and representation," "subject and object," "conscious and unconscious," etc. are among the most common examples.[38]

The specific dualities clustered together – and assailed – by Said are all in one way or another immediately germane to his critical project in that they pertain either to the split between "theory" and "practice" – a distinction which, though recently challenged, has had a profound impact on the Western intellectual tradition – or to matters of privilege and its absence. For example, an "original," as I have already pointed out, has traditionally been credited with a purity, simplicity, and completeness that are denied to its issue, which is often implicitly or explicitly demoted to the status of a mere copy. But also paradoxically that same self-subsistent original is often made to bestow legitimacy on its progeny by virtue of its filiatively transmitted authority. It is as a consequence of such strategic enactments that various cultures have been able to maintain such things as the purity of the bloodline, the continuity of history, the unity of traditions and canons, and the validity of preferred interpretations –

all of them exclusionary, hieratic, and often imperialistic. Similar observations can be made about the other dualities. The result (in part) of all this is that, "[f]or most of my generation [of intellectuals], *mind, culture, history, tradition*, and *the humanities*, both as words and as ideas, carry an authentic ring of truth, even if for one or another reason they do not lie easily within our grasp."[39] My point in drawing attention to these and similar details is that, in oblique (and often cryptic) but clearly specifiable ways, Said repeatedly deconstructs various aspects of empiricism and idealism, both in *Beginnings* and elsewhere in his oeuvre.

Said's critique of empiricism and idealism is not unique to him, and in the course of the debates about modernity which I outlined earlier, other thinkers have made powerful assaults on one or both of these two traditions. What makes Said's critique interesting is that, first of all, it is not restricted to literature or philosophy but rather cuts a wide swathe across a multiplicity of disciplines, registers, traditions, and locales; this is something to which I have drawn attention right from the outset, and I will reflect on it in various contexts. Second, Said appears to deposit empiricism and idealism under the umbrella of a shared realist or foundationalist epistemology. He suggests that empiricist and idealist attitudes at once short-circuit themselves in different ways and interact with each other in the construction of ideologies. On the one hand, the empiricist mode, in its own lights, presents the world "as it truly is" (or "was") in a transparent language that delivers reality to an objective, disinterested subject who has (presumably) already suspended his prejudices. By virtue of an easygoing, comfortable correspondence theory, the philosopher, anthropologist, historian, or journalist can thus claim to be merely transcribing or describing accurately what is or was "out there" or, if not that, then analyzing and (scientifically) "explaining" the chosen object domain; word and object are at one and together dispose of Truth. The duality in operation here takes the form of an omniscient, self-assured subject and a passive, knowable object delivered by means of a transparent medium. On this view, the relationship between commonsense empiricism and scientific positivism is one of conceptual reduction, not one of opposition or contradiction.

On the other hand, the idealist (or quasi-idealist, such as the Zionist or the refining critic) denies any substance to the brute materiality of the external world, which can be shrugged off as irrelevant, posited as mere appearance, or construed as malleable data available for transformation by ideas. Thereby he or she is enabled to insist on the inward clarity and distinctness of ideas, the mind (individual or collective) being afforded primacy. An inner reality of ideas – essences, forms, unsullied origins, etc. – can be proposed in this way and kept fundamentally uncontaminated by the messy affairs of worldly praxis. Like the bracketed-off world, language itself offers no resistance to these idealized images of reality, formalistically whipping them into shape but otherwise letting them shine through in their full glory (that is, if the ideas are supposedly good) or expose themselves in the full capacity of their evil (if they fall into the category of the disapproved). The result, broadly speaking, is a coherence theory of Truth capable of building imposing functionalist systems that always find ways of stabilizing themselves – despite the resistance that subverts these totalizations.

Both in *Beginnings* and elsewhere, Said suggests that these two different ways of generating knowledge have been conveniently employed in constructing a whole constellation of meanings and values that have had a powerful impact on the modern world. For example, Said's critique of Orientalist epistemology, which he characterizes as a species of radical realism, is based in large part on the claim that Orientalist discourse has, over the ages, found ways of combining an essentialized, negatively encoded, ahistorical Orient with syncretically assembled, historically variable, empirical details almost all of which are intended to demonstrate the radical Otherness of the Orient. The objectifying, reifying power of the empiricist attitude is made to buttress – sometimes directly, at other times through multiple mediations – the purifying, refining, essentializing substance of ideas and ideals, whereby the term ideas (in contradistinction to ideals) can refer to either culturally approved conceptions or negative valuations. The duplicities and mechanisms involved in this construction – the rhetorical ruses, the crude motivations, the trails of scent, the hierarchies of power, the facticity and contingency of circumstance, the capacity for accident and error, the brute materiality of cultural institutions (including language): these and similar matters are occluded forthwith. In a carefully regulated equilibration between "knowledge" and "truth," the "idea" is more or less literally made to cohere with the "fact." In short, an airtight mimetic "fit" is discovered rationalistically between reality and representation. The whole of *Beginnings* is ultimately an attack on rationality understood in these terms.

Reason as Intentionality: Towards an Experimental Rationality

The other type of rationality, which apparently partakes of both "surrationalism" and sound reasoning, is "enlivened" by "rational sentiment, passion, and urgency." Reason conceived in this manner will allow the intellectual to "multiply the occasions for thought" (Bachelard's phrasing). It can also be used "as a means of setting tasks" and as a way of "generat[ing] thought in order to activate itself beyond the bounds and limits set by the mere historical conventions of reason." Never narrowly mimetic, this version of rationality manifests itself in the socio-historically determined, dramatic uses of language – where language is no longer a passive medium but rather an event occasioned by (and caught up in) a whole constellation of worldly events. More specifically, rationality understood in this light operates in written works which enter "a realm of gentile history, to use Vico's phrase for secular history, where [there are] extraordinary possibilities of variety and diversity" in human cultural forms.[40] Although it is neither metaphysical nor divine, it is both more speculative and more rigorous than mere rationalism; it is equipped with a demystifying capacity which allows it to lay bare the instrumental dimension of thought. It is "earthbound" – and therefore subject to the historical and cultural constraints that circumscribe human agency – but it is also desire-laden, experimental, and expansive.

More appetite than intellection (in the narrow, rationalist sense), this type of rationality incorporates such impulses as will, dream, myth, emotion, and phantasy. Above all, it dissolves the dualities that plague empiricism and idealism, substituting for both a single "order of reality" which is shaped by the eccentricities, repetitions, and irregularities of writing – where writing "includes the production of meaning, the method of composition, the distribution of emphasis, as well as the tendency to produce mistakes, inconsistencies, and so on."[41] It is this type of rationality that Said describes as intention:

> By *intention* I mean an appetite at the beginning intellectually to do some-
> thing in a characteristic way – either consciously or unconsciously, but at any
> rate in a language that always (or nearly always) shows signs of the beginning
> intention in some form and is always engaged purposefully in the production
> of meaning.[42]

What does rationality understood in this way – that is, as a desire caught up in the operations of language qua writing – effectuate in practical and theoretical terms? This question has a long answer, which will occupy me throughout the remaining sections of this chapter as well as the next one. A considerable part of that answer will be devoted to Said's conception of language in general and textuality in particular. As will become clearer later on, crucial to this conception are insights drawn not only from contemporary structuralism and poststructuralism but also from the philological tradition of an earlier era. At this point, however, a short response to the above question is possible – one which has direct relevance for the status of knowledge as such, for the creation of ideologies, and for the responsibilities of the critical intellectual. Modern, postmetaphysical thinkers, Said tells us, have of necessity been obliged to deploy three heuristic principles all of which register tropes of arbitrariness and inauthenticity and all of which preserve their inaugural transgression as enactments of anthropomorphic volition. These principles are supposition, construction, and fiction.

Insofar as the modernist sentiment has, in a manner of speaking, arrogated to itself a large measure of freedom – the freedom to "intend" its beginning or define itself – the overweening power behind it is "a large supposition," a sort of optimism or initiative whose ultimate aim is to enable human agency to achieve both self-liberation and self-authorization.[43] Once that objective has been realized, then it becomes possible "to effect (or dream)" the construction of intellectual projects mandated by "formal beginnings" – or specific methodological beginnings arrived at by fiat. It is particularly important to note that, even though Said is not directly concerned with imperialism here – as was the case in *The Fiction of Autobiography* – he nevertheless ascribes an enormous amount of egoism to this intellectual enactment, at least insofar as it is an inaugural desire or thought experiment initially dreamt up by the mind: "Consciousness, whether as pure universality, insurmountable generality, or eternal actuality, has the character of an imperial ego ... The starting point is the reflexive action of the mind attending to itself, allowing itself to effect (or dream) a construction of a world whose seed totally implicates its offspring."[44] The notion of fictionality subsumes the provisional status of knowledge in general, the fact that methodological beginnings themselves are constructs or working hypotheses (since they cannot be confirmed or refuted by an appeal to empirical reality), and the progressive negation or exhaustion of the inaugural freedom "insofar as [a beginning intention] says or avows much more *at* the beginning than it in fact is."[45] This entire process is roughly equivalent to (but much greater in scope than) what Said described in *The Fiction* in the following terms: the total immersion of the self in the deep shadow of truth; the self's gradual awakening as the intellect forms an image of the self in possession of the truth; the elevation of that image to an idea of truth; the project of conquest according to that idea of truth; and, finally, the onset of skepticism as the intellectual distinctions collapse.

It is clear, then, that Said's provisionalization of knowledge seems to place him solidly in the camp of those (post)Nietzschean – rather than Kantian or neo-Kantian – thinkers (including poststructuralists and postmodernists alike) who don't conceal their profound distrust of the claim (made by various thinkers from Descartes down to Habermas) that the *rational* subject, individually or collectively, can in principle have access to theoretical truth – provided, that is, the proper methodological road map is followed. Said's view on this matter is this: "reason" is the stepchild of conatus; the human desire for certainty – rather than the possession of some theological, onto-logical, or epistemological privilege or capacity comprehensible as certainty – is responsible for what we call knowledge; "truth," that norm, foundation, or essence supposedly captured (and vouched for) by "certainty," is nothing more than the will to truth, a suasive ruse of self-endowment. And once this self-persuasion has taken place, it almost automatically authorizes self-elevation and conquest.

Ideological Currency Versus Critical Knowledge

Yet it should be equally clear by now that Said's critique of foun-dationalism is intended not so much as a mechanism for destroying epistemology (and, along with it, normativity as such) but rather as a means of initiating an important methodological transformation – a transformation, it must be added, which he did not achieve in *The Fiction of Autobiography*. By virtue of this methodological advance, he is now able to make an effective, clear-cut distinction between two types of knowledge, as well as the processes, strategies, and instru-mentalities of their formation. One variety could, broadly speaking, be called ideological; the other, critical. And therein lies the funda-mental bifurcation that Said has observed right in the heart of inau-gural intentions: namely, the split between transitive and intransitive beginnings, characterized by him as two sides of the same coin.

It may be recalled that Said himself leans towards transitive beginnings because they are – in his own words – "problem- or project-oriented" and are therefore "suited for work, for polemic, for discovery." In effect, they are purposive, goal-directed, historically sensitive tools which can be used to produce quantifiable, secular knowledge in the world of modernity. Their aims and consequences can be sensibly evaluated in spatio-temporal circumstances. An intransitive beginning, on the other hand, is a "purely conceptual," "summational fiction" which stands aloof from history and historicity. It should also be remembered that, despite its intransitivity, it is as much a product of human intentions as is its transitive counterpart – after all, as an inevitable consequence of modernist skepticism, metaphysical and theological origins have been so thoroughly eclipsed that they can no longer be invoked as sources of legitimacy, and what we are therefore left with is a transcendentally homeless human consciousness.

The question then arises: what exactly is the function of an intransitive beginning, and why is Said suspicious of it anyway? To answer that question and, at the same time, sharpen the distinction between the two types of knowledge to which I referred earlier, I would like to juxtapose two crucial passages in *Beginnings*:

> For most of my generation [of literary-critical intellectuals], *mind, culture, history, tradition,* and *the humanities*, both as words and as ideas, carry an authentic ring of truth, even if for one or another reason they do not lie easily within our grasp. I have no desire to have done with them, if only because as words and ideas they still seem partially to anchor the world we inhabit, if only because they also are still objects of our regard – and also because, to adapt a phrase coined by I. A. Richards, they are machines to think with. Temperamentally, I have an equal amount of intolerance, on the one hand, for manifestos of delight in the culture, history, and tradition of a given society, and, on the other hand, for vehement attacks on culture, history, and tradition as instruments of outright repression. Both these moods – and they are scarcely more than that – are irresponsible; worse, they are uninteresting. Occasionally they are useful as reminders of the fact that the tradition somehow continues to exist, and that it can sometimes also be repressive. More often, however, it is better not to treat such attitudes simply as objects of praise or blame at all – in order, as Merleau-Ponty says of a verbal phrase, *to hear what they say.*[46]

> Beginnings and continuities conceived in [a formal, and methodologically enabling] spirit are an appetite and a courage capable of taking in much of what is ordinarily indigestible ... [T]his is why Swift's "[A] Modest Proposal" is so perfectly illustrative both of itself as a cannibalist tract as well as of the operations of criticism as formal rethinking. For the obduracy of the Irish peasant bodies that are coerced into a marvelously fluent prose [is] not

unlike the obduracy of books and ideas coexisting in something we call verbal reality or verbal history. A literary critic ... who is fastened on to a text is a critic who, in demonstrating his right to speak, makes the text something continuous with his own discourse; he does this first by discovering, then rationalizing, a beginning. Thus the critic's prose, like Swift's as it mimics the cannibalism it propounds by showing how easily human bodies can be assimilated by an amiable prose appetite, swallows resisting works, passes into passages that decorate its own course, because it has found a beginning that allows such an operation. In the cheerful optimism that it sometimes gives rise to, the beginning resembles a magical point that links critic and work criticized. The point is the meeting of critic and work and it coaxes the work into the critic's prose.[47]

One of the few overtly political (but still only indirectly critical) statements in *Beginnings*, the first passage has a significance that far surpasses the view which is explicitly expressed in it. In both what it says and what it leaves unsaid, the passage is bound by a subtle web of allusions to a number of concerns which have been central to Said's critique of ideology and to his revitalized conception of human community. His deep ambivalence towards such large identitarian constructs as "culture, history, and tradition" here takes the form of an equipoised "intolerance" both for "manifestos of delight in" strategically valorized versions of these institutionalized ideas and for outright condemnations of them. These extreme positions – or "moods" – are both "irresponsible" and "uninteresting," Said tells us, adding in a Merleau-Pontyan frame of mind that it is far more preferable "to hear what they say." Etched out on the flipside of this ambivalence is what could be called an equally deep-seated appreciation of the multiple, variously crisscrossing connections that bind all societies together in an ongoing drama at once incorporating unity and diversity. As I have already hinted, much more will be said about this *sensus communis* in the next chapter, as I treat the final chapter of *Beginnings* in which Said pays homage to Vico.

My immediate objective in citing the passage here is to shed more light on what Said has called intransitive beginnings. Even though he does not make direct methodological or thematic connections between intransitive beginnings, on the one hand, and such broad matters as *"mind, culture, history, tradition*, and the *humanities,"* on the other, it is possible, by virtue of both the meditational structure of *Beginnings* and the web of allusions I have just referred to, to forge oblique links between these two sets of concerns. That is to say, it can be inferred that (in Said's view) interest in intransitive beginnings is not restricted, as might have been suggested by his singling out of

Husserl and Heidegger, to the odd philosopher here and there, who is obsessively – and perhaps delusionally – searching for the perfect, absolute beginning, the ontological or epistemological moment of inauguration that presumably authorizes all lesser beginnings. On the contrary, such recondite labors, as well as their implications (immediate or otherwise), resonate throughout the larger society in all kinds of ways precisely because they have broad, more readily accessible analogues which happen to make available ideologically useful, endlessly recyclable currency in various spheres of cultural life. For, unlike origins (with which, as we shall see presently, they have a great deal in common), beginnings of this kind can be domesticated for modernity, while at the same time somehow maintaining their essential purity. They can be rendered in the terminology of disciplinary fields as different as philosophy, historiography, anthropology, philology, literature, biology, and journalism, to name just a few.

And therein lie their peculiar potency and scandal: they can be neatly tailored in order to cover (and cover over) "the culture, history, and tradition of a given society" such that seemingly objective knowledge generated by disinterested scientists, historians, journalists, and experts of various hues can be delivered about that society, whereas on closer examination this "knowledge" may turn out to be little more than a calculated whitewash or a carefully concealed act of intellectual aggression. In other words, there is a sense in which such "purely conceptual," "summational fictions" as "Western culture," "Islam," "the English literary tradition," "the American way of life," "the Orient," "Zionism," or "the Arab mind" – all of them grand, totalizing ideologies – are constructed as words and ideas (that is, as beginning intentions) by an a posteriori act of the will, either as sources of ultimate authority or as objects of ultimate opprobrium. More specifically, they are made to sustain filiative lines of descent which are carefully protected from lateral contaminations or enhancements; they are also invested with positive or negative valuations that gradually become part of their constitutive substance. In the meantime, the enormous collective energies expended in constructing these economies, as well as the strategies of their construction, are continually effaced so that the unsullied character of these words and ideas for good or ill can be maintained. This, even if at the same time their concrete actualization is supposedly taking place in circumstances of space and time – with all the accompanying drama and messiness (what Said would later describe as worldliness). In short, these large concerns are at once historicized and de-historicized – a feat of ideological mystification without parallel.

The immediate implication of all this is that, for all practical purposes, intransitive beginnings inhabit the site vacated by meta-physical and theological origins – either as stand-ins, as allies, or as resurrections – and dispose the same absolutist functions that origins did before the era of modernity: they serve as horizons of ultimate restoration, celebration, or redemption (if they are "ours") or as the targets of ultimate demonization and excommunication (if they belong to the "other"). It also goes without saying that – by Said's own lights – this subtle alignment of silent origins, intransitive beginnings, and ideologically manufactured knowledge systems is largely (if not wholly) due to foundationalist rationalism and the empiricist/idealist epistemological models it ratifies. Said's major political writings, including *Orientalism*; *The World, the Text, and the Critic*; *The Question of Palestine*; and *Culture and Imperialism*, are all in one way or another attempts to come to terms with the unflattering consequences of such ideological mystifications and the project of realism which made them possible.

The remarkable second passage, which requires little immediate commentary, constitutes one of Said's earliest and most cogent statements about the function of critical consciousness as he under-stands it – a problem to which he has returned repeatedly over the decades. That function, or more precisely that responsibility, *begins* with unconstrained methodological freedom: that is, the capacity and willingness to inaugurate one's own methodologically delimited intellectual projects such that the "beginnings and continuities" thus authorized are "capable of taking in much of what is ordinarily indigestible ... Books, names, ideas, passages, quotations ... adjust to a system of relationships formally postulated for them" by critical intentionality.[48] The result is the almost magical transformation of what could be called the assembled raw materials into one's own discourse. The invocation of Swift's *A Modest Proposal* is not entirely incidental. This is what Said says of that maverick satirist in "Secular Criticism," the introductory article of *The World, the Text, and the Critic*:

> For me [Swift] represents the critical consciousness in a raw form, a large-scale model of the dilemmas facing the contemporary critical consciousness that has tended to be too cloistered and too attracted to easy systematizing. He stands so far outside the world of contemporary critical discourse as to serve as one of its best critics, methodologically unarmed though he may have been. In its

energy and unparalleled verbal wit, its restlessness, its agitational and unacademic designs on its political and social context, Swift's writing supplies modern criticism with what it has sorely needed since Arnold covered critical writing with the mantle of cultural authority and reactionary political quietism.[49]

Said's confrontation with contemporary academic criticism will be the topic of a later chapter. What will become clear is that, of the many challenges involved in interpreting his multifaceted work, arguably the most difficult – and potentially most fruitful – relates to his understanding of critical consciousness and its role in the world. The point I want to emphasize here, though, is that – once again – it is primarily in *Beginnings* that Said clears the theoretical space from which the later, more politically explicit projects were to be launched. In our immediate context, the divergence, even opposition, between the two types of beginning seems to be justified by Said as follows. Either by commission or by omission, intellectual projects modeled on intransitive beginnings almost inevitably lead to consensually validated knowledge indistinguishable from ideological dogma, to critical system-building and political quietism, and ultimately to totalitarian imperialism. A transitive beginning has the potentiality of effecting disengagement and autonomy from one's cultural identity. Beyond that initial establishment of distance, it can lead to critical self-empowerment, to the kind of methodological rigor crucial to serious ideology critique, and ultimately to the possibility of socio-political transformation. It is with this distinction in mind that I would like to examine more closely an important theme that my analysis has been engaging indirectly throughout this chapter: Said's understanding of the place occupied by language in human culture.

Language as Event: The Dynamics of Textuality

Next to critical consciousness, the most difficult interpretive challenge to be faced by any commentator on Said will undoubtedly concern his views on language in general and on textuality in particular. One of the reasons for this difficulty can be inferred from my discussion of consciousness as such, in the context of both *Beginnings* and the early work on Conrad. As I have already pointed out, a partial methodological transformation separates the two texts as concerns the meaning(s) designated by consciousness: the Sartrean and Schopenhauerian nuances which were central to the argument of *The*

Fiction – nuances which gave that book a decidedly existentialist, even pessimistic cast – are manifestly absent from *Beginnings*. The other aspect of this partial transformation, which I have characterized as a "linguistic turn," constitutes an entirely new dimension in Said's criticism. Unlike *The Fiction of Autobiography*, *Beginnings* is caught up in the structuralist debates of the Sixties and Seventies, as well as the emergence of what has since come to be known as poststructuralism.

Despite this dual methodological shift, it is also the case that Said's *primary* philosophical/theoretical underpinnings in both books (and indeed throughout his career) have remained fundamentally phenomenological: his well-known eclecticism, which enables him to cross various kinds of methodological and thematic boundaries, is always carried out with an explicit or implicit understanding that human cultural life is, in the first and final instances, an affair of the mind performing meaningful acts in specific socio-historical circumstances. Hence, even though my discussion in this chapter has not drawn attention to the Husserlian technique of *epoche* (in part because in *Beginnings*, other than the important concept of intentionality, Said does not use Husserlian terminology), there is a sense in which the implications of that same technique are as crucial to an evaluation of *Beginnings* as they were to the interpretation of *The Fiction*: that is to say, the suspension of the natural, commonsensical attitude; the institution of eidetic and apodictic reductions through bracketing; the activation of the noetic and noematic poles of consciousness in order to map out the contours of the experiential field, etc. – these and similar methodological tools, which were directly utilized in uncovering Conrad's difficult dialectic, are also at work in *Beginnings*, though they are presupposed rather than explicitly invoked.

Said's radicalized conception of rationality (or intentionality) – a conception which, though profoundly speculative, is constitutively enmeshed in the material realities of culture (including the eccentric operations of language) – should therefore be seen both as a further working out of the phenomenological view of mental activity expressed in *The Fiction* and as a strategic complementation of it. That close coordination of word, idea, and action weaves through Said's entire corpus of writing from *Beginnings* onwards. Hence when (in *Beginnings*) he describes "language as an intentional structure";[50] or when (in *Orientalism* and elsewhere) he insists that Orientalist discourse embodies, and articulates, an imperial–hegemonic intention emanating from the West;[51] or when (in *The World*) he endorses the argument of the Zahirite school of medieval Arab linguists – namely, that words report a *khabar* (i.e., a verbalized intention) about the world:[52] in all these cases, as in others, Said is deliberately fusing phenomenologically derived insights with others which, as we shall see presently, are drawn primarily from language-based theories.

The interpretive challenge entailed in this twinning of thought and language in the service of agency can be presented interrogatively: should Said's methodological eclecticism be seen as an empowerment or as an impoverishment? Granted that Said is trying to undercut or bypass the unwieldy dichotomies of empiricism and idealism, has he gone too far in the opposite direction? What, in practical terms, are the interpretive gains (or losses) that result from the elision of such traditional demarcations as those between externality and internality, theory and practice, or pure description and the pure gaze? Given Said's leveling of intention and signification, how does one tell word from idea, concept from realization, or object from image? The task of working through the implications of these questions at this point requires a slight shift of focus, from consciousness to language. What we find is that, rather than providing straightforward answers or solutions, this shift only duplicates and intensifies the challenge.

For, in confronting the power and problem of language, Said has found it necessary to appropriate (and collapse) divergent, even opposing theoretical positions, which are largely taken over from structuralism and poststructuralism. The resulting tensions and ambiguities of written language can be cast along a number of different axes: at times Said suggests that texts, by virtue of their interrelatedness, coagulate as a structure into a vast intertextual "system" – a homeostatically self-sustaining universe operating according to its own functionalist protocols. A closely related but slightly different view is that language is an invented totality which parallels, displaces, and caricatures the natural order. At other times, however, Said lays the emphasis on what could be described as a "process" – that is, texts as instances of a shifting, luxuriating chain of signifiers caught up in a repetitive, self-parodying play. On this view, the activity (or reality) of writing is being conceived as an endlessly interacting series of performative events with the capacity to disregard everything save the exigencies of the moment and to insist, if only as rhetorical ruses, on their own beginning authority. Finally, writing (and texts) can also be viewed discursively: as a shared, contested intellectual space saturated with energy – a space which, though having its own whims and caprices, can also be strategically harnessed for ethico-political ends. Here, too, language is an activity – or, more

precisely, an ensemble of events – but rather than being a disembodied signifier-chain performance, it "happens" (or makes things
happen) in a world of socio-cultural agents, institutions, and formations.

All these different conceptions of language, textuality, and writing
lie in an uneasy tension with one another between the covers of
Beginnings. What impresses us about this heterogeneous cluster of
nuances and inflections is that, even though both in *Beginnings* and in
later texts Said mounts a withering critique against such major theorists as Lévi-Strauss, Barthes, Lacan, Derrida, and (to a lesser extent)
even Foucault, to whom Said is particularly indebted, his own pronouncements about language (or writing, textuality, etc.) often seem
to endorse, at least on the surface, structuralist and poststructuralist
views associated with these thinkers. Intentionality, along with subjectivity – indeed the entire category of human agency – comes very
close to being occluded altogether. Here is an example of what I am
getting at:

> Words ... stand at the beginning, *are* the beginning, of a series of sub-
> stitutions. Words signify a movement away from and around ... reality. This
> is another way of characterizing the human capacity for language. To use
> words is to substitute them for something else – call it reality, historical
> truth, or a kernel of actuality. For Freud, and Valéry – as for Mallarmé,
> Nietzsche, Conrad, and others whose project is a radical one – language is the
> beginning of *another* enterprise which, despite its seeming irrationality, has
> method. The difficulty of this method is that it does not imitate nature, but
> rather displaces it. This method does not center about a *cogito*, nor does it issue
> from the *cogito*; in fact, the individual subject has little more than a provi-
> sional authority to construct hypotheses (substitutions).[53]

Elsewhere in the book, Said argues that, because of the sheer presence and pressure of intertextual influence, "the modern writer's
energies are caught up in writing over, rewriting, writing about, or
writing to other writing."[54] And there is this statement: "Once
writing-as-text is thought of as energy on the one hand, or as a specific
monument belonging to a specific series of like monuments on the
other, authority cannot reside simply in the speaker's anterior privilege. Either authority is ... a property of discourse and not of writing
... or authority is an analytical concept and not an actual available
object."[55] And this: "I think that writers have thought and still do
think of writing as a type of cosmos precisely because within the
discontinuous system of quotation, reference, duplication, parallel,
and allusion which makes up writing, authority – or the specific

power of a specific act of writing – can be thought of as something whole and as something invented."[56] Finally note how in the following passage Said brings together all (or nearly all) the above nuances:

> To begin to write . . . is to work a set of instruments, to invent a field of play for them, to enable performance . . . If writers today do not explicitly invoke the Muse at the outset, they are nevertheless still perfectly aware that some force other than physiological causation usually impels them to write. Writing is not a fact of nature [but rather] has its own kind of action, its own dreams, its own restrictions – all doubtless acquired, all doubtless connected to a psychological, social, and historical context.[57]

Said does arrive at his own carefully circumscribed thesis, which broadly speaking revolves around the idea of textual dynamics. Presented most forcefully in the fourth chapter of *Beginnings*, which is pointedly titled "Beginning with a Text," this argument is especially honed to provide what could safely be called a textualist accounting of the intensely lived, often extremely private dilemmas embodied by the literature of high modernism (more about which later). However, because this particular thesis is itself embedded within a broader argument about textuality as such, its implications resonate throughout the book – and indeed throughout Said's oeuvre from *Beginnings* onwards. By virtue of this palimpsestic thesis, Said is able to insist on two seemingly opposed assumptions which in his hands become complementary: on the one hand, language (or more precisely the text) is endowed with its own preponderance – that is, its own defamiliarizing, transformative power; its own perdurable presence and recalcitrance; and even its own transgressive waywardness – as a result of its palpable materiality and energy. But on the other hand, that materiality is neither opaque nor monolithic; and its peculiar energy is not insusceptible to human intervention. On the contrary, the text can be supple and sensitive enough to register multiple historical, epistemological, and psychological articulations and consolidations that obtain as human consciousness interacts with the world in the spatio-temporal circumstances given to it.

According to Said, texts have an immanent, active force which manifests itself in a text's capacity to preserve, transmute, and ultimately displace the source of its authority. Closely related to, and following from, the above predication is that a text, as an actual positivity – i.e., as a sheer, concrete "presence" and force – is an entity that demands attention, hence activating the desire for more texts. In effect, texts – and this is especially true to the extent that they invoke a communal, formative ideal – create a transhuman, overdetermined dimension, a field of excess where the retention, introjection, revision, and repetition of various kinds of enactment take place. These textual traits, for example, account for the solemnity that has attended the process of collecting, tracing, codifying, and standardizing biblical and classical manuscripts and related materials. They also explain the conflicting, often impassioned responses elicited from various thinkers by texts or specific textual engagements. This is, in effect, another way of describing what Said has called an intentional structure. A particularly cogent example of the power of textual authority is offered in this passage, in which Said is encapsulating Renan's argument in *Vie de Jésus*:

> Let us try now to articulate in another way what Renan says he is doing. The true origin of his biography [of Jesus] is a living, speaking man who, except as the author of a continuing spiritual revolution, has disappeared forever. Then there emerges a series of texts consequent upon this life *and* this disappearance. Renan imagines the texts as first continuing, then replacing, then displacing a textless original (i.e., one spoken and lived) that is inaccessible through ordinary, natural means. That is, in the early stages of Christian history, Jesus' life was the common spiritual property of friends and apostles; no one document contained his life complete. Each version in its own way continued his life, gently and silently replacing a previous version with a "fuller" one, which everyone presumably welcomed. Authority appears, or begins, when this process of silent replacement stops. *The authority of a text, according to Renan, is tied to the realization that a text has outlived whomever* [sic] *participated in its original making.* This rift between textual authority and the historical individual lifetime further means that a document becomes a text with authority when emendations, excisions, additions, editions, and revisions of it become intentional textual acts displacing earlier textual acts instead of, as before, matters of communal tacit agreement. For the communal document there can be no question of textuality, since anyone who intervenes in it does so out of love and common memory: such a document increases in value each time something (an anecdote) is added to it and fills it out. For the text, however, each change is viewed as making its "textuality" more secure, safer from willy-nilly rifling (or displacement) of its contents.[58]

Said offers other examples of textual power – indeed a whole constellation. In a tightly structured survey of the different, often conflicting ways in which ideas of texts, textual criticism, or scholarship as such have been appropriated or resisted, he shows how textuality as a category has tended to function as the beginning of certain attitudes, conceptions or interpretations which have had wide ramifications. For instance, an unverifiable but productive notion underlies each of the following: Kuhn's idea of "scientific paradigms," which are embodied in scientific texts and ratify the shifts and transformations of scientific revolutions; Nietzsche's Apollonian metaphor, which turns on a characterization of Greek tragic plays in terms of textual mediations of the past; Paul Maas's notion of "stemmatics," a genealogical method in which interrelated texts can be traced to an "archetypal" first copy; A. E. Housman's condemnation of "textual criticism as a sort of internal space inhabited largely by 'deplorably intellectual objects' "; Keats's description of Chapman's rendering of Homer as a "voice-text."[59] The list could continue, but the point is that this constellation of notions puts the concept of textuality in a new perspective. Always anonymous but powerfully insistent and creative, these new determinations, argues Said, govern what could – or could not – be said not only about writing as such but also (though not always explicitly) about a wide range of human activities and interests. In other words, what emerges is a text's peculiar ability to produce and shape, whether negatively or positively, the whole realm of fact and value, or the very idea of reality itself, in relation to which individuals and societies describe themselves and their environment. That is to say, a given text produced at a given time determines a given community's originary and teleological moments; what constitutes its ethical, aesthetic, and epistemological self-definition; as well as its representation of the Other. A "text," then, is not just a static container of "knowledge" about the world but, on the contrary, its creator, preserver, energizer, or mediator. It dissolves, recovers, rejects, transposes, projects – all at the same time.

Said's thesis affords him several advantages that neither mainstream structuralism nor its poststructuralist extensions (including Foucault's) could have made available – a fact which also explains his critique of structuralism (this critique will be treated in the following chapter). It is at once synchronic and diachronic, multidimensional but unified as a field, oriented towards eccentricity and performativity rather than referentiality and stability, fissured and discontinuous yet interfaced and sufficiently interactive. In other words, Said's version of intentional structure draws attention to textual events – texts as an active field surging with intellectual energy – rather than to the idea of intertextuality as a passive, self-sufficient system. It is also, however, far less impersonal than Foucault's alignment of discourse and power. The implications of this Saidian thesis (not just for literary theory and practice, but also for cultural criticism in general, for historiography, and for philosophical reflection) should henceforth be borne in mind – they are vital not only to my further explication of *Beginnings* in the next chapter but also to the later chapters of this study, which deal with Said's more politically oriented writings.

3

Beginnings and Authority: Ideology, Critique, and Community (II)

Narrativity and the Natural Order: The Fate of the Classical Novel

The third chapter of *Beginnings* is a re-engagement of the novel – or more precisely the novelistic technique. It is both a deconstruction of what Said would consider naively descriptive and, therefore, inevitably mystifying histories of the novel and a recuperation of a radicalized version of novelistic history which retraces the routes traveled by this new kind of consciousness whose very inauguration in a sense signals the advent of modernity as we have come to know it. Said's study of the novel is also, however, intended as a serious indictment of the genre – an indictment based as much on the novel's epistemology as on its politics. Hence, the chapter on the novel is permeated by an ambivalence on Said's part: to the extent that the novel's beginning condition – its reflectiveness as a new intention – instantiates a self-conferred secular freedom, an agenda of emancipation from originary dogma, to that extent it has some of the features of modernity which are generally endorsed by Said. In the end, however, his suspicion of the realist novel is profoundly deepened.

Said's critique of the novel turns on a subthesis which has been implicit in my analysis of intentionality and textuality: that narration qua narration (whether in the novel, in historiography, in biography, or in any other disciplinary branch) must submit to the exigencies of writing, and as such has far less to do with the portrayal of referential, ostensive reality than with the production of meaning. Ultimately intended by Said to buttress his demystification of realism in all its forms, this particular argument is primarily designed to unmask the enormous hubris that licensed the self-invention of the classical (or

realist) novel, whose very birth in the eighteenth century was premised on two divergent – even potentially contradictory – proposi-
tions: on the one hand, the assumption that empirical reality, with all
its vastness, complexity, and diversity, could be captured between the
covers of a book, and on the other, the implicit insistence that this
entire intellectual venture was itself necessary because it somehow
augmented – and hence enriched – that reality rather than the other
way around. Such a project, according to Said, was bound to fail for a
number of fairly obvious but often disregarded reasons: the discontinuous relationship that obtains between human intention and
the temporal movements that determine the rhythms of the natural
order; the fact that language, as we have already noted, does not serve
as a transparent glass window affording access to an independent
reality unsullied by words but rather as a power-laden structuring
device that shapes – and often transforms in eccentric ways – the very
constitution of that reality; and, finally, humanity's incurable predilection for making images, myths, and metaphors. As a result of
these factors, the narrative techniques employed by writers almost
automatically activate built-in mechanisms of resistance. In short, the
movements, contours, and transformations of narration are determined (not by a natural, ready-to-hand blueprint that harmonizes
language with what we call reality but) by strategies of control and
manipulation; hence the project of realism, primarily in the novel but
also in non-literary disciplines, carried within itself, from the very
beginning, the seeds of its own negation and transformation.

Said's version of novelistic history is therefore meant both to give a
rigorous accounting of the tensions that weave through what he
sometimes calls novelistic consciousness and to show that this genre,
which – more than any other – has given form and substance to
bourgeois subjectivity, is at once self-empowering and self-scuttling.
According to Said, two antithetical forces between them created the
"beginning conditions" for the classical novel, determined its largely
conservative trajectory, and ultimately brought about its exhaustion.
That is to say, the novels of Stendhal, Richardson, Balzac, Dickens,
and other writers of the realistic mode embodied a new kind of desire
in Western (as opposed to, for instance, Islamic) literary discourse;
that this enactment of inaugural freedom was an attempt to fashion an
aesthetic, alternate totality, one which both mimicked and departed
from the order of common discourse; that the move was aimed at
embellishing, extending, and complementing reality, hence satisfying
a perceived lack in it; that the massive sizes of eighteenth- and

nineteenth-century novels, the expansive narrations of individual, family, and social histories, as well as the profusion of foundlings and outcasts as protagonists, all attest to the birth of a new form of autonomous subjectivity which is, at the same time, bent on delivering itself of an imaginative world potentially coextensive with the known one. The point to be stressed is that the natural order, which the silent Origin had brought into being, is at once taken as an ultimate referential model (hence the notion of realism) and superseded by the new textual one.

A similar disjunction is to be found in the novel's project of self-legitimation, its attempt to bestow normativity on itself. To the extent that this grand enterprise is committed to its vision of creativity and self-propulsion, it is sanctioned by a force that can best be described as an "authority" – a term equipped, as I pointed out, with a fertile "constellation of linked meanings": "beginning or inauguration, augmentation by extension, possession and continuity" are all in this case genealogically conceived designations capturing such nuances as progeniture, power, knowledge, and growth.[1] "Authority," a concept often used restrictively in literary analysis, is afforded by Said the widest inventive latitude, especially in his discussion of novelistic consciousness. It is particularly instructive that this "authority" is not natural but invented and is manifested by both novelists and characters.

And the problem arises precisely at this point. Because this authority is a borrowed one; because it is a pseudonym that "stands in" for a displaced, suppressed, or otherwise absent originary myth, it immediately activates a counter-force which can be designated as "molestation." This suggestive term denotes "consciousness of one's duplicity, one's confinement to a fictive, scriptive realm,"[2] a sham whose illusiveness is discovered once it is compared with reality. Molestation is the parodic subscript negatively encoded on the underside of the main narrative; it is the submerged alter ego that knowingly winks behind the back of the "author/father," or the major characters, of a novel. It is the eccentric, even disturbing text (say, a *Tristram Shandy*) that, seemingly sprouting out of nowhere, impishly deflates the stolid solemnity of realism, laying bare the tenuous foundations of the genre. It is "the bother and responsibility" of authorship, the potentially debilitating challenges of initiation, the anxiety which follows autonomy, the uncertainty about legitimacy that accompanies transgression. Molestation is ultimately the contingency of circumstance, the textual web – or the power of discourse

– that ensnares human intentions. Said suggests that this demystifying force dogs the project of realism right from its inaugural
moments, but it sharply intensifies towards the end of the nineteenth
century and the beginning of the twentieth, by which time the
symptomatic rift is too jagged to smooth over. By then, modernism
has erupted upon the literary scene.

According to Said's account, this tension between authority and
molestation disperses and refracts novelistic intentionality, resulting
in the co-presence of the dialogic and ironic impulses in authors and
characters, a condition that blunts the revolutionary potential of the
genre and undermines the classical novel in three different ways. First,
there is a persistent doubt about the sufficiency of one viewpoint –
whether that be the author's, the protagonist's, or any other character's. In important respects confirming more empirically oriented
theories (those of Bakhtin and Lukacs immediately come to mind),
this novelistic suspension of univocality allows for, even insists on, a
dispersion of meaning that acknowledges multiplicity of perspectives,
necessitates compromises, and establishes irony as a constitutive element in the novelistic tradition. Often essential to maturity, this
condition circumscribes overarching forms of freedom by counter-
vailing unrealizable hopes and hallucinations. Second, never directly
available to the pure gaze, novelistic truth can be approached only
through a meandering maze of oblique routes and sidelong glances.
The author's (or character's) attempt to gain knowledge is implicated
in, and mediated by, a web of obfuscations consisting of errors, distractions, and false starts. The inherent paradox, suggests Said, is that
these delusions are crucial to authenticity, which in any case turns out
to be either an absent factor or, at best, an inadequate approximation:
despite the novelistic agency's determination to play the role of the
father, originary plenitude is decidedly absent. Finally, there "is an
extraordinary fear of the void that antedates private authority."[3] This
point, which is essential to Said's central idea of transitive beginnings,
refers to the rupture that inaugurates the birth of the novelistic
consciousness, the empty background out of which it emerges – one
that, paradoxically, guarantees its very self-invention but also constantly reminds it of its illegitimate and precarious status.

These three related strands together create the vacillation between
authority and molestation, eventually tipping the scales in favor of the
latter. Note the exorbitance of the price paid for daring to create
oneself:

> The novelistic character gains his fictional authority . . . in the desire to escape death; therefore, the narrative process endures so long as that essentially procreative will persists. Yet because a character's real beginning takes place in the avoidance of the anonymity of pure negation . . . there is a simultaneous pressure exerted upon him by that which he is always resisting. The demystification, the decreation or education, of illusions, which is the novel's central theme – and, paradoxically, its own alternate theme – is thus an enactment of the character's increasing molestation by a truer process pushing him to an ending that resembles his beginning in the midst of negation.[4]

Instead of revealing an ontological ground, the peregrinations of novelistic consciousness are progressively enmeshed in profound inauthenticity. Escape from nullity, obscurity, or death inevitably rounds in upon itself, leading back to a point of "maturity" whose value is equivalent to zero or death. At once an ending and a beginning but never an origin or a terminus, the point that completes the cycle of novelistic maturity also constitutes both a beginning-again and a rupture.

Another way of formulating this entire problematic is to say that this consummation of molestation is inevitable, given the classical novel's lack of the ontological substance necessary for sustained unity and self-propagation. That is to say, there is a fundamental divergence between the natural order, which is at once being mimicked and embellished by the novelistic narrative, and the textual order in which that narrative resides. Unlike the natural realm, which has its own immanent temporal continuity and generative power, the intertextual world of the novel depends as much on sameness as novelty or innovation. The result of this tension is a continual inner multi-plication of generic examplars, a process which ultimately strains novelistic authority itself through self-distanciation and parody. There is, in other words, an inevitability to this process: the final rupture is bound to occur sooner or later. Also, having inaugurated itself in a fallen world of death and decay, fictional narrative charts out a movement away from the sacred, self-identical Word of religious discourse. Novelistic consciousness privileges a secular agenda that must, in the end, come to grips with its own facticity, illegitimacy, and dispersion. Playing the roles of both creator and created, this abbreviated entity eventually trips itself.

This gradual intensification of self-abnegation and maturation determines the genealogical trajectory of the novel reconstructed by Said. In the early stages of its trajectory, novelistic consciousness fathers forth relatively successful characters such as Tom Jones, who

are capable of inventing and reinventing themselves without completely succumbing to molestation. Later on in its progressively
problematized history, however, the novel produces such renunciative,
anti-life characters as Ahab, Ishmael, Emma Bovary, Pip, and other
great nineteenth-century archetypal egoists. Their destiny describes
both the novelists' increasing artistic self-consciousness and the arti-
ficiality, blockage, and interruption that gradually exhaust the realistic novel.

In the creation of all of these characters, time is an important
category, either as a potentially rich vein to be appropriated for a
private vision of freedom or, as becomes increasingly clear from the
late nineteenth century onwards, as evidence of loss, absence, or
negation. The ultimate implication of this temporal double-valency,
according to Said, is perfectly allegorized in the tragedy of little
Father Time in *Jude the Obscure*: that the collective will of the great
egoists – where "will" denotes both inheritance and volition – should
come into its own in the shrivelled body of a man-child should come
as no surprise. Hardy's Father Time incarnates both a strange form of
maturity and a recognition of complete exhaustion. The equivalent
state of penury and disinheritance inscribed on the other side of this
discursive space – that is, the fate of the artist – is the unrelentingly
pessimistic vision memorialized in Gissing's *New Grub Street*: "Every
writer in this grim vision of the economics of narrative manuscript is
either sterile, blind, or celibate ... The books produced are a wilderness of mirrors that reflect the doomed effort to produce without
originality, to originate without energy, and to fable without bread."[5]

A significant, though largely implicit, strand in Said's argument is
that, despite the apparently unlimited possibilities of free creativity,
the novelistic venture has been a largely cautious, even conservative
affair – and perhaps inevitably so, given the tension between authority
and molestation. Said is implying that, inasmuch as the novel as a
genre, especially in its formative mode, has adhered to an agenda of
duplication, it has willy-nilly ratified established hierarchies and
continuities. (As we shall see in my final chapter, Said's critique of the
novel's conservatism – as of that of narrativity in general – becomes
sharper and more explicit in subsequent studies. In *Culture and
Imperialism*, for example, he closely implicates the narrative mode,
especially as it is exemplified in the nineteenth-century English novel,
with the twin ideologies of Eurocentrism and high European
imperialism.) That this agenda had, of necessity, to be abandoned is a
measure of the aridity underlying the dogma of realism. The great

arch of the classical novel, whose monumental achievements are
celebrated by Lukacs as genuine articulations (and hence indictments)
of the tensions and contradictions of bourgeois society, is redrawn by
Said as a movement of the self-constitution and impoverishment of
bourgeois subjecthood. Despite the fact that both of them are in a
sense interrogating the bourgeois consciousness that launched the
project of realism, Lukacs was fighting a rearguard action against what
he considered to be a modernist inwardness and world-weariness that
had sapped the robust, holistic, socially responsible realism of earlier
times. Said's anti-realism critique, however, is ultimately undertaken
so that a version of modernism can be instituted.

Said's account of novelistic consciousness allows him to establish
oblique, lateral relationships between the novel, on the one hand, and
on the other such fields as philosophy, psychoanalysis, and biography
– all of which are, it should be clear by now, caught up in the same
broad discursive formation. It should also be equally clear, however,
that Said's insistence on critical freedom – explicitly stated in an
earlier section, but also generally implicit in the roving, nomadic
maneuvers of the meditating mind – is designed to enable him to
institute a principle of selectivity that suits his specific agenda. Hence
even though he alludes to, or briefly analyzes, a large corpus of writing
produced in the last three centuries or so, the number of works that he
discusses in detail in the context of novelistic intentionality is actually
fairly small (they include *Great Expectations*, *Nostromo*, *Jude the Obscure*,
The Interpretation of Dreams, and *Seven Pillars of Wisdom*).

The High Drama of Modernism: Textual Production and the Dilemmas of Modernity

We have brought the discussion to a point where we can re-examine
more closely the full implications of Said's fusion of insights drawn
from two barely compatible tributaries of modern thought: namely
phenomenology and structuralism/poststructuralism. The occasion for
this re-examination is, as I indicated earlier, Said's eccentric (yet in its
own way compelling) reconstruction of high modernism – the his-
torico-textual factors that, in his opinion, led to the emergence of this
tortuous mode of literary writing. In the course of this close scrutiny,
we become informed about the extent of Said's partiality to the
densely packed, multidimensional writings of such thinkers as Conrad, Proust, Hopkins, and Eliot, among others: for, even though Said

does not say so explicitly, it is (I think) valid to insist that, within the immediate province of literature (in contradistinction to, for example, philosophy or historiography), he considers the texts of high modernism as being particularly exemplary in capturing the haunted spirit of modern times: they register, articulate, and dramatize – rather than synthesize or resolve – the enormously challenging dilemmas of modernity. This, in effect, is what Said means when he identifies the four fundamental oppositions of modernist discourse (or, what amounts to the same thing in this context, modernist consciousness), an exposition of which will constitute the core of my discussion in this section.

The rationale behind Said's dual methodological strategy – the leveling and activation of what could be called pure intention and the pure sign – now becomes clear: on the one hand, he must find a way to come to grips with the intense introspection that has traditionally been associated with high modernism; this heightened form of consciousness, as we have come to know it from various studies of modernism, takes the form of disjunctive configurations: a curiously reflective, divided mind; an awareness of the passage of time as evidence of permanent loss; a feeling of anxiety and inauthenticity; the adoption of a hesitant, ironic, often difficult style of presentation; a continual search for innovation and renewal. On the other hand, however, Said's primary aim is to attract attention to modernist literature qua text. There is a sense, then, in which this heightened awareness on the part of the modernist thinker is closely (perhaps inversely?) related to an unusually high threshold condition for (the emergence of) what could properly be called a text. The difficulty confronted – and dramatized – by major modernist writers, suggests Said, increases to the extent that they "aspire toward a highly specialized ideal of textual achievement as the *beginning* condition of their work."[6] The very activity of writing itself becomes a near-impossibility because of the enormously rarefied definition of texts. My own subthesis at this point is that, if it were possible to identify a specific segment of *Beginnings* in which Said employs his difficult compound technique – namely, agonistic dialectic and genealogy/archaeology – in its most intense form, his analysis of high modernism in the fourth chapter of *Beginnings* would have to be it: the full range of modernist dilemmas – psychological, logico-epistemological, and historico-sociological – are addressed in the context of a textualist interpretation of modernism:

My notion is thus that certain writers for whom producing a text is an achievement fraught with problems represent and are constantly troubled by [a] curious mixture of affirmation and rarity. For them the text is the statement of a career fully commanded by neither public pressure (even though that plays a part) nor the ordinary conventions that prescribe a literary vocation. On the contrary, the career is aboriginal; hence its problems. To write for Grub Street is abhorrent, as is also the idea of writing a mere collection of works. The desired goal is a true whole, in which individual segments are subordinated to the totality of collective affirmation. Further, the career in its rarity is even thought of as aberrant, not to say criminal. Thus whatever work is in fact produced suffers from radical uncertainty at the beginning; it is highly unconventional; it possesses its own inner dynamic; it is a constantly experienced but strangely impalpable whole partially revealing itself in individual works; it is haunted by antecedence, difference, sameness, and the future; and it never finally accomplishes its ideal aims, at least in its author's opinion. The writer's life, his career, and his text form a system of relationships whose configuration in *real human time* becomes progressively stronger (i.e., more distinct, more individualized and exacerbated). In fact, these relationships gradually become the writer's all-encompassing subject. On a pragmatic level, then, his text is his statement of the temporal course of his career, inscribed in language, and shot through and through with precisely these matters.[7]

Said argues that, unlike most of the writers in other eras, modernists developed a weirdly exaggerated idea about what constitutes a literary text. To the extent that the transvaluating power of the text assumed its own privative immanence, it became both performative and difficult. Because of the extreme idealization of the text's beginning condition and because of the heightened awareness resulting from the writer's intense reflection, writing itself emerged as a mode of living which paralleled – and often conflicted with – the writer's empirical self. No longer a vocation, the writer's calling tended to be transformed into an all-consuming "career"; and, in the end, the text served as a pure sign – a kind of extended signature – of its author. Formulated in traditional philosophical terms, this means that ethical, epistemological, existential, and ontological concerns merged coextensively to form a shared textual space.

It is this extraordinary relationship between author and text that Said intends to convey when he invokes Foucault's idea of "statement." The idea of statement in a discursive formation is particularly useful to Said because it enables him to describe texts as rarefied epistemological judgements made as *"conditions met* at a particular cultural time and place in a particular way [which are] rarer than mere speaking and writing."[8] The Foucauldian universe of discourse is the subject of a later section in this chapter; it is also central to the idea of textual worldliness, the broad topic of my next chapter. Here what is important is that the discursive space captures the historicity of modernity, the eccentricity of the modernist text, and the idiosyncrasy (or egocentricity) of the individual author, hence creating a coextension between a writer's textual production and the idea of a career – all without recourse to such concepts as stylistics, the cogito, or traditional literary history. By eliding self, sign, and space-time, *Beginnings* therefore ratifies itself on grounds whose existence is also under suspicion.

All of this means that the discursive field is not just the orthogonally engaged locus of the pure gaze (as in Foucault's texts, for example); it is also an animated inner domain of struggle where the energy acquired by virtue of transgression is redistributed, channeled, wasted, or dispersed – all within the compass of a given modernist writer's personal experience. The problematic that Said is trying to do justice to is, I think, philosophically at its most challenging at this point: the uncovered space on the one hand gives full vent to a thoroughgoing determinism enunciated in the form of an anonymous, yet power-laden, discursive field. On the other hand, it releases an intensely individuated, autodidactic subjectivity whose stoic freedom is buttressed by assumptions ultimately drawn from Vico. The multiple crises thrown up on this plane, where absolute self-creation is unnerved by a terrifying lack, account for a great deal of what seems otherwise intractable in modernism – for example, Conrad's cosmological homelessness, or Kafka's allegorization of the desire and nightmare of an astoundingly arbitrary anteriority. Since there is always a tension among several variables – the writer as an agency with a pre-discursive biography; the ongoing emergence of the writer and his writing as an unfolding career; the career perceived as a finished corpus of works – this struggle can best be described in terms of four oppositions that give shape and orientation to modernist writing. Though overlapping one another and coextensive with the writer's entire oeuvre, these oppositions each map out the limits and pressure points of the intellectual and emotional concerns that determine the writer's immediate field of engagement in various phases of his career.

The first opposition relates to the conflict that develops between "an author's career as a productive writer and either the beginning or the end of that career."[9] Presented in brief, transposed terms, this conflict between "career and non-career"[10] can be cast along bipolar axes revolving around the relationship between the writer as an empirical human being and his inevitable belief that he can live meaningfully only through his writing. The questions implied here can be phrased in the following way: Is the author's pre-literary experience a preparation for the career – or a lost opportunity? What particular enactments – memories, ruptures, projections, or transformations – must be effected in order for the rarefied text, "the pure sign" of the author, to appear? Conversely, if writing, as an activity guided by its own discursive logic, departs from, transgresses against, and ultimately displaces the empirical dimension of reality, isn't it in fact a negation of the writer's existence rather than an affirmation or augmentation of it? Beset by worries of this kind, the writer is condemned to a duality of perspectives, engaging himself in a perpetual inner dialogue. In a discussion involving Wilde, Conrad, and Joyce among others, Said investigates the way in which extreme forms of originality and repetition alternate with each other in the writer's evolving oeuvre. He closes his analysis of the first opposition with an extended examination of the refractive, ironic affinity among Proust as an individual and as a self-defining writer; his character Marcel, the would-be writer who forever abides in the realm of potentiality; and *La recherche*, the massive, seven-volume text that constitutes both Marcel's recovered memory and Proust's artistic achievement.

Building on, and intensifying, the pressures of the first, the second opposition turns on the incompatibility between public expectations and the left-handed imperatives of the modernist text. On the one hand, the writer is aware that, as a product of a given social climate, his writing is expected to be directed towards a readership; that therefore lucidity, referentiality, and catholicity of structure should be paramount. On the other, he is engaged in a project that, when all is said and done, has no object other than the creation of a textual field, one that alludes only to other textual fields. With no originary model or blueprint – except its own radical point of departure – and with no telos, writing becomes a specific writer's way of achieving the total fulfillment of meaning within the immanent arrangement of an artistic text – that is to say, his unique, self-investigative production of meaning in a discursive space. It therefore tends to be irregular, idiosyncratic, and opaque, even while it unfolds as part of a broad discursive formation. The second opposition, then, results from this conflict between what can, loosely, be called the public and the private spheres: the writer periodically plagues himself with questions about the ethical and artistic implications of the methodological choices he has made in the course of his career.

And, suggests Said, given the peculiar intensity and centripetality of modernism, it is the immanent configuration of writing that, in the end, determines the writer's gaze. The crisis engendered by the opposition is inscribed in the writer's oeuvre, not resolved by it. More specifically, the rifts, reversals, and repetitions enunciated in this conflict are registered (and should be investigated by the critic) in terms of a tension between a preparatory text (or "paratext") and a rarefied "final draft"; between a text's status and its volume; between the inevitable impoverishment (one must forgo certain consoling beliefs) and the "problematical enrichment" that textuality brings; between the performativity of writing and the ultimately metatextual omnivore that eventually swallows up individual texts. In other words, the modernist text is a particular sort of personal style, an idiolect, that defines a writer's uniqueness but at the same time enacts the writer's pain and alienation. Moreover, observed from a broader perspective, the movements of modernism can be seen to encourage "an artistic monism" that the writer cannot disregard except at the risk of "idolatry." It is with these parameters in mind that Said comments on the writings of James, Mallarmé, Eliot, and especially Kafka. Said believes that a modernist text tends to be lean in volume but dense, that its irregularity and elusiveness heighten its status.

The third opposition can be presented – with some modification – as a mid-career act of stock-taking. To a great extent, the resolution of what Said calls a tension between "speech" and "non-speech" depends on the writer's attitude towards a delicately balanced set of relationships that are already in place thanks to the special artistic idiom that has secured his reputation as a writer in the first half of his career. Said's appropriation of a highly finessed description of "speech" – one that takes its cue from formulations by Benveniste and Foucault but also echoes Austin's speech acts theory – is particularly apposite here: he purposefully equips the term with existential – and even ontological – significance. Inasmuch as a writer has earned credit as an author with a distinctive style; inasmuch as the audience – however limited – has come to associate him with specific investments, patterns, and problematics, the trajectory of his career reaches a point of maturity at which writing becomes a discourse defining personhood. No longer just unraveling in a temporal movement, writing disseminates meaning in a manner that privileges the achieved voice of subjecthood; it is as though writer, text, and audience knowingly engage one another in an eternal present.

The opposition here, then, turns on the role of subject positions, authenticity, and originality. How does (or should) the writer adjudicate between habit and innovation such that the validity of the already established equipoise – between author and text, text and reader, text and style – remains intact while new events are accommodated by the writer's own discourse? Hence the issue is not one of speech and silence in the traditional senses of these terms; rather it is one of discovering a way of fashioning techniques that enhance the writer's canonized subjectivity, while also yielding to the subtle pressures of the distinctively new – even potentially revolutionary – mode or impulse: hence the necessity of the resilient consistency of "voice" in the second half of the career. Although earlier examples can be cited (Swift succeeds in negotiating the tension superbly while Pope remains largely monologic throughout his career), it is the modernist writers that have almost invariably had to come to grips with this dialectic. Said focuses on Hopkins's lifelong obsession with sprung rhythm and on Eliot's later "delocutory" poetry in which the persona uses the text as an occasion to speak directly to the audience – even while echoing some of the subtlety and complexity of the poetry written in earlier phases of the poet's career.

The above transformation in Eliot's later poetry leads us directly to the fourth – and final – opposition that Said identifies in modernist literature. Eliot's adoption, especially in the *Four Quartets* of "explanation" – that is, a deictic, prosy style that both sublates and purges the obliqueness and polyvocality of earlier poetry – is laced with a certain weariness. Having known fame but now conscious of atrophy, the aged poet ponders whether a waning talent should be derailed permanently or whether a long, productive career should be permitted to totter along dodderingly. The resolution – or lack thereof – of this opposition can take different thematic forms, from Eliot's religious affirmation to Yeats's meditations on frail senescence. As a general rule, the sentiment expressed most often in this last phase of the career is one of bitterness and fatigue, an impulse usually articulated in language that draws attention to its poetic impotence. Said concludes the fourth chapter with a programmatic examination of Hopkins's extraordinary commingling of divine plenitude, sexual insemination, and poetic creativity – a bold, mildly transgressive intentional act that underpins the greatness of the early poems but signals sterility in the later sonnets.

The four oppositions, then, define the initiation, progression, culmination, and exhaustion of the typical career of the modernist writer, a tortured career that, in effect, marks the emergence of absolute exteriority: the rebellious animus that, sometime in the eighteenth century, wrested the reins of control from a senile parent, launched itself into an orbit of freedom, and initially reveled in the luxuriance of its own creativity, has finally come full circle. It has woken up to the painful realization that complete automony cannot be achieved without complete deracination. In the end, an overdetermined text reigns supreme. And it is the progressive rarefaction of that animus through several cycles, from the early realistic novel to the contorted modernist performance, that is described in the swerves, repetitions, and ruptures enunciated in both Foucault's and Vico's analyses. (Said here particularly underscores the extent to which the four modernist phases instantiate Vichian cyclicality.)

By way of conclusion, I would like to digress from *Beginnings* (or, more precisely, to leap ahead) and reflect on Said's re-examination in the Nineties of some of the broad topics we have discussed in the preceding two sections – a re-examination which, on the one hand, neatly exemplifies the uses he has put to the logic of beginnings and repetitions but, on the other, shows that the repetition is sometimes so radical that it amounts to a more or less complete transformation of the original problematic rather than the addition of a new inflection to it. Two specific instances can be cited here – one about a brief note on modernism in *Culture and Imperialism*, the other about the idea of lateness, the main theme of several articles written in the early and middle Nineties.

In a brief discussion in *Culture and Imperialism*, Said offers a new account of what he considers to be the historical, artistic, and thematic transformation from the mode of realism – the provenance of the classical novel – to that of the tortured modernist consciousness, which we have just examined. He argues that, whereas the realist novel generally collaborated with the mission, process, and con- solidation of empire-building in complex ways (more about all of this in the final chapter of my study), modernist literature signals a new awareness of uncertainty, even disillusionment, in European culture about imperialism. The nineteenth-century novel, and the narrative mode in general, revels in its endorsement of "frank exoticism and confident empire"[11] building; a large number of novels and travel documents (Said specifically cites the writings of Kipling, Haggard, and Loti) "are based on the exhilaration and interest of adventure in the colonial world ... [and] serve to confirm and celebrate" the spectacular successes of the imperial venture.[12] The unmistakable impression one gets from reading these texts is that the European imperialist is in total control, and the opposing native has been permanently disabled. Instead of "this optimism, affirmation, and serene confidence," modernist writings are suffused with profound irony. Conrad's texts, for example, "radiate an extreme, unsettling anxiety"[13] – even at the same time that he fails to offer an alternative to the actualities of imperialism. Modernism, Said insists, instantiates an artistic transformation of realism, an enactment which also creates an open, "encyclopedic form,"[14] "a new inclusiveness."[15] Phrased differently, this means that modernism recognized that the fates of Europeans and natives are closely implicated in ironic, tragic, and comic ways: "the hallmark of modernist form is the strange juxta-position of comic and tragic, high and low, commonplace and exotic, familiar and alien whose most ingenious resolution is Joyce's fusion of the *Odyssey* with the Wandering Jew, advertising and Virgil (or Dante), perfect symmetry and the salesman's catalogue."[16]

Said's point in this brief discussion coheres at one level with a broad affirmative argument that permeates his entire career: that all cultures are interrelated, and there are no such things as unsullied originary sources or essences dynastically transmitting their issue and authority down the ages. In the context of *Beginnings*, he particularly stresses this theme in the chapter on Vico (to be discussed below). At a more circumscribed level, the brief revisit to modernism in *Culture and Imperialism* is meant to illustrate Said's specific thesis in this late text: that high European imperialism was so spectacular and thorough-going that it at once transformed the entire world into a global village and established socio-political realities so discrepant and hierarchical as to be scandalous and unseemly. At its most immediately pertinent level, the note on modernism resonates with the idea of beginnings and what transpires in their wake. Just as the unity and self-endowed freedom of the early realist novels were followed (as we saw earlier) by the disillusionment and self-abnegation of later novels – an attitude that manifested itself in the form of irony, fragmentation, sterility, and blockage, eventually leading to the tortured forms of modernity – so the realist novel's enthusiasm for empire is transformed into the more nuanced, doubtful, refracted consciousness of modernism. Ear-lier forms, attitudes, enactments, locales, etc. are rearranged – or "affiliated," as Said puts it in *The World, the Text, and the Critic* – in a new way that, paradoxically, affords new insights but also registers loss and fatigue. As we shall see both in this chapter and in the remaining two chapters, these later transformations can also harden into ossified dogmas – so ambiguous is the meaning of modernity.

Another name for modernity is coming after – the reality of

emerging on the cultural scene at a later date or age; it is precisely this idea that Said has in mind in his reference to what he has called the style of lateness, especially with respect to Adorno. By "lateness" Said seems to mean an idea (and intellectual practice) which has both quantitative and qualitative dimensions to it – quantitative in the sense of arriving or appearing on the intellectual–historical scene at a later point in time, qualitative because disabusing and laden with deep (perhaps irreversible) awareness of finality. Conscious of exhaustion, loss, senescence, and the impending catastrophe of death, certain thinkers (for example Adorno in his piece on Beethoven's *late* compositions) meditate on – even embrace – the impress of aging, hence in their own heroic way giving full measure to the occasion of absolute finality and making lateness an emblem of authenticity, a personal signature symbolizing *the* terminus as lived and experienced. The work produced (by Adorno as by Beethoven) is therefore not only fragmentary and opaque, but also the exact antithesis of positive totality – that is, totality as absence but also as absolutely insistent on its own terms:

> Here [Adorno] is at his most paradoxical: you cannot say what connects the parts [of either Beethoven's musical compositions or Adorno's meditations on them] other than by invoking "the figure they create together". Neither can you minimize the differences between the parts, and it would appear, you cannot actually *name* the unity, or give it a specific identity, which would then reduce its catastrophic force. Thus the power of Beethoven's late style is negative, or rather, it *is* negativity; where one would expect serenity and maturity, one finds a bristling, difficult and unyielding – perhaps even inhuman challenge. "The maturity of the late works," Adorno says, "does not resemble the kind one finds in fruit. They are ... not round, but furrowed, even ravaged. Devoid of sweetness, bitter and spiny, they do not surrender themselves to mere delectation" ... Beethoven's late works remain unco-opted: they do not fit any scheme, and they cannot be reconciled or resolved, since their irresolution and unsynthesized fragmentariness are constitutive, not ornamental or symbolic of something else. Beethoven's late compositions are about, are in fact "lost totality", and therefore catastrophic.[17]

A brief comparison with the fourth (and final) modernist opposition that we discussed earlier shows that, in both tone and inflection, these words from "Adorno as Lateness Itself" (1995) are a far cry from the daylight world of *Beginnings*. In the earlier text, the final opposition indicated exhaustion, not doom; the bitterness expressed by the modernist author primarily related to the loss of poetic genius, but the language of the aging poet still retained its deictic capacity, its ability to formulate a statement. In Adorno (and in Beethoven), almost absolute interiority and incommunicability are the norm. The modernists rarely ever meditated on aging as a long, catastrophic zone to be abided in for "its own sake." On the other hand, "Adorno [and apparently Beethoven before him] is, I think, prepared to endure ending in the [ontological] form of *lateness* but *for itself*, its own sake, not as a preparation for or obliteration of something else. Lateness is being at the end, fully conscious, full of memory, and also very (even preternaturally) aware of the present. Adorno as lateness itself ... as scandalous, even catastrophic commentator on the present."[18] For the modernists, the final opposition was in its own way integrated to the earlier oppositions and hence to the career as a whole; the logic of lateness appears to have its own detached yet self-contained integrity. It is almost an internally dynamic, implosive mode of existence, almost entirely incommensurable with the conventions of the social world: "for Adorno *lateness* includes the idea of surviving beyond what is acceptable and normal; in addition, lateness includes the idea that one cannot really go beyond lateness at all, not transcending or lifting oneself out of lateness but rather deepening the lateness."[19] It is this mode of living and intellectual practice, Said tells us, that is articulated in Adorno's analysis of Schoenberg's atonal music.

Said notes repeatedly the profound pessimism that lies at the heart of Adorno's style of lateness, with the further possible risk of nihilism and cynicism. Said wrote "Adorno as Lateness Itself," as well as a few other articles (among them "On Lost Causes" and "Traveling Theory Reconsidered"[20]) in the early and middle Nineties – that is, in the wake of both his own diagnosis with cancer and the signing of the Oslo Agreements between the leaders of the Palestine Liberation Organization and Israel, an agreement which he has denounced as fraudulent. The fact that these articles in different ways take up the topic of lateness may therefore prompt us to give them an auto-biographical reading. This view is, I think, valid – but only up to a certain point; in passages like the following, we sense that Said not only endorses but in a manner of speaking appropriates Adorno's defiance:

> In the performance of individual critical thinking there is the "force of pro-test." Yes, such critical thought as Adorno's is very idiosyncratic and often very obscure, but, he wrote in "Resignation," his last essay[,] "the uncompromisingly critical thinker, who neither superscribes his conscience nor permits himself to be terrorized into action, is in truth the one who does not give up" ... To work through the silences and fissures is to avoid packaging and administration, and is in fact to accept and perform the *lateness* of his position.[21]

The voice that needs to be heard beyond (and above) the auto-biographical note is, I think, that of the critic par excellence, the voice of the erudite scholar as an oppositional public intellectual. In the remaining two chapters of my study, that voice will become far more clearly audible, far more precisely articulated.

The Grand Gesture of Structuralism: Much Ado About Nothing

Said's association with structuralist linguistics and its extensions has been both very fruitful and fairly contentious. My discussion of the crucial notion of textuality both in the preceding section and in the second chapter reflected that dual relationship to some degree; I noted that the various tensions in Said's views on language, textuality, and writing – for example, the tension between "system" and "process" – are due as much to an ambivalence on Said's part as to an ambiguity in structuralism itself. In this section, I wish to foreground the notion of structure itself; more specifically, I will concentrate on Said's critique of the structuralist project (and French linguistic theory in general) in the context of *Beginnings*, but I will also insist that – this critique notwithstanding – at least some of the assumptions underlying structuralism, including the notion of structure itself, have also been quite useful to Said, hence further contributing to the multiple tensions weaving through the entire text of *Beginnings*.

The idea of structure, as Said is using it, delivers meaning on at least two distinct levels: at a broad level, it has the features of a totality – something analogous to what would traditionally be called history, society, or culture at large. His characterization of language as "an intentional structure" would cohere with this holistic definition. More often, however, he seems to have something narrower and more focused in mind – something comparable to "form" or "shaping principle," as these terms were popularized by the New Critics and neo-Aristotelians respectively. Hence, for example, the "real" beginning of a given intellectual project (an intentional event) ultimately determines not only the "formal" beginning of that project but also its further development and its limits that is, its structural dimensions. Said has, therefore, appropriated the idea of structure in *Beginnings* (and elsewhere) as part of his repertoire of legitimate conceptual armor – and has done so in ambiguous, often eccentric ways. Nevertheless, his assessment of structuralism is on the whole negative.

Presented in the most general terms, his complaint concerns the uses that have been made of the central idea of structure itself. He believes that, in the hands of such thinkers as Lévi-Strauss, Barthes, and Lacan (though not Foucault), "structure" has become an anaemic, fundamentally passive heuristic device that neutralizes the powerful energies of human agency and domesticates them for harmless intellectual games. A related criticism is that structuralists are "linguacentric" – that is, they rely too heavily on the interpretive resources made available by language and as a consequence distort (or minimize) the function of other, equally important cultural forms. Said's criticism of what he calls structuralism or semiology (two terms used interchangeably by him) perhaps should come as no surprise – given his enduring interest in both consciousness and ethico-political matters. There may, however, be a historical factor in the equation: Said finished *Beginnings* at a time when mainstream structuralism, with all its scientific garb and its claims to formalist rigor, was about to give way to the onslaught of poststructuralism and postmodernism in American literary circles. Hence, his exposition and appropriation of French linguistic theories seem to straddle a threshold: the residual uneasily abuts the emergent. All of these factors need to be considered in contextualizing the following summary.

Said identifies a set of four assumptions (or "features") that undergird structuralist theories: "radical discontinuity" as an inescapable condition for the generation of knowledge; post-narrativity and a concomitant rarefaction; the strategic fusion of "uncertainty and invention" in the production of knowledge; and "a supposition that rational knowledge is possible."[22] These principles together inaugurate the structuralist project and its Foucauldian extensions – a project in which language acts as both the "beginning" and the "center," in the process all but abolishing human subjectivity, inflicting enormous violence on the substance of nature, and fashioning a monolithic "ontology of nothingness."[23] What must be noted here is that, Said's backhanded slap notwithstanding, these same principles have mandated (admittedly to unequal degrees) his own study from the outset. Sometimes buttressing, but often undermining, his central concept of intentionality, they have shaped the orientation of his argument, directing such variables as "transitive beginning," repetition, reversal, as well as the other fine-tunings and transformations we have analyzed above. In other words, what finally emerge into full theoretical view – as a sustained critique and as an explication – are the hitherto largely submerged theoretical assumptions which (in part) authorized the textual-discursive thesis we have discussed in the preceding section.

At a more specific level, Said's critique of structuralism can be stated thus: first, the Saussurian assumptions appropriated by the structuralists – that the link between the two components of a linguistic sign, the signifier and the signified, is not truly referential but arbitrary; that meaning is, therefore, to be found not in the world but only in the differential relationships amongst the various elements that constitute the structure of a given language; that the total system (or langue) of a language is an unknowable, self-regulating, subterranean entity that, nevertheless, ratifies the particular instances of language use (or parole) – these assumptions are enormously productive in their own way but are, in the last analysis, simply tautologous. Freed from its subservience to the grand debate between the subject and the object, language now becomes a quasi-independent storehouse of ideas whose capacity for variety and inventiveness is virtually unlimited. Yet in the end one wonders whether any really worthwhile insights have been delivered by structuralist linguistics.

Describing the project of structuralism as "linguacentricity pushed very far,"[24] Said coins his own neologism for it: linguicity. He tells us that linguicity does indeed have an analytic "quality" (his term) which performs "very valuable services," but (he suggests) that very capacity itself turns structuralism into a virtually closed exercise that has no viable goal beyond its own self-perpetuation:

> Among other things, [linguicity] informs the activity of what Lévi-Strauss calls the totemic operator, that rational instrument carried within the primitive mind that enables him [sic] to divide the observed world into a logic of finely organized species ... It also insures the availability to language of unlimited signifying opportunities, despite the impoverishment of what is being signified; it guarantees language unlimited linguistic discovery – that is, a sort of permanent finding power; and it provides the links between the dimensions of investigation (say, from particular to general, or from discontinuity to discontinuity). In short, linguicity is a privilege taken for granted by structuralist activity; its perpetuation, however, is structuralism's project and purpose. Linguicity is the consequence of the radical discontinuity [which is] also presupposed by structuralism.[25]

Let us schematize the implications of the passage. According to Said, linguicity is an enabling presupposition that opens up a vast universe for analysis. Instituting itself as a fundamental grammar for human thinking, language becomes a rational tool that, through strategic oppositions, structurations, and transformations, explains various spheres of human activity as instances of its own mode of functioning.

Structuralists can, therefore, quite comfortably talk virtually about any subject under the sun: from the myth-bound kinship systems of "primitive" tribes (Lévi-Strauss), to the "overdetermined" character of dominant ideologies (Althusser), to the latest models of the Paris fashion industry (Barthes). The claim that structuralist analysis provides a rational explanation of society can be based on the fact that the various structural realms in a sense act as mirror-reflections of one another.

But it is also conceivable that structuralists, having explained everything, may have explained nothing at all. The reason is that linguicity, the empowering presupposition of the entire structuralist project, is also a mechanism of radical foreclosure. Since linguistics, the presumed scientific "ground" of structuralist truth claims, uses the elements of language or homologies thereof (phonemes, morphemes, mythemes, ideologemes, etc.) both as the problem of investigation and as the medium of study, the various models, codes, and conventions conform to the peculiar prejudices of a self-validating system: "What linguicity cannot do ... is show us why structure structures: structure is always revealed in the condition of having structured, but never ... in the condition of structuring, or of *being structured*, or of failing to structure. The main structuralist weakness, which is not Foucault's, is that linguicity must remain outside the constitutive structure, even to the point of being rejected by structure, yet it is presumed by structuralism as a precondition for order."[26] Structuralism can, in a swift enactment of "découpage" (roughly, delimitation or definition), cut through a great mass of details, generate "pertinent" "information" for its immediate purposes, and hew a realm of order out of chaos. In the process, however, it ends up begging too many questions – about history, society, and the material weight of culture; about the corrosive, dynamic energies of the human mind; about power, politics, and social combat; and about a whole array of forces, agencies, conflicts, agendas, and institutions that form the very substance of human cultural life. In short, structuralists can exploit the conveniences language offers, but they cannot break out of its circularity. Linguicity "permits language" to become "a totalitarian system."

Another way of formulating this point is to say that structuralism is hampered by the anti-historicist, anti-humanist imperatives of its logic, a curious logic which encourages both a quietist aestheticism and a nihilistic determinism. On the one hand, the structuralists' obsession with the synchronicity, relationality, and arbitrariness of

language obliges them to dodge causal and teleological issues. Very
often, a divine or mythic originary plenitude before writing – variously described as "zero degree," "zero point," or "floating signifier"
– is posited but then suppressed forthwith: coextensive with thought,
language (especially in its written form) cannot grasp the "pure
meaning" of the self-identical Word. Even more ominous, language,
which marks the actual beginning of human culture, is found to
condemn man to a post-lapsarian state of dispersion and contingency.
Hence the purposefulness of action, the authenticity of values, the
claims of belief – all those matters which are essential to subjectivity –
are neutralized and woven into a passive textual web. A grand
superscript displaces human intentionality. Man as he is portrayed by
Lévi-Strauss, Barthes, Lacan, and other French thinkers, argues Said, is
an enslaved entity, "a speaking pronoun," whose self-definition can be
executed only in terms of refracted, hopelessly strung-out subject
positions. And to entertain any freedom from the signifier–signified
chain is to seek for something outside the compass of human
experience. Like Kafka's castle, it can never be realized even if it must
be pursued.

But on the other hand, that same fascination with the operations of
language authorizes structuralists to disown the burdens of empirical
reality: "What is especially interesting about Saussure's discovery
[about language] – at least so far as it carries over into structuralist
writing – is that . . . the sheer oppressive mass of historical, biological,
or psychic determinism is first lifted, then frittered away, then
brought back as weightless gamelike rules or protocols."[27] Instead of
genuinely interrogating society's matrix of contexts, structuralist
thinkers have invented a form of rationality that decouples the spheres
of thought and praxis, substituting a neutered, self-sustaining system
for both. "Linguicity discounts memory, and history, in the interests
of total recall, for structure, which is the child of language and linguicity, has no way of containing its past, but only of delivering its
present by 'laying all its cards on the table.'"[28] Recovering scraps and
fragments, which are recombined into a totalizing shell that abides in
an unchanging present, semiology is essentially a descriptive model of
analysis that, in effect, inscribes an acknowledgment of loss, absence,
and impoverishment – even if at times it pretends to be doing much
more than that.

Said's general conclusion is that, even though structuralism "is a
kind of positivism," it cannot be considered a philosophical method
with any serious claims to powers of explanation or interrogation:

"*structure* is neither a spatial term nor, for that matter, a temporal one"; rather, it is "an activity" or "a general tendency of thought" which "is attracted to the elusive in-betweenness of order" – where "order" in this case has less to do with the complex realities of human existence than with what Said calls "a complement" to that existence.[29] In other words, structure is a quasi-metaphysical, deodorized entity suspended in a twilight zone, a zone precariously poised between metaphor and metonymy. Structuralist thinkers, then, have erected an imposing but passive bricolage that leaves the world pretty much as they have found it:

> In most structuralist writing we rarely have any sense of Freud's tragic realization that civilization and language both serve to repress man's instinctual nature, nor do we sense any of the pain of Nietzsche's assaults against an obdurate wall of history and custom, nor any of Heidegger's patient yet agonized doom within language. For the most part, the structuralists are adjusted to language and civilization (they see the two as coterminous); they take culture for what it rationally appears to be instead of rebelling against it.[30]

Said detects a certain comedy in the structuralists' production of insouciant energy, suggesting that they engender a false sense of security, control, and freedom. In structuralism, interpretation has become "an aesthetic activity, a release, so to speak, from the tyranny of time and history."[31]

As we shall see in my next chapter, Said's impatience with French language theorists and their American fellow travelers intensified in his later writings. At this point, however, two points need to be noted. One is that Said's analysis of "structuralism" amalgamates mainstream structuralism with the theories of a number of writers who have since come to be known as poststructuralists. The other is that Said believed – at least in the late Sixties and early Seventies – that the far greater demystificatory and explanatory power of the theories proposed by the latter group could be domesticated for humanistic purposes. This is especially true of Said's attitude towards Foucault (more about him shortly), but even Derrida, whose idea of deconstruction is subjected to strong criticism in *The World, the Text, and the Critic*, is reviewed favorably in *Beginnings*. Derrida's metaphors ("trace," "decentering," "differance," etc.) are characterized by Said as an ingenious exaggeration of structuralist models, a playful parody that punctures the scientistic stolidity of structuralism. At any rate, beyond Said's immediate commentary and beyond the fact that the provenance of structuralism as an intellectual enterprise has shrunk considerably since the Seventies, it is also the case that his reliance (acknowledged or otherwise) on structuralist and poststructuralist assumptions comes very close to forestalling his own humanistic ideals. This problem, which more than anything else turns on the ambiguity in Said's appropriation of "rationality," reappears in his career in various guises. What must be stressed, however, is that Said's ambivalence – here and elsewhere in his oeuvre – needs to be contextualized in the broad methodological infrastructure that I have described as an activated confrontation between agonistic dialectic and archaeology/genealogy. That dynamic, conflictual attitude lies behind his critique of structuralism and his more appreciative analysis of Foucauldian and Vichian speculations.

Vico and Foucault: The "Space" Between Philosophy, Language, and History

I have argued throughout this study that the philosophical spine that runs through Said's entire career is the phenomenological idea of intentionality. But I have also insisted that Said has appropriated that Husserlian term in a highly eccentric fashion – that he has found it necessary to complement, extend, fine-tune, and depart from it in various ways; that the introduction of linguistically derived insights into his interpretive repertoire is part of that strategy of eclecticism which has allowed him to move "in and out of things." Finally, I have maintained that both the claims of history on what might otherwise become a disembodied, purified chain of ideas and the equally insistent claims of ideology critique have necessitated the deployment of interrogative tools far more critically sensitive than those provided by Husserlian phenomenology and structuralist linguistics. Hence Said's juxtaposition of conceptions of historical movement (and situationality), the operations of the human mind, and the double-bladed character of language as these were proposed by maverick thinkers separated by two centuries: Vico and Foucault. At its most cogent – and yet in some ways most problematic – moment, the methodological discordance of *Beginnings* is the result of Said's appropriating Vico's and Foucault's anti-originary, anti-mimetic, and anti-linear heuristics in order to account for the phenomenon of modernity over the past three centuries or so.

Even though Said does not treat either Vico or Foucault until the very last chapters of *Beginnings*, it is important to note that, in the context of *Beginnings*, he is indebted to these two thinkers more than to any others. The interactions between various determinations of "beginning," as an intellectually enabling fulcrum, and broad conceptions of "intention" and "method," as well as most of the specific theoretical insights he uses in the study, are ultimately traceable to Foucauldian and especially Vichian assumptions. Equally important, these assumptions, similar though they are in some ways, nevertheless entail unbridgeable gaps and divergences. Behind Said's persistent attempt to "go beyond" Foucault – both in *Beginnings* and in such later texts as *The World, the Text, and the Critic* – is a conscious decision that, for ideology critique to be effective, the intellectual must posit a utopian moment beyond Foucault's powerfully effective but largely negative criticism. Said's utilization of Vichian insights in *Beginnings*, as well as his repeated (though often cursory) invocations of these insights in later works, is meant to provide that utopian space.

It is not difficult to see why the heuristic techniques of these two renegade intellectuals would be useful to Said. Both of them launch assaults on originary mythologies, whether philosophical or theological, in a manner that is – in Said's estimation – far more compelling than anything mustered by advocates of empiricism or idealism. This effectiveness can be formulated in several different ways. First, although neither Vico nor Foucault is materialist in the crude, absolutist sense (of Mettrie or of "vulgar" Marxism, for example), both enmesh the operations of the human mind and language in the circumstances of place and time. As I pointed out in earlier parts of my study, this fusion of space and time, which can be described as a historical activation of geography or a geographical intervention into history, has been an indispensable methodological device throughout Said's entire career. The whole issue of human culture – its relationship to ideas, to moments of history, to institutions; the forms of its manifestation, the processes and mechanisms that empower it or exhaust it – this entire problematic, which has become the arena of direct attention in the 1980s and 90s, can be opened up for investigation with the help of the spatio-temporal approach. It is primarily for this reason that Said has deployed this technique repeatedly, both in relatively unpoliticized works like *Beginnings* and in avowedly political texts – most notably *Culture and Imperialism*.

Second, Vico and Foucault use the technique of historical retrieval as an immanent instrument of destruction. That is to say, there is a sense in which Vico was conducting genealogical investigations into the cultural archives of language and mind – and their collaborative production of provisionalized, power-laden knowledge – long before Nietzsche's perspectivalism and Foucauldian discursivity came along. In this respect, Vico's speculations about the recursive cycles and stages of history are roughly equivalent to – though clearly not identical with – the historical discontinuities, thresholds of emergence, and sedimentations described by Foucault. In both cases, a certain unity and transparency (of divine purposiveness, of word and intention, etc.) are displaced as dispersion, disharmony, and mutation take place: a field of refracted representation, constituted as a spatio-temporal network or gestalt, appears. Hence it becomes possible to establish interstices, lateral connections, and overlappings. This drama, in which human agency is caught up, has been utilized by Said in *Beginnings* and elsewhere. He uses it to counteract what he considers to be the univocality, linearity, and evolutionism of traditional historiography; and it empowers him to envision the possibility of multiple narratives – rather than a privileged, totalizing history – which are performed, often in a contestatory fashion, in a series of tableaux vivants. More than anything else, these particular aspects of Foucault's and Vico's philological, historical, and philosophical speculations have been appropriated by Said to reconfigure ideas and their relationships, not as a vertical chain transmitting unsullied wisdom, but in the form of multiplicity in unity: Said describes this configuration as that of adjacency, correlation, and complementarity conceived dynamically rather than statically.

And yet, of course, there are irreconcilable differences between Vico and Foucault, and Said's conflation of their views of history, the mind, and language has greatly intensified the tensions and ambiguities of *Beginnings*. If Vico's sense of "poetic history" is fundamentally a gesture of liberation (admittedly of a limited kind), Foucault's understanding of history and historicity is ultimately deterministic. Vico empowers humanity, both as individuals and as a collectivity, to invent itself. Language, or what he calls eloquence – together with the awakening of consciousness among the early giants – becomes a tool with which to shape civilization in progressive stages. To Foucault, the disciplinary invention of man in the discursive network of the human sciences does not constitute liberation; on the contrary, man becomes an oddity, a thing divided against itself. Harboring the will to truth (and by implication to power), where "will" is to be understood as an impersonal construct, the unfoldings and transmutations of discourse determine what and who man turns out to be. To him, what is proclaimed as rational subjectivity is little more than the effect of institutionally sustained microphysical technologies. In short, Vichian and Foucauldian approaches to the phenomena of history, mind, and language are in some important respects antithetical to each other. How does Said negotiate this divergence? The short answer is that he leans towards Vico, to whom he devotes the entire final chapter, but as I have insisted throughout this study, juxtaposing the "negative" Foucauldian moment (the moment of pure critique) with the more "affirmative" Vichian moment can be seen as yet another way in which Said has come to terms with the predicament of modernity.

The Power of Discourse: Foucault on Truth, Knowledge, History

Foucault's writings receive a good deal of attention from Said (almost an entire half of Chapter 5 is devoted to him) clearly because of the provocative, even revolutionary character of the French thinker's analytic techniques. Since the publication of *Beginnings*, Foucauldian conceptions (about discursivity and power, about history and his- toricity, about knowledge and truth, etc.) have undergone consider- able domestication in American intellectual circles, but they have also been denounced heartily. Like Derrida's notion of deconstruction, Foucault's left-handed analytics have caused a good deal of worry among some humanistic circles but have also been used as empow- ering critical levers. All of this despite the fact that Foucault's reflections are not presented as "theories" applicable in the conven- tional sense. Said's own appropriation of Foucauldian ideas has been crucial to some of his specific critical projects – for example, his critique of Orientalist discourse – but as we shall see in Chapter 4, he has also registered strong reservations about some aspects of Foucault's work. In *Beginnings*, his explication of Foucault's early writings is on the whole sympathetic.

He argues that Foucault's transmutation of textual relationality into a discursive force, while admittedly confirming a view of humanity as bleak as that portrayed by structuralists (if not bleaker), permits us to scrutinize the constitutive workings of language as it fashions reality, as it were, before our eyes. That is to say, instead of passively describing systems of structuration in order ultimately to install a finished product, analysis in the Foucauldian sense becomes an "event": "Foucault's central effort is to consider thoughts taking place *primarily as events*, to consider them precisely, consciously, painstakingly as being mastered in his writing in their aleatory and necessary character as occurrences."[32] Dissevering the link between signifier and signified and honing the coercive capacity of language, Foucault awakens what could have been a formal arrangement into an energy-laden spatio-temporal theatre, in the process creating "a new mental domain" – or archaeology – and "a new habit of thought" – or discourse.[33] Foucault in effect achieves an almost total "reperception" of the way in which mind, language, and world interact by fashioning "a primordial mental space":

> On a primary epistemological plane, therefore, Foucault sets out to redispose and redeploy thought in a primordial mental space much as an artist takes the representational space of his work in an active manner, rather than passively as an inert surface. The filled, activated space of a given epoch Foucault calls an *episteme*; the filling is *discourse*, a body that has temporal duration and is comprised of *énoncés* (statements)."[34]

That idea of space – or more precisely a spatio-temporal field or gestalt seething with intellectual energy – is one of the most important contributions of the Foucauldian legacy. This space partakes (among other things) of the specific institutional features of the library, the prison, the mental hospital, and the stage. As we shall see, Said highlights some of these features. According to him, this spatio-temporal technique gives a far better accounting of "the tyranny of time and history" than do traditional methodologies. Said believes that Foucault's fascinating technique – "a technique of trouble,"[35] as he puts it – derives its effectiveness from the compelling description of the interplay among language, knowledge, and "truth," as well as the conception of man that this interplay sanctions within – and across – the discontinuities of history. Hence Foucault's formulations, while in a special sense related to structuralism, are qualitative radicalizations of that project.

Foucault, argues Said, recasts the centrality of language by insisting that it forms both a "constituting horizon" and an "energizing atmosphere,"[36] a range in which humanity attempts to generate and organize knowledge about itself and its environment. By virtue of the fact that it is something always already begun – something into which the facticity of human affairs is inserted as a "temporary interruption" – but at the same time providing the very tools with which man fashions myths, meanings, and images, language possesses its own impersonal rational power whose pressure dissolves everything except man himself. Formulated thus, the argument does not seem all that different from the claims of such structuralists as Lévi-Strauss or Jakobson – that is, despite the final proviso. But it is Foucault's compelling regrounding of the strategic relationship between language, knowledge, and validity that enables him to effect a critique of realist claims at the epistemological and ethical levels: "the most notable thing about [Foucault's] definition of *knowledge* is that it is a series of denials. Knowledge is not constitutive of anything, can be referred neither to an origin nor to a *telos*, is detached from any particular subjectivity. In a certain sense, then, knowledge is epistemologically neutral – not value-*free*, but saturated with *all* values; perhaps it would be better to say not that knowledge *is* anything, but is rather the *possibility* of everything we know."[37] This negative but nevertheless value-laden characterization of knowledge illustrates "Foucault's profound distrust of mimetic representation and theological givens"[38] – while also directing attention, if only obliquely, to the almost total inseparability of "knowledge" and valuation.

The issue, then, turns on what representation of "truth" is warranted by language at various historical epochs; what particular styles, concepts, and tactics are deployed to contain or channel these representations; and what strategic poses man adopts in order to determine his own status vis-à-vis these "truths." Hence the special potency of Foucault's methodology of archaeology, which enables him to create a logic of correlation, adjacency, and complementarity through the crucial concept of discursivity:

> Correlation, adjacency, and complementarity are ... the relationships that interest him, but what lies behind them and permits such relationships is no scheme of imitation conceived as representation. A discourse does not represent an idea, nor does it embody a figure: it simply repeats, in a different mode, another discourse ... The extraordinary variety of discourses today is a result of the decline in [mimetic] representation ... When language is no longer thought of as a kind of secondary transparency through which shines Being, then the past, for example, becomes only the cumulative repetition of designated words. Such a past lasts only so long as its elements – which make the past possible, and not the other way around – are of value. Thus each epoch defines its forms and its limits of expression, of conservation, of memory, of the reactivation of preceding cultures or foreign ones, of appropriation ... And since the very notion of an epoch is itself a function of these limits and forms, it is even more accurate to say that each discursive formulation articulates the limits and forms of its own existence, inseparable from others.[39]

In short, every epoch manufactures its own validity claims according to the specifications of its own discourse. There is no ontological substance that "shines" "through" language. Rather language qua discourse defines the scope – and limits – of legitimate currency, otherwise known as knowledge and value, at a given historical and socio-cultural conjuncture. To phrase the point differently, what passes for "truth" at any given time acquires its status as such precisely to the degree that it is *made* to become so by virtue of the power invested in – and dispersed by – language: "A will to truth is above all a will to place things in language, which in the ongoing discipline of a discourse is a phenomenon we might justifiably call 'knowledge.'"[40] Even though Said does not foreground in *Beginnings* (as he does, for example, in *Orientalism*) the surging presence of power in Foucault's understanding of discourse, his analysis of knowledge, history, language, and ideas in general repeatedly evokes power as the ultimate arbiter. That is to say, the close, interactive relationship between power and knowledge that Foucault so compellingly describes in his various studies derives from the disciplinary co-activation of the will to truth and the will to control.

Devising a host of terms invested with specially refined (or "rarefied") meanings, Foucault positions himself at a cuspidated point from which he can unflinchingly interrogate the powerful interaction of history, language, and philosophy as they manufacture – and authenticate – knowledge between them in the form of discourse. In effect, Foucault's "profoundly imaginative" analytic tears up such legitimizing ruses as linearity, interiority, and progression and, instead, "redistributes" their recovered raw materials according to an anti-dynastic arrangement that privileges parallelizations, overlappings, and lateral relations. Sharpened in order to come to grips with the "ontological discontinuities," Foucault's method is (in his own words) fundamentally an "analytic of finitude."[41]

Here is a summary of Said's exposition of Foucault's argument, especially as it has been presented in such early works as *Madness and Civilization*, *The Order of Things*, and *The Rise of the Clinic*, as well as in several seminal articles. The socio-cultural history of the West must be formulated, not in terms of natural continuities, but in terms of discontinuous, interfaced epistemes, or active epistemological fields. A depthless exteriority, each episteme – or historical a priori, as it is sometimes called – is composed of statements, which are extremely rarefied units of knowledge whose specific rule-bound configurations determine the discursive formation of a particular era. In other words, Foucault considers discourse as the anonymous constitutive force in society; this force, which is equipped with protocols of inclusion and exclusion, fashions knowledge with the help of an ever-increasing constellation of elaborations, transformations, and refinements caught up in a broad systemic field. Sometime in the eighteenth century, a relatively unproblematized episteme, in which the leak-proof correspondence of words and meanings was guaranteed by a transcendently sanctioned discursive unity, came to an end, hence opening up a rift. Consequently, the assumed harmony, linearity, and transparency of the earlier episteme disappeared, along with the sense of "spatial togetherness" it had bestowed on objects of knowledge. Instead, "a vacant space [appeared] between things, words, and ideas," introducing the disequilibrium and inadequacy that we have come to associate with the modern, or post-classical, episteme.[42]

Another way of phrasing this problematic is to say that the new discursive threshold ushered in an era during which the mimetic – or representational – power of words was displaced by interpretation, in part because new knowledge systems – specifically the "human sciences," which resulted from the loss of origins – had to be accommodated. This accommodation necessarily stipulates that man, like all the elements engaged by discourse, is an "object" of study that can be represented, but since he also considers himself to be the "representer" – that is, the agent who creates, and remains outside, the field of representation itself – man becomes an oddity of discourse. Caught in an "empirico-transcendent doublet"[43] (Foucault's phrase), man assumes the shape of a "problem," "an irrationality". This is Said's summation: "Man is a problem defined in terms of an alternation between impersonal biological functions and psychological norms, between standardized economic rules and sociological conflict, and between language as system and the signification of myth and literature ... Modern man is the enigmatic structure that with difficulty knits them together."[44] Man fails to be accounted for by the powers of an episteme whose ultimate ontological correlative, no longer supported by an absolute authority outside discourse, is strictly speaking a lack or an absence. Neither a subject nor an object, man therefore acquires the properties of a generalized structure that uneasily occupies the discursive interstices between the three major "human sciences" – biology, economics, and philology – disciplines whose validity claims are, for this reason, at best dubious. The earliest signs of discomfort on Said's part with some of Foucault's formulations come through fitfully in this commentary on Foucault's dissolution of man:

[I]f tradition and education train us to take man as the concrete universal, the
pivot and the center of awareness, then Foucault's prose, and concurrently his
argument, makes us lose our grip on man. If we are inclined to think of man
as an entity resisting the flux of experience, then because of Foucault and what
he says of linguistics, ethnology, and psychoanalysis, man is dissolved in the
overarching waves, the quanta, the striations of language itself, turning finally
into little more than a constituted subject, a speaking pronoun, fixed inde-
cisively in the external, ongoing rush of discourse.[45]

On the whole, however, Said finds Foucault's critique of realist and
idealist epistemology powerfully compelling. What, in the end,
becomes plain in the play of post-classical discursive practices is the
extent to which the dimensions of intelligibility are determined, not
by the availability of truth (neither philosophy nor religion has privileged access to it anymore), but by the workings of an effaced, yet
powerful, will to truth.

Although Said himself has used the genealogical method extensively throughout his career, in his exposition of Foucault's writings
he is primarily concerned with the archaeological method that Foucault employed in the early works. Leveling, despite the resulting
paradoxicality, what I have earlier called the pure descriptivity of
language and the pure intention (or gaze) of agency into a series of
single, unified planes layered on top of one another, this method
enables the scholar, who obviously must recognize the limitations
imposed on his or her work by the historically determined epistemic
necessity, to frame the very idea of being in terms of discursive
archives. Permitting – and insisting upon – a comprehensive reperception, this peculiarly imaginative form of inquiry explains the great
importance Foucault attaches to the site of discovery: "the library
holds, in ways Foucault tries to specify, a staggeringly vast array of
discursive formulations, an array whose essence is that no source,
origin, or provenance, no goal, teleology, or purpose can be thought
through for it."[46] Fusing an enormously abstractive power with
extreme forms of specification and articulation, archaeology is
designed both to expose the lowest epistemological common
denominator and to register the relative strangeness of a past separated
from us, not by a temporal distance, but by a discursive mutation.

The special forte of the method lies in its ability to bring to life a
succession of theaters where discursive events can be staged. "The
image of theater," Said tells us, "serves to fix study in one place and to
make study as self-conscious as possible from the very beginning."[47]
But it also has another function – one with far greater implications:

[T]he theater offers a spectacular event, an event divisible into lesser events, each playing a part on the stage, each moving with reference to every other event on a number of different axes; in short, the theater's stage is where there occurs a play of events, embodied either in gestures, characters, groups of actions, or even a changing scene. All this precisely fits Foucault's attitude toward what he calls the existence of discursive events in a culture, their status as events, and also their density as things – that is, their duration and, paradoxically, their monumentality, their character as monuments.[48]

What was traditionally conceived as a unified, linear history is, therefore, fragmented into thickly tessellated discursive networks, rearranged discontinuously as a series of activated intellectual spaces, and deprivileged into the status of mini-histories. That is to say, the discursive formations of "history," integrated as they are with the dominant epistemes, do not have an independent explanatory force. Philosophically, this methodology entails, not just the subversion of traditional versions of conceptualization, but also an attempt to incorporate the fugitive accident, the moment of unreason, into the effective enunciations of discursive analysis. To that end, Foucault engineers a complex enactment of strategic couplings arranged according to the logic of adjacency, complementation, and correlation. The aim of this enactment is to help the scholar to investigate the progressive rarefaction of material entities into the incorporeal; to examine the way discontinuity and system collude with each other even as they modulate each other; to determine the extent to which "chance as a category" is inevitably absorbed into the operations of thought. The very performativity of this intellectual exercise institutes coextension between modality and substance.

Most of Said's exposition of Foucault's early work is schematically clustered around four "exigences de méthode"[49] – reversibility, discontinuity, specificity, and exteriority – all of which support Foucault's grim vision and uncover "the history of the present" as a scene of incarceration and terror. In the panoptically engineered world unmasked by Foucault, even the stoic freedom of existentialism no longer seems viable. To Foucault, as has often been noted, the versions of domination engendered by modern rationality are far more insidiously effective than earlier uses and abuses of power because of their anonymity and diffuseness. As we shall see in later chapters, Said puts this particular insight, which turns on Foucault's twinning of discursive practices and power relations, to good use in his own political criticism – the argument of *Orientalism*, for example, is largely (though by no means exclusively) supported by Foucauldian assumptions.

More immediately germane to my discussion at this point is that the carefully arranged reconstruction of intellectual history in *Beginnings* is fundamentally Foucauldian – even if, as we shall see presently, Said gives more credit to Vico. Determined by the broad, but fissured, inaugurations of successive epistemes, this anti-mimetic, anti-genetic presentation of historical recovery is what Said has called a "discontinuous series." In other words, even if most of the terminology that Said employs casts a distinctly literary/critical hue over the entire discussion, what matters most at the metaleptic level is his utilization of the following Foucauldian analytics: a series of active fields of discursive practice composed of laterally related disciplinary clusters; the qualitative mutation of these fields at points of historical inevitability, a mutation resulting from progressive rarefactions, repetitions, and differentiations; the notion of discursive sedimentation; and, finally, the necessity of excavating archives. No longer a continuous linearity but "a succession of functional conditions," the history of ideas assumes the traits of an impersonal field of energy whose distinctive features amalgamate the anonymity of paradigms; the incremental, overlapping accumulations of commentary and interpretation that might be found on a palimpsest; and the absent presence of an archaeological site or a tableau vivant. This is essentially the approach Said takes, especially in the middle four chapters.

Vico's Poetic History: Humanity as Autodidact

But Said is also fully aware of the limitations imposed on him by such a deterministic schema – for a number of reasons which should be obvious by now. One is that, in order for his meditational structure to come alive, there has to be a meditating mind, an individuated self with its own intentional force – however refracted and hemmed in that self may be. Foucault's analytics preclude even that limited autonomy. Second, theories of language – even those as persuasive as Foucault's – cannot exhaust and (what is worse) may even distort the dense materiality and sheer complexity of human cultural life, with its vast multiplicity of agents, objects, institutions, and teleologies. In short, linguicity – an idea whose power and limitations have already been examined – cannot contain human cultural life in its entirety, even if the two are constitutively implicated in each other. Hence the need for theoretical insights far more suited to the task of better understanding what may simply be called culture.

And therein lies Vico's importance to Said's project. As we shall see in the next two chapters, Said's head-on confrontation with the problematical concept of culture – both in the affirmative, life-enhancing sense of community and in the sense of a hegemonic, supremacist sensibility – takes place in such later texts as *The World, the Text, and the Critic*; *Orientalism*; and *Culture and Imperialism*. Vico's value lies in the fact that the Neapolitan thinker's speculations provide Said with a cogent point of departure – *a formal beginning* so to speak – for a historical and epistemological understanding of human cultural life. There is a sense, therefore, in which it is incumbent, in ways I have been suggesting, on Said's interlocutors to study *Beginnings* seriously, and more specifically the last chapter of that text, in order to form a much more informed opinion about his critical position on a whole range of topics.

The following passage, in which he itemizes seven vital "signposts," gives us a good idea about Vico's enormous significance for the argument of *Beginnings* and, beyond it, for Said's criticism as a whole:

> Vico's thought ... is extraordinarily useful at this stage in that it parallels my key arguments throughout the preceding five chapters [of *Beginnings*]. Here is a schematic list of seven Vichian signposts that have helped me, from the beginning, to discuss beginnings and to sketch a method:
>
> a.   The initial distinction between the gentile or historical and the sacred or original – paralleling my distinction between [a] beginning and an origin.
>
> b.   The combination in intellectual work of a special, idiosyncratic problem and a very strong interest in human collectivity – a combination that occurs in this text from the beginning.
>
> c.   An acute awareness not only of genealogical succession (except as its biological foundations obviously persist), but also parallelism, adjacency, and complementarity – that is, all those relationships that emphasize the lateral and the dispersed rather than the linear and the sequential.
>
> d.   A central interplay between beginning and repetition, or between beginning and beginning-again.
>
> e.   Language as *rewriting*, as history conditioned by repetition, as encipherment and dissemination – the instability, and the richness, of a text as practice and an idea.
>
> f.   Topics for critical analysis that do not fall neatly into the categories of commentary, chronicle, or thematic tracings.
>
> g.   The beginning in writing as inaugurating and subsequently maintaining *another* order of meaning from previous or already existing writing. Here, once again, the distinction (made in *a*, above) between gentile and sacred becomes relevant.[50]

Though not always exactly corresponding with my own inter-

pretive schemata, these are in essence the topics which I have been
treating in my analysis of *Beginnings*. Instead of recapitulating these
topics, I would like to focus on a set of three major impulses (or
"tributaries," as Said calls them) which constitute the spine of Vico's
speculations: (a) the contiguity and, by implication, interchange-
ability of "theory" and "actual experience" in the generation of
knowledge; (b) the recognition that studying and understanding
humanity, whether as individuals or as members of groups, must be
undertaken "in terms of a collective fate"; (c) the necessity of an
interpretive mode of presentation that accommodates the infinite
multiplicity and variety of human affairs and yet responds to the
rigors and pressures of an internally imposed form of methodological
discipline. What immediately impresses us (that is, Vico's fore-
grounding of the distinctly "human" notwithstanding) is the extent
to which the ideas of this eighteenth-century maverick thinker pre-
figure modern theories. Clearly the suppression of Origins, the contingency, and the relationality of mainstream structuralism can be
detected even in these broad outlines of Vico's reflections. However,
the power of these insights – and hence their usefulness for Said's
project – can be found in the way they amalgamate the closely
interrogative, demystifying techniques of the suspicious hermeneutics
characteristic of such thinkers as Nietzsche, Freud, and Foucault with
a subjectified, intentionally grounded will. That Said finds it necessary
to conclude his study with a discussion of Vico has, therefore, its own
strategic significance. Besides offering a generously appreciative
reading of Vico, the chapter also becomes the site of a full theoretical
accounting: the grand cycle inaugurated by the first two chapters of
Beginnings, and charted out by the middle three, fulfills its methodological imperatives by earning its theoretical validity, even if it does
not claim privileged access to truth.

According to Said, the cogent, yet problematic, point of departure
for Vico's speculations is his "discovery," after a long search, of the
"poetic" model of history and the centrality of language in the evolution of that history. Vico argues that the dawn of human consciousness took the form of "indefinite" stirrings that only vaguely
grasped their environment; that this hazy awakening started with an
understanding of the "object" closest at hand – the human body itself
– and gradually strengthened its purchase on the natural surroundings;
that precise articulations and broad abstractions are relative latecomers
which took a long period of time to develop; that, to the extent the
mind forged its own intellectual armor, ideas gradually became dera-

cinated from their concrete beginnings; that, therefore, for modern human beings it is extremely difficult to capture intellectually those primitive gropings. The analogy Vico uses is that of the child and the philosopher; the mental distance between them is such that it can be bridged only through a sympathetic imagination. Despite that historical and intellectual distance, Vico is insisting that thought – however sophisticated it may have become over the centuries – cannot afford to lose sight of its material beginnings. "Man's world," observes Said, summarizing a crucial passage from *The New Science*, "begins among stones, rocks, frogs, and cicadas ... This is quite another world from Plato's realm of forms or from Descartes's clear and distinct ideas. All of Vico's great book is an effort to give substance to the otherwise banished beginnings of human reality."[51]

According to Said, Vico's curious, yet gripping, argument derives its power from a provocative metaphysic with far-reaching implications. On the one hand, this metaphysic enables him not only to challenge more orthodox philosophical conceptions of origination but also to go through the motions of a pious exercise that, for all intents and purposes, allows him to deliver God, quite respectfully, into a domain of virtual irrelevance. On the other hand, humankind becomes its own author – an "autodidact" – though at an enormous price. Vico's vision in part rests on a distinction he makes between Jews and "gentiles"; the former, having accepted the injunction against "divination," earned the status of being God's chosen people. Their province is that of "sacred history." The latter – apparently the rest of humanity – were, in the absence of divine revelation, condemned to improvization: they had to invent deities that, through the sheer terror they visited on men's hearts, curbed the unbridled naive freedom they would otherwise have enjoyed. By harnessing the animal-like propensities of the early fathers, those initial enactments of human intentionality created an atmosphere conducive to the growth of social institutions, hence heralding the idea of community. The important point about this distinction between Jews and "gentiles," then, is that the latter's history began in an act of transgression and that its subsequent evolution is, in its fundamentals, a necessarily contaminated further working out of that act. Inasmuch as that beginning violation of "divine" authority both empowered man for self-realization and sowed the seeds of further alienation, modern culture is a repetition – at several removes – of the first breach. The neonate and the philosopher are found to be after all implicated much more closely than might appear to be the case at first glance: these oblique relationships have become vital to Said's entire critical project. Both the seven signposts listed earlier and such concepts as affiliation and contrapuntality are traceable to this multilateral logic.

Consonant with the above distinction between sacred and profane history is Vico's equally intriguing conception of the human mind. Making a series of shrewd, if not always accurate, philological moves, he concludes that, at the point where the early giants' form of semi-conscious slumber gave birth to self-consciousness and reflexivity, the mind assumed the symbolic equivalence of a wedge. The crucial point is that the "wedge" is, in human terms, a sharp, efficient tool, but it is also artificial and therefore inferior in comparison to divine power. Hence the puny human mind pales in comparison to God's vast intentional power but nevertheless in its own way echoes that power. Here is Said's paraphrase of the distinction made by Vico:

> God, conceived of as pure mind, wills intentionally, and then matter or nature comes into existence from that beginning act of will. Man, in his mind, wills intentionally, and then, not nature, but a different version of it comes into existence from *that* beginning or intentional act of will ... Human will, or conation, then, is precisely like an initial, or beginning, or inaugural wedge between man and nature. That is why every metaphysical theory attempts intellectual mastery of impenetrable nature and succeeds only in providing a certain but different version of nature, which the mind then pronounces to be true. Thus human intellectual activity is, to use Coleridge's terms in the thirteenth chapter of the *Biographia Literaria*, "a repetition in the finite mind of the eternal act of creation in the infinite I AM." ... When God says *cogito ergo sum*, he wills himself into material and spiritual existence. When man says it at the beginning, he wills only himself and *his* world – quite another thing – into existence. From a reflective, historical standpoint, all human things (or institutions) are, from the beginning, created by the mind, *mind* understood as that which can begin intentionally to act in the world of men.[52]

Despite Descartes' hubristic claims for the cogito, Vico announces, the human mind wields no control or influence over nature – that is God's prerogative. Born out of His powerful will, nature essentially functions as His perception. And though echoing the movements of this pure consciousness of divinity, the perception brought forth by the human will is a second-rate entity confined to the "geometrical," shadowy dimension of images. Hence the curiously fitting characterization of the wedge as a metaphor with a double purpose: it stopped a potentially overwhelming divine flood but also enabled man to ignite the initial flash of self-recognition as a result of the anxieties occasioned by that flood. It is this exercise of the human will that Said identifies, both in Vico's work and in his own, as the "beginning

intention." Yet, of course, the mind – however powerful and purposive – does not have the full capacity to bring forth that human
world by itself. For that eventuality to be realized, language must play
its role:

> Human will has, to be sure, a real effect on what is intellectual and human;
> yet the substance of thought is sense perception, which is recorded in the
> mind as imagery of one kind or another. Men, however, are gifted with
> language; and language, because it is associated with the mind, expresses the
> result of sense perception ... Each linguistic expression represents a begin-
> ning act of choice, of will, for in making a sound man is confirming a sense
> impression, becoming conscious of it.[53]

From this close relationship of mind and language, it is therefore
possible to reach the following conclusion: "History's records are
primarily verbal; language itself is the foremost historical document."[54]

Human civilization was therefore born out of this interaction
between mind, language, and the circumstances of place and time.
The first step in the dawn of history launched the slow but sure-footed
process of self-education in which the enormous bodies of our primitive forebears were gradually toned down, eventually assuming the
proper human proportions, while at the same time the mind sharpened its cognitive powers and widened its purposive scope. What is
paradoxical about this formulation is that, for Vico as for Said, it is
not the rational capacity of the mind that is privileged but rather the
will, or "conation"; the intellect, Vico claims, is a second-tier affair
that, though necessary for abstraction and universalization (roughly
what he calls "scienza" or "philosophy"), is nevertheless fundamentally passive. The motor of consciousness (or "conscienza"), according
to Vico, is the active will. Presumably accessible to the supersensible
zones as well as to the passions, it is energy-laden, corrosive, and
creative; its province is that of the imagination and of desire. This
characterization of rationality is repeatedly endorsed by Said (in
opposition to what he has called rigid, "dry-as-dust"rationalism) in
order to account for both the nightmare and the achievement of
secular modernity.

Nevertheless, reason and conation act as two interactive dimensions
of the mind – and here "mind" refers to a property of human collectivity as well as of discrete selfhoods – working together in order to
form the substance of human history. Between them the two faculties
enable mankind to be both "philosophical" and "philological":

Vico's way of pairing philology and philosophy ... suggests the necessary complementarity of the two sciences. Not only are they close because love motivates the adherents of both – or "conceit" is an affliction their adherents both share – but also because philosophy deals with the true, philology with the certain. These are subjects that Vico intends us to see as practically close: both the true and the certain lay claim to belief, both to urgency, both to conviction – most of all, both to man's mind, which can, and ought, to live with both.[55]

In other words (and at the risk of simplifying Said's complex and suggestive exposition), Vico seems to argue that both the intellect and the will are essential for matters related to belief and values, that they both respond to urgent needs as well as long-term memories and plans. Yet he insists that, since the intellect is at its best in concretizing "synchronous structures" and in stabilizing perdurable systems, it lacks the energy that generates the pressures necessary for progress. It is conation that brings forth these diachronous advancements, together with the inevitable shifts and mutations that accompany them. These two aspects of the psyche between them shape and deliver human history, which is properly speaking a flawed, second-order, yet in its own way impressive, achievement. This, Vico declares, is "gentile history." Anti-linear and anti-Platonic, but not reductively materialist, this history follows a "poetic" route, where the idea of poeticality is being used (in Said's words) "in three ways: as imagistic and hence inadequate, as creative and hence human and grand, and as descriptive of the beginning."[56] Said points out that, Vico's instinctive piety aside, God is effectively overthrown, while man assumes the authority of a rogue hero who courageously copes with post-lapsarian, post-diluvian disinheritance and loss. Gingerly picking his way between dangerous pitfalls, man by and large succeeds in spite of the great odds stacked against him. Said endorses Vico's ideas more than he does those of any other thinker we have discussed so far.

According to Said, Vico proposes a flexible, provisional conception of beginnings which allows him to conceive of civilization in two complementary ways: on the one hand, the inventiveness of the human mind luxuriates in its mythic creativity and polysemy. On the other, the eventuality of self-destruction is precluded precisely by that same enactment: humanity imposes on itself laws designed to protect – and build on – such early institutions as marriage, the burial of the dead, the settled community, and so on. Language, in the meantime, serves both as the initial lightning rod and as the means of later absorption and assimilation. It is that combination of cornucopia and constraint, as well as the progressive rarefaction thereof, that Vico charts out in the three broad cycles – the ages of gods, of heroes, and of men – and the multiple repetitions and fine-tunings implicit in them. Transmitted through verbal branchings, transmutations, and splicings, this history cannot – according to Vico – be reconstructed through traditional scholarship; on the contrary, only with the help of deft etymological tracings and the capacity to sniff out affinities in the multiplicity of human cultural forms can we hope to succeed in recapturing what amounts to an obscure, alien past.

All of this means that the three "tributaries" identified earlier form both a historical confluence of impulses and a methodological configuration: normatively, the successive topical constellations of "poetic" knowledge (for example, "poetic morals," "poetic economy," etc.) are launched, stabilized, and transfigured in laterally congruent turns, in the process programmatically creating their structures within the context of the three "poetic" phases of history. Historically, the predictable cadence of the three phases interacts with the profusion of concrete details and nuanced inflections in a specific social setting at a given time. What emerges as a unity-in-multiplicity is a leveling, self-refining collective will, one which bears a symbolic, universal mental language. The features of this common language can be detected in the "proverbs and maxims of vulgar wisdom"[57] (Vico's phrasing) but are best preserved in fables, which are encapsulated recapitulations of insights from the past. This is how Said sums up the methodology we have been describing: "thus *adjacency, complementarity, parallelism, and correlation* [are employed by Vico] *in the interests of a genealogical goal*."[58] The striking thing about this summation is the extent to which it corresponds with the methodological arrangements proposed by Foucault. Said's appropriation – and extension – of ideas from two unorthodox thinkers separated by more than two centuries of intellectual history is, therefore, a calculated assault on unicentric, linear, and hierarchical visions of socio-historical reality. Nevertheless, he is drawn more to the recuperative, and hence affirmative, humanism of the one than to the (de)humanized bleakness of the other.

To sum up, then, Said's strong endorsement of Vico stems largely from his belief that the Neapolitan philosopher's life and ideas are an embodiment of several themes that constitute important strands in Said's own work. One of them is the notion of a confident, self-made man who is, nevertheless, acutely aware that he is also a participant in

146   E D W A R D   S A I D

a larger human drama, a drama that endlessly manufactures opportunities but also courts trouble. Said sees an "organic" link, in both
method and content, between *The New Science*, which has been the
focus of my discussion, and the *Autobiography*, a book in which Vico
meditates on his own personal experiences and intellectual evolution.
Vico characterizes himself as an autodidact, just as he does humanity
at large. His is a powerfully original mind, Said says appreciatively of
Vico, which is also at once critical of itself and cognizant of long-held
validity claims. Another theme, which is closely related to the above
one, is Vico's methodological eccentricity. Said believes that Vico is
one of the first anti-dynastic thinkers – perhaps even the first among
many (another is Rousseau, a close contemporary of Vico's) – in
modern intellectual history. His insistence on a version of cyclicality
that ratifies both development and recovery – and hence allows for
sameness and difference; his ability to recognize both the willfulness
of the human enterprise and the fact that it stands on feet of clay; his
privileging of a hard-won, problematized freedom over blithely
enthusiastic utopianism; and his resistance to rationalistic schemas –
all of these intentionally bifurcated, yet promising, strategies attest to
Vico's uncanny understanding of the hidden, often unseemly, element
that gets domesticated or ignored by neat continuities and closures.
Finally, Vico's argument that human culture must be studied under
the refracted light of a historicized, thoroughly pragmatized theory of
language – one that deliberately undercuts theologically and metaphysically conceived doctrines – marks him as a quintessentially
modern thinker.

All of these assumptions are, as we have seen above, crucial to Said's
project. He points out that Vico's pairing of philology and philosophy
as constitutive partners in the generation of meaning and value, as
well as the superior status he has reserved for eloquence (Vico was a
professor of oratory), has authorized both the deployment of a severe,
self-demystifying form of rationality and the projection of a large-
minded, "copious" attitude. Both are enunciative capabilities inherent
in the operations of mind-in-language, and both are woven, in an
emphatic fashion, into the fabric of Said's study.

4

The Struggle for the World: Culture, Hegemony, and Intellectuals

Early on in "Secular Criticism," Said identifies four dominant forms of criticism: practical criticism, which is principally employed in literary journalism and book-reviewing; academic literary history, a descendant of philology largely restricted to academia; appreciation and interpretation, a branch of criticism which every student of literature is familiar with: it "is what is taught and performed by teachers of literature ... and its beneficiaries in a literal sense are those millions who have learned in a classroom how to read a poem, how to enjoy a metaphysical conceit, how to think of literature and figurative language as having characteristics that are unique and not reducible to a simple word or political message"; and finally literary theory, a late arrival on the American literary scene which reached maturity only in the Seventies. An interdisciplinary field, it appropriated philosophical models imported from Europe and in the process acclimated them for American academic consumption. Said tells us that he has employed in his own work techniques traceable to all four forms of criticism – but quickly comes to the main point of his discussion: his aim in writing this and the other articles in the book is to go beyond all four of them. And exactly where should this beyond be? The world, replies Said, simply and emphatically.[1]

Thus opens the introductory article of one of Said's most polemical books. Unlike the two works which I have discussed so far, *The World, the Text, and the Critic* can hardly be described as a conventional book in the strict sense of the term – that is, a unified study with individual chapters related together thematically and structurally. Indeed, it instantiates what could be called a strategic dispersal: it consists of fourteen articles most of which had already appeared in various literary-critical journals and were later revised – in some cases substantially – for inclusion in the book. Hence one of the striking features of *The World* is its kaleidoscopic character in both presentation and subject matter. Among the disparate topics it engages are the stubbornly resistant, endlessly anarchic torsions of a typical Swiftian text; the ingeniously dodgy ways in which contemporary critical energy is (in Said's view) domesticated for theoretical elaboration; and the appropriating power of French Orientalism. Some of the articles are relatively narrow and circumscribed (focusing, for example, on a single author's oeuvre or on a specific topic – hence "Conrad: The Presentation of Narrative," "On Originality," etc.); others treat multiple authors, themes, disciplines, and cultures. Some are historical reconstructions – though obviously in a highly eccentric, Saidian fashion. Others directly intervene in the critical debates of the Seventies and Eighties. Despite this diversity, all the articles are clearly intended to give force and substance to a single thesis: that texts in general, including those of literature (a field whose domain is supposedly that of the imagination), have particular modes of worldly existence, particular ways of being *and* acting in the world.

Presented in these broad terms, Said's argument may not strike us as either unduly alarming or unusually compelling. It is at the level of articulation that the full import of his challenge can be registered: the unconventional, yet in its own way cogent interpretation; the intensely felt dilemmas of an individual thinker – dilemmas that almost always occasion an extended methodological drama rather than a neat resolution; the powerful, conflicting socio-cultural energies that shape a specific historical moment; the multiple tensions harbored by a seemingly unified text: these and similar foci are used by Said not only to bestow global significance on what might otherwise appear to be localized phenomena but also to establish oblique links and parallel movements between various domains of cultural life.

Several short examples can suffice here to illustrate what I mean. In an attempt to help us re-examine the slippery notion of culture in a new, more insightful light, Said recounts the difficult circumstances under which Erich Auerbach wrote his masterpiece, *Mimesis*. An erudite classicist whose very identity had been nurtured by a commitment to an ideal of humanistic learning and a common European heritage, Auerbach had to come to grips with the painful actualities of the mid-twentieth century; he was stranded in Istanbul – the Byzantium of another era, now in Muslim hands – exiled physically and intellectually from Nazi-occupied Europe. Yet, on Auerbach's own admission, the book might never have been written *but* for that banishment from home and hearth. "In writing *Mimesis*," observes Said, "Auerbach was not merely practicing his profession despite adversity." Rather, he may actually have been "performing an act of cultural, even civilizational, survival of the highest order"[2] at a time when there was precious little to celebrate for a Europeanist, a scholar, or a Jew. Culture here has become both a burden and a boon (a "possessing possession,"[3] as Said phrases it), something to be affirmed, transformed, and transcended all at once. As we shall see later, the idea of distance (and its necessary connection with criticism) is central to this understanding of culture.

Elsewhere in the book, Said reflects on Swift's lifelong fascination with the recalcitrance of language, as well as its capacity for abuse by the powers that be: "We are ... forced to take seriously Swift's discovery that words and objects in the world are not simply interchangeable, since words extend away from objects into an entirely verbal world of their own. If words and objects ever coincide, it is because at certain propitious times both converge into what the prevailing polity can readily identify as an event, which does not necessarily involve exchange or communication."[4] Statements such as this one may at first glance seem to vitiate Said's main thesis – that texts are worldly – but then we are obliged to remember that, right from the beginning of his career, one of Said's major objectives has been to unmask the submarine collaboration between epistemology and ideology. (This, though Swift could not have seen himself, for obvious personal and historical reasons, as a critic of ideology or a skeptical philosopher, but rather as a literary satirist.) In other words, Said's aim here and elsewhere is – at least in part – to show that "what the prevailing polity can readily identify as an event" may not always correspond with what actually obtains in the world; that ruses, diversions, and ventriloquisms are often officially billed as the real thing, while other important matters (effective instruments, illicit gains, forensic evidence) are carefully camouflaged; that, in a state of lopsided power relations, what is proclaimed as an uncoerced exchange of ideas between equal partners may, on closer examination, turn out to be undercover diktat. Despite this profound and continuing suspicion of epistemological realism and its ethico-political consequences, Said's foregrounding of worldliness as such appears to have necessitated some revision: at certain points in his argument, he endorses a brand of phenomenalism strikingly similar to the very object of his critique.

Finally, there is Said's claim, ultimately stemming from *Beginnings*,

that originality is nothing other than an acknowledgment of absence –
a lacuna – coupled with a desire to repeat: "Originality in one primal
sense ... has to be loss, or else it would be repetition; or we can say
that, insofar as it is apprehended as such, originality is the difference
between primordial vacancy and temporal, sustained repetition."[5]
Said's point here is that originality is not some rare, cornucopic
profundity, essence, or quality residing in great works of literary
genius (in contradistinction to, for example, mere critical interpretation) but rather a given writer's "irreducible intention to perform
a specific [intellectual] activity" combined with "an irreplaceable
action giving forth the writing" instantiating this intention.[6]

I am drawing attention to these almost randomly selected citations
to indicate the extent to which the disparate articles in *The World* are
intended by Said as a multi-vectored, multidimensional interpretive
collage – an ensemble of focused insights working in tandem with
(and at times in opposition to) one another across a varied range of
epistemic and ethico-political problems. It is perhaps as a recognition
of this activated heterogeneity that Said, echoing Lukacs, singles out
the essay as the form ideally suited to critical thinking in general and,
in particular, to the kind of investigation he is conducting in this text.
The essay is brief, tentative, ironic; parasitic in status, it is mindful of
its lateness, occasionality, and transitoriness. It does not deal con-
clusively or in detail with weighty issues that confront humankind –
as tragedy does, for example. But it is also fundamentally Socratic; it
is the "ultraviolet light" of literary-critical writing, the distillation of
pure "conceptuality and intellectuality";[7] it is primed for propaedeutic subversion and questioning: "the essayist," in Lukacs's phrasing, "is a pure instance of the precursor."[8] Insofar as it inaugurates
radical reflection; insofar as it goes beyond (or behind) the taken-for-
granted "image," in the process also proposing (if only adumbratively)
alternative conceptions of socio-political reality, the essay form is
considered by Said as being crucial to his strategy.

But that is not all; for there is another equally eccentric concept,
operating at the infrastructural level, that ultimately mandates Said's
argument: it is what he has described as affiliation. At a later stage of
my discussion, I will provide a more detailed evaluation of its
implications. At this point what needs emphasis is that the notion of
affiliation (a) further crystallizes the meditatively guided, intentional-
discursive network of ideas which we encountered in *Beginnings* and
(b) shifts the focus of the interpretive lens from the rarefied locale of
intellectual history in which the argument of the earlier text unfolded

to the far more immediately contested space of social history and political culture. It should also be noted immediately that the idea of affiliation, in conjunction with worldliness, maps out the difficult interaction between what I have been calling agonistic dialectic and archaeology/genealogy. Hence, as we shall see, affiliation marks the flashpoints where critique confronts ideology, lodging in the process what may be described as utopian moments.

There is another sense in which the later book manifests a strategic shift of critical priorities: it is openly combative and polemical. Most of the articles in *The World*, it should be remembered, were composed at a time when Said was also occupied with the Orientalism trilogy. *Orientalism, The Question of Palestine*, and *Covering Islam* (all to be treated in my final chapter) are extended reflections on the saturating, and – in Said's opinion – generally poisonous presence of Orientalist discourse, a seemingly disinterested but ideologically motivated disciplinary language constructed over the past several centuries by Western scholars, artists, journalists, and colonial functionaries about the Orient in general and the world of Islam in particular. Although only two of the articles in *The World, the Text, and the Critic* directly treat this topic, the book is caught up in this broad political turn in Said's career. Unlike the comparatively level-toned, largely tolerant analysis of *Beginnings*, most of the discussion in *The World* is suffused with a spirit of impatience, even bitter disillusion. One comes across charged, contentious assertions about "the regulated, not to say calculated, irrelevance" of academic criticism as a result of "specialization and professionalization"; about the "ostrich like and retrograde" view that the canon of the "Eurocentric humanities" – a tiny fragment of the knowledge available to humanity in the modern world – should constitute the heart of any viable intellectual life;[9] about the hegemonic collaboration of what Said calls "system" and "culture," that is, the subterranean collusion between critical system-building and theories of knowledge production, on the one hand, and the institutions and power structures of the dominant culture, on the other.

Said reserves his harshest criticism for the clubby advocates of what has come to be known as literary or critical theory, a small but (at least for a time) influential group of advanced critics with whom he himself has often been classed. In his quarrel with de Man, Derrida, Foucault, and other poststructuralists, Said's principal complaint is that these self-declared "radical" thinkers (including even Marxists) have, perhaps unwittingly, helped create various allies, alibis, and surrogates for the very dogmas against which they purportedly took up arms in the first place. Said's indictment of fellow theorists, however, should not be interpreted as a rejection of theory but rather as an attempt to refocus attention on the multiple relationships between criticism (or critical consciousness) and theoretical models – relationships that can be used either as opportunities for an incisive interrogation of "the prevailing polity" or as a license for elaboration, refinement, and the nurturing of aesthetic sensibilities. More precisely, his major objective is to help effect theoretically informed debates about an entire constellation of topics – debates about culture, identity, and canon-formation; about intellectuals, critique, and responsibility; about power, hegemony, and coercion; about literature and its connections with the socio-political world. And it is precisely such debates that The World has provoked, or at least considerably energized, since its publication in 1983. These debates have in turn become part of the ongoing interdisciplinary discussions that have come to dominate the Anglo-American literary-critical scene in the Eighties, Nineties, and beyond. What was in the Seventies and early Eighties known simply as literary or critical theory has since evolved into the separate but affiliated fields of cultural studies, postcolonial discourse, feminist theory, and so on. Although the remaining chapter of my study will be devoted to Said's enormous contribution to postcolonial theory (as distinct from postcolonial studies in general), most of these broader debates fall outside the limited purview of my analysis. Nevertheless, it must be stressed here that – because of the multiplicity of topics it engages and because of its polemical style of presentation – The World, the Text, and the Critic has had a far-reaching (though not always exactly determinable) impact on these literary-critical discussions.

There is another reason for the influence of the book: the propitiating historical circumstances of its publication and reception. By 1983, the student insurgency of the previous decade and a half, whose justifiable call for relevance had in large part instigated the theoretical upheaval in English studies, was in a state of exhaustion, giving way to a profound loss of nerve and direction among intellectuals on the left and an equally profound upsurge in reactionary politics and apologetics. The Vietnam fiasco was still fresh in the American national psyche, but apart from the lonely efforts of a few valiant scholars (prominent among them Noam Chomsky), the close diagnostic examination which the war solicited from the political and cultural elites had not taken place. To top it all, Ronald Reagan, the new apostle of conservatism, Cold Warriorism, and neo-imperialism, had been swept into the White House on the crest of a vast wave of patriotic pride and collective amnesia. Much of the electrifying tension that surges through the articles in *The World* is the result of Said's disenchantment with the intellectuals' conduct in the face of these historical developments. A similar tension weaves through the debates generated in the wake of Said's text. It is perhaps for this reason that *The World, the Text, and the Critic* has been far more frequently linked to *Orientalism*, Said's most controversial book, than either of them has been to *Beginnings* – a study which clears a theoretical space for both later works.

Apropos of the debates about *The World*, it is regrettable that some of the participants have shown themselves to be almost entirely indifferent to the protocols of serious debating, the complexities of literary theory, and the rigors of careful reading. Thus in a piece published in *Philosophy and Literature*, one A. R. Louch dismisses both Said's study and literary theory in general with unceremonious dispatch, even derision. At one point he delivers himself of this little summation: "Said's book and the genre of which it is an instance suggest two ideas to me, one that literary theorists simply misunderstand science [which he says Said has misrepresented], the other that he, and the rest, are victims of bad philosophy."[10] Louch enlightens us neither on the proper way of understanding science nor on the distinguishing marks of good philosophy. An almost identical strain of hostility to literary theory and to Said's project pervades a review by Gerald Weales, who opens his diatribe with a mildly racist parable.[11] And there are others of similar feather – critics who, though not always as unsympathetic to critical theory as these two, have over the years written about Said with venom. (The most notorious is probably the author of "Professor of Terror."[12]) They need not detain us here any longer, although at a later stage of my discussion I will reflect on the ideological animus that licenses some of their violent rhetoric.

Other reviewers have been more judicious in their remarks about *The World*. Denis Donoghue, for example, expresses regret at the "contempt" (his term) with which Said treats religious criticism in the brief, concluding article of the book. He adds: "The rest of the book is, in the best senses of the words, provocative and exacting; the essays provoke due interrogation of contemporary theory, and exact from the reader the care and conscientiousness the questions at issue warrant."[13] William E. Cain observes that Said has written "a book of great power and distinction," and uses adjectives such as "suggestive," "valuable," "brilliant," and "cogent" in assessing its critical insightfulness.[14] He does, however, identify some "difficulties" in it, and argues at one point that in his almost total rejection of systematic knowledge Said "comes dangerously close to disabling himself." Said, in other words, "defines himself in 'opposition' to orthodoxy so adamantly that he does not really allow for a firm statement of an alternative to orthodoxy."[15] Similarly nuanced, reflective evaluations are made by Bruce Robbins, Dan Latimer, and Abdul R. JanMohamed.[16] The most unreserved praise comes from Daniel O'Hara, who, at the end of a wide-ranging article, declares that "*The World, the Text, and the Critic* [is] far and away the finest work of American criticism since *The Liberal Imagination*."[17] O'Hara is one of the few interpreters of *The World* who particularly emphasize the dialectical character of Said's thought both here and elsewhere, hence providing a much-needed complement to the prevailing view that Said is at heart a poststructuralist unhappy with the ethico-political implications of his theoretical tools.

Since these early reviews, the controversy over Said's text has intensified. Quite apart from the general intra- (and inter-) disciplinary soul-searching that it has helped occasion, along with *Orientalism*, the book has also prompted several polemical exchanges between prominent critics. The sharpest critique of Said has been made by Paul Bové, who (it must be immediately added) has elsewhere both defended Said and praised some of his other writings.[18] In the context of *The World*, Bové particularly castigates Said for being critical of Foucault (see pp. 199–201 below), whose idea of discursivity and power is central to Bové's own thesis in *Intellectuals in Power: A Genealogy of Critical Humanism*.[19] Beyond this specific disagreement, Bové places Said in an unholy pantheon of "sublime," "humanistic intellectuals" who – intent on disciplinary self-promotion and the projection of power – smother the weaker voices of common humanity and thereby lead to "essentially antidemocratic forms and practices."[20] Bové's list of culprits includes thinkers as different as I. A. Richards, Erich Auerbach, and Marshall Hodgson, as well as Said. Bové's attack on Said and other oppositional intellectuals has elicited a counter-critique from Jim Merod, who at one point observes that "everything Bové says about Said's self-promotion can be turned against Bové also."[21]

In an earlier exchange, Bruce Robbins and Catherine Gallagher had squared off. Responding to Robbins's seminal review of Said's writings, "Homelessness and Worldliness," Gallagher identifies what she considers to be a serious weakness in Said's criticism: "since *Orient-alism* Said has been writing himself into a dilemma that has ontolo-gical, epistemological, political, and literary-critical dimensions."[22] Robbins's fault is that he helps resolve this otherwise insoluble dilemma by nodding agreement to Said's unwarranted haranguing of the literary-critical profession and the university that houses it. "But," she adds, Robbins's "very success [in resolving this dilemma] testifies to the dubiousness of the premise at the base of Said's position: that a unity of one's critical-intellectual and political identity is possible and desirable."[23] In other words, Said and Robbins want to claim the impossible for criticism as an academic profession: that it is at once exilic – unhoused, nomadic, unencumbered by socio-cultural burdens and particularities, etc. – and politically committed; that it is both worldless and worldly. In contrast, she holds that a critic's specific political inclinations, while to a certain extent germane to his or her professional work, are neither entirely exhausted by nor completely commensurable with his or her literary-critical practice. In her opi-nion, the idea of professionalism can best serve its legitimate function as a limit and not as a general license – that is, as a filtering membrane enabling us to enact a certain set of activities which help us fashion our "professional identity" but also empowering us to disallow "a high proportion of our political interests, analyses, and activities."[24] These excluded matters presumably belong to a wider arena governed by a logic alien to that of one's critical practice: "As a self-limiting system, my professionalism [as a critic] creates a political 'outside,' the contents of which it is then *prohibited* by its own logic from deter-mining."[25] By ignoring this demarcation line, Said is therefore advocating an incoherent, and ultimately empty brand of universalist intellectualism, in the process also resurrecting a naive species of pluralist humanism. Robbins in turn applauds such an impractical (and perhaps ultimately idealistic) project.

Robbins's rejoinder needs to be quoted from at length, since it lights up with uncommon clarity the heart of what has come to be known as the politics of interpretation:

> For Gallagher, clearing a space for politics in the profession serves only to circumscribe the limits of that (secondary) space, thereby marking off a (primary) political arena outside it ... An empty politics, for her, is a politics without imperatives. But where do these imperatives come from? "Outside" is not really satisfactory, but it is all we get. Here Gallagher falls into the other "emptiness" ... which opens a miraculous space of freedom and ideality in the midst of formative and social institutions. Gallagher's critique of Edward Said

is all the more bizarre in that it is just such an ideal freedom that she accuses him of claiming for oppositional intellectuals. Yet Said's social affiliations are hardly hidden. Gallagher's, on the other hand, seem restricted to a normative Never-Never Land, and one not offered as a provisional hypothesis or wager . . . but as an unquestionable plenitude that can judge the politics of others as empty.[26]

It should be noted right off that Robbins is as suspicious of the grand claims made for the universal intellectual as Gallagher is – though for somewhat different reasons. A crucial strand of his argument in various texts, including his recent book *Secular Vocations: Intellectuals, Professionalism, Culture*,[27] is that the much-vaunted independent intellectual, whose supposed demise has been lamented in recent years (by Russell Jacoby in *The Last Intellectuals*,[28] for example), has rarely ever existed except as a fictional character; that intellectuals, as much as anyone else, have always been supported by (and hence supportive of) identifiable socio-cultural groups; that more often than not carefully packaged ideological wares and vested interests have been peddled under the seal of independence; that the absorption of intellectuals from various cultural backgrounds into the university system is not an unmitigated disaster (as is often claimed by both rightwing and leftwing critics) but a solid achievement for all – and therefore should not be denounced either as a massive sell-out of the intellectuals or as a threat to Western civilization. The upshot of all this seems to be that the interminable debate about intellectual vocations is a tiresome affair and the sooner we're done with it the better. There is obviously a hint of caricature in my quick review of Robbins's fairly nuanced, complex argument; my immediate point, though, is that Robbins's position is ultimately closer to Gallagher's than to Said's.

Robbins's disagreement with Gallagher centers on what could be called her strategic (and tautologous) alignment of normativity and political practice such that a certain set of privileges, preferences, and promotions as well as a balancing set of dodges, silences, and prohibitions can be tolerated, even encouraged, in the name of professionalism. In other words, Gallagher's simultaneous insistence on a carefully policed professional space, a systematic division of intellectual labor, and a selectively invoked ethico-epistemic normativity in practical terms translates into the following. A localized, self-interested politics – the politics of difference – is embraced within and without the profession, a step that obviates, or at least discourages, the reality (if not the possibility) of a common political agenda between various socio-cultural groups in opposition to the powers that be. Nevertheless, it is asserted that (epistemically ascertainable?) ethical imperatives ascribed to the societal whole (apparently under such rubrics as justice, freedom, the will of the people, and so forth) govern this political practice, hence bestowing legitimacy on the political gains of particular groups at the expense of (or at least in competition with) other groups. And yet critical intelligence is prohibited, in advance and by virtue of its self-limitation as a professional activity, from prying too closely into the constitution of these regulative imperatives or into the institutions and practices of society at large. Gallagher, in effect, has embraced the political agenda of pragmatic liberalism, or to phrase the point in ethical parlance, the attitude of enlightened self-interest. Her position precludes any viable critique of ideology qua ideology.

As I have tried to demonstrate throughout this study, Said's position is that such a critique of ideology is not only possible but also absolutely necessary: given that we are neither omniscient nor omnipresent but instead live in the contingent circumstances of space-time; given humanity's capacity for all kinds of delinquency and folly, among them injustice, vanity, and self-delusion; and given the global but asymmetrical expansion of modernity – given these obvious but generally overlooked realities, it is the irreducible and non-negotiable responsibility of radical intellectuals to wage such a critique whenever and wherever possible. To do otherwise is to commit treason, as Julien Benda put it nearly eighty years ago. This is the message that the essays in *The World, the Text, and the Critic* emphatically underscore. It is no wonder, then, that the book has had such an at once unnerving and exhilarating effect on literary-critical intellectuals who – with a few exceptions – had traditionally cast themselves in the far less ambitious role of literary handmaid.

At its broadest level, my thesis is that the book brings to a high point of articulation – though certainly not to a point of resolution or synthesis (which has never been Said's objective) – the confrontation between radical intentionality, in its capacity as suspicious intelligence and critical knowledge, and what could be called the totalizations of theory and culture. That is to say, the book enacts both a continuation and a transmutation of the aesthetic, epistemological, and ethico-political problematics which Said reflected on in *The Fiction of Autobiography* and in *Beginnings*. Said himself draws attention to the interconnections between *The World* and the major theoretical text that preceded it:

> With the exception of two essays, all of the essays collected [in *The World, the
> Text, and the Critic*] were written during the period immediately following the
> completion of my book *Beginnings: Intention and Method*, which argued the
> practical and theoretical necessity of a reasoned point of departure for any
> intellectual and creative job of work, given that we exist in secular history, as
> the always-already begun realm of continuously human history. Thus each
> essay presupposes that book.[29]

The brief passage can be read in two slightly different ways, both of
which are central to my explication, though to different degrees. One
is that the later text is at least in part an exercise in autocritique. That
is to say, Said is conducting a theoretical self-accounting intended at
once as a *post hoc* inventory, an internal dismantling, and a strategic
transformation of the theoretical insights that have gone into the
creation of the early stages of his own career. To recapitulate one of the
crucial subtheses of *Beginnings*, he is in effect beginning *again*, revi-
siting an already established intellectual landscape – but this time
with a difference. Consistent both with Said's preference for repetition
over pure origins (and hence for multiplicity, discontinuity, and
dispersion over unity and dynastic descent) and with his own
acknowledgment that he tends to go "in and out of things," this mid-
career stock-taking involves a shift of emphasis from structuralist/
poststructuralist thought to Marxism – with ideas from Lukacs,
Gramsci, and Williams featuring strongly in his analysis.

A slightly different, and in my opinion more valid, way of glossing
the above passage is to consider the two books as not only thematically and methodologically related but actually *requisite* to each other
philosophically. In other words, the argument of *Beginnings* in a
manner of speaking constitutes, if not a theoretical ground, then the
condition of possibility for the argument of *The World* – a ground-
clearing exercise without which, in Said's understanding of human
endeavor in history, any discussion of worldliness in general and
textual worldliness in particular would be incomplete. Since, given
the vast wealth of material available, a single study could not have
done justice to both intellectual history and the matter of worldliness,
a meditation on the fundamental problems of rationality in the
context of modernity had to precede any confrontation with the
pressing issues of the public domain. The exposition of metaphysical
and theological origins and their silent self-subsistence; the distinction between intransitive (i.e., obsessively self-referring, centripetal,
airless, ultimately ideological) beginnings and the transitive, "pro-
blem- or project-oriented" beginnings necessary for critical self-

empowerment; the investigation into the transgressive, desire-laden, at once speculative and ironic modern intentionality; the discussion of discursive emergences and mutations, a process in which the self-authorizing transparency of the realistic narrative gradually gives way to the severe tortuousness of modernism and to linguicity: all these interacting theoretical insights, which effectively banish all forms of transcendent authority from the realm of humanity and instead empower a sutured, desacralized authority premised on the notion of mind-in-language-and-history, establish, if not a philosophical foundation, then a contextual justification for further inquiries into human situationality in various local and global contexts. This theoretical background ultimately ratifies Said's insistence that texts have a profoundly worldly dimension.

Traceable in equal measure to Vico's seminal idea of a profane, cyclical history; hermeneutic phenomenology; poststructuralist theories informed by Nietzschean and Freudian suspicion; and revisionist Marxism, this at once constructivist and deconstructive understanding of human culture enables Said to argue that human agency, singly and collectively, creates meaning and value in constitutively materialist categories; that language, like all other aspects of the distinctively human, is caught up in a network or affiliation of cultural self-creation in space and time. The short passage from "Secular Criticism" alerts us, if only allusively, to all these presuppositions. It is particularly apposite to stress this affinity between Said's early writings and his later, more politically explicit works since most of his interlocutors have not afforded it more than a passing gloss.

My own explication of *The World, the Text, and the Critic* – and indeed the remaining chapter of my study – will take this assumption as its point of departure. My interpretive approach will be on the whole relational and interactive rather than episodic; that is, rather than focusing on specific articles (or clusters of articles), I will present my explication as an attempt to elucidate an ensemble of themes. (I should add immediately that the articles on Orientalism will not feature significantly in this chapter, since strictly speaking they belong to the topic of the next one.) After an analysis of the two important notions of worldliness and affiliation, I will examine Said's interrogation of culture as hegemony, affording special attention to his reflections on Gramsci, Williams, and Arnold. The next section will treat the contentious problem of language and its purchase (or lack thereof) on the world. Thereafter, my discussion will focus on what Said considers to be the serious failings of contemporary criticism. This section will begin with a summary of Said's comparative treatment of the two most influential poststructuralist thinkers: Foucault and Derrida. Next, I will provide a review of his less charitable account of Anglo-American criticism and "the ideology of refinement" that in his opinion dominates it. I will close the chapter with an examination of what Said calls critical consciousness – that is, critical intelligence and critical knowledge as the embodiment of a form of judgement which is at once situated, skeptical, value-laden, self-interrogating, and close to socio-historical reality. In this final section of the chapter, I will reflect on Said's somewhat eccentric appropriation of insights drawn from Swift and Lukacs, two thinkers separated by more than two centuries of intellectual history, by diametrically opposed methodological orientations, and by diverging socio-political inclinations.

Should Worldliness Be an Issue?

One of the most unusual aspects of Said's study is his choice of worldliness as a central problematic. Prior to Said's study, the idea of worldliness had been occasionally used in discussions of literature but, as Bruce Robbins points out, in a far more circumscribed, more immediately anchored fashion. Robbins insists that, in Said's book, worldliness comes across as slippery, off-centered, and somewhat fuzzy – a broad idea that points to textual worldliness in general but somehow doesn't quite deliver anything more precise or specific.[30] Yet Said himself suggests otherwise. In an interview conducted several years after the publication of *The World, The Text, and the Critic*, Said glosses the idea of worldliness thus: "Worldliness originally meant to me, at any rate, some location of oneself or one's work, or the work itself, the literary work, the text, and so on, in the world, as opposed to some extra worldly, private, ethereal context. Worldliness was meant to be a rather crude and bludgeon-like term to enforce the location of cultural practices back in the mundane, the quotidian, the secular."[31] This means that worldliness, in an immediate sense, simply names the brute, irreducible thereness of empirical reality and human cultural life in it – roughly what Heidegger calls *Dasein*, or the unavoidable, ontic thrownness of human beings into their world. But as Said's dismissal of the "extra worldly, private, ethereal context" suggests, his analysis is generally not presented in an existentialist mode (Said's brief discussion of Hopkins is a rare exception). Rather, worldliness functions as a maneuverable device which, operating globally and locally, primarily relates to public concerns in civil and political culture – concerns which have traditionally been discussed (for example, in historiography and social theory) without much overt worry about their "worldliness," which would have been assumed as a given.

Indeed, as Denis Donoghue observes in his generally favorable review, Said's claim that texts and their authors are worldly "sounds fairly conventional."[32] A similar comment is made by Tom Conley, one of the most hostile reviewers of Said's book. He avers that the "grandiose" title of the book acts as a cover for bland "truisms," one of which is the idea of worldliness.[33] Although Conley himself does not pursue this issue as rigorously as might be expected, it could well be argued that what Said dresses up as worldliness already underlies not just our understanding of ourselves but also our use of words, our very idea of language itself: literary critics – not to mention historians, anthropologists, sociologists, and newscasters, among others – have taught us that language, in both its written and spoken forms, engages aspects of the world we live in. Whether one views it as a transparent medium, as a reflexive mirror, or as a precision tool, language coincides with true knowledge about ourselves and our world – provided, of course, it is used with enough integrity, clarity, and sincerity. The same applies to our ideas and institutions in general – indeed to our very conceptions of society, history, and reality.

Hence, as every schoolboy knows, good history books bring the past alive: different historians may disagree about the best way to execute that task (for example, should one aim for the retrieval of value-neutral, objective information or for the reconstruction of "clear and distinct ideas" about the world of the past? Does the historian describe or interpret? etc.). There is, however, a solid consensus on the nature of the desired end: to reveal the truth about past cultures. Likewise, trusted, avuncular anchormen and selfless reporters daily convey to us the business of the present world, "the way it is," in accurate journalistic language. And even literature, no matter how fictional its immediate content may be, ultimately refers to an empirical, socio-historically recognizable world. So *Great Expectations*, to take a well-known realistic novel, is realistic precisely to the degree that it reflects, emulates, or at least evokes the actualities of Dickensian London. One could also take an exemplary work from the other end of the literary spectrum – *The Waste Land* – and still arrive at the same worldly destination. Even the most formalist of the New Critics would acknowledge that Eliot's great poem is in the first instance part and parcel of its moment in history – however timeless, transcendent, or mythic its ultimate dimensions may be: it was written at a particularly wrenching moment in modern European history, a moment which its author was both alluding to in multiple ways and making uncompromising judgements about. What all these different examples demonstrate – the argument might conclude – is that Said's talk about the worldliness of texts is old hat, that anybody with half an eye already knows that texts are worldly through and through (what else *could* they be?), that belaboring this point is just a lot of polemical shadow-boxing, that Said has entangled himself in a species of rhetorical overkill.

An appropriate way of addressing these criticisms might start with the following anecdote, in which Said recounts a brief but telling exchange between him and "an old college friend":

> The degree to which the cultural realm and its expertise are institutionally divorced from their real connections with power was wonderfully illustrated for me by an exchange with an old college friend who worked in the Department of Defense for a period during the Vietnam war. The bombings were in full course then, and I was naively trying to understand the kind of person who could order daily B-52 strikes over a distant Asian country in the name of the American interest in defending freedom and stopping communism. "You know," my friend said, "the Secretary is a complex human being: he doesn't fit the picture you may have formed of the cold-blooded imperialist murderer. The last time I was in his office I noticed Durrell's *Alexandria Quartet* on his desk." He paused meaningfully, as if to let Durrell's presence on that desk work its awful power alone. The further implication of my friend's story was that no one who read and presumably appreciated a novel could be the cold-blooded butcher one might suppose him to have been ... Many years later this whole implausible anecdote (I do not remember my response to the complex conjunction of Durrell with the ordering of bombing in the sixties) strikes me as typical of what actually obtains: humanists and intellectuals accept the idea that you can read classy fiction as well as kill and maim because the cultural world is available for that particular sort of camouflaging, and because cultural types are not supposed to interfere in matters for which the social system has not certified them. What the anecdote illustrates is the approved separation of high-level bureaucrat from the reader of novels of questionable worth and definite status.[34]

The passage from "Secular Criticism" is particularly instructive in that it sheds light on a number of related concerns all of which are germane to the argument of *The World, the Text, and the Critic*. First, it draws attention in a stark fashion to the socio-political realities of the late twentieth century, what has come to be known as the asymmetrical power relations of a globalized context. One can cite Vietnam, Panama, the West Bank, or South Africa under apartheid – the pattern is pretty much the same: some groups and nations (or, to be more precise, their political elites) have access to military, economic, or technological power, and they often exercise it with almost total abandon. Others are not only deprived of it but also victimized by it. Second, the anecdote gives us – if only adumbratively – an idea of the various kinds of rhetorical footwork deployed in order to justify the enormous waste of human life and natural resources which has resulted from such power trips. Said mentions two ready-to-hand guises assumed by the rhetoric of legitimation with respect to the Vietnam adventure ("defending freedom and stopping communism"), but as will become clearer both in this chapter and in the final one, he believes that a whole clutch of these scandalous ruses have been put into circulation in the course of high European imperialism and in what has more recently been called the American century. Third, Said's account illustrates a specific way in which literature as a category of "high" culture has been made both to reveal and to conceal its worldliness in equal measure: it serves to ennoble and elevate an enactment which, in Marlow's memorable words, "is not a pretty thing when you look into it too much." Said recalls how his friend had described the then Secretary of Defense as "a complex human being" who didn't quite fit the image of a "cold-blooded imperialist murderer. The last time I was in his office I noticed Durrell's *Alexandria Quartet* on his desk." Having delivered this important piece of inside information, Said's unnamed interlocutor "then paused meaningfully, as if to let Durrell's presence on that desk work its awful power alone." What has been trotted out here is of course akin to the rhetorical bromides that I alluded to a little earlier. In both cases, an act of intellectual laundering has been executed.

Finally, there is the habitual alibi of "humanists and intellectuals," among them literary critics: Said suggests that these self-anointed missionaries of secular knowledge and humane values can (with the exception of a tiny minority mentioned elsewhere in his writing)[35] somehow live with "the idea that you can read classy fiction as well as kill and maim." Why such docility in the face of what is patently unconscionable? "[B]ecause cultural types are not supposed to interfere in matters for which the social system has not certified them." It could of course be objected that Said has no right to lecture anybody about the Vietnam war – after all, he didn't write about it himself except on rare occasions, and even then only in passing. The larger point though is that, as an actual historical conflict which consumed the lives of millions, the Vietnam adventure was a nonpareil example of the kinds of degenerative crises (among them the Israeli–Palestinian struggle) that Said's attention has repeatedly turned to – crises which in his opinion serious criticism disregards at its own peril. And yet neither the Vietnam tragedy nor other conflicts of comparable magnitude now or in the past have ever seemed to disturb, except in trivial ways, the peace of garden-variety critics, heavyweight "theorists" included.

The immediate implications of the anecdote for Said's interpretive project should be clear enough: a proper accounting of literary-critical worldliness cannot be achieved by using either formalist or realist techniques of analysis, familiar techniques underlying the imagined critique of Said's thesis. To the extent that formalism encourages an abstractive, compartmentalist, often work-centered understanding of the literary artifact – an enactment usually undertaken in the name of disciplinary autonomy – to that extent it severs (or at least de-emphasizes) the powerful ties that bind literature both to other intellectual fields and to society at large. Formalism, then, embraces a species of cultural idealism – creating in the process an antiseptic universe cleansed of any contamination by history and social reality. Literary realism, on the other hand, commits the opposite error: it appeals to a naive reflection theory that takes the common flow of everyday experience at face value, hence misrecognizing the profoundly motivational dimension of the normalized common sense operating in society (another name for which is the dominant ideological dogma) as well as the often disastrous consequences of that normalization. Instead of both, Said's conception of worldliness calls for a historicist–materialist interpretation of literature – that is, a careful examination of the socio-cultural formations, practices, institutions, and agencies in which texts in general, literary texts included, are caught up at a given historical moment. Said is not particularly well known for providing precise definitions of important critical concepts used in his oeuvre (his forte lies in de-defining, dismantling, etc. normalized concepts and formulae), but in this case the following brief discussion of *materiality* gives us a good idea of what is entailed by his approach:

> By "material" ... I mean the ways, for example, in which [a given] text is a monument, a cultural object sought after, fought over, possessed, rejected, or achieved in time. The text's materiality also includes the range of its authority. Why does a text enjoy currency at one time, recurrence at others,

oblivion at others? By the same token, an author's *fama*, his reputation and status, is by no means a constant thing. Is an account of this inconstancy, or at least this inconsistency, within the critic's job? It is, I believe, the more so now as the possibilities of archeological historical research have been so extended and refined by Foucault.[36]

In the case cited above, for example, "Durrell's presence on that desk" willy-nilly ensnares his work, by virtue of the "definite status" conferred on it and in spite of its "questionable worth," in an intricate network of privileges and culpabilities. It has become an important component in a complex alignment of power, self-approving idiom, cultural capital, and systematic acquiescence which – along with the almost inevitable demonization of the "enemy" – sustains a grand ideology in the name of which bombs can be dropped "over a distant Asian country." It should be added immediately that this interpretive approach to literature has become common currency in the past decade and a half, especially among the new historicists and cultural materialists (among them Steven Greenblatt, Alan Sinfield, Catherine Gallagher, and Catherine Belsey), but it is usually applied with far less attention than in Said's writing to the powerful ideological forces that sustain the perdurable inequalities of the contemporary world. It should also be borne in mind that Said's version of this interpretive approach is strongly tinged with phenomenology: the mind is *always* a powerful motor in the world; it also acts as its own monitor and demystifier. Later on I will provide more details about Said's own appropriation of this technique, paying special attention to what might be called its two complementary dimensions or moments – namely, the cultural and the linguistic/textual. At this point, however, I would like to use the same anecdote as an opportunity to reflect further on Said's infrastructural concept of affiliation, a concept instantiated in one of its many forms by the undercover ideological arrangement we have just identified in the Vietnam war context.

Mapping Affiliations: The Genealogy of Modernity

The term *affiliation* is used by Said in a wide variety of contexts. It designates, sometimes simultaneously, the idea of repetition in history, the discursive formations of modern disciplines, the oblique insights of Freudian psychoanalysis, as well as a number of other formations. In its most cogent, densely packed form, affiliation appears in a discussion of literary modernism; elsewhere in the book,

it is proposed as an alternative methodological tool that would cir-
cumvent the constrictive formalism and naive positivism that Said
associates with modern and contemporary literary criticism. Said has
also glossed the idea of affiliation in informal conversations outside
the immediate context of *The World*. In the interview I cited above, he
distinguishes it from, but also links it directly with, the notion of
worldliness:

> "Affiliation" is a rather more subtle term [than worldliness] that has to do
> with mapping and drawing connections *in* the world between practices,
> individuals, classes, formations – that whole range of structures that Raymond
> Williams has studied so well in books like *The Long Revolution* and *The Country
> and the City*. Above all affiliation is a dynamic concept; it is not meant to
> circumscribe but rather to make explicit all kinds of connections that we tend
> to forget and that have to be made explicit and even dramatic in order for
> political change to take place.[37]

What emerges out of this constellation of inflections is that affiliation
broadly designates the dramatic enactments – i.e. vectors, intersections, transformations, and consolidations – of modernity as such, that
is, modernity understood as an ongoing intellectual and societal
change and reconstitution, a process capable of accommodating
multiple institutional imbrications, ideological constructions, and
counter-hegemonic positions. Like the notion of meditation in
Beginnings (and contrapuntality in *Culture and Imperialism*), affiliation
is therefore resilient enough to avoid the rigidity which Said associates
with systematic theorizing, but it also has the capacity to deliver
valuable theoretical and historical insights. This cogency results in
part from the fact that affiliation is related to filiation by both etymological echo and dialectical transformation. More specifically, the
two terms recover and extend, at least in the context of literary
modernism, a tension already present in the heart of novelistic consciousness and in narrativity as such, a tension which in *Beginnings*
Said designated as *authority* and *molestation*.

It may be recalled from my earlier discussion that authority, in one
of its important guises, names the will to power driving the classical
or realist novel, the genre's desire to inaugurate itself by appropriating
the prerogatives of an originary paterfamilias who had long since been
pronounced dead or silent. Molestation, on the other hand, was
described as the ironic double, the fictive subtext that continually
undercut this transgressive authority, reminding it of its inauthentic
status (since it concealed an ontological lack) and warning it that it
could not be both father and son. Molestation eventually exhausted

realism, replacing it with the multi-layered texts of modernity. In *The World, the Text, and the Critic, filiation* and *affiliation* are intended by Said to re-encapsulate and subtly rearrange what was originally designated as authority and molestation respectively.

> What I am describing is the transition from a failed idea or possibility of filiation to a kind of compensatory order that, whether it is a party, an institution, a culture, a set of beliefs, or even a world-vision, provides men and women with a new form of relationship which I have been calling affiliation, but which is also a new system. Now whether we look at this affiliative mode of relationship as it is to be found among conservative writers like Eliot or among progressive writers like Lukacs and, in his own special way, Freud, we will find the deliberately explicit goal of using that new order to reinstate vestiges of the kind of authority associated in the past with filiative order. This, finally, is the third part of the pattern. Freud's psychoanalytic guild and Lukacs' notion of the vanguard party are no less providers of what we might call a restored authority. The new hierarchy or, if it is less a hierarchy than a community, the new community is greater than the individual adherent or member, just as the father is greater by virtue of seniority than the sons and daughters; the ideas, the values, and the systematic totalizing world-view validated by the new affiliative order are all bearers of authority too, with the result that something resembling a cultural system is established. Thus, if a filial relationship was held together by natural bonds and natural forms of authority – involving obedience, fear, love, respect, and instinctual conflict – the new affiliative relationship changes these bonds into what seem to be transpersonal forms, such as guild consciousness, consensus, collegiality, professional respect, class, and the hegemony of a dominant culture. The filiative scheme belongs to the realms of nature and of "life" whereas affiliation belongs exclusively to culture and society.[38]

Like the notion of authority in *Beginnings*, filiation is premised on narrative linearity, familial procreation, biological succession, and the "vertical" transmission of traditionary authority. Somewhat transforming this family-based notion, Said allegorizes it into the authority of an immediate community or specific culture, to which one belongs "by birth, nationality, profession."[39] In the context of modernity, this authority is gradually eroded and transformed into "horizontal" or spatialized structures premised on adjacency, parallelism, and complementarity – a process roughly equivalent to molestation. It is these lateral, affiliative structures that Said broadly characterizes as system or method – namely, a theoretical model that one affirms "by social and political conviction, economic and historical circumstance, voluntary effort and willed deliberation."[40]

The new inflection that Said foregrounds in the revised terminology consists in this: first, the ethico-political implications of the new dialectical process are far more greatly emphasized than was the case in *Beginnings* – a text that, as we saw, was largely restricted to intellectual history. Second, whereas molestation was in the main an ironic, self-deflating form of consciousness, affiliation congeals into a new authority which is every bit as coercive, as appropriative, and as dogmatic as the old, superseded orthodoxy: the "filial relationship . . . once held together by natural bonds and natural forms of authority – involving obedience, fear, love, respect, and instinctual conflict" – now cedes ground to a transpersonal relationship enforced through "guild consciousness, consensus, collegiality, professional respect, class, and the hegemony of a dominant culture." What is happening here is that a largely submerged streak of aridity and conservatism that in *Beginnings* Said etched out within the authority–molestation trajectory of the novel has now been vastly expanded into the terrain of modern rationality as a whole. This is in effect another way of saying that the logic of modernity – the affiliative rule of "culture and society" as such (in contradistinction to a specific culture), which during the past three centuries has been presided over by a rationalistic consciousness shaped by the assimilative dialectic of idealism and empiricism – has not progressed far beyond the logic of "nature and 'of life,'" the rule of the tribal bloodline.

As I have already pointed out, the anecdote about the Vietnam war provides a revealing example of such an ossified, coercive affiliation in operation, showing us how it crystallized into a self-fortifying dogma at a particular historico-cultural intersection in the United States. In the course of his career, Said has furnished other examples of such rigid dogmas brought about by the filiation–affiliation dialectic – among them European imperialism and Zionism, but also Islamism and nativism – ideologies which in his view have unleashed (or have the capacity to unleash) powerfully destructive forces. It is particularly instructive that Said detects this tendency towards congealment and domination in the writings of both conservative thinkers, like Eliot, and their progressive counterparts – Lukacs, for example. This is clearly meant as a wake-up call to oppositional intellectuals, who – in Said's general scheme – are enjoined to view with suspicion the already realized, always ambiguous consolidations of modernity. The radical intellectual, that is, must stand between the totalizations of (filiative) cultures and (affiliative) systems.

Yet it would be a mistake to conclude from all this that Said is irreconcilably hostile to the idea of affiliation as such. Bruce Robbins is undoubtedly right in pointing out that the term largely functions as a neutral, descriptive marker in Said's book.[41] I would like to gloss this observation by bringing out the positive nuances which can be teased out of the term for, although this is not obvious in the passage quoted above, there is a sense in which Said does endorse, ever so subtly, the idea of affiliation (as opposed to filiation) throughout *The World*. Unlike the "failed idea" of filiation, which openly insisted on the unilinear, unicentric, dynastic authority of fatherhood (and, by extension, on the purity of a specific culture, the unity of a given tradition, the exclusive validity of monarchical rule, or the transcendent rule of a divine origin), affiliation at least in principle affirms an open, hybrid plurality – an autodidactic brotherhood fashioning itself in the *corsi* and *ricorsi* of a secularized history. It is this Vichian vision of human community, which was central to *Beginnings*, that Said also recapitulates in one of the various formulations of the filiation–affiliation dialectic:

> What is historically important about marriage [as well as other institutions considered by Vico as being crucial to the development of human culture] is not that it enables procreation; rather, since procreation takes place naturally anyway (and wastefully, at least by intention), marriage as an institution interdicts sexual desire so that affiliations, other than purely filial ones, can take place. The father's place therefore loses its unassailable eminence. The paternal and filial roles, necessary to each other as much in their natural concomitance as in their natural hostility, seem to give rise to other relationships, affiliative ones, whose undoubted historical and factual presence in human society concerns the historian, philosopher, social theorist, novelist, poet.[42]

Within the dialectical tension between filiation and affiliation – a tension which historically manifests itself as the cyclically repeated articulations of sameness and difference – one can detect utopian possibilities which (Said suggests) can be enhanced by the interpretive/critical efforts of "the historian, philosopher, social theorist, novelist, poet." These utopian projections are justified because – even though human insight is too contingent and too context-bound to predict a definitive, totalizing telos – one can still study "the concrete facts of human history" (as conceived by Vico) and solicit pointers and signposts out of them. Such a Vichian conception of history, Said tells us, "reveals a principle or force of inner discipline within an otherwise disorganized series of events." History, that is, turns out to be neither a depressing parade of "gratuitous events" nor a "boring" process of progress "realizing a foreordained blueprint"; rather it is a "dramatic sequence of dialectical stages, enacted by an inconsistent but persistent humanity."[43] And the powerful, yet self-monitoring motor

propelling this dialectic is the human mind (especially as an embodiment of conative desire or will). Equipped with an intentional (i.e.,
filiative) impulse which almost ineluctably leads to an unintentional
(i.e., affiliative) counter-action, the mind "is the general system of
brakes that restrains the always accelerating action of human behavior." The broad cyclical repetitions – or, in Vichian parlance, *corsi*
and *ricorsi* – of the mind's evolutionary stages manifest themselves as
changes "from pure bestiality, to moderate rationality, to overrefined
intellectuality, to new barbarism." The mind's "ultimate purpose,"
Said paraphrases Vico, "is to preserve the human race," and it achieves
this end in historical time by acting against the folly in which human
beings often indulge singly and collectively.[44]

According to Vico, these mental laws of progress, restraint, and
consolidation are not directly accessible to philosophers, philologists,
and other students of culture; still, it seems, they can be reconstructed
obliquely by indirect methods of mapping. Said's more urgent, more
interventionist agenda obliges him to stress the role of criticism in
society; criticism in and of itself is a reflexive form of inquiry which,
used effectively, has the capacity to furnish valuable *knowledge* about
itself, its prehistory, and its immediate socio-cultural horizons. And it
is in this sense of critical practice that the notion of affiliation serves
Said's project most effectively:

> Let me try to suggest the general importance of this notion to contemporary
> critical activity. In the first place, as a general interpretive principle affiliation
> mitigates somewhat the facile theories of homology and filiation, which have
> created the homogeneously utopian domain of texts connected serially,
> seamlessly, and immediately only with other texts. By contrast affiliation is
> what enables a text to maintain itself as a text, and this is covered by a range
> of circumstances: status of the author, historical moment, conditions of
> publication, diffusion and reception, values drawn upon, values and ideas
> assumed, a framework of consensually held tacit assumptions, presumed
> background, and so on and on. In the second place, to study affiliation is to
> study and to recreate the bonds between texts and the world, bonds that
> specialization and the institutions of literature have all but completely effaced.
> Every text is an act of will to some extent, but what has not been very much
> studied is the degree to which texts are made permissible. To recreate the
> affiliative network is therefore to make visible, to give materiality back to, the
> strands holding the texts to society, author, and culture. In the third place,
> affiliation releases a text from its isolation and imposes upon the scholar or
> critic the presentational problem of historically recreating or reconstructing
> the possibilities from which the text arose. Here is the place for intentional
> analysis and for the effort to place a text in homological, dialogical, or
> antithetical relationships with other texts, classes, and institutions.[45]

Studying the affiliative relationships of a given text does not deny its textuality – on the contrary, its material positivity *as a text* is stressed – but rather rescues it from "the facile theories of homology and filiation" which have made it possible for critics to create a seamless, artificially purified universe of texts. But at the same time, the text is released from its privileged formalist isolation as "an autonomous work"; placing a text in its affiliative network entails a heterogeneous "range of circumstances" which mark its historicality and situationality. It also entails the recognition that texts are not available of their own accord but "are made permissible" precisely to the degree that they carry the normative weight of those who wield cultural authority and socio-political power. Hence, it becomes necessary to unmask "the values" normalized by a given text – its ideological stripes, the uses that have been made of it, the complicities in which it has been involved, the prohibitions and promotions it has enacted. It also becomes equally necessary to recognize a text's recalcitrance – its capacity to resist cultural dogma or to unleash radical energy. In other words, to pay careful attention to the variously arranged, often crisscrossing affiliations of a given text is to at once activate its archival sites and determine its genealogical descent, with the critic *intentionally* placing it "in homological, dialogical, or antithetical relationships with other texts, classes, and institutions" – that is to say, with the critic having an acute awareness of the various ways (for example, oppositional or assimilative) in which it has, or could have, interacted dialectically with its socio-historical world. It should be clear that the emphasis here falls on the text's function as a public agency acting in the world (rather than primarily on its epistemological status, as the case would have been in *Beginnings*).

Later in this chapter I will provide more details about Said's conception of critical consciousness, a methodological element of which is constituted by this idea of affiliation. What needs emphasis here is the extent to which Vichian assumptions undergird even this highly prescriptive appropriation of affiliation: the seven methodological "signposts" that Said derived from Vico's thought in *Beginnings* are equally (though indirectly) crucial to an understanding of criticism as a worldly practice – a cultural energy purposively directed to help prevent the congealment of the filiative–affiliative dialectic into a set of rigid dogmas or repressive institutions. With this discussion of affiliation and Vichian insights as a general background, we can now examine Said's utilization of conceptions of culture drawn from the twentieth-century Marxist tradition.

Demystifying Culture: Hegemony or Community?

The tensions we have identified in the filiation–affiliation process –
and within affiliation itself – can also be found in Said's treatment of
culture as a descriptive/interpretive category. This ambiguity is not
difficult to understand, given the semantic sedimentations the term
has acquired since the eighteenth century – sedimentations which, as
Raymond Williams has shown,[46] lead back to various geneses and
tributaries of modern thought and practice. The term *culture* has
therefore become somewhat vague and slippery. Like the notion of
worldliness, it seems to refer to everything and hence runs the risk of
referring to nothing in particular. More serious, it carries its own
considerable baggage, most of it in the form of unattractive ideological secrets; all kinds of enactments (political, ethical, aesthetic,
epistemological) have been made in the name of culture – enactments
both legitimate and illegitimate. For these reasons, Said's treatment of
what is designated as "culture" has been ambivalent. Perhaps it would
be more accurate to say that, in his writing, it comes across as a
challenge – to be confronted, interrogated, unpacked, and scrutinized
both as a substantive idea and as a boundary condition or zone.

That challenge can be articulated interrogatively: how does one
resolve the tension between the broad and narrow senses of culture, or
distinguish between its generally benign (even positive) meaning and
the malignant uses that have historically been made of it? Is it possible to conceive broadly of culture in such a way that it can be
rendered useful, perhaps even crucial, to a radical critical intellectual
without also summoning the seamier associations of the word? Can it
be, for example, purged of its "social-scientific" appropriation, the
kind of strategic disciplining of knowledge that, in one of its forms,
distinguishes between "sociology" and "anthropology" – the former
being reserved for the "advanced" societies of the West while the
latter, as the study of "primitive cultures," has continually been
activated in conjunction with openly imperialistic programs of action?
If this strategic purgation of "culture" can be achieved, is it also
possible to retain – and perhaps even enhance – a favorable sense of the
word, for example in the sense of an interconnected plurality of
human communities as envisioned by Vico? Can one posit an
understanding of the term that turns on the belief that "culture"
properly names that which binds us all together, identifying the
common – or analogous – formations that distinguish us, say, from

nature, and yet does not erase the various boundaries, articulations, overlappings, and interrelationships between (and within) *cultures* and specific cultural *forms*?

To phrase the point differently, can we think of ways of describing the concrete rootedness of the local community – the sense of being at home, in place – as well as a (physical or imaginative) distanciation from it, through an appreciation of the diversity, multiplicity, and correlation of human creations and self-creations? If so, how can this be realized without falling back upon or (re)instituting the dubious holism of yesteryear, the kind of talk (Kant's ethical universalism and Lukacs's totality are good examples) that has been repeatedly – and justifiably – deconstructed in postmodernist, poststructuralist, feminist, and anti-colonialist critiques?

To shift the perspective slightly, how has the idea of culture in the narrow but privileged sense – i.e., high or elite culture – been deployed in Western society? What kinds of overt and covert relationships have obtained between culture in this ideologically valenced sense, on the one hand, and the culture at large (that is, as an enveloping socio-historical environment), on the other? In what ways, for example, have etherealized intellectual productions – say literature or philosophy – been positioned vis-à-vis the matrix of technological, military, and political power? Apropos of all this, how has the relationship between culture and critique been configured? More specifically, how have literary *critics* conducted themselves? Have they acted as demystifiers of high culture, and of power, or as guardians and beneficiaries? What ought to be the *proper vocation* of secular intellectuals as a class, given the various aesthetic, ethical, and political transactions that command their attention and especially given the testimony of modern history, a history which has stood witness both to the nightmare of racism, imperialism, and genocide, and to the grand claims made for the Enlightenment?

Although strategically complemented by poststructuralist conceptions of language (more about which later), Said's investigation into the idea of culture, its stripes and morphologies, and its multiple relationships takes place on an intellectual site consecrated from the right by Matthew Arnold and demystified from the left by Antonio Gramsci and Raymond Williams. To avoid unnecessary repetition, I will organize my synoptic analysis around the Gramscian notion of hegemony – but I will filter it through Saidian and Williamsian interpretive lenses; Said's critique of the Arnoldian valorization of high culture will be considered last. Seen in this multiple light, culture-as-hegemony acquires the dimensions of a massively saturating (and saturated) repository of authority which, in order to legitimize itself as a naturalized common sense, relies less on the instruments of raw power than on the subtler suasions of habit and consensus.

Writing in the turbulent years of European Fascism, a period during which socialism was especially vulnerable to a brand of dictatorship that at once exploited populism and maintained the hierarchical structures of capitalism, Gramsci realized that a conceptual rethinking was necessary to rescue Marxism from terminal theoretical paucity and political erosion. The idea of hegemonic control came out of these reflections – as did such other by now well-domesticated notions as organic and traditional intellectuals, civil and political society, historico-cultural blocks, emergence, and so on. The notion of hegemony is not entirely unproblematic. Interpretable as an enveloping idea, a process, a set of practices and relationships, or a historical and cultural unconscious, it has over the years absorbed an unhelpful residue of ambiguities and obfuscations, but its usefulness to Gramsci (as to Williams and Said) primarily lies in the fact that it is fine-grained and sensitive enough to register subtle distinctions which the far more familiar term of ideology cannot. These distinctions can in turn be exposed to the light of day with the help of incisive, equally sensitive critical instruments. Without surrendering the powerful macrological insights of traditional Marxist thought, the analyst of hegemonic control can – through a strategy of filtering, defamiliarizing, and X-raying – unmask a vast network of cultural minutiae which often becomes available for ideological use by virtue of its capacity for mediation, absorption, camouflage.

This vital ideological tissue would not normally have been accounted for under the mere economism and historical determinism of what has come to be known as vulgar Marxism. Hegemony is therefore marked by suppleness, resilience, and accommodativeness – qualities which enable its adherents not only to immunize themselves to but also to embrace, knowingly or otherwise, serious multiple pathologies in the name of a rational order of society. Above all, hegemonic control instantiates immense depth and saturation. This combination of hegemonic elasticity, perdurability, and sheer presence in the modern West has been made possible, Said tells us, because of the crucial role of elaboration as a cultural activity:

> By elaboration Gramsci means two seemingly contradictory but actually complementary things. First, to elaborate means to refine, to work out (*e-*

laborare) some prior or more powerful idea, to perpetuate a world view. Second, to elaborate means something more qualitatively positive, the proposition that culture itself or thought or art is a highly complex and quasi-autonomous extension of political reality and, given the extraordinary importance attached by Gramsci to intellectuals, culture, and philosophy, it has a density, complexity, and historical-semantic value that is so strong as to make politics possible. Elaboration is the ensemble of patterns making it feasible for society to maintain itself ... Far from denigrating elaboration to the status of ornament, Gramsci makes it the very reason for the strength of what he calls civil society, which in the industrial West plays a role no less important than that of political society. Thus elaboration is the central cultural activity and, whether or not one views it as little more than intellectual propaganda for ruling-class interests, it is the material making a society a society. In other words, elaboration is a great part of the social web of which George Eliot spoke in her late novels. Gramsci's insight is to have recognized that subordination, fracturing, diffusing, reproducing, as much as producing, creating, forcing, guiding, are all necessary aspects of elaboration.[47]

Whether one identifies it primarily with civil institutions or coextends it with the entire socio-cultural domain, culture as hegemonic authority insinuates itself into individuals and collectivities through this process of elaboration and diffusion, normalizing itself as part of the internalized experience of socialization. Yet it entails multiple forms of domination and subordination. Gramsci, argues Said, "loses sight neither of the great central facts of power and how they flow through a whole network of agencies operating by rational consent, nor of the detail – diffuse, quotidian, unsystematic, thick – from which inevitably power draws its sustenance." Gramsci, in other words, recognized that "culture serves authority not because it represses and coerces but because it is affirmative, positive, and persuasive."[48] Culture-as-hegemony is the malleable, transparent, power-laden glue holding together – and lubricating – the different spheres and strata of society. In effect, culture is the very stuff of which individual and collective identities are made. It is this enormous capacity for self-occultation and saturation that is captured with remarkable clarity in this definition of hegemony by Williams. Ideology is abstractive and formal, Williams tells us, hence suggesting conscious manipulation of the public by the ruling classes. Hegemony, on the other hand,

> sees the relations of domination and subordination, in their forms as practical consciousness; as in effect a saturation of the whole process of living – not only of political and economic activity, nor only of manifest social activity, but of the whole substance of lived identities and relationships, to such a depth that the pressures and limits of what can ultimately be seen as a specific economic,

political, and cultural system seem to most of us the pressures and limits of simple experience and common sense ... It is a lived system of meanings and values – constitutive and constituting – which as they are experienced as practices appear as reciprocally confirming. It thus constitutes a sense of reality for most people in society, a sense of absolute because experienced reality beyond which it is very difficult for most members of the society to move, in most areas of their lives. It is, that is to say, in the strongest sense "a culture", but a culture which has also to be seen as the lived dominance and subordination of particular classes.[49]

Hegemony, in short, is a mode of living and intelligibility – a way of making sense of oneself and the world one lives in – which has evolved over a long period of time as a result of continual repetition and reinforcement. It has so effaced itself as to appear to be the absolutely logical view of things. Like the air we breathe, it is both invisible and all-enveloping, becoming part of the natural substance and rhythm of life. For all these reasons, its demystification is also absolutely necessary.

I have laid unusual stress on the notion of culture-as-hegemony not only because (as we shall see more clearly in a later section) such an emphasis brings into sharp focus the reasons for Said's indictment of contemporary intellectuals – who he thinks are hegemonically colla-borating with "the prevailing polity" – but also because I specifically wanted to bring out the Marxist-culturalist dimension of Said's cri-ticism. This affinity with Gramsci and Williams is very strong, both in *The World* and in *Orientalism*, a text which is often reductively characterized as Foucauldian in inspiration.

Said's debt to Williams is of course not particularly difficult to explain. Unlike Foucault, Derrida, and other poststructuralists, who never concealed their distaste for humanism, Williams was a public intellectual committed to humanistic ideals. On the other hand, unlike most academic American Marxists and other leftists, Williams did not forget that political battles could – indeed had to – be fought both tactically and strategically, that one could practice serious aca-demic criticism which also had a sharp edge designed for immediate socio-political combat. Said, I think, would find particularly com-mendable Williams's ability to combine a working-class brand of activism – a brand thoroughly infused with the subtle ironies of a Welsh Marxist ensconced, and contained, in the bastion of English Tradition – with the considerable sophistication of Continental thought without, however, surrendering to the officialized dogma of Orthodox Marxism or falling into what might be called the casuistic snares of contemporary critical theory. Thanks to this combination of independence, rigor, self-interrogation, and commitment to broad humanistic ideals, Williams was able to energize the study of culture as a legitimate area of radical thought – rescuing it from Arnoldian valorization, Leavisian mystification, and left suspicion. Cultural studies is now more charged and vibrant than ever on both sides of the Atlantic, despite the presumed – and much gloated-over – burial of Marxism proper.

Williams's voluminous, diverse work attests to his remarkable energy and to the persistence with which he pursued his twin objectives: to "materialize" culture and to help rescue Marxism from its own ossified dogma before rigor mortis set in. The broad outlines of his argument – revised and fine-tuned over the years – are well known: that the literary tradition is not something passively received and transmitted but is actively shaped through selection, valorization, censorship; that economic and political stakes – issues of class interest, governance, direct or indirect control, etc. – as much as innate literary merit have been considered in the construction of that tradition; that "literature," "aesthetic experience," and the like are by and large illegitimate forms of hegemonic concealment; that this concealment program has succeeded – through categorization, rarefaction, deflection, and suppression – in creating a mode of understanding in which the established order of inequality is naturalized and institutionalized; that what is ultimately extirpated from literature and from all other privileged intellectual productions is the brute materiality of human culture. With respect to Marxism specifically, Williams argued that such reductionist – and ultimately dualistic – categories as base and superstructure, the economic basis of production, ideology as false consciousness, literary theories of reflection, and so forth are no longer by themselves useful and must be replaced by, or fine-tuned with the help of, subtler, more insightful terms like hegemony, cultural materialism, and structures of feeling.

I have summarized a complicated series of arguments which interactively unfold in different texts written over a fairly long stretch of time. The point I want to stress here, though, is that Said's general thesis of worldliness, as well as the subtler concept of socio-cultural affiliation, is informed to a great extent by these Williamsian insights. Notice how in the following passage Said lines up for interrogation an entire constellation of cultural forms and practices (literary realism, restorative interpretation, aestheticism, the hegemonic concealment of "dispossessions and theft," etc.) by carefully deploying a highly

appreciative summary of *The Country and the City*. One of the things
he is opposed to in contemporary criticism, he tells us, is

> the assumption that the principal relationships in the study of literature –
> those I have identified as based on representation [or realism broadly under-
> stood] – ought to obliterate the traces of other relationships within literary
> structures that are based principally upon acquisition and appropriation. This
> is the great lesson of Raymond Williams' *The Country and the City*. His
> extraordinarily illuminating discussion there of the seventeenth-century
> English country-house poems does not concentrate on what those poems
> represent, but on what they *are* as the result of contested social and political
> relationships. Descriptions of the rural mansion, for example, do not at bot-
> tom entail only what is to be admired by way of harmony, repose, and beauty;
> they should also entail for the modern reader what in fact has been excluded
> from the poems, the labor that created the mansion, the social processes of
> which they are the culmination, the dispossessions and theft they actually
> signified. Although he does not come out and say it, Williams' book is a
> remarkable attempt at a dislodgement of the very ethos of system, which has
> reified relationships and stripped them of their social density. What he tries to
> put in its place is the great dialectic of acquisition and representation, by
> which even realism – as it is manifest in Jane Austen's novels – has gained its
> durable status as the result of contests involving money and power. Williams
> teaches us to read in a different way and to remember that for every poem or
> novel in the canon there is a social fact being requisitioned for the page, a
> human life engaged, a class suppressed or elevated – none of which can be
> accounted for in the framework rigidly maintained by the processes of
> representation and affiliation doing above-ground work for the conservation of
> filiation. And for every critical system grinding on there are events, hetero-
> geneous and unorthodox social configurations, human beings and texts dis-
> puting the possibility of a sovereign methodology of system.[50]

In short, Williams has turned conceptions of culture inside out.
Through historically informed studies and carefully researched alternative reconstructions of the genealogy of such terms as culture,
society, civilization, ideology, literature, institutions, and formations
in the light of insights derived from Lukacs, Goldmann, and Gramsci,
among others, Williams shows that none of these terms are static; in
other words, their meanings and "values" have not been settled once
and for all, but are subject to revision because they are all caught up in
the continuous, changing, contested process of (British) society's self-
creation in history.

Said has indeed occasionally expressed disappointment in Williams's silence about the nexus between culture and worldwide
imperialism.[51] It is clear, however, that he considers his own brand of

cultural criticism, both in *The World* and elsewhere, as being in important respects an application (and extension) of Williamsian insights. More specifically, there is a sense in which Said is in agreement with Williams's reconstitution of different designations of *culture* on a single, hierarchically contoured plane which Said calls "an environment, process, and hegemony."[52] That is to say, culture approximates Williams's idea of a broad "way of life" which (Said implies) covers "the nuances, principally of reassurance, fitness, belonging, association, and community, entailed in the phrase *at home or in place*."[53] Coextensive with this notion is culture as a vast intellectual–material *constellation* of agents, practices, institutions, and formations; and finally there is culture as a *process* of societal movement and change in history. In effect, this is a reconstruction by other means of the filiation–affiliation dialectic we discussed earlier, and as such it is meant both to alert us to the asymmetrical socio-cultural consolidations of modernity and to suggest alternative ways of conceptualizing human community. Such notions as *structures of attitudes and references* (itself inspired by Williams's structures of feeling) and *contrapuntality*, both of which Said has used in *Culture and Imperialism*, are clearly intended to fine-tune these historical insights and utopian possibilities further.

It should also be clear, however, that Said's primary objective in citing Williams – and Gramsci – is to enact what he has described in the above passage as "a dislodgement of the very ethos of system" – an enactment for which my analysis of hegemonic control has been preparing the way. What exactly is being dislodged? The idea of high culture in the Arnoldian sense: culture as "sweetness and light" – "the best thought and knowledge" of Europe; its ability to determine the good and not so good, and to hold sway over both; its self-adulation, self-idealization, and self-fortification; its demotions and ex-communications; its insatiable appetite as "possessing possession" (Said's phrase);[54] and above all its explicit identification with politico-military power. Arnold, argues Said, helped create the doctrine of high culture and at the same time captured it for the state, hence combatively legitimizing political power exerted from above:

> The question raised by Arnold's passion for culture ... is the relationship between culture and society. He argues that society is the actual, material base over which culture tries, through the great men of culture, to extend its sway. The optimum relationship between culture and society then is *correspondence*, the former covering the latter. What is too often overlooked by Arnold's readers is that he views this ambition combatively: "the best that is thought

and known" must contend with competing ideologies, philosophies, dogmas, notions, and values, and it is Arnold's insight that what is at stake in society is not merely the cultivation of individuals, or the development of a class of finely tuned sensibilities, or the renaissance of interest in the classics, but rather the assertively achieved and *won* hegemony of an identifiable set of ideas, which Arnold honorifically calls culture, over all other ideas in society.[55]

This self-endowed legislative capacity of culture-as-hegemony – "the power of culture by virtue of its elevated or superior position to authorize, to dominate, to legitimate, demote, interdict, and validate"[56] – is indicted directly and uncompromisingly in all of Said's political works, including *Orientalism*, *The Question of Palestine*, *Covering Islam*, and *Culture and Imperialism* – a fact which is often overlooked by some of his critics (among them the nativist-Marxist Aijaz Ahmad), who, in pointing to various alleged ambivalences and obfuscations on Said's part, elide the multiple designations of culture which I have just outlined. Said's often-noted reverence for "high" culture must be complemented with the fact that it is precisely this valorized notion of culture-as-hegemony (and not culture as such) that comes in for his own severest criticism. It is the locus where, in his view, unseemly practices in the world – practices which have had social, political, and economic consequences both locally and globally – have historically been cleansed of their base contaminations, the place where they have been intellectually laundered. Culture here has become "a system of values *saturating* downward almost everything within its purview; yet, paradoxically, culture dominates from above without at the same time being available to everything and everyone it dominates";[57] it is "a system of discriminations and evaluations" which, though "perhaps mainly aesthetic," is also above all tyrannical and exclusionary: "a system of exclusions from above but enacted throughout its polity, by which such things as anarchy, disorder, irrationality, inferiority, bad taste, and immorality are identified, then deposited outside the [approved] culture and kept there by the power of the State and its institutions."[58]

Culture in this hieratic, appropriative sense is identified by Said not only with multiple oppressions inside Europe itself – as theorized by thinkers as different as Marx and Foucault – but also with worldwide European imperialism and its unacknowledged transumption in contemporary America. He finds its impress in the vast, tessellated discourse of Orientalism. And he associates it with Zionist political philosophy – a carefully packaged theocentric ideology largely born out of European anti-Semitism and the European imperial venture but more recently sustained with American-made instruments of power and with residual Orientalism. Culture as embodied in these valorized policies, practices, and institutions enables its adherents to make quasi-theological distinctions between the West and the non-West – distinctions "between what is fitting for us and what is fitting for them, the former designated as inside, in place, common, belonging, in a word *above*, the latter, who are designated as outside, excluded, aberrant, inferior, in a word *below*."[59]

The controversy generated in the wake of Said's indictment of Orientalism, Zionism, and imperial culture in general will be considered in the remaining chapter of my study. Now, however, I would like to make explicit a question to which I have been alluding throughout this section: just exactly what is entailed in *critically* coming to terms with the hegemonic control of society? Said's answer appears to take two main lines.

First, positing – or recognizing, to be more precise – the subtle but saturating presence of hegemonic authority alerts us to the *political* dimension of culture – without, however, reducing everything to politics. That is to say, political power and cultural practices constitute distinct (and in some respects quite independent) but nevertheless closely entwined spheres. Hence, for example, there is an obvious sense in which the production and reception of literary works take place primarily in a disciplinary space where neither science, philosophy, nor politics can feel at home in any immediate fashion. Yet the boundary around that space is neither hermetically sealed nor rigidly static – on the contrary, it is both porous and fluid: it is caught up in a vast field of moving socio-cultural forces, a field which is being fought over and appropriated all the time. "Durrell's presence" on the Defense Secretary's desk is a perfect example of what can – and often does – happen as a result of these contests. A specific cultural artifact, which belongs to a valorized canon – an immense reserve of cultural capital accumulated, idealized, and preserved over a long period of time – has become available as a screen for an extremely noxious exercise of political, technological, and military power – itself the end-product of long-evolving, stored-up social energies. It therefore stands to reason that literary critics should pay close attention as much to what lies *outside* the boundary of their professional space as to what is inside it. It also follows that this "outside" is by no means exhausted by the explication of a few recondite passages from Kant, or Nietzsche, or Derrida – that it actually also includes such minor distractions as the killing and maiming of people in a distant country in the name of American national interest.

The second point is implicit in the first. Intellectuals are both members of multiple communities and autonomous agents – and since they, more than any other group, can sharpen their insight into these hegemonic operations in the context of modernity, they have a vital role to play as either defenders or demystifiers of power. They have the option, for example, of openly siding with the dominant culture (oppression and all) – as experts, functionaries, rationalizers, spin doctors, and the like. Henry Kissinger is a famous contemporary example of this group. They can collude with it surreptitiously, as most media operatives, academic professionals, and other quasi-independent humanists do. Or they can openly and uncompromisingly oppose it in the name of our common humanity. Noam Chomsky is a towering exemplar in this category. Some of the most passionate passages in *The World, the Text, and the Critic* are intended as an unstinting appreciation of critical intellectuals as well as a barely disguised denunciation of collusive intellectuals:

> [I]f we allow that it has been the historical fate of such collective sentiments as "my country right or wrong" and "we are whites and therefore belong to a higher race than blacks" and "European or Islamic or Hindu culture is superior to all others" to coarsen and brutalize the individual, then it is probably true that an isolated individual consciousness, going against the surrounding environment as well as allied to contesting classes, movements, and values, is an isolated voice out of place but very much *of* that place, standing consciously against the prevailing orthodoxy and very much for a professedly universal or humane set of values, which has provided significant local resistance to the hegemony of one culture.[60]

The Worldliness of Language: Texts as Bearers of Authority

We have brought the discussion to a point where the second strand of Said's worldliness thesis – namely, textual worldliness – can be examined more closely. As I tried to demonstrate in my analysis of *Beginnings*, Said's treatment of language is a very complex affair. Both in that text and elsewhere in his oeuvre, one can find multiple inflections of what language entails: language as an intertextual, self-stabilizing system; as an invented totality displacing reality – often violently; as instances of an iterable signifier chain, a process broadly designated as writing, etc. I also pointed out that, in order to arrive at a more insightful understanding of language, he has found it necessary to complement these linguistically derived formulations with ideas drawn from phenomenology. The result, at a broad level, is the thesis that language constitutes an *intentional structure*. This formulation has been necessitated by Said's insistence on a wide latitude of freedom for human agency – a latitude disallowed by the very logic of what he has described as linguacentricity or linguicity. Finally, a satisfactory description of language has to account for history and socio-political reality. What emerges out of these multiple configurations is, as I stressed in my discussion of *Beginnings*, a conception of textual power and dynamics which is not, however, immune to human intervention – a discursive conception which I characterized as being broadly Foucauldian. That discursivity is also central to the thesis of textual worldliness.

For there is a way in which Said is ultimately appealing to that poststructuralist thinker's genealogical alignment of language-as-knowledge – the regime of Truth – with the omnipresence of political and cultural power. Foucault's left-handed analytics of historically conditioned epistemic discontinuities, mutations, and emergences; of statements or discursive formations dispersed – and controlled – by rules and strategies; of modern power as a pervasive, panoptically impersonal socio-political energy twinned with knowledge systems which are disciplinary (in both senses of the word); of the pure descriptivity of a rarefied, effaced language and the pure gaze of the disinterested professional together enunciatively activating a spatio-temporal cultural archive: all these heuristics are being deployed by Said. In fact, the importance for Said of this compelling cluster of analytic tools can hardly be overestimated. They go a long way in buttressing his argument that texts are culturally embedded intentional constructs whose force is never simply neutral but works in conjunction with active, even combative, socio-political forces that ineluctably dictate legislations, interdictions, and suppressions – in order to install and maintain a set of highly naturalized, strictly observed, hierarchically structured inclusions and exclusions. In other words, I am arguing that, even though as we shall see later Said does express strong reservations about some of Foucault's specific assumptions, he finds Foucault's analytics extremely useful inasmuch as they together mark an unsurpassed theoretical limit where the often unrecognized or otherwise ideologically sublimated complicities of knowledge and power are unmasked in the most cogent and, one might add, most emphatically damning way.

A sense of this discursive power, and of Foucault's importance to Said's conception of textual worldliness, is conveyed by this passage:

> [I]t is now certain that Foucault's greatest intellectual contribution is to an understanding of how the will to exercise dominant control in society and history has also discovered a way to clothe, disguise, rarefy and wrap itself systematically in the language of truth, discipline, rationality, utilitarian value, and knowledge. And this language, in its naturalness, professionalism, assertiveness, and antitheoretical directness, is what Foucault has called *discourse*. The difference between discourse and such coarser yet no less significant fields of social combat as the class struggle is that discourse works its productions, discriminations, censorship, interdictions, and invalidations on the intellectual, at the level of base not of superstructure. The power of discourse is that it is at once the object of struggle and the tool by which the struggle is conducted.[61]

In short, discourse functions in exact conjunction with – indeed *as* – hegemony. Not merely a matter of individual authors and their oeuvres – or even of genres, autonomous fields, or styles of presentation – discourse in this sense constitutes subjectivity, the claims of epistemology, historical consciousness, and political imbrications into great, impersonal, rule-governed gestalts: vast, densely packed tableaux vivants slowly emerge, unfold, mutate, and displace one another as discontinuous, sedimented archaeological fields. Hence the need for an archaeological investigator rather than a traditional historian of ideas.

Discourse, then, is obliged to disclose – indeed turns out to be – the reverse side of the Enlightenment, the counter-memory of the modern master-narrative: reason, clarity, scientific truth, technological progress, the democratic social order, freedom – all these high-toned commonplaces of modernity are exposed to the withering scrutiny of their own carefully suppressed negative light. And both in Foucault's narrowly European (or more precisely almost exclusively French) focus of intellectual history and in Said's extension of it, the extent to which utopian scopic vision has actualized dystopian reality is underlined. To Said specifically that reality – its scandalous duplicity, its extremely heavy toll, its tenacity and persistence – is to be found largely in the consolidated vision of imperium (more about which in the final chapter).

In a later section devoted entirely to contemporary criticism and its discontents, I will provide more specific details about the strengths that Said sees in Foucault's analytics (in opposition, for example, to Derrida's deconstruction). I will also comment on what Said considers to be unsalable Foucauldian baggage. Here, I would like to examine Said's appropriation of this broad thesis of discursivity for his own argument of textual worldliness – an idea which, it should be clear by now, acquires a far greater culturalist emphasis than it would have in a strictly Foucauldian rendering. Hence in considering the following discussion of textual worldliness, we should bear in mind my earlier observations about Said's views on Gramsci, Williams, and Arnold.

Said argues for a textual (or verbal) logic – a linguistics, if you will – of events in which meaning, though important in itself, is anchored to the vicissitudes of place and time and gauged in terms of its occasion and its effect. Seen in this light, language happens – or makes things happen – in the world by virtue of the fact that it is used by living agents who are themselves active in that world. At the instant of speaking or writing, language locates an action (that of speaking or writing) undertaken in a physical socio-cultural setting and at a specific time, an action carried out, not merely by a speaking pronoun whose subjectivity amounts to a signature, but by a conscious individual who makes certain choices – about subject matter, about aims and ends, about styles and strategies of presentation, etc. – and who, being also a member of a community, is therefore implying, even soliciting, an audience. It follows that this discursive action has consequences, sometimes unintended, in the world (for individuals, communities, cultural formations, nature, etc.) because the meaning embodied in that utterance (or exteriorized intention) does not simply repose in suspension or potentiality as structuralists and other formalists suggest; nor is the process of recovering that meaning just a matter of a lone, disinterested critic reading, understanding, and translating faithfully a stable set of discoverable ideas patiently waiting, hidden in the text. On the contrary, what the text *means* or *says* is being continually received, retransmitted, processed, revised, and appropriated (or disappropriated) for various projects, plans, and purposes. And in a very literal sense, texts, no less than dialogically verbalized exchanges, mark – indeed *are* – positions of contestation in a public domain where they are no longer just the property of their individual authors but are subject to the discursive pressures of that domain. At a minimum level, then, texts are caught up in a concatenation of production, reception, appropriation, and reproduction that places author, text, and critic in historical, geographical, and cultural circumstances which both bestow authority and impose constraints. This is the broad thesis emphatically stated – though of course inflected differently – in essay after essay. The following pas-

sage, in which Said is directly challenging Paul Ricoeur's narrowly
hermeneutic understanding of texts, presents the gist of the argument
with exemplary brevity and clarity.

> My contention is that [textual] worldliness does not come and go [as Ricoeur
> suggests]; nor is it here and there in the apologetic and soupy way by which
> we often designate history, a euphemism in such cases for the impossibly
> vague notion that all things take place in time. Moreover, critics are not
> merely alchemical translators of texts into circumstantial reality or worldli-
> ness; for they too are subject to and producers of circumstances, which are felt
> regardless of whatever objectivity the critic's methods possess. The point is
> that texts have ways of existing that even in their most rarefied form are
> always enmeshed in circumstance, time, place, and society – in short, they are
> in the world, and hence worldly.[62]

It is this dialectical conception of language that Said invokes in his
effort to overturn formalism in general and structuralist/post-
structuralist systematicity in particular. It allows him to activate the
energy which has – in his view – been reduced to a state of virtuality,
absorbed into the construction of a quasi-transcendent structure, or
frozen into articulations adorning systems and subsystems: the energy,
in other words, that is denied to language as a result of its manifestly
pragmatic, even instrumental, uses being either de-emphasized or
ignored altogether by formalists of all stripes.

One specific way in which Said tries to buttress this thesis is to
show that texts of "literature," even those written by the most self-
consciously eccentric of authors, attest to their presence in the lifeworld – a feature which is not incidental but vital to their very
positivity as texts. Phrased differently, this means that authorial
intention is implicated, by virtue of the discursivity of its constructed
site (i.e. the text), in the very business of the world. Hence, it is by no
means a mere coincidence that Said has brought together for illustration Hopkins, Wilde, and Conrad, three authors who are well
known as much for the extreme eccentricity of their styles as for their
participation (in different ways and for different reasons) in the turn-
of-the-century movement of modernism. It is an attempt to dispel
what Said considers to be a carefully constructed and ultimately
insidious myth: the dubious assumption that literary works somehow
transcend their socio-historical reality. There is an obvious sense in
which these three writers each effect a highly personalized enactment
of literary defamiliarization – each creating his own idiolect, as it
were. Hopkins's sprung rhythm, Wilde's effete aestheticism and love
of epigrams, and Conrad's multi-vectored narratives are in their own

different ways attempts to dislodge – or at least disengage from – what could broadly be called the nineteenth-century poetics of realism and romanticism. Though vastly different in other ways, these two traditions had one thing in common: the belief that language is a transparent medium capable of delivering (empirical or ideal) knowledge about its immediate subject matter (the title of M. H. Abrams's book, *The Mirror and the Lamp*,[63] suggests some of that shared attitude about language's mediatory or reflexive capacity). As my analysis of *Beginnings* has tried to demonstrate, literary modernist texts, including those written by Hopkins, Wilde, and Conrad, shatter that belief.

Yet, according to Said, each of these three writers "deliberately conceives the text as supported by a discursive situation involving speaker and audience; the designed interplay between speech and reception, between verbality and textuality, *is* the text's situation, its placing of itself in the world."[64] In Hopkins's case, the "dialectic of [poetic] production" is so intimately intertwined with God's intention, as manifested in the very configuration of the natural order (the layer of frost covering the earth, for example), that it takes on an existential significance for him: "So close is the identification in Hopkins' mind among world, word, and the utterance, the three coming together alive, that he envisages little need for critical intervention." His own style of sprung rhythm becomes a reanimation of poetry, an attempt to give "back to poetry its true soul and self." The text, therefore, is not a "lifeless, worldless" object but in a manner of speaking Hopkins's own child.[65]

Wilde, on the other hand, tries to transform himself – and the world – into an art form but is instead ensnared by worldliness in the most nightmarish way. And the author of this nightmare is none other than himself – his own text: "Having forsworn action, life, and nature for their incompleteness and diffusion, Wilde took as his province a theoretical, ideal world," a Platonic universe where civilized people cultivated the art of conversation – which in its distilled, crystallized form could be summed up in the quotable epigram. That utopia is destroyed when a letter he has written to a young friend falls into the wrong hands: "When the communication between men no longer possesses the freedom of conversation, when it is confined to the merely legal liability of print, which is not ingeniously quotable but, because it has been signed, is now criminally actionable, the utopia crumbles." The world's unwanted attention has been invited precisely because of the circumstances in which an extremely private text was produced and thereafter publicly appropriated as a "criminally actionable" document.[66]

Said's discussion of worldliness as exemplified in Conrad's writing needs to be examined a little more closely – for two reasons. The first, more obvious one is that the old Conradian dialectic – a dialectic which in *The Fiction of Autobiography* took the form of an existentialist agonism – is reformulated in starkly textualist terminology. The second, more immediately relevant reason is that, along with the analysis of the Zahirite School of Arab grammarians, the treatment of Conrad manifests Said's deep ambivalence toward epistemological realism: on the one hand, Said seems to be insisting – at least insofar as an implicit position can be derived from his Conradian analysis – that it is extremely difficult to make things visible, to disclose them as entities in the world through the use of language. On the other hand, he unambiguously endorses the phenomenalism of the Zahirites, whose linguistic theories were premised on a strict correspondence between words and objects.

Conrad, Said argues in an article entirely devoted to this author, confronted "the duplicity of language" which has become such an important topic in twentieth-century philosophy: that "the chasm between words saying and words meaning was widened, not lessened, by a talent for words written."[67] To Conrad, writing was as much a "presentational" challenge, relating to problems of motivation and occasion, as it was an attempt to "represent," or render accurately, a slice of reality. At the same time, however, his own use of language was a palpable demonstration that it was well-nigh impossible to accomplish either of these objectives. The result was an "interplay of antitheses"[68] which took the form of an almost unparalleled virtuosic performance, a brilliant dramatization of language which commands attention, not because it delivers satisfactory knowledge about the professed objects of the narrative, but precisely because it *is* a textual locale:

> Quite literally, therefore, Conrad was able to see his narratives as the place in which the motivated, the occasional, the methodical, and the rational are brought together with the aleatory, the unpredictable, the inexplicable. On the one hand, there are conditions presented by which a story's telling becomes necessary; on the other hand, the essential story itself seems opposite to the conditions of its telling. The interplay of one with the other – and Conrad's attention to the persuasively realistic setting of the tale's presentation enforces our attention to this – makes the narrative the unique thing it is.[69]

Conrad, Said believes, was obliged to come to terms, as no other modernist fiction writer was, with "the change from storytelling as useful, communal art to novel writing as essentialized, solitary art." The consequences of this transformation manifest themselves in several different ways: (a) to the extent that "the status of information has become problematical," the medium of delivery itself is progressively accented; (b) writers try to find ways of creating interest by a variety of means (variation in the tone of words, "narrative management," etc.); (c) since there is no ready-to-hand audience, the author has to dramatize it, creating it on the page, as it were; (d) finally, the "narrative is presented as utterance, as something in the actual process of being delivered" in the form of spoken words.[70] Said suggests that all these modernist tensions are far more greatly amplified in Conrad's writing than in that of any other novelist of his time. In Conrad's stories the desire to tell a story, described by Said as "wanting-to-speak" through *written* "narrative utterances,"[71] must contend with the fact that writing as such – because of its manifest materiality and temporal differentiality – is incapable of making visible (or audible) anything around which it wraps itself. Conrad's narrative method is also characterized by Said as "the alternation in language of presence and absence,"[72] a process which reveals "the exact contours"[73] of an obscurity rather than a clear-cut image. The following statement about *Lord Jim* can, with some modification, apply to Conrad's other tales; they are all "inconclusive" in one way or another:

Jim's appetite for disastrous adventure, like Marlow's narrative, like our attention to the tale, corresponds not to any communicable pattern of linear progress from, say, ambition to accomplishment, but conforms rather to a more abstract impulse. The impulse can find no expression in action, and no image, other than the vague rubric of Romance, conveys the aim of Jim's troubled quest ... In all cases the dominating factor is not narrative energy but a fatalistic desire to behold the self passively as an object told about, mused on, puzzled over, marveled at fully, in utterance. That is, having everywhere conceded that one can neither completely realize one's own nor fully grasp someone else's life experience, Jim, Marlow, and Conrad are left with a desire to fashion verbally and approximately their individual experience in terms unique to each.[74]

The details of Said's discussion need not be pursued further, since in the main they echo, and textually transform, the existentialist analysis of *The Fiction of Autobiography*. What does need emphasis here is that Conrad's verbal dramatization of personal dilemmas is used by Said as an occasion to restate – admittedly in a cursory fashion – his own strong belief that "a general loss of faith in the mimetic powers of language"[75] has progressively taken place in the context of modernity – a change he detects not only in other modernist novelists but also in the work of such diverse thinkers as Marx, Freud, Nietzsche, Foucault, and others. The same negative attitude towards mimesis, however, is not expressed in Said's discussion of the Zahirites. Indeed the exact opposite is the case.

Said's appreciative summary of the exegetical theory espoused by these eleventh-century Spanish Arab linguists may at first strike some readers as a bit far-fetched. After all, neither the Zahirites (or externalists) nor their Batinist (or internalist) opponents said much about literature, and they certainly didn't concern themselves with such matters as culture-as-hegemony, worldwide imperialism, and so forth. Besides, unlike Augustine, Kant, and Derrida, the Zahirites are not part of *our* tradition – no one in your typical English department has ever heard of them. So, why drag them in? The answer to this question takes two slightly different forms both of which are germane to the theme of worldliness. One is that Said's discussion constitutes a pointed, though brief, intervention in the recent debates about the canon; it indirectly reinforces his insistence, both in *The World* and elsewhere, that there is a vast multiplicity of intellectual traditions in the world, each capable of offering valuable insights in its own way, and the more *affiliations* we consciously establish among them, the better for all of us. The convocation of canons and cultures that he endorses in *Culture and Imperialism* is probably the best example in his oeuvre of an attempt to present an alternative to a filiatively created tradition. Ferial Ghazoul puts this point succinctly:

> By introducing Arab-Islamic thought into his writing, Said brings in parallel views, and, in order to show affinities, draws insights from them to solve intellectual problems in metropolitan thought. This is not a matter, in my opinion, of noting that Said adorns his discourse with Arab-Islamic touches, the way someone may have a thoroughly modern urban house decorated with a few Bedouin cushions. Said is clearly feeling his way towards ushering in a more global comparative approach that goes beyond the cosmopolitan, essentially European approach.[76]

It is particularly instructive that, in this case, he has chosen linguistics as the object of immediate inquiry: as he reminds us in *Orientalism* and elsewhere, European linguistic theories (as expounded by Renan, for example) have historically been deeply implicated in multiple forms of European supremacism. The Andalusian Zahirites, on the other hand, were encumbered neither by race theory nor by imperialism.

The second reason for Said's choice relates to the vigor and persuasiveness with which the Zahirites embed texts – even religious ones – in their irreducibly worldly circumstances, whence their remarkable prescience and their relevance for the debates swirling around analogous issues ten centuries later. In contradistinction to the Batinists, who maintained that meaning inheres in the multiple semantic possibilities of words and sentences, and therefore insisted on a polysemous, depth interpretation of the Koranic text, the Zahirites steadfastly defended an exigetics premised on both the divinely ordained semantic integrity of the Koran and the historicity of its message. Since, they argued, the Koran "was a sacred text whose authority derived from its being the uncreated word of God, directly and unilaterally transmitted to a Messenger [Prophet Mohammed] at a particular moment in time," then it must be considered "a unique event."[77] It follows that its meaning is at once "stable and complete"[78] by virtue of the very particularity of that event – its unsullied uniqueness as an enactment of divine will. As such, the Koran is an embodiment of Absolute Truth. But there is also a sense in which this same event constituted "a descent" into human history.[79] The Prophet was entrusted to deliver God's message into the circumstances of time and place, the factitious situationality of the Muslim community. The same event can, therefore, also be viewed as pure contingency. That is to say, for example, the same privileged language (Arabic) that God chose as the vehicle of divine will is also used by human beings who are inserted in temporality. Hence the Koran embodies what could be called a dialectic of the eternal and temporal in terms of both validity and occasion:

> [T]he Koran speaks of historical events, yet is not itself historical. It repeats past events, which it condenses and particularizes, yet is not itself an actually lived experience; it ruptures the human continuity of life, yet God does not enter temporality by a sustained or concerted act. The Koran evokes the memory of actions whose content repeats itself eternally in ways identical with itself, as warnings, orders, imperatives, punishments ... In short, the Zahirite position adopts a view of the Koran that is absolutely circumstantial without at the same time making that worldliness dominate the actual sense of the text: all this is the ultimate avoidance of vulgar determinism in the Zahirite position.[80]

That dual understanding of the significance of the sacred text obliges the Zahirites to put in place a hermeneutics of total phenomenality and clarity, one that puts severe limits on the potentially virtuosic freedom of the lone interpreter: "A word has a strict meaning ... and with that meaning there also goes a strictly ordained series of resemblances (correspondences) to other words and meanings, which, strictly speaking, play around the first word."[81] Language, in short, is a grammatically structured system which, by virtue of its being *in use* in a vast world of objects, agents, actions, and intentions, must deliver meaning – including the divine message of the sacred book – in as precise a fashion as possible. There is no room here for ambiguity, fuzziness, or polysemy. This sharply controlled interpretive regime, Said tells us, summarizing Roger Arnaldez's detailed exposition, is firmly wedged at the verbal level between "the two paradigmatic imperatives, *iqra* (read or recite) and *qul* (tell)" – the imperative being the mode in which God addressed His Messenger – together with the delimiting juridical power of *hudd* (limit or definition). Within these strict parameters, according to the Zahirites, the Koranic text is to be understood as the deliverance of a *khabar* (utterance) "which is the verbalization of a signifying intention, or *niyah*," a conception which endorses the Koran's irreducible occasionality and its compelling pertinence.[82]

What impresses us about Said's summary of Zahirite phenomenalism is that – despite the sustained, transformative presence of a rigorous dialectic – it comes across as a historicized version of epistemological empiricism, a species of normativity which (along with idealism) he has repeatedly denounced as being ideological, delusional, rationalist (in a negative sense). In other words, he seems to be negating positions he has taken elsewhere in his oeuvre – the proposition, for example, that truth is inaccessible to insight; that language is not a transparent window pane, a reflexive mirror, or a shining lamp, but a cultural *material* produced and reproduced continually; that the mimetic or representational tradition is dead as a doornail, etc. Indeed Said reaffirms this anti-realist position in *The World* as well, as we saw in his summary of Raymond Williams's *The Country and The City* and in his discussion of Conrad. Hence, the question arises: is Said deliberately contradicting himself – and if so why? – or is he unaware of the philosophical conundrum in which he has entangled himself? How can he reconcile, for example, the Conradian "interplay of antitheses" which, we were told, ultimately reveals only the exact contours of an obscurity, on the one hand, and on the other the Zahirite claim that words referentially *correspond* to entities in the world? Why has the dialectical operation produced a profound negativity in one case and lucid knowledge in the other? Above all, isn't Said in the latter case peddling a version of knowledge which is remarkably similar to the ideological currencies he has denounced elsewhere?

Said rarely responds to questions like these in the typically formalistic fashion common in Anglo-American mainstream philosophy and literary criticism. This, I believe, is at least in some respects a potential weakness in his work – and I will reflect on it in the conclusion of this study. What is clear, however, is that – as I have noted repeatedly – oppositions like these are fairly common in Said's writing. They form an important component in the agonistic dialectic that partially guides all of his studies. Beyond that, it is important to note that he has often criticized in no uncertain terms religious and political conservatism in the Arab-Islamic world. His endorsement of the Zahirites is therefore not so much an expression of approval for a particular dogma (religious or otherwise) as it is an attempt to illustrate a theoretically forceful way in which an important text was anchored in its worldly circumstances.

Collusion and Amnesia: Refining Critics, "Radical" Theory, and the Liberal Consensus

Said does, of course, provide answers to the above questions in his own way – answers which create a space for critique qua critique between the hegemonically totalizing tendencies of culture and system. Early on in *The World*, he offers a brief but cogent description of what constitutes to him criticism properly understood:

> Criticism in short is always situated; it is skeptical, secular, reflectively open to its own failings. This is by no means to say that it is value-free. Quite the contrary, for the inevitable trajectory of critical consciousness is to arrive at some acute sense of what political, social, and human values are entailed in the reading, production, and transmission of every text. To stand between culture and system is therefore to stand *close to* – closeness itself having a particular value for me – a concrete reality about which political, moral, and social judgements have to be made and, if not only made, then exposed and demystified.[83]

Starting with a discussion of Foucault and Derrida, the rest of this chapter will explore the implications of this conception of critical practice as instantiated, approximated, mimed, dodged, or otherwise disregarded by modern and contemporary critics.

In a long article devoted almost exclusively to Foucault and Derrida, especially in the context of the rancorous exchange between them in the wake of the publication of Foucault's *Madness and Civilization*, Said commends both for practicing a brand of criticism whose cogency and energy are almost never matched by their American fellow travelers. In its technical prowess, its performative brilliance, its uncanny incisiveness, its sheer rigor and difficulty, its hostility to orthodoxy, and its alertness both to the problems of textuality and to the conditions in which all knowledge is produced, the kind of critical power fielded by Foucault and Derrida commands our attention both as a register of congenital crisis in the socio-political domain and a (potential) tool of intervention into that domain's institutional structures. Said argues that both critics show different – but exemplary – ways in which radical thought can be interrogatively positioned between cultural hegemonism and theoretical system-building:

> Each in his own way has attempted to devise what is a form of critical openness and repeatedly renewed theoretical resourcefulness, designed first to provide knowledge of a very specific sort; second, to provide an opportunity for further critical work; third, to avoid if possible both the self-confirming operations of culture and the wholly predictable monotony of a disengaged critical system.[84]

And they try to achieve these ends largely by uncovering what the normalized text conceals from the light of day: they "make visible . . . the various mysteries, rules, and play"[85] which, though structured into the very constitution of textuality, are almost never acknowledged by texts:

> [F]or both writers, their work is meant to replace the tyranny and the fiction of direct reference – to what Derrida calls *presence* or the transcendental signified – with the rigor and practice of textuality mastered on its highly eccentric ground and in Foucault's case, *in* its highly protracted persistence.[86]

At once empirical and perspectival, this double-paced strategy of engaging texts alerts the reader to the narcotizing effect of lucidity (so called), leading instead to a more radical form of clarity. These anti-positivist, anti-originary textual enactments enable Foucault and Derrida to defy, de-define, derail, and dissolve the conceptual fictions that have been used to construct – and maintain – tyrannical pieties. In short, Foucault and Derrida, according to Said, differ from American poststructuralists in that these two thinkers are not only conscious of the way in which cultural authority actively harnesses critical energy, transforming it into methodological elaboration, but also consciously try to hone their powerfully tensive insights against the possibility of their being submitted to this type of domestication.

But Said is also critical of both in different ways – being harsher on Derrida than on Foucault. According to Said, Derrida in the end fails in his critical project, and his enormously influential method has become "an extremely pronounced self-limitation, an ascesis of a very inhibiting and crippling sort":[87] he continually attenuates, even pre-empts, the effectiveness of his radical critique by at once recognizing and suspending the hieratic, and ultimately worldly force of the philosophic authority he tries to dismantle. Said believes that Derrida's anticonceptual "theatrical metaphors" – differance, pharmakon, trace, supplement, hymen, dissemination, etc. – at first glance have a compellingly unsettling effect; they "reveal the *entame* – tear, incision – in every one of the solid structures put up by" the logocentric tradition of the West, from Plato to Heidegger.[88] The incision, which according to Derrida is constitutively inscribed into the temporality of writing (ecriture) as an irreducibly differential activity, is persistently (and duplicitously) suppressed or covered over by the philosophers' hubristic insistence on pure presence. Deconstruction, Derrida's "unbalanced and unbalancing"[89] method of reading, exposes that duplicity: ideal forms, the prime mover, the cogito, being, essence, the transcendental ego – these and other foundationalist concepts are shown to be nothing more than philosophic (and ultimately rhetorical) ruses enacted to privilege pure origination, the centrality of the subject, the directness of speech, and the plenitude of meaning. Philosophy, like every field which owes its authority, indeed its very existence, to textuality, is found to be riddled with self-irony; its "great," "classic" texts never deliver what they promise because the aporias, elisions, and confusions which are built into the very structure of signification reduce meaning to a refracted play of signifiers that never submit to closure but rather at once produce difference and surplus. So far, suggests Said, the critique is right on target. He also points out that Derrida, to his credit, repeatedly attacks – if only briefly and in passing – not only these metaphysical fictions but also the oppressive hierarchies which have been put in place in their name.

But to the extent that he has been unable or unwilling to take seriously the actual material implications of these hierarchies, Derrida pre-empts the potentially enormous impact of his critique, transforming it instead into a jocoserious, purely semantic, textual exercise which in effect leaves those very hierarchies in place. Said argues that both Foucault and Derrida regrettably reduce the thinking and acting subject to a mere effect of language. However, unlike Foucault, who describes the close, interfaced imbrications of institutional authority, disciplinary protocols, the production of knowledge, and the machinery of political power as all these are discursively activated to structure social formations and practices in broad terms and to shape subjectivities (i.e., individual human beings) often in a manner that authorizes the infliction of great violence, Derrida skirts the entire issue of praxis altogether. He ignores, in other words, historical density; the concrete, local operations of institutional hierarchy; the individual writer's status in that hierarchy – the subtle but real pressures that oblige him or her to contribute to (or resist) these operations; the network of contesting forces that both mandate the production of philosophical (and all other) texts and legislate the abiding and often unambiguous ways in which these texts are used in society; the broader socio-political arrangements which determine the convergence of textual, personal, and institutional authority; the strategies and apparatuses of bureaucratic control and administration in whose legitimation the intellectual as much as the political functionary participates.

In short, Derrida occludes the world itself as we have been describing it. Having made the duplicity of the text palpably visible, he fails to make visible the equally duplicitous transactions it carries out as a conduit for certain policies, strategies, and protocols which regulate its manifestly worldly energy within the structure of "circumstance, time, place, and society."[90] Foucault's entire project has been to uncover textual duplicity as well as its duplicitous deployment in the world:

> Whereas Derrida's theory of textuality brings criticism to bear on a signifier freed from any obligation to a transcendental signified, Foucault's theories move from a consideration of the signifier to a description of the signifier's place, a place rarely innocent, dimensionless, or without the affirmative authority of discursive discipline. In other words, Foucault is concerned with describing the force by which the signifier occupies a place, so that in [for example] *Discipline and Punish* he can show how penal discourse in its turn was able to assign felons to their places in the structural, administrative, psychological, and moral economy of the prison's panoptic architecture.[91]

Said traces Derrida's weakness to an unadvertised but self-serving involuntarism that at once launches and scuttles his entire project. By obviating the transitivity of such potent ideas as presence, meaning, and identity; by at once pronouncing them fictional in advance and invalidating their operational utility in socio-historical reality; by radically foreclosing the possibility of any purchase on the text from the outside; by putting all these interdictions in place and all the while pursuing textual minutiae, Derrida permanently brackets off both the *intentional force* of all texts – their will to power – and their *place* in the world, a place they occupy precisely because of that will. At the same time, Derrida's own authorial intention – his cogito – is smuggled into the text, a move that the deconstructive footwork, which is at bottom nothing but an endlessly recycled series of efficient tautologies, both enacts and disavows by fiat. Said equates Derrida's privileging of undecidabilities with theology – a negative one, to be sure, but not the less binding for that, given the dogma that has been built around him by his disciples.

The critique of Foucault comes in the wake of Said's own appropriation of Foucauldian ideas in much of his own work, including *Beginnings* and *Orientalism*. And, as I pointed out earlier in this chapter, Foucault's reflections on discursivity and power are crucial to the argument of textual worldliness. Still, however, even as early *Beginnings* we were able to detect a certain degree of latent dissatisfaction on Said's part with the hidebound rigidity of some of Foucault's assumptions. That dissatisfaction becomes explicit here. Said targets three closely related shortcomings in Foucault's "theoretical overtotalization."[92] First, Foucault "is unable to deal with, or provide an account of historical change" which is not governed by a strict regime of rules.[93] His version of history – and his conception of historicity in general – at once overemphasizes dramatic change in history and overtextualizes historical understanding. In other words, by collapsing temporality into a rule-governed, spatialized field of discourse and power, Foucault reconstructs a successive series of archival fields and transformations which – though overlaid with thick, diffuse detail – establish rigid regularities incapable of accommodating the vast range of possible variations in historico-cultural changes. Foucault disregards the fluidity of the moment; the local drama of specific situations, cultures, and transformations – including uncertainties, hesitations, and sudden consolidations; the particularity of cadence and destination; the variously organized arrangements; and the lived tensions between the past, present, and future. He cannot explain, for example, the experiential dynamic – the pressure points, the limits, the losses and gains, etc. – that obtains in a given cultural domain as a result of the interplay between strategies of socio-political combat and the palpable differences in the pace of change. He can't account, that is, for, the relationship between, on the one hand, long periods of stability, stretches of decline and exhaustion, and moments of crisis, and, on the other, the contending sociopolitical forces and societal change in general.

I am extrapolating from Said's cursory rebuke of Foucault, but as his attention to culture-as-hegemony and his abiding interest in individual autonomy have shown, he is insisting, I think, that Foucault's epistemic uniformities and mutations are too rigid to form the basis for a more reflexive, nuanced understanding of epochal change as experienced by those caught up in it, an understanding sensitive to broad movements as well as local conditions and specific situations. "Gramsci," Said tells us at one point, would find Foucault's Borgesian history "uncongenial. He would certainly appreciate the fineness of Foucault's archeologies but would find it odd that they make not even a nominal allowance for emergent movements, and none for revolutions, counterhegemony, or historical blocks."[94]

Second, Foucault offers an account of modernity which alerts us to the pervasiveness and surreptitiousness of power but simply disregards the often insidious human motivation behind it. Power, Said insists, is not an impersonal, invisible substance that, like the air we breathe, is at once everywhere and nowhere. Nor does it inhere only in a rarefied space called discourse which disperses it – democratically, as it were – in such a manner that its effects are felt in identical ways by all those involved in it: "power can be made analogous neither to a spider's web without the spider nor to a smoothly functioning flow diagram; a great deal of power remains in such coarse items as the relationship between ruler and ruled, wealth and privilege, monopolies of coercion, and the central state aparatus."[95] In other words, despite Foucault's annihilation of agency, power is exercised by identifiable groups and for specific political and economic ends, and the convergence of discourse and power that Foucault so ably describes takes place precisely because of this fact: dominant groups realize that power cannot always be dispensed from the barrel of a gun – that, to be effective, it has to be legitimized, camouflaged, rendered palatable. That is to say, the most rarefied type of discourse may act as a conduit for such crude passions as ambition and greed, which – however much they may be disavowed, decontaminated, disguised, or clothed in the language of righteousness, reason, and the like – can never be made to lose their true stripes. In short, power is always profoundly motivated – no matter where it resides and what configuration it assumes. More precisely, as the Marxist tradition which Foucault cavalierly dismisses has insisted all along, the exercise of power is inextricably entwined with the operations of ideology, and ideological arrangements always privilege certain groups – call them classes, if you like – and demote others. Another name for these "others" is victims.

Finally – and this is strictly speaking a corollary to the preceding two points – Foucault, according to Said, fails to realize that where there is power, there is resistance, and resistance implies a change for the better. This particular point is of course crucial to Said's understanding of the radical critic's place in society: as a doubly alienated intellectual – one who, though professionally affiliated to the great institutions of high culture in the West, is obliged both by his subaltern filiation and by his commitment to human dignity to effect a trenchant critique of that culture's insidious conservatism and imperialism – he is unwilling to surrender freedom of intention and action to the bureaucratic machinery of impersonalized power. According to Said, by universalizing power, by inflating it to such Spinozist proportions, Foucault has failed to provide a point of purchase – a lever – for the oppositional critical intellectual or for the victims of power. Hence, power is characterized as a panoptically structured totality that swallows up all agency, an omnipotence that no one can challenge or escape from. That view, suggests Said, is simply not defensible either historically or philosophically. Likewise, Foucault's dystopian vision precludes the possibility of any struggle for a less dismal tomorrow.

Foucault, Said maintains, should understand that history does not make itself, nor does it always move on its bad side; he should also realize that he is not in possession of Truth unmediated: "There is . . . a sensible difference between Hope and hope, just as there is between the Logos and words; we must not let Foucault get away with confusing them with each other, nor with letting us forget that history does not get made without work, intention, resistance, effort, or conflict, and that none of these things is silently absorbable into the micronetworks of power."[96] Said, then, finds Foucault's determinism and pessimism untenable – despite the efficiency and cogency of Foucault's critique. In other words, Said is distancing himself from Foucault's anti-humanism, a virulent form of cynicism that blights recent French theory, taking its severest form in Foucault's analytics.

As I pointed out earlier in the chapter, Said's chiding of Foucault has drawn a sharp response from Paul Bové. Bové, who has also found fault with *Orientalism*,[97] does not present a sustained analysis of (as distinct from brief allusions to) Said's various explications, evaluations, and appropriations of Foucauldian insights. Rather he restricts his remarks about Said's alleged anti-Foucauldian bias to what he calls "a coda," a brief discussion at the end of "Traveling Theory" where Said offers most of the critical remarks I have summarized above. Such a narrow focus allows Bové to reduce what is in fact a very complex critical reception to a drastically simplified thesis honed specifically for polemical purposes: that Said's attack on Foucault is at bottom an attempt to score points against the competition; that the assault has very little to do with the soundness (or lack thereof) of Foucault's insights – since Said himself has extracted considerable mileage out of them; that the real problem here is Said's agonism (and – Bové gently suggests – perhaps envy); that, because Foucault's ideas have gained wide currency, they are seen by Said as a threat to his own standing and agenda; that he subtly distorts Foucault's message the better to show himself in a positive light; that Said's deficiencies and excesses are none other than those of a delusional character well known in the history of ideas: the sublime, hubristic intellectual of critical humanism, whose addiction to utopian fantasies has remained incurable despite the disabusements of history. According to Bové, Said's characterization of criticism as an "unstoppable" commitment to finding alternatives is, when all is said and done, nothing more than a self-promoting project intended by Said to accomplish two related objectives: to enhance his own status vis-à-vis other intellectuals and to maintain the collective privilege of intellectuals in general:

> At the risk of being reductive, let me be as clear as possible: despite its oppositional commitments, Said's image of critical consciousness is essentially a legitimation of the status quo of intellectual life; imagining alternatives means competing against other intellectuals and their work; being "unstoppable" means being free to reposition oneself whenever the felt need to preserve authority or identity requires it; and judging theories on the basis of their "insurgent" power means granting the intellectual and self-interested judge an unfortunate amount of authority. And in all, this adds up to a model of intellectual life, more revealing of the current state of intellectual life than any *specific* image of the intellectual offered as legitimate by any critic at any given time.[98]

What is remarkable about Bové's summation is not so much its polemical assertiveness (this kind of combativeness is very common these days) as the fact that it is based largely on assumptions drawn from a few pages of Said's vastly complicated work. Said's difficult, often idiosyncratic methodology; the multiplicity of topics he has treated in *The World* and elsewhere; the various relationships that obtain between these topics; his strategic, highly nuanced expositions of other thinkers' ideas; the problems of history, theory, and culture and their complex interactions with ideology and criticism – all these matters are pretty much ignored by Bové in the heat of polemical battle. His defense of Foucault, his chosen intellectual, against what he considers to be a malign assault somehow obliges him to disregard not only these broad concerns but also the fact that Said is indeed highly appreciative of Foucault's enormous contribution to modern thought in ways I have tried to illustrate.

To be fair, Bové is not always as harsh on Said as he is in *Intellectuals in Power*. On the contrary, he has written about Said in glowing terms on a number of occasions. In a recent issue of *Boundary 2* (edited by Bové) which was entirely devoted to Said, Bové makes this generous assessment of Said's critical career: "Said's work embodies three values essential to intellectual responsibility: breadth and depth of knowledge, historical and scholarly rigor, and a profound basis in political morality of a kind that alone makes civilization possible. Minus any one of these virtues intellectuals become clerks, professionals with specialized interests, and career ambitions."[99] Elsewhere, Bové offers a highly favorable review of *Culture and Imperialism* and defends Said against ideologically motivated attacks (by the likes of Edward Alexander, for example).[100] And yet it is not terribly clear – to me at any rate – what divergent premises and assumptions have enabled Bové to make all these conflicting evaluations of Said's writing. What values, for example, does *Culture and Imperialism* (described by Bové as "a monumental book"[101]) embody in contradistinction to *The World, the Text, and the Critic* or *Orientalism*? My intention is not to impugn Bové's sincerity or perspicacity. Nor am I insisting that any or all of Said's writings, polemical or otherwise, are beyond blame: as I have noted repeatedly, Said's combination of agonistic dialectic and archaeology/genealogy can lead to all kinds of torsions which can be viewed either as unnecessary – and ultimately symptomatic – obfuscations or as timely interventions which help defamiliarize normalized dogmas. Either way, however, they are interpretive challenges that require careful study. Unfortunately, most of Said's interlocutors – hostile or sympathetic – have shown little inclination for the kind of rigorous, judicious analysis which would alone lead to a more insightful decision about his work – a problem which has helped create what I have been calling a misrecognition. More will be said about the consequences of this misrecognition in various contexts. At

this point, however, I would like to shift the focus to Said's reflections
on contemporary American criticism.

Said's evaluation of contemporary American criticism has a sharp
edge to it. Consider the following passage:

> As it is now practiced and as I treat it, criticism is an academic thing, located
> for the most part away from the questions that trouble the reader of a daily
> newspaper ... [We] have reached the stage at which specialization and pro-
> fessionalization, allied with cultural dogma, barely sublimated ethnocentrism
> and nationalism, as well as a surprisingly insistent quasi-religious quietism,
> have transported the professional and academic critic of literature – the most
> focused and intensely trained interpreter of texts produced by the culture –
> into another world altogether. In that relatively untroubled and secluded
> world there seems to be no contact with the world of events and societies.
> Instead, contemporary criticism is an institution for publicly affirming the
> values of our, that is, European, dominant elite culture, and for privately
> setting loose the unrestrained interpretation of a universe defined in advance
> as the endless misreading of a misinterpretation. The result has been the
> regulated, not to say calculated, irrelevance of criticism, except as an adorn-
> ment to what the power of modern industrial society transacts: the hegemony
> of militarism and a new cold war, the depoliticization of the citizenry, the
> overall compliance of the intellectual class to which critics belong.[102]

The polemicism of the passage appears to be warranted by the discrepancy that Said sees between what serious academic critics ought to
have been doing, on the one hand, and on the other, what the literary-
critical profession has in fact become "ever since Arnold covered
critical writing with the mantle of cultural authority and reactionary
political quietism."[103] To phrase the point differently, a process of
decontamination and idealization which has been gathering pace for
more than a century has neutralized critical energy, substituting what
could be called a narrow ethics of professionalism for the broader
ethics of critical responsibility and involvement in society at large.

According to Said, contemporary American criticism, even in its
ostensibly revolutionary versions, has largely turned into an apolitical,
ahistorical affair written by – and for – the members of a small,
privileged community ensconced in academia. The assumption war-
ranting this sort of intellectual labor is apparently that literary texts
deliver signification at a locale safely distanced from socio-political
reality and from what is presumed to be the coarser aspects of life. In
this etherealized, jealously policed zone, the critic can go about the
important business of codifying "great," "original" works of literature, explicating, unpacking, and evaluating them for aesthetic or
moral consumption. In the Anglo-American context, this critical bias

has historically led to what Said describes as literary refinement – a form of belletristic writing marked as much by intense attention to the formal features of the literary work as by an almost total vacuity of theoretical insight and an almost equally total disregard for the historical, social, and political dimensions of literature. This, according to Said, is largely the legacy of literary modernism and (by implication) New Criticism. It could at times be brilliant (witness Northrop Frye, whose archetypal criticism is seen by Said as a species of formalism);[104] it could also occasionally be rigorously technical (Said cites Richards and Empson);[105] on the whole, however, literary refinement was "dull and enervating": "a huge agglomeration of various literary industries" grew up around Joyce, Conrad, Pound, and Eliot, churning out "a virtually unassimilable secondary elaboration of a body of [modernist] writings universally accepted as primary."[106]

One consequence of all this activity, Said argues, is that these primary texts gradually came to represent, not just a specifiable literary style which happened to be described as modernist, but the very idea of literary modernity itself (or the irreducibly new and hence original) – a belief which persisted long after the modernist writers had all become part of history: "in a unique and perhaps puzzling way then, literary modernity was associated ... not with the present but with an immediate past which was endlessly validated and revalidated."[107] Another consequence is that critical practice thus understood was (and continues to be) undertaken for a professedly modest end; the patently derivative text of criticism was presumed to be a supplement which would stand parallel to the literary work but could never match it in importance: "The point to be made is that this body of secondary elaborations ... was demystified from the start." Literary refinement "pretended to no illusion about itself; it was secondary, harmless, and ideologically neutral, except within the internal confines of the more and more professionalized profession."[108]

An interesting set of questions now present themselves. How does one account for this deliberate lowering of intellectual horizons? Why was it possible for criticism to be reduced to the role of literary handmaid? Granted that critical evaluation is normally occasioned by an event (textual or otherwise) which predates it; granted that it is necessarily a late-arriving, temporally secondary enactment, does it therefore have to be qualitatively secondary too? Why was it that the idea of critique – a powerfully corrosive form of intellectual energy which (at least since Kant's Copernican revolution) had been deployed against various kinds of socio-cultural orthodoxy – could so easily have been converted into the aesthetic assessment of a few literary texts? Exactly what does criticism conceived in this manner ulti- mately amount to anyway? Why would anyone in his or her right mind invest so much time and effort in something which, on the face of it, didn't seem to have much relevance or weight?

These questions bring us to an important factor alluded to in the passage I cited earlier: the strategic (apparently historically specific) transformation of the critical profession, not just into a relatively harmless activity going on in an obscure corner of academia, but into what Said calls "an adornment" to "the power of modern industrial society." In other words, literary refinement, along with other forms of "high" culture, served from the modernist period through the Sixties (and in a transformed guise even beyond) an unacknowledged hegemonic function: this laborious, seemingly secondary activity in reality constituted a crucial component in a much larger ideological program by virtue of which literary interpreters occupied a carefully circumscribed intellectual space where certain financial and symbolic rewards accrued to them while certain constraints were imposed on them. On this view, the literary-critical tradition would count as something quite other than a relatively impracticable corpus of writing fussed about by a few professors and their protégés. Rather it was part of the Great Canon of the West – that immense reservoir of unadulterated wisdom stretching from Homer to Joyce and beyond. It almost automatically followed that this filiatively received repository of knowledge should be venerated, its flanks protected, its enligh- tening message enhanced, its hieratic injunctions enforced.

Two obvious conclusions can be drawn from all this with respect to the issue of worldliness and the intellectuals' responsibilities. One is that the practitioners of literary refinement cannot, strictly speaking, be described as *critics* – if by "criticism" one means the kind of demystification, de-definition, conceptual dismantling, and (direct or indirect) political action carried out in different ways by such thinkers as Gramsci, Williams, Foucault, and Derrida. On the contrary, it would be more accurate to characterize Anglo-American formalists generally as guardians of elite culture in the Arnoldian sense, although most of them might not be as belligerently assertive about their role as Arnold was. In other words, their interpretive efforts are not merely exegetical in the narrow sense of interpreting texts; they are also acts of profound affirmation, celebration, and redemption – what Said sardonically describes (in *Beginnings*) as a "manifesto of delight"[109] in the culture one identifies with. The literary interpreter has become an active, though in some respects undercover, agent working on behalf of "high" culture – one who delimits, authorizes, authenticates, and sanitizes what properly belongs to "literature" or "the humanities" in accordance with well-rehearsed disciplinary protocols.

The underlying assumption is that – quite aside from the financial gains – the transmission of elite culture is in and of itself an edifying experience inasmuch as the professor-interpreter believes himself to be accomplishing two goals at the same time: cultivating a finely honed aesthetic and ethical sensibility in himself and his young students while also discharging an august civilizational mission. Perhaps ultimately more insidious, this combination of idealization and internalized censorship has helped create (and sustain) the vast, osmotic hegemony we discussed earlier, a complex arrangement whereby potentially troublesome intellectuals are effectively defanged by the culture at large in return for creature comforts and other kudos. "My disappointment," Said laments at one point, " ... stems from a conviction that it is our technical skill as critics and intellectuals that the culture has wanted to neutralize, and if we have cooperated in this project, perhaps unconsciously, it is because that is where the money has been."[110] In short, "the refining critic" strengthens (rather than exposes) the supple ideology of liberal humanism:

> What is created as a result is what can reasonably be called a liberal consensus: the formal restricted analysis of literary aesthetic works validates the culture, the culture validates the humanist, the humanist the critic, and the whole enterprise the State. Thus authority is maintained by virtue of the cultural process, and anything more than refining power is denied the refining critic. By the same token, it has been true that "literature" as a cultural agency has become more and more blind to its actual complicities.[111]

Quietism, specialization, elaboration, non-interference, rarefaction – all these devoutly observed rituals of literary refinement, suggests Said, were (and are) on the one hand ways of enhancing the critic's personal standing and strengthening the university's institutional authority while at the same time increasing the normative weight of the culture as a whole, and on the other comfortable cushions and screens keeping out the world's unpleasant din but also letting in the considerable benefits which the political institutions made (and continue to make) available by virtue of their professed worldliness and the overwhelming geopolitical power of the culture at large. The second implication relates to the canon; this is what Said has to say about it: The "great texts [of the West] have an authority that compels respectful attention not so much by virtue of their content but because they are old or they have power, they have been handed on in time or seem to have no time, and they have traditionally been revered, as priests, scientists, or efficient bureaucrats have taught."[112] So much for the innate superiority of the "great texts," "great theories," and "great teachers"!

Thus far, my discussion has been restricted to Said's critique of what might justifiably be dismissed as a straw man. Home-made Anglo-American formalism has repeatedly come under fire ever since the Sixties, and even though Said has on occasion defended the New Critics and their achievements (or at least their initial rebellion against what they considered to be exclusionism and academicism),[113] there is a sense in which he could, in the context of *The World*, be open to the charge that he is beating on a dead horse. After all, one could argue, critical theory has wrought tremendous transformation in the way literary and other texts are interpreted. Thanks to the enormous collective talent and erudition of such critics as Geoffrey Hartman, Harold Bloom, J. Hillis Miller, Jonathan Culler, Frederic Jameson, and Paul de Man (among others), highly sophisticated European philosophical models have been domesticated for the Anglo-American market. These methodologies cover a wide range of epistemological assumptions, techniques of analysis, and ethico-political commitments – they include, for example, phenomenological, hermeneutic, linguistic, and historical models. Surely Said is well aware of these new developments, since he himself has been one of the importers and interpreters of literary theory. We have now arrived at the heart of Said's indictment of the literary-critical enterprise.

For, as I have already noted, by far the most caustic passages in *The World, the Text, and the Critic* are concerned with the reception of literary theory in the United States. Said's major complaint against the practitioners of literary theory can be summarized thus: on the one hand, these critics indulge in the fantasy that their efforts are contributing to the emergence of a genuine counter-hegemonic authority and effective opposition. This kind of talk in turn galvanizes remnants of the old guard, who put up a spirited resistance in the name of "humanism, tact, good sense, and the like."[114] In this considerable exertion on both sides, there is a good deal of exaggeration and excess baggage – excess of interpretive labor, of claims to the ultimate definitive formula or deconstructive key, of polemical massacres and bad blood, of rhetorical ingenuity and verbal fog. On the other hand, in their actual practice of criticism, theorists are almost indistinguishable from their presumed adversaries: more precisely, they have helped install a voracious, theoretically armed species of hermeticism which not only replicates and fortifies the old formalism of the New Critics but also reaffirms the profoundly conservative politics of elite culture:

> [W]hat I am trying to say ... is that the oppositional manner of new New Criticism does not accurately represent its ideas and practice, which, after all is said and done, further solidify and guarantee the social structure and the culture that produced it. Deconstruction, for example, is practiced as if Western culture was being dismantled; semiotic analysis argues that its work amounts to a scientific and hence social revolution in the sciences of man. The examples can be multiplied, but I think what I am saying will be readily understood. There is oppositional debate without real opposition. In this setting, even Marxism has often been accommodated into the wild exigencies of rhetoric while surrendering its true radical prerogatives.[115]

The sharp tone of this and similar passages scattered throughout the fourteen articles of the book is in part evidence of disillusionment – an insider's feeling that the powerful energies made available by theoretical and historical insight have been dammed up, corralled, and frozen so that they can be converted into self-stabilizing systems.

Said does in passing mention some of the "salutary" consequences of theory. At one point he suggests that a certain element of fuzziness and sentimentalism which had formed part of the repertoire of English studies has been swept away by a far more rigorous international terminology that "makes an extremely sharp break between the community of critics and the general public."[116] Henceforth, instead of making "empty rhetorical testimonials merely proclaiming a work's greatness, humanistic worth, and such," critics will be obliged "to talk seriously and technically and precisely about the text."[117] It is also the case that a process of deregionalization has accompanied the arrival of the new theories, as hitherto autonomous fiefdoms are overrun by interdisciplinary collations, confluences, conflicts, and cross-overs. Hence, it is not unusual these days for literary critics to appropriate non-literary texts for close reading, while at the same time also deploying methodologies derived from entirely different disciplines. The shortcomings of contemporary theory are therefore not exactly the same as those of literary refinement: theoretical naiveté wedded to formalistic minutiae and pontifical opinion.

The problem, according to Said, is that – in the process of this

theoretically informed interpretation – the critical, literary, philosophical, and other texts are all hijacked into a seamless, polysemous
wilderness known as textuality, where endless iterations and refractions echo and displace one another ad absurdum. The result is that,
whether as hermeneutic fields; as detachable idiolects; as structural
elements supporting a master-code; or as instances of a wayward play
of ecriture giving birth to aporias, misrecognitions, and other metaphysical pleasures, texts are consigned to their own autonomous locus
where they are hermetically sealed from the socio-political context in
which all literary, critical, and philosophical productions and recep-
tions take place. It is this self-contained but internally expandable
universe – a universe where "unrestrained interpretation" is aligned
with a severely constricting brand of formalism and *de rigeur* terminology – that Said designates as a form of "functionalism":

> A functionalist attitude pays too much attention to the text's formal opera-
> tions, but far too little to its materiality. In other words, the range assumed
> for the text's operations tends to be either wholly internal or wholly rheto-
> rical, with the critic serving as a sort of one-person *Rezeptionsgeschichte*. On the
> one hand, the text is imagined as working alone within itself, as containing a
> privileged, or if not privileged then unexamined and *a priori* principle of
> internal coherence, *Zusammenhang*; on the other hand, the text is considered as
> in itself a sufficient cause for certain precise effects it has on an ideal reader. In
> both cases, the text does not remain but is metamorphosed into what Stanley
> Fish has called a self-consuming artifact. A perhaps unforeseen consequence is
> that the text becomes idealized, essentialized, instead of remaining as the
> special kind of cultural object it really is, with a causation, durability, and
> social presence quite its own.[118]

The possibility that the language employed in these texts is entwined
with the world of bodies, objects, agencies, and institutions; that it
can be (and has been) used to represent or misrepresent aspects of that
world; that men and women happen to utilize it as a handy tool of
communication (though not always successfully or in good faith); that
texts are caught up in a dialectical, ongoing socio-historical drama
some of whose many vectors we have already examined – all these facts
are, according to Said, almost completely ignored by the advocates of
theory. In effect, the cultural currency of texts – their embeddedness
in, embodiment of, and transitivity for cultural authority – is
somehow alchemically abstracted and made to undergo a remarkable
disappearing act. Said notes that – thanks to the prevailing functionalist attitude – even phenomenological critics (like Georges
Poulet) have been obliged to acknowledge "before anything else the

eccentricity, contingency, and instability of [the] self, its mutability and powerlessness before the text."[119] Likewise, historically alert theorists like Harold Bloom recover an almost exclusively literary version of history. Among the American critical theorists, Said singles out Paul de Man for valorizing the most rigorous, and yet most peculiarly crippling, brand of all formalisms: "The literary work for [de Man] stands in a position of almost unconditional superiority over historical facticity, not by virtue of its power but by virtue of its admitted powerlessness; its originality resides in the premise that it has disarmed itself 'from the start,' as if by having said in advance that it had no illusions about itself and its fictions it directly accedes to the realm of acceptable form."[120] For de Man, Said argues, the world has pretty much ceased to exist; if it "exists at all, it must have ended up in or as a book" à la Mallarmé. Literature, on the other hand, "expresses only itself" or else nothing at all.[121]

Said is a bit ambivalent about the causal relationship between the pre-theoretical and post-theoretical formalisms: at one point he suggests that the ideology of refinement is so strong and resilient that it has "absorbed" and hence neutralized even the powerful challenge of radical theory; elsewhere, however, he argues that theory itself – or more precisely its appropriation by self-censoring critics – has put in place an entirely new orthodoxy which is all the more beguiling and persuasive because of its claims to compelling new insights. The important point, though, is that, in Said's estimation, the theorists, no less than the refining critics before them, are guardians of elite culture – protestations to the contrary notwithstanding. They are every bit as protective of the canon as any Arnoldian now or in the past; they are committed to rarefaction, compartmentalization, and idealization; above all, they have made their peace with "the prevailing polity." In this undignified sell-out, a distinguished civil institution, namely the university, acts as the site of hegemonic transaction, the ground where the pre-emption, capture, and domestication of ideologically dangerous species of knowledge like critical theory take place. As a result of this compromise, the possibility of deploying serious, advanced, academic criticism in the public arena is practically obviated – leaving the field to the narcotizing, instant discourse of the mass media and to the rhetoric of politicians on the stump.

Critical Consciousness, Methodology, and History

We have brought the discussion to a point where we can examine more closely what it is that Said designates as criticism properly understood. It should now be clear that, of the three terms that together constitute the title of the book, the word "critic" – that who professes criticism – is considered by Said to be the most crucial, or at least of most immediate concern. For this reason (or perhaps in spite of it), the idea of criticism or critical consciousness presents arguably the most intractable interpretive challenge in a book that has more than its share of eccentric concepts. The reason for this difficulty is that the Saidian notion of criticism is not strictly identifiable with any one specific political or theoretical viewpoint, contrary to what has recently been suggested by some commentators.[122] Rather it involves a multiplicity of disjunctions which inscribe themselves as irreducible paradoxes: it is intended to act as an insurrenctionary form of energy – an index of congenital crisis that at once unmasks and dissolves dogmatic ossification; yet at times it acquires the properties of a measuring rod, a positive criterion. It partakes of methodology, often very eclectically; yet it is meant to negate – or at least problematize – method as such: perhaps it would be more precise to say that method is turned inside out, upside down, or against itself. Criticism is enjoined to furnish knowledge (about mind, world, text, etc.), yet the relationship of that knowledge to the best-known – and most often approved – epistemological models is emphatically contentious. It is historically and culturally situated, conditions which make it necessarily contingent, local, specific; yet Said repeatedly insists that criticism can (and ought to) cross boundaries, sever intellectual hobbles, appeal to universal values.

The list could be extended, but the point to be made is that criticism is never at one with itself; one could say that it is both p and not-p, breaching the "law of non-contradiction", one of the most basic principles of the kind of coherentist logic often touted as an important desideratum for a successful argument. Questions like the following are therefore inevitably bound to arise: Is such a slippery, nomadic concept useful at all? Isn't Said, as it were, continually cutting the ground from under his feet at the same time that he is proposing what he claims to be a viable critical project?

One way of responding to these questions is to consider the idea of criticism as it is treated in *The World* in the light of my explication of

Said's earlier texts. I have repeatedly stressed these connections between Said's writings, and I don't intend to tarry with them at this late stage of my study. What needs particular emphasis here is that "criticism" perfectly illustrates what I have been calling Said's own technique of trouble – namely, the dramatized confrontation of agonistic dialectic and archaeology/genealogy. More than any other single concept used by Said, including the very important idea of beginnings, criticism approximates that technique in its starkest, most unqualified form. Applying to Said's own writing an observation that he has made about Conrad's narratives, we could say that criticism names the site where "the motivated, the occasional, the methodical, and the rational are brought together with the aleatory, the unpredictable, the inexplicable."[123] It is no accident, therefore, that to him true "criticism is reducible neither to a doctrine nor to a political position on a particular question,"[124] that it is of necessity – by definition as it were – a declaration of opposition both to theoretical closure and to cultural dogma. It is no accident either that, even though leftist thought generally and more specifically Marxism – the tradition which historically made it possible for the very question of ideology critique to be broached at all – have provided Said with powerful tools (in our immediate context Lukacsian insights are vital, as we shall see later), he has by no means restricted himself to that friendly climate, an attitude that has fallen afoul of some Marxist critics.[125] In fact, he has often found it necessary to go to great interpretive lengths in order to salvage – or amplify – the radical streak in the writings of thinkers who have traditionally been cast in a conservative, and in some cases profoundly reactionary, mold: in Said's estimation, Conrad, Vico, Auerbach, and Swift at their best instantiate the kind of reflexive openness, resourcefulness, and drama that he considers to be absolutely indispensable to any thought worthy of being called criticism.

Said's attempt to de-domesticate Swift is particularly instructive in this regard. Swift, Said tells us in a passage I cited in an earlier chapter, "represents the critical consciousness in a raw form, a large-scale model of the dilemmas facing the contemporary critical consciousness that has tended to be too cloistered and too attracted to easy systematizing."[126] Said is certainly aware that Swift was, as he puts it, a "tragically compromised"[127] figure, a highly controversial thinker whose many serious flaws cannot be ignored or easily dismissed. At one point, he observes that nearly "all of Swift's work does in fact support a fairly strict, not to say uninteresting, conservative philosophy" which revolves around "the loss of normality" in human

beings.[128] Said, in other words, recognizes that there is a good deal of
validity to the charge often made against Swift – that his almost
unmitigated misanthropy so infects his thought that it is difficult to
extract out of it any insights unsullied by grim negativism. And yet it
is in the multiple implications of that very negativity that Said finds a
much-needed antidote to the tameness, amnesia, and pretension that
he detects in contemporary criticism.

In Said's view, Swift's work exemplifies critical consciousness in
action in two complementary ways: methodologically and socio-
politically. With respect to the first, Swift's writing epitomizes
ultimate resistance to the kind of restorative interpretation that takes
the form of explicative clarity, neat alignments, and putative judgements. What Said calls "the restorative method" is, in broad terms, a
totalizing formula or an overarching principle which – whether biographical, psychological, historical, or formal – empowers a critic to
deliver the object of interpretation whole, without residue or excess.
That is to say, through a process of what might be characterized as
conceptual reduction in reverse, the critic effects the conversion of a
given author's writing into the constitutive elements of a "literal
pretext" where every detail fits its assigned place. According to Said,
restorative critics approach texts "as problematic in every way except
as texts"; exploit temporality as an ordering device that helps establish
continuities; and place "text, pretext, and criticism" in a common site
"in which important hidden things become visible, in which nothing
crucial is lost, and in which whatever merits saying can be said and
connected."[129] This way the author's corpus of writing is restored to a
definitive "text," "a chronology of events," "a set of characteristics,"
"an age," and so on.[130] Said observes that, although it can be
"extraordinarily absorptive and catholic," the restorative method can
also "become reductive and exclusive."[131] His immediate point in this
context, though, is that too many critics have made the mistake of
applying this essentially appropriative methodology to Swift despite
the fact that it is fundamentally unsuited to him. Why unsuited?
Because his writing dramatizes the extreme tension between "the
anarchy of resistance" and the conservatism of "tory order":

> His work can be approached and characterized as the highly dramatic
> encounter between the anarchy of resistance to the written page and the
> abiding tory order of the page. This is the most literally basic form of
> encounter: it is capable of great multiplication, going from the difference
> between waste and conservation, absence and presence, obscenity and dec-
> orum, to the negative and positive dimensions of language, imagination,

unity, and identity. The life of such an encounter is, so to speak, the active content of Swift's mind as we are able to grasp it in its essential resistance to any fixed boundaries.[132]

Such confrontations are the very life and breath of critical thought as conceived by Said, the very stuff of which it is made. Another way of phrasing this point is to say that critical consciousness is not just diametrically opposed to orthodoxy as such; it is actually in close and (potentially) total combat with multiple dogmas. In other words, Swift may have been theoretically handicapped and historically hemmed in by his immediate historical circumstances. But (suggests Said) he was far in advance *as a critic* of today's garden-variety critical scribbler.

If one takes the resistance thesis as an unavoidable point of departure, then the "canonical view" of Swift's politics and general vision of life is greatly problematized. Said's aim here is to overturn, or at least substantially qualify, what he suggests to be two related dogmas: (a) that Swift is permanently identifiable as a Tory satirist who held a stable set of political beliefs which he consistently defended, and (b) that he was a disenchanted teleological thinker whose pessimistic ruminations on humanity can be broadly described as systematically worked out philosophical positions. Swift, Said insists, can best be seen as a "local activist, a columnist, a pamphleteer, a caricaturist";[133] more specifically, he was a reactive writer most of whose texts wear their irreducible occasionality and worldliness precisely to the extent that each of them was deployed as an interventionary instrument at a particular moment, for a particular purpose, and in a particular manner. For that reason, they are strictly speaking neither creative literary works in the modern sense nor long-view, definitive reflections offered by a "pipesmoking armchair philosopher."[134]

Seen in this revisionary light, much of what we find disturbing or inexplicable in Swift can be accounted for: "his [alleged] misanthropic craziness";[135] "his dryness, severity, [and] intensity";[136] his tendency to turn things into their exact opposites; his intense awareness about the power, limitation, and debasement of language-*as-event*; his use of personae, digressions, and other extreme forms of irony; the great capacity of his work to defy generic classification – these and similar Swiftian quirks can be interpreted, not as the symptoms of a peculiar sort of dislocation and obsession, but as part of a deliberate strategy to shock readers into recognition – a strategy adopted by someone who had come to witness (though not to possess) both the weight and authority of power and the misery which that power often inflicted on those (like the peasants in Ireland) who were unfortunate enough to become its victims: typically Swift greatly exaggerates "the implications of a book, a position, or a situation, all of which are otherwise likely to be mindlessly digested,"[137] thereby raising his readers' consciousness to a high degree. It is this "agitational method" – a technique of extremes allowing for the use of excoriating satire in a manner that draws attention both to the occasion of an event and to the pertinence of what is being said about it "at that moment" – that Said characterizes as being paradigmatic of Swift's writing. To give us a more schematic understanding of Swift's technique, Said offers the following "three theses":

> (1) Swift has no reserve capital: his writing brings to the surface all he has to say. His fictions, his personae, his self-irony turn around the scandal ... that what is being said is being said at that moment, for that moment, by a creature of that moment ... (2) Swift is invariably attacking what he impersonates. In other words, his technique is to become the thing he attacks, which is normally not a message or a political doctrine but a style or a manner of discourse ... (3) Ahead of his critics, Swift is always aware – and troubles the reader with the awareness – that what he is doing above all is *writing* in a world of power.[138]

Said's sympathetic reading of Swift is not meant to remold this eighteenth-century satirist into the unlikely shape of a twentieth-century critic of ideology. On the contrary, his entire argument, which unfolds in two interfaced articles, in a sense moves in the *opposite* direction. Swift, Said reminds us, was a man of his time; and the issues, occasions, and problems which commanded his attention are separated from us by multiple historico-epistemic discontinuities and transformations. Perhaps equally important, they are also in a manner of speaking separated from each other by virtue of the unique particularity that each assumes as a direct consequence of Swift's anarchic method, a spontaneous technique which according to Said bestows total externality, specificity, and instantaneity on every text Swift wrote. It is this extremely radical historicism, which has an uncanny affinity with Nietzschean perspectivalism and Lacan's notion of refracted subjectivity, that Said invokes against Swift's detractors (Orwell, for example) – even as he himself acknowledges Swift's often repellent conservatism.

Still, however, Said's rescue of Swift from systematic appropriation by restorative critics is clearly intended as a long-overdue (re)activation of a radical form of intellectual energy. That is to say, Swift's critical challenge is an open challenge, one which is not restricted to his era but is also *ours* to confront: to the extent that he alerted readers to humanity's great potential for folly and delinquency; to the extent that his ire was always directed against "anything connected with human aggression or organized human violence"[139] – including war, conquest, colonialism, and the oppression of the poor; to the extent that he knew that his writing involved contestations of power in the world, to that extent Swift instantiates a model of intellectual agency which, in Said's estimation, is sorely missing in contemporary America. "To read Swift seriously," Said maintains, "is to try to apprehend a series of events in all their messy force, not to admire and then calmly to decode a string of high monuments. In addition, his own social role was that of the critic involved with, but never possessing, power: alert, forceful, undogmatic, ironic, unafraid of orthodoxies and dogmas, respectful of settled uncoercive community, anarchic in his sense of the range of alternatives to the status quo."[140]

It is that coexistence of awareness about worldly circumstance, principled intervention, methodological openness, and suspicion of dogma that Said commends not only in conservative thinkers like Swift, Conrad, and Auerbach, but also in liberals like I. F. Stone and Noam Chomsky, and in Marxists like Gramsci and Williams. Critical reflexivity of this kind is seen by Said as an empowering yet self-monitoring form of intentionality whose rhythms and transformations we have already examined in various contexts. Involving the dialectical activation of extreme irony with speculative freedom – a dialectic also operating in the material circumstances of space-time – critical intentionality has the capacity to negotiate between the local and the global, between affirmation and negation, between theoretical insight and resistance to theory, between history as burden and as opportunity, between culture as privilege and as life-enhancing community. In short, criticism names that which allows a given writer optimally to come to grips with distance – where "distance" is to be understood, not only geographically and culturally (as was the case, for example, with Auerbach's state of exile in Instanbul), but also historically, epistemologically, and politically. The entire problematic of strategically crossing (or erasing) boundaries is therefore entailed in the idea of criticism. It is an extremely difficult operation which few contemporary critics have been inclined to commit themselves to. And that brings us to Lukacs, theoretically the single most important thinker in Said's conception of criticism and its relationship to theory.

Said's reflections on Lukacs's early masterpiece, *History and Class Consciousness*, as well as its reception in later years by other Western Marxists, are offered in "Traveling Theory," one of the most influential but in my opinion least well-understood articles in *The World*. Apart from providing a cogent point of departure for nuanced investigations into the nomadic, endlessly transformable phenomenon of modern and contemporary critical theory,[141] the article has prompted some bemused comments. Critics often cite it to support the claim that Said's writing is shot through with "ambivalence" – without, however, shedding much light on the broader methodological strategy that this alleged ambivalence might be contributing to or for what reasons. The broad thesis of the article at first glance appears to be (and indeed in certain respects *is*) fairly traditional. Theories, Said tells us, undergo a change when they "travel" from one socio-historical climate to another. The reason for this mutation is that the difference – however small – between the inaugural conditions of a given theory and the circumstances of its later peregrinations takes the form of either accommodation, incorporation, or resistance, hence leading to a transformation of the theory itself. It is as an illustration of this relatively uncomplicated argument, which doesn't seem terribly different from countless other claims premised on such common places as zeitgeist, teleological progression, and epochal change, that Said introduces Lukacsian ideas and their impact on Lucien Goldmann and Raymond Williams.

As we unpack this dense, highly synoptic article, we gradually realize that this relaying transaction is being used by Said as a vehicle for an interacting – and sometimes antithetical – ensemble of theses all of which have been examined at one point or another in my discussion. To avoid any unnecessary repetition, I would like to restate them briefly and schematically: the irreducible situationality and occasionality of ideas (critical or otherwise) as distinct from – though not exclusive of – their capacity to cross boundaries, traverse distances, effect (or absorb) change; insurrectionary critical consciousness in contradistinction to reflective critical judgement; radical theoretical insight as opposed to theoretical elaboration and closure; and finally criticism (as suspicious consciousness, knowledge, practice, etc.) as distinct from – and in opposition to – the totalizations of system and culture. These are the major problematics dramatized by "Traveling Theory" in characteristic Saidian fashion – with ruptures, juxtapositions, turns, and loose ends working together in a methodical yet unpredictable way that makes an easy or appropriative reading of the article fairly difficult. It is particularly instructive that, in what might be called his own rereading of the article (in "Traveling Theory Reconsidered")[142] more than ten years after its appearance in *The World*, Said adds a radical new inflection to the original argument, an inflection which partakes of the interpretive attitude of *Culture and Imperialism*, published shortly before the revised article. Suffused with the Adornian-inspired idea of lateness that I discussed in an earlier chapter, "Traveling Theory Reconsidered" is more uncompromising in its emphasis on criticism-as-negation, more atonal than symphonic. But as we shall see presently, "Traveling Theory" itself remains vital to Said's conception of criticism.

Much of "Traveling Theory" is occupied with Lukacs's theoretical opposition between a reified bourgeois culture ripe for destruction and the insurgent proletarian energies conceived as the future instrument of that destruction – as well as the wholesale application, elaboration, and domestication of that theory by Goldmann. The distance – temporal, epistemological, cultural, political – traveled by the theory in its transplantation from a revolutionary situation in early twen-tieth-century Hungary to the staid academic setting of mid-twen-tieth-century France is considered crucial by Said: the theory loses its urgency – its sense of drama, immediacy, and missionary zeal – but also acquires the dimensions and paraphernalia of a systematic methodology – with all that this type of change entails for Said's understanding of critical theory. Said tells us that, in its original version (whose Hegelian–Weberian assumptions Lukacs later repu-diated in favor of "socialist realism"), the profound socio-political crises engendered by capitalism are transmuted into a powerful cri-tique of the system as a whole, and not just its specific failings. According to Lukacs, capitalism has the tendency to turn everything human agency undertakes, including thought, into quantifiable, mechanical objects measurable for their use-value in a market econ-omy. As a result, a dissociation (of subject from object, sentiment from reason, producer from product, etc.) manifests itself; the pro-cesses of socio-economic life congeal into multiple pathologies; and experience takes the form of articulation, fragmentation, and aliena-tion. Even human beings and their relationships with one another become object-like. In short, social reality is reified. As Said points out in the following passage, Lukacs's antidote for this state of ossi-fication and blockage is proletarian consciousness strategically trans-formed into powerful critical intelligence: "Consciousness goes beyond empirical givens and comprehends, without actually experiencing, history, totality, and society as a whole – precisely those unities that reification had both concealed and denied. At bottom, class consciousness is thought thinking its way through fragmentation to unity; it is also thought aware of its own subjectivity as something active, energetic, and, in a profound sense, poetic."[143] According to Said, Goldmann at once de-dramatizes Lukacs's theory and amplifies its totalistic tendencies.

In Goldmann's *Le Dieu caché*, a text in which he tries to demonstrate that Pascal's and Racine's writings served as a conduit for tragic Jansenist doctrines, "class consciousness has been changed to 'vision du monde,' something that is not an immediate, but a collective consciousness expressed in the works of highly gifted writers."[144] Goldmann effects this change by taking two interrelated steps, one quasi-metaphysical, the other historical: he operationalizes the idea of totality – itself the product of the sublational syntheses of Lukacs's (Hegelian-Marxian) dialectic – into a coherentist, determinative principle which foregrounds the unity thus posited rather than the smoldering crisis registered by thought. Having put this general logic in place, he now historicizes it by applying it to a specific period in French history which he presumes to have had its own unique vision – a sort of dominant ideology (in this case the theological beliefs of the Jansenists) – expressed in the works of great representative writers (an honor conferred on Pascal and Racine). This way, Goldmann establishes an interconnected series of correspondences between totality and its constituent parts, and Lukacs's revolutionary theory is stabilized into a static set of expressivist homologies: "for Lukacs theory originates as a kind of irreducible dissonance between mind and object, whereas for Goldmann theory is the homological relationship between individual part and coherent whole."[145] In short, Goldmann has converted a dynamic, transgressive theory into a restorative method.

The implications of this transformation for criticism, theory, and historical context are cast by Said along several axes which bring the distinctions and oppositions I alluded to earlier into sharp focus. One of these implications – perhaps the most obvious – concerns the academicization of critical theory and the attendant neutralization of its subversive power. In Said's estimation, Goldmann's appropriation amounts to a regrettable impoverishment of Lukacs's theory, a "degradation" (Said's term)[146] remarkably similar to those enacted by Anglo-American recipients of Continental thought over the past three decades or so. In both cases, the process of acclimating radical theory turns out to be little more than an exercise in academic formalization and routinization – an exercise Said sometimes describes as professionalization. As the cliché goes, the sting has been taken out of the theory, and as a result it has become docile, familiar, harmless. Despite the explicit or implicit claims made by both its proponents and its opponents that it continues to be a dangerous enemy of authority, the theory has been subjected to a strategy of ideological containment – a strategy which involves a calculated procedure of normalization, institutionalization, and marginalization. In effect, it has been academically ghettoized.

Could this downward revision of a once-revolutionary theory into a lackluster imitation have been prevented? Is this academic domestication inevitable as part of *any* theory's migration from the locale of its birth to other times and climes? Such questions might not arise at all if it weren't for the radically historicist accounting that Said offers for the above mutation:

> [I]t seems to me perfectly possible to judge misreadings (as they occur) as part of a historical transfer of ideas and theories from one setting to another. Lukacs wrote *for* as well as *in* a situation that produced ideas about consciousness and theory that are very different from the ideas produced by Goldmann in his situation. To call Goldmann's work a misreading of Lukacs', and then to go on immediately to relate that misreading to a general theory of interpretation as misinterpretation, is to pay no critical attention to history and to situation, both of which play an important determining role in changing Lukacs' ideas into Goldmann's. The Hungary of 1919 and post-World War II Paris are quite different environments. To the degree that Lukacs and Goldmann are read carefully, then to that precise degree we can understand the critical change – in time and in place – that occurs between one writer and another, both of whom depend on theory to accomplish a particular job of intellectual work. I see no need here to resort to the theory of limitless intertextuality as an Archimedean point outside the two situations. The particular voyage from Hungary to Paris, with all that entails, seems compelling enough, adequate enough for critical scrutiny, unless we want to give up critical consciousness for critical hermeticism.[147]

Considered in the light of what we have just noted about academicization, this is a remarkably odd passage. It has the immediate, and perhaps unintended, effect of saving Goldmann from conviction. This "ambivalence" elicits the following protest from Abdul R. JanMohamed, who (as I pointed out in the context of *Beginnings*) characterizes Said's criticism as a worldless exercise on cultural borders:

> [Goldmann's] transmutation of a complex theory into a vague, formulaic metaphor is rightly characterized by Said as a "degradation." Yet he seems

unwilling to consider the possibility that this change may be produced by the failure of individual understanding or imagination; instead, he argues, it is "just that the situation has changed sufficiently for the degradation to have occurred." One waits [in vain] to see what specific modifications in the situation are responsible for this, what kind of border has in fact been crossed, what are the socio-political differences between the two locations that can bring about such changes.[148]

Goldmann, Said seems to be saying, couldn't have done otherwise than he in fact did with Lukacs's theory, even if he had wanted to. Why? Because his own historical circumstances made it not only possible but necessary for him to appropriate the theory in exactly the way he did – just as Lukacs's original inauguration had been propitiated (and constrained) by inescapable historical conditions. On the face of it, this is a form of historical determinism that flies in the face of Said's entire critical project as I have been describing it.

Nevertheless, if we consider the passage in the context of Said's broad argument, we realize that it constitutes just one vector of his complex methodology, a technique which I have described as a confrontation between an agonistic, either/or dialectic and archaeology/genealogy; it also becomes clear that the extraordinary stress Said lays on history in this article is intended to demystify theory in general, Lukacs's radical variety included. Hence, of course, the polemical jabs scattered throughout the passage – the references to "misreadings" and "misinterpretations," to "limitless intertextuality," and to "critical hermeticism" are pointed allusions to Bloomian, Derridean, and other species of formalist, mystical, or disembodied theory which have been denounced elsewhere in *The World*. More immediately relevant, Said's aim is to detach theory of any kind from what he has called critical consciousness, a step he considers crucial for determining the difference between theoretical closure (in collusion with cultural dogma) and critical insight and its relationship with theoretical cogency. It is at this point that Williams's reception of Lukacs's theory (via Goldmann) becomes crucial.

For unlike Goldmann, whose attempt at the faithful transumption of a once "liberating idea" has transformed the idea itself into "a trap of its own," Williams is "a reflective critic" with the canniness and perspicacity to identify the weakness harbored by the original idea at its very roots.[149] Williams, Said tells us, expresses considerable appreciation for Lukacs's highly sophisticated and revolutionary theory (as well as Goldmann's extensions of it), but he finds the idea and "practice of totality ... profoundly and even obviously difficult" to accept (Williams's phrasing).[150] Williams is objecting to Lukacs's simultaneous insistence on two incompatible assumptions. On the one hand, there is a sense in which totality qua bourgeois culture is assumed to be already reified completely and without remainder – even if this state of total reification (as distinct from its specific articulations) cannot be experienced directly. On the other hand, however, we are given to understand that something does escape reification after all – else how would any critique be possible? What all of this means for Said is that Williams "has the critical recognition" not to copy an imported theory slavishly but "consciously to qualify, shape, and refine his borrowings from Lukacs and Goldmann."[151] It also means that theory – however powerful, radical, or timely – "can never be complete"[152] and that Lukacs's talk of totality as part of his theory's condition of possibility had, from the very beginning, the potentiality of becoming either an ideological straitjacket or "a bad infinity."[153]

In other words, in evaluating the insightfulness of any theory, critics need to consider the full range of material connections that – through resistance, dislodgement, and transformation – prevent it from becoming a self-stabilizing, reductive system: "status of the author, historical moment, conditions of publication, diffusion and reception, values drawn upon, values and ideas assumed," and so on. That is to say, the entire constellation of ideas, agencies, institutions, movements, and formations that Said identified as worldly affiliations needs to be activated *by the critic* in order both to gain the most cogent insights a given theory can offer and to resist the temptation of turning the theory into a self-sustaining, but internally expandable totality.[154] Finally, it means that critical *intentionality* is closely caught up with but not reducible to theory, critical or otherwise. Rather, critical consciousness is a roving, perpetually active, "measuring faculty" which places – but also goes behind, below, and beyond – theory, opening (it) up into the socio-political world of common humanity which is ignored by most theorists:

> No reading is neutral or innocent, and by the same token every text and every reader is to some extent the product of a theoretical standpoint, however implicit or unconscious such a standpoint may be. I am arguing, however, that we distinguish theory from critical consciousness by saying that the latter is a sort of spatial sense, a sort of measuring faculty for locating or situating theory, and this means that theory has to be grasped in the place and time out of which it emerges as a part of that time, working in and for it, responding to it; then, consequently, that first place can be measured against subsequent

places where the theory turns up for use. The critical consciousness is awareness of the differences between situations, awareness too of the fact that no system or theory exhausts the situation out of which it emerges or to which it is transported. And, above all, critical consciousness is awareness of the resistances to theory, reactions to it elicited by those concrete experiences or interpretations with which it is in conflict. Indeed, I would go as far as saying that it is the critic's job to provide resistances to theory, to open it up toward historical reality, toward society, toward human needs and interests, to point up those concrete instances drawn from everyday reality that lie outside or just beyond the interpretive area necessarily designated in advance and thereafter circumscribed by every theory.[155]

This is one of the most cogent statements of Said's critical project to be found anywhere in his oeuvre. The passage obviously at one level reflects his prolonged interest in the phenomenological attitude; however, the repetition of such words as "consciousness" and "awareness" should not be misconstrued as a desperate resort to a naive species of phenomenologism, a hypostatization of pure consciousness. On the contrary, the entire passage is imbued not only with the radical historicism we have repeatedly noted but also with the radical reflexivity which Said considers to be crucial to critical thinking. Understood in these terms, critical intentionality is meant to be an advance on empiricist and idealist conceptions (of the mind, history, socio-cultural reality, etc.), but it also parts ways with methodologies based on hermeneutics: it echoes but also radicalizes Heidegger's ontology of worldliness, sharpening it into a publicly utilizable epistemological and ethico-political weapon; and it is far more sensitive to rifts and interruptions than Gadamer's restorative, tradition-bound understanding of historical consciousness (what he calls the fusion of horizons) as well as Jauss's extensions of it. Finally, it is much more alert to the powerful operations of ideology in the contemporary world than much of the criticism known as the new historicism and cultural materialism.

For all these reasons, Said's strategic juxtaposition of history, theory, and suspicious consciousness goes to the very heart of his argument that criticism should at once interrogate and map (the cartographic metaphor is – I think – very crucial here) the historical, cultural, political, and epistemological ground which has been covered and covered over in the context of modernity. It is this critical consciousness as *energy* that is initially made available by Lukacs's revolutionary theory – despite the totalitarianism of that theory; it is also this critical energy that is translated by Goldmann into totalizing homologies devoid of critical bite; finally, it is this same critical consciousness that is recovered by Williams and enhanced into a sharp, fine-grained measuring faculty. The point to be made about all this is that genuine critical intelligence configures an active, irreducible dissonance: it opposes – by unmasking, subverting, dissolving, defamiliarizing, turning inside out – all formulaic solutions and syntheses, whether they be theoretical or cultural. "Theoretical closure," Said observes at one point, is "like social convention or cultural dogma." Together they constitute the substance and modality of ideological formations and are therefore "anathema to critical consciousness, which loses its profession when it loses its active sense of an open world in which its faculties are exercised."[156] Critical consciousness thus understood entails *"interference"* in the business of the world, "a crossing of borders and obstacles, a determined attempt to generalize exactly at those points where generalizations seem impossible to make."[157] This is exactly what Said has been doing in his various political writings – from his critiques of Orientalism, imperialism, and Zionism, to his condemnation of the current peace process as a fraud.

In the conclusion of my study, I will have the occasion to reflect on the specifically philosophical implications of criticism understood in these terms. I will argue that, minus this form of at once insurrectionary and rigorous intentionality, philosophical thinking ends up being a second-rate, manifestly impoverished affair – technical minutiae wedded to what Charles Taylor calls "wordy elaborations of the obvious."[158] In my next (and final) chapter, however, I want to turn my attention to Said's specifically political writings.

5

Culture and Barbarism: Eurocentric Thought and Imperialism

Critical Misreception: The Case of *Orientalism*

In an attempt to give us the ultimate insight into Conrad's *Heart of Darkness*, Walter Allen delivers himself of this remarkable sentence: "The heart of darkness of the title is at once the heart of Africa, the heart of evil – everything that is nihilistic, corrupt, and malign – and perhaps the heart of man." In the next sentence, after a passing gloss on the unhealthiness of imperialist exploitation, Allen unpacks his tidy little summation with the same relish and self-approval: the story, he tells us, "relates the effect on Marlow of the blackness of Africa, its otherness – everything that lies beyond the concept of fidelity – and of the presence, terrifying even when unseen, of Mr. Kurtz, the figure of evil who is worshipped by the natives as a god."[1] Quite apart from the logical contradictions thrown up at a primary level (What formula has allowed Allen to translate "the heart of Africa" into "the heart of evil"? Is it Africa that actually causes the evil? Or is it Kurtz, "the figure of evil," that visits it on the "natives"?), what is striking about this passage is that it could have been conceived, and then delivered, and then published in this manner at all. That such a piece of "literary analysis" could have been offered by an eminent scholar in the middle of the twentieth century; that such broad, unqualified judgements could have been made about an entire continent and its peoples; that the Truth unmediated is revealed to us with such theological assurance and enthusiasm; that neither the publisher, nor the political authorities, nor the audience raised so much as a whisper in protest against what is, after all, intellectual aggression of the most malignant kind; that these commissions and omissions were being enacted in the wake of the Holocaust – the century's most horrendous European supremacist crime – and at a time during which hundreds of thousands of natives were being slaughtered (in Algeria and Vietnam, for example) to maintain European colonial rule – that all of this could have come to pass is an extremely disconcerting but historically undeniable fact.

And yet if the Said of *Orientalism, Covering Islam,* and *Culture and Imperialism* is right, one should not be particularly surprised that scandalous statements like these were (and continue to be) made by scholars, journalists, politicians, and fellow travelers. For, rather than being isolated, anachronistic indiscretions made by a lone, "prejudiced" individual, such pronouncements form part of a vast, carefully woven discourse whose genealogy stretches across a period of several centuries and whose perdurable effects are being felt in multiple ways right up to the present. Intimately entwined with the narrative of modernity and the story of Western imperialism and racism, this discourse has in recent decades come to be known as Eurocentrism. And in delivering his pontifications, Allen is right at home in it. It is no accident that the author he is citing – a homeless Pole who at once became a British gentleman and came to adopt the whole of Europe as his homeland – is best known for arrogating to himself the artistic ability to render familiar the exotic and the alien. Nor is it an accident that, in accordance with the Hegelian protocols of possessing "otherness," Marlow and Kurtz – two projections of a European cultural will – between them serve the function of proprietor and commentator. Still, as befits the odd logic of master–slave relationships, we are not surprised that neither of them quite delivers the object of his search, that the "god" of the natives is claimed by "the blackness of Africa," that "the horror" (Kurtz's final gasp) and mystery of Africa are in the end profoundly deepened.

I have once again used Conrad as an important point of purchase in my study for two related reasons. First, I want to illustrate, if only briefly, the kind of ideologically driven "interpretation" of literature and other cultural agencies in opposition to which Said's political writings were deployed in the Seventies, Eighties, and beyond. Said has never cited Allen personally in the Conradian context (or for that matter anywhere else), but his own reflections on Conrad's dilemmas, which I have already discussed in earlier chapters, shed a sufficiently demystifying light on Eurocentric critics like Allen. A second more important reason is that the Conradian connection can be used as an opportunity to reiterate emphatically a contention which I have made repeatedly throughout this study: that Said's so-called postcolonial writings cannot be fully appreciated without a careful study of the early works, including *Joseph Conrad and the Fiction of Autobiography*.

Admittedly the political texts of the later period have their own distinct critical flavor: such books as *Orientalism*, *The Question of Palestine*, *Covering Islam*, *Culture and Imperialism*, and *The Politics of Dispossession* are all informed by a number of related concerns which Said sometimes clusters under the disjunctive notion of "discrepancies":[2] discrepancy between what is often claimed for – and by – the West (democracy, Western values, humanism, and the like) and what Westerners have actually done in the non-West (literally millions of natives were – and continue to be – killed, displaced, or otherwise victimized); between the privileged colonial or neo-colonial official's experience (feelings of racial and cultural superiority; peremptory, disciplinary power; self-assurance, ease, comfort) and that of the colonial or otherwise victimized subject (daily drudgery, economic deprivation, humiliation; implacable hatred of the foreign intruder; cultural and military resistance); between the grand illusions of the imperial mentality, "the rhetoric of power" (George Bush's "New World Order" talk during the Gulf War is a perfect recent example) and the disabusing lessons of history (virtually every inch of land captured for European imperialism in Africa, Asia, and elsewhere was subsequently recaptured by the natives, and resistance to neo-imperialism continues to this day); between the omnivorous complacency of the Western metanarrative and the multitude of non-Western voices who have always been there but are now more than ever determined to be heard and reckoned with. Perhaps the most invidious version of the discrepancy is to be found in the heart of the literary-critical establishment: as we noted in the preceding chapter, it has the resilience to accommodate not only the Walter Allens of the profession but also more sophisticated types – the refining critic, the self-cocooning theorist, the ideologically "alert" new historicist, etc. – all of whom are, in Said's view, collaborating with "the prevailing polity" to one degree or another.

But the point I am stressing here is that, in order to come to terms with the full significance of these discrepancies for Said, in order to understand what they entail to him not just ethically and politically but also epistemologically, historically, and culturally, we must place them in the context of his career as a whole. I have argued that this contextualization has not been enacted except in very limited ways. The result is what I have called a misrecognition of his critical project

– an enactment which I have been trying to counteract, directly or indirectly, throughout this study.

In terms of both commission and omission, this misapprehension is illustrated by the unusual trajectory of *Orientalism*, a complex, richly suggestive text whose wrenching critical impact is being felt more than twenty years after its original publication. Even though it was primarily concerned with a relatively specialized domain of inquiry – namely, the discourse in which the Orient and Orientals have been for ages represented by and for the West – *Orientalism* has turned out to be an intellectual event of far-reaching implications. The peculiarly unnerving and enabling quality of this event is attested to by the enormous controversy it has generated since its publication in 1978. It has scandalized many – some of them Orientalists – who have denounced it in no uncertain terms: Bernard Lewis, who has written extensively on Arabs and Muslims, dismissed it as a "coarse polemic";[3] and the Sinologist Pierre Ryckmans described it as "three hundred pages of twisted, obscure, incoherent, ill-informed, and badly written diatribe."[4] More reflective scholars have also discovered a variety of faults with Said's text. Probably the most influential commentator on Said's various "ambivalences" is James Clifford, a respected anthropologist, who persistently notes the incompatibility between Said's Foucauldian thesis and his reluctant (and symptomatic) recognition that discourse does not exhaust human reality. Here is a typical passage from Clifford's review:

> This ambivalence [about what Orientalism is and is not], which sometimes becomes a confusion, informs much of Said's argument. Frequently he suggests that a text or tradition distorts, dominates, or ignores some real or authentic feature of the Orient. Elsewhere, however, he denies the existence of any "real Orient," and in this he is more rigorously faithful to Foucault and the other radical critics of representation whom he cites. Indeed the absence of anything more than a brief allusion to the "brute reality" of the "cultures and nations whose location is in the East ... their lives, histories and customs" represents a significant methodological choice on his part. Orientalist inauthenticity is not answered by any authenticity. Yet Said's concept of a "discourse" still vacillates between, on the one hand, the status of an ideological distortion of lives and cultures that are never concretized and, on the other, the condition of a persistent structure of signifiers that, like some extreme example of experimental writing, refers solely and endlessly to itself. Said is thus forced to rely on nearly tautological statements ... or on rather unhelpful specifications.[5]

Other reviewers – among them Dennis Porter, Sadik al-'Azm, Mahdi Amil, Paul Bové and Bart Moore-Gilbert – make similar criticisms.[6] The most common criticisms usually turn on logical, epistemological, or historical failings attributed to Said. It is claimed that he has committed the very sins for which he castigates Orientalists – for example, by drawing a neat binary divide between the West and the Orient, he essentializes both from the outset; that he deliberately de-emphasizes the importance of Orientalists who show empathy for the Orient and its peoples, while exaggerating the negative streak in the tradition; that while condemning Orientalist discourse for creating a simulacrum which, in the manner of a caricature, both stands in for and obfuscates the complex realities of the Orient, Said himself is incapable of telling us just exactly what the real Orient is and is not; that he knowingly or otherwise utilizes a species of epistemology which at once assumes and denies the possibility of neutrally communicable, intersubjectively shareable knowledge; that he posits an ethics of human emancipation but relies on a severely deterministic version of historicism which thwarts the achievability of that very goal. As was clear from the Clifford passage I cited above, most of these criticisms converge on one very crucial methodological aspect of *Orientalism*: Said's reliance on Foucault's enormously influential "disciplinary" history of Western modernity, and more particularly on the argument – most vigorously presented in *Discipline and Punish* – that knowledge and power, by virtue of their coeval and coextensive presence in the same discursive network, are so closely knitted together that it is virtually impossible to conceive of one without the other. Since its publication, *Orientalism* has repeatedly invited this kind of negative and rather reductive criticism.

The book, however, has been welcomed by others, among them "third world" anti-imperialist intellectuals and feminists like Homi Bhabha, Gayatri Spivak, and Partha Chatterjee. These writers have found its argument powerfully convincing and its critical technology unusually compelling. The power of *Orientalism* can be attributed not to (or not merely to) the specific content of its argument (although Said has marshaled a vast, almost encyclopedic repertoire of evidentiary material) but rather to its unconventional mode of presentation, a strategy which allows its author both to up-end received wisdom and to open up an old conceptual terrain for re-examination under a new, more corrosive light.

By this I mean that Said combines historical and theoretical insight, rhetorical force, and interrogative positionality – and combines them in such a manner that multiple disciplinary boundaries are erased and hitherto secure knowledge systems (for example, "social

science," "the humanities," "religious studies," and so forth) all come
under suspicion at once. The fruitful co-activation of critical instruments originally sharpened in different, and in some respects
mutually suspicious, domains of modern thought (i.e., poststructuralism and neo-Marxism); the unapologetic use of a hard-hit-
ting, polemical idiom largely unknown in the tame, supposedly
disinterested discourse of academic criticism; and the politically
interventionist character of the argument – the proposition that, in
the asymmetrical contest between socio-cultural power and its various
others, critical agency cannot afford to remain neutral but is, on the
contrary, ethically enjoined to side with (and offer explicit, active
support to) the victimized: this strategic conjunction of what has been
seen by many as methodological rigor and insurrectionary intentionality accounts for the unusual appeal of *Orientalism*. (As of early
1998, the book had been translated into seventeen languages worldwide.) It has served as an exemplary model of worldly criticism in
action, a demystification of power which both complements and goes
beyond traditional left criticism – a fact which explains its denunciation, some of it ferocious, by some Marxist critics, the best-known
of whom is Aijaz Ahmad.[7]

For all these reasons, a vast amount of literature has been generated
in the wake of *Orientalism*, either in direct response to the book itself
or as extensions, appropriations, and refinements of its argument or its
critical vocabulary. Its influence has been registered not only in so-
called area studies (including what nowadays remains of Orientalism
as an academic discipline) but also in the field of anthropology and
ethnography as a whole – as well as in historiography and feminism;
and of course it is often cited as the inaugural text of postcolonial
theory, hence complementing and considerably energizing an earlier
anti-imperialist tradition.

Yet most of the commentary on *Orientalism* has been presented in
such a manner that neither Said's *methodological* infrastructure nor his
complex, highly reflexive statements on matters of theory and critical
consciousness elicit more than a passing gloss (if any at all). This
theoretical misrecognition has been compounded by another one,
which revolves around *Orientalism*'s relationship to the explicitly
political works, most of which were written after 1978. Most of the
scholars, hostile or sympathetic, whose attention has turned to Said's
indictment of the Orientalist tradition have tended to restrict their
response to this text – failing to take into account (except in the form
of glosses and allusions) the direct methodological and thematic

connections between *Orientalism*, on the one hand, and, on the other, *The Question of Palestine* and *Covering Islam*, both of which were meant to clarify and refine the original thesis. More specifically, these two texts were primarily designed for one main objective: to furnish irreducibly contemporary – and for that reason indubitable – material evidence that would give direct, substantive support to the argument of *Orientalism*.

In fact, Said has since written a large number of texts which are in one way or another about Orientalist discourse (as a powerful instrument of imperialism and hegemonism) and its consequences for Muslims, Arabs, and especially Palestinians in the postcolonial era. Yet the debate provoked by *Orientalism* itself has largely been conducted in a way that, though vaguely understood in historical terms, is nevertheless strangely indifferent to the contentious *present* realities of the Middle East. Reading the otherwise generally perceptive analyses of *Orientalism* by such scholars as Homi Bhabha, James Clifford, Robert Young, and Moore-Gilbert,[8] for example, one wouldn't know that Said's critique – at once historical and interventionary – is intended as a dramatized retrieval of a contested past, an investigative report on an equally contested present, and a guerrilla attack on a status quo which is in his view based on multiple dominations. One wouldn't know that Orientalists, past and present, are being implicated, not just in what transpired in a bygone era of high imperialism, but also in the instigation of six major wars in the Middle East region over the past five decades, or in the plight of millions of refugees. None – or very little – of this sense of urgency features in the concatenation of commentary on the book, or in the various appropriations and extensions of its thesis and methodology. (One of the rare exceptions to this self-inflicted amnesia is to be found in *Colonialism's Culture*, whose author, Nicholas Thomas, characterizes both *Orientalism* and Said's other political writings as a direct response to the dehumanizing anti-Arab, anti-Muslim sentiment that pervades contemporary American culture.)[9]

The result has been doubly handicapping. *Orientalism*'s theoretical rigor and sophistication are bracketed off from the contemporary world – its transgressive energy corralled, diverted, or contained in a variety of ways. Its critical insights into ideology, history, power relations, and the presence of the past are rendered unavailable for deployment in the contemporary socio-political theatre – except in the limited sense of a fast-receding background. The argument of *Orientalism* and the theoretical debate it has fired up almost invariably seem to occur offstage, a zone which – though very close – is nevertheless somehow occluded from the arena of direct attention. In short, even though Said himself has not complained about this matter in such terms, it is clear that the fate of *Orientalism* is in an important sense analogous to the fate of much critical theory as he describes it in *The World, the Text, and the Critic*: it has been academicized in both senses of the word. A new discourse – self-consciously theoretical, ahistorical, formalistically elevated – has grown around it (Homi Bhabha's opaque reflections are an extreme example of such intellectual labors); yet one wonders whether any of it has any relevance beyond a limited audience of professors and graduate students – the mythical three thousand who read each other's books.

In the meantime, Said's further writing on Orientalism, including monographs, scholarly articles, reviews, and editorial interventions, scarcely attracts the attention of "serious" academic critics. Said's detailed, highly nuanced analyses of various individual scholars in the Orientalist tradition (including Ernest Renan, Raymond Schwab, Lewis Massignon, Bernard Lewis, and Albert Hourani),[10] as well as the implicit distinctions he makes among them; the differences he sees between European Orientalism and its American progeny; the specific suggestions which he offers (in *Covering Islam*,[11] for example) for a non-reductive, non-coercive alternative to Orientalist discourse; the transformations (both positive and negative) that he identifies in the field as a whole in recent years; and finally the distinction (again largely implicit) that he makes between, on the one hand, Orientalism as a highbrow, privileged activity – now and especially in the past – and, on the other, a vulgarized, popular version of it, especially in contemporary America: all of this highly articulated expansion and clarification of the original argument is virtually ignored by the vast majority of the critics who have found it necessary to respond to Said on the issue of Orientalism. The symptomatic nature of the academic response to *Orientalism* is perhaps best instantiated in the fact that the direct ideological transaction between Orientalism as a field of knowledge and Zionism as a specific program is rarely ever noted by advanced critics (again there are a few exceptions). Conversely, in exonerating Israel, Zionists and other supporters of Israeli policies – especially in the United States – have almost without exception failed to come to grips with the formidable challenge of *Orientalism*, even while many of them have pressed into service the most defamatory stereotypes to come out of the Orientalist tradition. (It should be noted, though, that – in Israel at least – the recent debates about the

Ashkenazi–Mizrahi tensions and about Zionism and post-Zionism are caught up in the broader discussions concerning Eurocentrism and European supremacism, as well as postcoloniality, postmodernity, and related problematics. *Orientalism* and Said's other political writings have, of course, contributed to all these intercultural debates in various ways.)[12]

As I have tried to demonstrate in the preceding chapters, *Orientalism* is methodologically and thematically affiliated to Said's earlier writings at various levels of generality and specificity and in a manner that always draws attention – whether directly or indirectly – to the modern intellectual's relationship with ideology. At the minimum, then, all the debates initiated (or contributed to) by *The World, the Text, and the Critic* are directly germane to *Orientalism* – debates about identity, culture, and hegemony; about the canon's symbolic value and its availability as a screen for power; about the irreducible worldliness of literary and all other cultural artifacts; about liberal humanism and its discontents; about the relationship between socio-cultural history, knowledge systems, and critique. Beyond these immediate concerns lies the entire problematic of rationality which Said meditated on in *Beginnings* – with reflections on intentionality, textuality, transitive and intransitive beginnings, and especially silent origins assuming special significance. The complex tensions suggested here, in both methodology and substance, are rarely ever given more than a cursory nod by most of the analysts of *Orientalism*.

One of the few critics to indicate some of Said's theoretical complexity (if not the vast range of topics treated by him) is Asha Varadharajan, whose recent book on Adorno, Said, and Spivak provides a welcome corrective to the thesis that Said is a Foucauldian (and hence anti-humanist) "third world" critic castigating the West in the name of a humanistic ideology – itself invented in the West. Despite the rather restricted scope of Varadharajan's study (most of the chapter on Said revolves around a few late texts dealing mostly with "post-colonial" themes), I have found her Adornian thesis particularly compelling. Varadharajan's analysis deepens our insight into Said's critical enterprise in several ways. First, by drawing attention to the remarkable similarities between Adorno's negative dialectic and Said's extremely radical, or (as she phrases it) "doubled," form of reflexivity, she helps throw into greater conceptual relief what I have been describing as the modernist or critical oppositions implicitly or explicitly endorsed by Said in all of his texts. Although Varadharajan does not directly treat the archaeological/genealogical dimension of

Said's writing, hers is one of the very few interpretive efforts to shed light on the dialectical infrastructure that (partially) guides my own analysis. Second, her concentration on subjectivity complements the emphasis laid on discourse by most commentators on Said; although her discussion is not, strictly speaking, presented in either existentialist or phenomenological terminology, it echoes (and in some respects radicalizes) my own observations in this regard. Finally, Varadharajan's invocation of Adorno enables her to employ what could be called a culturalist lens – without, however, framing the discussion in terms of the recent debates about multiculturalism, which are strongly tinged with postmodernist ahistoricism and differential politics. She places Said (and Spivak) in earlier, more historically conscious reflections on the nexus between culture and barbarism, a theme central to the thought of first-generation Frankfurt theorists, especially Horkheimer, Adorno, and Benjamin. This way, she bypasses the textualism, anti-humanism, and determinism often associated with poststructuralist theories while also recovering an extremely suspicious, powerfully corrosive variety of Marxism. In short, Varadharajan highlights certain intellectual affinities which have always been there but had previously been de-emphasized or ignored by most of Said's interlocutors.

The affinity between Adorno and Said may seem all the more surprising given the fact that, with the exception of a few late texts nearly all of which are primarily about music,[13] none of Said's studies – major or minor – contain extended analysis of Adorno's philosophy, social theory, or literary criticism. Nor is Adorno's "influence" discernible in any of Said's major works – with the possible exception of *Culture and Imperialism*, where the underlying musical idea of "contrapuntality" is described at one point as "atonal."[14] Yet the similarities are unmistakably there, as Said himself acknowledges: Adorno, he tells us in *Representations of the Intellectual*, was an intellectual exile par excellence, a man who – like Swift and Naipaul at his best – embraced the condition of permanent, even metaphysical homelessness as both boon and bane. He adds:

> [Adorno] was a forbidding but endlessly fascinating man, and for me, the dominating intellectual conscience of the middle twentieth century, whose entire career skirted and fought the dangers of fascism, communism and Western mass-consumerism ... Paradoxical, ironic, mercilessly critical: Adorno was the quintessential intellectual, hating *all* systems, whether on our side or on theirs, with equal distaste. For him life was at its most false in the aggregate – the whole is always the untrue, he once said – and this, he

continued, placed an even greater premium on subjectivity, on the individual's consciousness, on what could not be regimented in the totally administered world.[15]

It is this affinity that Varadharajan's analysis of determinate negation draws attention to, in both methodological and substantive terms. Clearly the idea of lateness (or late style) that I briefly discussed in an earlier chapter constitutes an important element in Said's belated interest in the brooding pessimism of this alienated mandarin.

In its specific operations as well as in the content it transforms, the Saidian dialectic – which can best be described as a protracted reflection on a double-bind or (as he puts it in the book on Conrad) a difficult "Either/Or" enactment – approximates to Adorno's negative dialectic in that both are designed to go beyond identitarianism. Varadharajan phrases this similarity thus: "Said shares with Adorno the concern for 'the liquidation of the particular' [which is] endemic to identity thinking, to self-affirmation that presides at the expense of whatever that self constitutes as other."[16] And of course both Adornian and Saidian versions of dialectical thinking are meant both to echo and to turn inside out Hegel's idealistic conception of the notion as well as Marx's materialist transformation of it – a transformation which (Adorno and Said would insist) is burdened with untenable positivistic pretensions. That is to say, both Adorno and Said sharpen the severely agonistic (rather than – in their view – facilely synthesizing) edge of dialectical sublation, hence sensitizing thought to the horrendous nightmares of history through which dialectic must work if it is to avoid the fate of becoming a vacuous exercise. The result, argues Varadharajan, is the constitution of a deracinated, scarred yet intensified subjectivity whose heightened awareness of human suffering impels it to transmute the very category of thought into critique, together with "a deep-seated commitment to the mitigation of" that suffering:

> The diagnostic character of Said's intellectual labors is a function of his insistence on worldliness, on the self-implicated mode of knowledge production in which the intellectual's entanglement in the travails of existence produces a deep-seated commitment to the mitigation of those travails. Adorno and Said share the position of the intellectual émigré, whose experience of displacement translates into the loss of history, language, and identity, but whose very "damaged life" becomes the occasion for reflection on the conditions that produced that "mutilation." Adorno and Said privilege a particular form of critical consciousness rather than the category of thought itself; for them, the position of exile makes the intellectual vitally attuned to

suffering, which enables a different articulation of one's position in the world. In short, the immersion in suffering produces its own repudiation in critique.[17]

It is this deep, all-imbuing suspicion – a sharp-edged version of rational cognition which transforms the homeless intellectual into a living indictment of domination and injustice – that has obliged Said (as it did Adorno before him) to forge a method of determinate negation, a method "which refuses to objectify what it seeks to know."[18]

Varadharajan's Adornian intervention sheds a particularly revealing light on the discrepancies I alluded to earlier – the stark contrast between the grand claims made for "Western civilization" and the concrete socio-historical realities created on the ground: "Said's texts gain their power from the uncompromising realization that the fact of Empire radically corrodes the claims of Western civilization. It is not possible, as Adorno well knew in the context of Nazism, 'to defame barbarism and rely on the health of culture. Rather, it is the barbaric element in culture itself which must be recognized.'"[19] In Varadharajan's view, "Said translates this 'shame' into a code of intellectual conduct."[20] In exposing the scandals of civilization, the intellectual makes a badge of integrity and moral courage for himself – even as he runs the risk of contamination by civilization's stain of dishonor. In other words, the nightmare of history exerts its enormous pressure on intellectuals like Adorno and Said, admonishing them to equate (or almost equate) the realm of actuality – what has been called "the administered world" by Adorno and the totalizations of "culture" and "system" by Said – with the consolidations of ideology against which the edge of critique must be sharpened. Varadharajan's brief but brilliant analysis shows us that, by effecting "a staged confrontation between dialectic and difference,"[21] we can make sense of the dramatic, multiple tensions that weave through Said's writing – the tension between affirmation and negation, between methodology and critical consciousness, between authority and transgression, between totality and what escapes it, as well as a large number of other tensions whose significance I have reflected on at various points of my study. My highly synoptic discussion of *Orientalism, The Question of Palestine, Covering Islam, Culture and Imperialism,* and other related writings will be premised on the assumptions I have outlined in the foregoing paragraphs.

I will begin with a very brief summary of *Orientalism,* which will be followed by a discussion of reflections on the Orientalist tradition elsewhere in Said's writings, especially those which came in the wake of *Orientalism*. The next three sections will concentrate on high European imperialism and American postwar hegemonism, giving special attention to the interplay between these two forms of ideological consolidation. The final cluster of sections will examine the genealogy of Zionism over the past century and a half – with emphasis in the first section falling on the gradually intensifying collusion, from the mid-1860s to 1948, between Zionists and European imperialists. The next section focuses on the so-called special relationship that has developed between Israel and America over the past several decades – a relationship which, though informed by the horrifying reality of the Holocaust, has largely been brought about by the strategic co-deployment of Orientalist discourse in its most dehumanizing forms, of American exceptionalism and superpowerism, and of a theologically ordained species of Jewish supremacism. The chapter will end with reflections on Said's suggestions for a just solution to the Middle East conflict.

Orientalist Discourse as Hegemonic Intention

The lineaments of Said's argument can be drawn in broad brush: Orientalism, he tells us, is not "a positive doctrine," but a specific family of ideas – a style of thought, a set of practices, and affiliated institutions – which together constitute a broad, interdisciplinary discourse that evolved in the common cultural consciousness of Europeans for centuries for the purpose of making imaginary and actual purchase on the Orient (especially the "Near East") and its inhabitants. The specifics of Said's thesis can be further schematized:

(1) Orientalism brought into being an ambivalent, bipolar understanding of the Orient according to whose definitions and terminology the region and its peoples were objectified globally and locally – through reductions, anatomizations, categorizations, and various forms of pigeonholing. On the one hand there was the morally attractive, privileged Orient (namely, the Orient of Origins – including Christianity; of truth and plenitude; of the Garden of Eden, Jerusalem, and Prester John, etc.). On the other, there was the repellent, even demonic, Orient of dangers and apostasies (such as the Yellow Peril and Islam).

(2) Alternating between modes of familiarity and strangeness, the bipolar

oscillation was particularly energized by the rise of Islam, whose prophet and doctrine were, for centuries, domesticated in terms that ensured either their demonization or their trivialization by a Europe dominated by Christian dogma.

(3) In the increasingly secular context of the past three centuries, Orientalist discourse has transmuted some aspects of its originally religious motivation. As more "eyewitness," empirical, or "scientific" knowledge (acquired through translation or study of Oriental texts, through travel, or through conquest) became available, some of the more imaginatively extravagant characterizations of the Orient were gradually pruned away. But Orientalist discourse also finally matured in the nineteenth century into a powerful, theoretically armed, highly conservative, "median category" that, in the hands of a technologically advanced Europe, became an ideological instrument with which to settle old scores, an instrument which has in more recent times been relayed to willing American hands.

Said detects a particularly revealing relationship between Orientalism and imperialism: whereas in their encounters with cultures farther afield Europeans did not feel compelled to divest themselves of prior historical burdens that might unduly complicate the relatively straightforward enterprise of grabbing land, the special Western investments in the Near East were such that a potent, almost implosive dynamic had already been installed before imperialism proper was launched. This dynamic manifested itself as a heightened form of awareness, a specialized rhetorical thrust, an ambience predisposed to transvaluation, an easily available dogma about what constitutes rectitude and error: in effect, almost every statement enunciated about that region, and every policy executed in terms of it, was from the outset strongly tinged with the pressures of polemical engagement

As a result, a complex, resilient, interrelated, specially finessed set of ideas, images, metaphors and mythologies came into being as a substantiation of the "Oriental" character; the ingredients of this set were co-activated with various projects, plans, and designs tailored for the Orient, particularly in the context of the colonial ambitions of Britain and France, the two Western powers with the greatest stakes in the region. Sometimes overlapping, often disparate and contradictory, the elements of this ensemble together served as a loose but efficient economy which on the one hand deployed enormous generalizations and on the other generated a multiplicity of eccentric particulars – and thus created a grotesque avatar that stood in for, and caricatured, the empirical Orient. Shaded with multiple tones and inflections; catering to the whims and desires of adventurers, pilgrims, artists, as well as academicians and official functionaries; profoundly imaginative and fantasy-prone and yet often exacting in its imposition of methodological discipline after its own fashion, this, the heritage of Orientalism, whose stalwarts include such scholars as Silvestre de Sacy, Ernest Renan, and William Lane, paved the way for – and underwrote – the grand imperial project that, by the end of the First World War, brought almost the entire Near East under European suzerainty.

The details of Said's argument need not detain us here – they have been unpacked and analyzed in ways, both favorable and hostile, which I have indicated above. The point I would like to stress here is that, as this remarkable paragraph demonstrates, *Orientalism*'s "message" cannot be fully grasped apart from the complex, often seemingly incompatible statements which Said has made elsewhere – statements about textual worldliness, about affiliations, about the nature of intentionality, about ideology, and about a whole constellation of other eccentric movements, concepts, and relationships large and small:

> Orientalism is not a mere political subject matter or field that is reflected passively by culture, scholarship, or institutions; nor is it a large and diffuse collection of texts about the Orient; nor is it representative and expressive of some nefarious "Western" imperialist plot to hold down the "Oriental" world. It is rather a *distribution* of geopolitical awareness into aesthetic, scholarly, economic, sociological, historical, and philological texts; it is an *elaboration* not only of a basic geographical distinction (the world is made up of two unequal halves, Orient and Occident) but also a whole series of "interests" which, by such means as scholarly discovery, philological reconstruction, psychological analysis, landscape and sociological description, it not only creates but also maintains; it is, rather than expresses, a certain *will* or *intention* to understand, in some cases to control, manipulate, even to incorporate, what is a manifestly different (or alternative and novel) world; it is, above all, a discourse that is by no means in direct, corresponding relationship with political power in the raw, but rather is produced and exists in an uneven exchange with various kinds of power, shaped to a degree by the exchange with power political (as with a colonial or imperial establishment), power intellectual (as with reigning sciences like comparative linguistics or anatomy, or any of the modern policy sciences), power cultural (as with orthodoxies and canons of taste, texts, values), power moral (as with ideas about what "we" do and what "they" cannot do or understand as "we" do). Indeed, my real argument is that Orientalism is – and does not simply represent – a considerable dimension of modern political-intellectual culture, and as such has less to do with the Orient than it does with "our" world.[22]

The passage at once describes and X-rays an already familiar intellectual space – a space where Gramscian and Foucauldian ideas have both intersected and meshed in mutually complementary and contrastive ways. Orientalism, Said suggests, is not (or is not merely) a bald-faced, easily recognizable bundle of lies and stereotypes which will melt away once they have been exposed to the light of truth; nor is it a flimsy, polemical figleaf designed to justify a crude, mechanical species of political or economic exploitation. Tempting – and to a degree valid – as they are, claims like these are bound to misrecognize the absorptive, fecund power of the field. Orientalism is rather a subtle, refractive *"distribution* of geopolitical awareness" which partakes of a multiplicity of methodologies and knowledge systems; it is also *"an elaboration"* by virtue of which a quasi-ontological distinction is made between "two unequal" cultures and by means of which certain vested interests are preserved. That is to say, Orientalism is a cultural will or intention – to understand, master, mold, manipulate – which operates hegemonically. As a socio-historical consciousness which – whether in the form of an enveloping environment or a fastidious, finely distilled, elite sensibility – filters through several orders of reality, Orientalism is the cultural substance which dispenses "knowledge" about the Orient in multiple comparatist ways.

Profoundly saturated with desires, suppressions, interdictions, and agendas, this irradiating, hegemonic outreach is marked by resilience, resourcefulness, and homeostatic stability, processing its admonitions consensually; "above all, [it is] a discourse," which works "in an uneven exchange with various kinds of power" – including "power political", "power intellectual," "power cultural," and "power moral"; in the series of enunciative events and sweeps that execute the gradual emergence and articulation of that discourse, the Orient is made to assume the dimensions of a textual archive, a site of discovery and rediscovery where ancient rituals can be re-enacted with a conscious difference; it is activated into a theater where history comes alive, a tableau vivant upon which dreams and fantasies can be realized. It becomes the raw materials of the classroom, the stuff of theory and conjecture. It is displayed as a vast cultural museum, dissected as a laboratory specimen, disciplined in both senses of the word. In short, Orientalism both covers and covers over the Orient.

It is particularly important to note that Said is careful to depart from Foucault in order to clear a space for independent choice and responsibility: "unlike Michel Foucault, to whose work I am greatly indebted, I do believe in the determining imprint of individual

writers upon the otherwise anonymous collective body of texts constituting a discursive formation like Orientalism."[23] Just as he did in
Beginnings – as well as in *The World, the Text, and the Critic* (and indeed
everywhere else in his oeuvre) – Said is conceptualizing the notion of
intentionality both at the level of collectivity and at the level of
individual agency, and the mediating mechanism between the two
tiers of thought and action is none other than the dialectical transformation which we have examined in various contexts: "Accordingly
my analyses employ close textual readings whose goal is to reveal the
dialectic between individual text or writer and the complex collective
formation to which his text is a contribution."[24] In other words, the
negating, agonistic dialectic of critical consciousness unmasks the
assimilative dialectic of Orientalism, which is at once a hegemony and
a discourse. In both cases, what is posited is this: the possibility of
freedom, of the intellectual's ability to think through any problematic
no matter how forbidding, to develop resistance to the tempting
conclusions of established dogma, and to make methodological
choices that will respond to the most exacting criteria of accountability. In Said's estimation, that resistance has rarely ever manifested
itself in the field of Orientalism now or in the past. Both in *Orientalism*
and in the numerous later texts about the Orientalist tradition, he
tries to show the extent to which Orientalist modes of representation
continue to permeate Euro-American public discourse, contributing
to an almost perpetual climate of hostility in relations between the
Arab-Islamic world and the West.

In the last chapter of *Orientalism*, Said argues that contemporary
Orientalist writing has become increasingly tension-ridden, exposing
a field which is progressively enmeshed in crisis. Dominated by
American social scientists and other "experts" on Islam, Orientalism
is characterized by him as a discipline which is no longer able to
smooth over epistemological, methodological, and ideological rifts
and discontinuities which an earlier generation would have had less
difficulty coping with. The field is, in effect, less univocal and less
surefooted than it was in its heyday in the nineteenth century and in
the early twentieth. This subthesis, which involves an assessment of
the transformations in the field in the past three to four decades, is
further worked out in subsequent writings – among them *The Question
of Palestine*, *Covering Islam*, and various shorter pieces.

Said sometimes suggests that these transformations are not always
for the worse, giving us tantalizing hints that a significant attempt at
self-interrogation (or at least the development of greater sensitivity to

the political dimension of the discourse) is gradually emerging, if only among a small number of writers. In *Culture and Imperialism* (1993), for example, he tells us that "the critical and anti-Orientalist discourse of an older generation like Anwar Abdel-Malek and Maxime Rodinson continues with a younger generation"; that in the Eighties "an important ideological transformation [to the left]" occurred in the Middle East Studies Association — which had hitherto been dominated by conservatives; that healthy debates about critical events in the Middle East are regularly conducted among scholars.[25] This kind of cautious optimism can be found in all of Said's major political writings — including *Orientalism* and *Covering Islam*. Nevertheless, his repeated analyses of Orientalism are by and large informed by a profound sense of pessimism.

In the works published since *Orientalism*, Said's argument can be broadly summarized thus: contemporary Orientalist writing (that is, of the Seventies, Eighties, and Nineties), particularly in the United States, is an attenuated, anemic, second-rate affair — with academic and popular varieties interacting in increasingly symptomatic ways. One reason for the general degeneration — it can be inferred — is that Orientalism as an ambitious, ideologically motivated field may be finding it difficult to justify its very existence in a postcolonial world. An important motif in Said's writing is that, despite repeated incursions into the heartland of the Arab-Islamic world as well as extended periods of direct political rule or military occupation, the West has never triumphed over Islam in a way comparable to its successes elsewhere in the world. The sense of crisis and disorientation in the field may therefore be in large part due to a loss of nerve, a realization that, in light of the successful eviction of European imperialists out of the Near East over the past several decades, as well as strong cultural challenges to the West by Muslims and Arabs, Orientalism may indeed not only have failed in its primary objective but also lost its very raison d'être as a field.

According to Said, contemporary Orientalist studies have become progressively narrower, more compartmentalized, less informed by the breadth of culture and great range of authority enjoyed by an earlier generation: today's Orientalists (in both Europe and America) "tend to know jurisprudential schools in tenth-century Baghdad or nineteenth-century Moroccan urban patterns, but never (or almost never) about the whole civilization of Islam — literature, law, politics, history, sociology, and so on."[26] This in itself — it might be argued — is hardly an unpardonable sin: after all (as Weber, Habermas, and

Foucault, among others have theorized in different terms), all fields of
modern knowledge have tended, for good or ill, to undergo a process
of internal, systematic differentiation, precision, and rarefaction.
Said's aim, though, is to point out what he considers to be an eccentric
discrepancy in Orientalism: despite this shrinkage and fragmentation
in the field, there is a sense – mainly a negative sense – in which
broad, reductive generalizations are still commonly made about Arab-
Islamic culture and religion. Nearly fourteen hundred years of Islamic
history – involving multiple narratives, local tensions, embeddings,
and transformations; dozens of cultures, languages, ethnicities and
climes; various competing schools of interpretation; antithetical
political orientations – including revolutionaries, reformists, and
traditional conservatives: this rich variety of the world of Islam past
and present, a world in which – in the vast majority of cases – firmly
established secular institutions mediate between the various pressures
and constraints of contemporary experience (a socio-cultural environment which has provoked heated debates about modernity and
tradition; about the role of women in society; about the relations
between nationalism, the state, and religious dogma; about governance and the rights of the citizenry; about the most appropriate way to
build intra- and inter-cultural bridges; and about countless other
aspects of public and private life among Islam's one billion adherents)
– all of this vast, variegated, massively hybrid socio-cultural life is
very often summed up in one or two formulations without so much as
a qualifying hiccough.

   In addition to this general decline, Said identifies other reasons for
what he characterizes as the mediocre performance of American
Orientalists. Like a great number of other cultural wares, Orientalism
did not emerge out of an American socio-political context. Rather,
American Orientalism is a long-distance echo of a once-grand but
currently embattled and exhausted European tradition. According to
Said, in the nineteenth century and early twentieth – the heyday of
European Orientalism – American intellectual and political elites did
not attach to the Middle East the kind of importance which their
European counterparts did. Whereas in Europe the ideological
imperatives of high imperialism, the geographical contiguity of the
two regions, and the unique cultural and historical resonance of the
Near East all combined to create a desire to generate a specialized
body of knowledge that would make the Orient and Orientals more
clearly intelligible, in America there were no such promptings. The
immediate national priorities of the United States were generally

assumed to lie elsewhere, usually closer to home.

Consequently, despite occasional encounters (Twain's jocularly dismissive little report about Palestine and the military expedition against the "Barbary Pirates" are cited by Said), and despite some Christian missionary activity – mainly in the Levant – most Americans knew very little about Islam, Muslims, or Arabs. What passed for Orientalism was by and large restricted to obscure corners of university departments of religion or schools of divinity. When Orientalism proper finally arrived on American shores in the middle decades of the twentieth century – in the form of geopolitically motivated Near Eastern studies departments established in such major universities as Harvard, Columbia, Princeton, UCLA, and Chicago – it was foreign (mostly European) scholars who both imported it and acclimated it. But even after its academic domestication, American Orientalism has remained disembodied, second-hand. A nurturing cultural, historical, and geographical context has not been there to support it.

In Said's view, American Orientalism has never developed into the kind of impressive, multifaceted, highly prestigious cultural institution which classical European Orientalism evolved into. America simply has not produced scholars comparable – in erudition or stature – to de Sacy, Lane, Schwab, Hitti, Massignon, Gibb, Grunebaum, Hourani, Berque, and Rodinson – all of whom had a vast wealth of knowledge about (and in some cases genuine sympathy for) Islam and Muslim peoples. Nor are there (or have ever been) American equivalents of such adventurers, poets, novelists, and empire-builders as Goethe, Nerval, Burton, Flaubert, and T. E. Lawrence – men who at their best showed both "imagination and refinement."[27] And yet in America there exists – and has existed for at least three decades – an obsessive, unhealthy sort of fascination with Islam and the Arab world, fascination which – especially in its popularized version – manifests itself almost exclusively in modes of hostility and aggression. The enormous generalizations, the selection and syncretic conjunction of the caricatural detail, the almost unqualified commitment to the view that Islam is the embodiment of the irreducibly alien Other, the locus of Oriental "mystery, exoticism, corruption, and latent power":[28] this crude staple of stereotypes has, in Said's view, been willingly inherited from Europe with almost none of the potentially redeeming qualities of classical Orientalism.

The most curious aspect of all this is that such defamations take place almost by rote at a time when the public expression of bigotry against any other racial, ethnic, or religious grouping would almost certainly unleash a firestorm of protest and a great deal of soul-searching:

> A corps of "experts" on the Islamic world has grown to prominence, and during a crisis they are brought out to pontificate on formulaic ideas about Islam on news programs or talk shows. There also seems to have been a strange revival of canonical, though previously discredited, Orientalist ideas about Muslim, generally non-white, people – ideas which have achieved a startling prominence at a time when racial or religious misrepresentations of every other cultural group are no longer circulated with such impunity. Malicious generalizations about Islam have become the last acceptable form of foreign culture in the West; what is said about the Muslim mind, or character, or religion, or culture as a whole cannot now be said in mainstream discussion about Africans, Jews, other Orientals, or Asians.[29]

These words come from the revised edition of *Covering Islam*, which came out in 1997 – sixteen years after that text's original edition was issued and more than twenty years after the publication of *Orientalism*. For Orientalism, it seems, history almost never changes – and if it does, it moves only on its bad side. This is the conclusion that Said has reached – yet again – after studying a large body of material on offer in the Eighties and Nineties: news and editorial pieces churned out by both the print and electronic media; scholarly, travel, and other species of instant, twopenny-halfpenny writing produced by noted Orientalists, journalists, and self-appointed experts; review and feature articles appearing in journals of opinion; and statements made by politicians and other public personalities.

According to Said, the most "perfervid anti-Muslim"[30] poison of recent years has been spread by the likes of Daniel Pipes, Peter Rodman, Conor Cruise O'Brien, Martin Peretz, Morton Zuckerman, Steven Emerson, Martin Kramer, A. M. Rosenthal, Milton Viorst, Elaine Sciolino, Samuel Huntington, and Judith Miller – all of them journalists and "scholars" whose demonization of Islam and Arabs regularly appears either in such major national publications as *US News and World Report*, *National Review*, *The National Interest*, *Foreign Affairs*, *The New York Times*, *The Washington Post*, *The Atlantic*, *The New Yorker*, and *The New Republic*; or (as movies, documentary films, "analysis," and "considered" opinion) on the major television networks. Among the academic Orientalists, Said singles out Bernard Lewis, whose ideas about Islam – publicized in a long series of articles and books – "have remained unchanged and indeed have become more reductionist" over a long stretch of time. Lewis's views, maintains Said, "have seeped into the discourse of the 'think' pieces and books undertaken by ambitious journalists and a few political scientists."[31] These "studies" of Islam and Arabs include such books as Uris's *The Hajj*, Friedman's *From Beirut to Jerusalem*, Pryce-Jones's *The Closed Circle*, Lewis's *Semites and Anti-Semites*, Viorst's *Sandcastles: The Arabs in Search of the Modern World*, Miller's *God Has Ninety-Nine Names*, Kelly's *Arabia, the Gulf and the West*, Laffin's *The Dagger of Islam*, Jansen's *Militant Islam*, as well as a large number of other books, think pieces, and films (among the films reviewed by Said are *Death of a Princess* and *Jihad in America*), all of which have enormously contributed to the hysteria about Islam and Arabs that has, in Said's view, engulfed the public imagination since the Seventies.

Said points out that occasionally a welcome exception does punctuate the concatenation of vulgar mediocrity. John Esposito's recent study, *The Islamic Threat: Myth or Reality?*, is "a sensible and cogently argued book [which] patiently deflates the menace theory of Islam."[32] Likewise, an article by Zachary Karabell, which appeared in *World Policy Journal* (Summer 1995), castigates the media for its obsession with fundamentalism and its negative characterization of Islam. Whatever effect this intelligent, sound scholarship might have had, however, is more than cancelled out by "scholarly" productions of the other sort, which by virtue of their sheer volume and repetitiveness have shaped public perceptions of Islam. Few (if any) of these representations of Islam or Arabs have any serious claims to the minimal putative protocols of sound scholarship ("fairness," "disinterest," "objectivity," etc.); nor do they embody a healthy curiosity about another culture considered as equal to (but different from) one's own – the need to understand better so as to communicate with those who hold different beliefs. Nor, finally, have they been prompted by a genuine commitment to human emancipation from religious and cultural dogma as such (if that were the case, one would naturally expect to find, for example, serious critiques by these authors of Christian *and* Jewish fundamentalism or fanaticism – as well as Islamic). And yet the "scholars" who produce this lamentably impoverished material arrogate to themselves the ability to deliver weighty truths about Islam, Muslims, or Arabs: that Islam is a stagnant civilization impervious to modernity; that atavism, fanaticism, and mindless violence are inherent in Islam; that Muslims and Arabs are beset by feelings of inferiority in the face of Western power and influence; that only rage, irrationality, and terrorism are to be expected from them; that the West should squarely confront this challenge; that two-bit dictators, sleazy sheikhs, and bloodthirsty ayatollahs should not be allowed to push us around.

In short, Islam, Muslims, and Arabs are continually demonized, defamed, and trivialized in equal measure. The following two passages – a tiny sample of the vast amount of documentary material that Said cites to support his argument – will give us an idea of how he thinks Orientalism works in the contemporary setting. (For purposes of the palimpsestic integrity of the text, I have retained Said's internal commentary where that occurs.)

> It should by now be clear that we are facing a mood and a movement far transcending the level of issues and policies and the governments that pursue them. This is no less than a clash of civilizations – the perhaps irrational but surely historic reaction of an ancient rival against our "Judeo-Christian" heritage, our secular present, and the worldwide expansion of both. It is crucially important that we on our side should not be provoked into an equally historic but also equally irrational reaction against that rival.[33]

This quote is from "The Roots of Muslim Rage," a piece written in 1990 by Bernard Lewis, a well-known academic Orientalist. Let us compare it with what Conor Cruise O'Brien delivers himself of in this passage from an article entitled "Thinking about Terrorism," which appeared in *The Atlantic* in 1986:

> Certain cultures and subcultures, homes of frustrated causes, are destined breeding grounds for terrorism. The Islamic culture [O'Brien does not inform us how he makes the jump from religion to culture in this instance, nor does he specify where the limits of each lie] is the most notable example. That culture's view of its own rightful position in the world is profoundly at variance with the actual order of the contemporary world. [O'Brien does not tell us how or where he managed to glean this particularly privileged bit of information.] It is God's will that the House of Islam should triumph over the House of War (the non-Moslem world), and not just by spiritual means. "Islam Means Victory" is a slogan of the Iranian fundamentalists in the Gulf [i.e., Iran–Iraq war, 1980–88]. To strike a blow against the House of War is meritorious; consequently, there is widespread support for activities con-demned in the West as terrorist. [Note that O'Brien has not vouchsafed his reader one fact, source, quotation, or context, and he does not seem concerned at all by this rather peculiar procedure or method of argument.] Israel is one main target for these activities [what Israel has done or continues to do is never the issue: it is just pure Islamic terror], but the activities would not be likely to cease even if Israel came to an end.[34]

In Said's view, this defamation of Islam is so common that it hardly raises any eyebrows in the West. The crudest aspects of Orientalist discourse, the positivistic jargon of "social science," the various pressures of the news and entertainment industry – including "newsworthiness" (with all that this fuzzy term implies) and the almighty bottom line – as well as unacknowledged yet powerfully insistent special pleading: these factors converge to forge an instrument for effecting – and sustaining – a neat divide between "us" and "them" – a state of affairs "signifying the triumph of unthinking Manicheanism over rational as well as self-critical analysis."[35] This stock of scurrilities most of the time lies below the threshold of public consciousness – a subliminal collective non-place where it is, as it were, incubated in cold storage. During a crisis in the Middle East (or a terrorist attack in the United States, no matter who its author might be), it is dragged out to invade the public space, saturating in the process the psyche of a large, ill-informed audience which – though generally passive and apolitical – can be massively transformed into de facto enemies of Arabs and Muslims almost overnight.

As I pointed out earlier, most of the academic critics who have commented on *Orientalism* have very little to say either about Said's other writings on the Orientalist tradition or about the extent to which anti-Islamic, anti-Arab sentiment is openly nurtured by people (like Lewis) who consider themselves as objective students of Islam and by others who have been influenced by them. One of the few scholars to draw attention both to Said's continuing indictment of Orientalism and to the prevailing hostility to Arab-Islamic culture is Nicholas Thomas. He writes that Said's various writings on the Orientalist tradition over the past several decades may have been "crude and repetitive." But, he adds, "they were no more so than the works in the Middle Eastern studies that he discussed, which were situated largely within the agendas of American foreign policy, and for the most part reflected the extremely negative views of Arabs and Arab perspectives then prevalent."[36] Thomas specifically stresses the connection between the negative transformation in the tradition during the second half of the twentieth century, on the one hand, and the consolidation of the Zionist political agenda in the United States, on the other:

> Said's over-emphasis on the negative dimensions of Orientalism needs to be placed in its context. While black Africans and Australian Aborigines are often portrayed in sympathetic or humanistic ways at present, in contrast to the highly racist images typical of the nineteenth and early twentieth centuries ... the trajectory with respect to the Middle East is virtually the reverse: there was a distinct "arabophile" strand in nineteenth century views, that continues to be conspicuous up to say the 1950s in books such as those of Charles Doughty and Wilfred Thesiger, and in films like Frank Hurley's 1948

Cradle of Creation ... that sentimentally idealized the biblical lifestyle of marsh-dwellers, pastoralists and Jerusalem potters. While these texts mostly failed to question the privilege of Western perception, and often rendered Middle Eastern societies as archaic, picturesque and decaying, they frequently dealt with individuals rather than types, and oscillated between approbation and denigration. But the circumstances of the Arab–Israeli conflict from 1948 on led to a consolidation of the most negative of prior images, which were later augmented by deeply dehumanizing constructions of the terrorists who, it was explicitly suggested, took up where Hitler had left off. These images were (and still are) circulated like other cultural products in a diverse and uncoordinated way through feature films, novels, journalistic commentary and many other means, but the specifically political effectiveness of such representations was ensured by the efforts of the pro-Israel lobby in the United States to silence and discredit pro-Palestinian voices – efforts which were remarkably successful up until the invasion of Lebanon in 1982.[37]

At a later stage of my discussion, I will reflect on the affiliations that Said identifies between Zionism and Orientalism. At this point, however, I would like to turn to the broad issue of imperialism as a specific ideological phenomenon – its genesis and morphology, its connections with Eurocentrism in general, the historical grounds it traversed, its manifestations in the contemporary world. Although *Orientalism*, *The Question of Palestine*, and a large number of shorter pieces deal indirectly (or in specific ways) with this topic, Said's most sustained, direct confrontation with imperialism takes place in *Culture and Imperialism*, a fascinating late book whose "contrapuntal" structure draws out to their logical extremes such earlier notions as meditation and affiliation. Like his other political writings, the book revisits – through casual allusions; partial recoveries; substantial expansions, clarifications, and rearrangements – such broad topics as the intellectual's ethico-political role in society, the construction of identities and canons, the complicity between political power and humanistic disciplines, and the (mis)representation of otherness. These re-engagements, however, take place in such a manner that, this time, they all shed light on one major theme: political-cultural imperialism as idea and practice.

The Birth of Hierarchism: Identity, Imperialism, and the Canon

As its title indicates, the book deals with the often submerged connections between culture – in the broad sense certainly, but more significantly in the narrower, privileged sense – and imperialism as a historical problem of the modern world, an unevenly experienced relationship between the West and the non-West. More precisely, the study is an investigation into the cultural archive of high European imperialism, an attempt not just to describe the brutalizing everyday presence of colonialism as an established political fact but to account for the extraordinary vitality of organized imperialism as an ideology both during the nineteenth century – its heyday – and in the twentieth. As such the argument of the book responds to questions like these: how is it that such a coarsening political program of action could have been conceived by the very same culture that also nurtured the philosophes, Kant, and Marx? What idea or ensemble of ideas eventuated its inaugural audacity? Is it possible to locate this inaugural moment at a particular historical and cultural intersection? Did the imperial mentality come into being, full-blown, in the late nineteenth century, as is commonly believed, or does it in fact have a much longer genealogy? Having been established – and actually experienced as a historical-political reality in Africa, Asia, and elsewhere – and hence given its enormous cost, why was it tolerated for such a long time by European society? In what way did rarefied intellectual productions directly rationalize, or otherwise camouflage, the use of power? What particular role did literature, for example, play in this rationalization and concealment? Is the era of imperialism really over yet? If so, why is it that even today, long after colonialism was pronounced dead, its residuum exercises such a powerful hold on Westerners and non-Westerners alike, stirring unedifying passions and often leading to catastrophic wars?

From a slightly different perspective, we can ask: is the United States an imperial nation or not? Are there any significant qualitative differences between what openly imperialistic nations like Britain and France did in their respective colonies and what America has undertaken to do in more recent times, say, in Korea or Nicaragua?

Addressing these questions could begin with the following passage:

> For the European of the late nineteenth century, an interesting range of options are offered, all premised upon the subordination and victimization of the native. One is a self-forgetting delight in the use of power – the power to observe, rule, hold, and profit from distant territories and people. From these come voyages of discovery, lucrative trade, administration, annexation, learned expeditions and exhibitions, local spectacles, a new class of colonial rulers and experts. Another is an ideological rationale for reducing, then reconstituting the native as someone to be ruled and managed. There are styles of rule ... And one finds them inscribed within the humanistic

enterprise itself: the various colonial schools, colleges, and universities, the
native elites created and manipulated throughout Africa and Asia. Third is the
idea of Western salvation and redemption through its "civilizing mission."
Supported jointly by the experts in ideas (missionaries, teachers, advisers,
scholars) and in modern industry and communication, the imperial idea of
westernizing the backward achieved permanent status world-wide, but ... it
was always accompanied by domination. Fourth is the security of a situation
that permits the conqueror not to look into the truth of the violence he does.
The idea of culture itself, as Arnold refined it, is designed to elevate practice
to the level of theory, to liberate ideological coercion against rebellious elements – at home and abroad – from the mundane and historical to the abstract
and general. "The best that is thought and done" is considered an unassailable
position, at home and abroad. Fifth is the process by which, after the natives
have been displaced from their historical location on their land, their history
is rewritten as a function of the imperial one. This process uses narrative to
dispel contradictory memories and occlude violence – the exotic replaces the
impress of power with the blandishments of curiosity – with the imperial
presence so dominating as to make impossible any effort to separate it from
historical necessity. All these together create an amalgam of the arts of narrative and observation about the accumulated, dominated, and ruled territories whose inhabitants seem destined never to escape, to remain creatures of
European will.[38]

This highly schematized summation is intended to show in a stark
fashion the extent to which the imperial ideology was, in Said's view,
sustained by a carefully concealed transaction between two greatly
valorized poles of a European cultural axis: a multi-inflectioned, finely
nuanced elaboration (and distribution) of an aesthetic/ethical pole
refracts its beautifying, Arnoldian sweetness and light over consolidations actualized by a power pole of political rule and military
force; thereby, the crudeness and raw brutality of imperial practice
are antiseptically transfigured into an economy of values; the power
of technological efficiency begets profit, induces enjoyment, and
confers rectitude. My brief analysis of *Culture and Imperialism* will
highlight what Said considers to be the dimensions and vectors of
this dialectic, in the process also elucidating three important metaphors
that together act as a dynamic methodological guide for the text:
"structures of attitudes and references," the cartographic attitude of
reconstructing historical understanding geographically, and the musical
notion of "contrapuntality." All three metaphors instantiate – and fine-
tune in specific ways – what I have been describing as a confrontation
between agonistic dialectic and archaeology/genealogy, a confrontation
which has epistemological, historical, cultural, and ethico-political
implications.

Said's book deals with a curious paradox which he argues was historically incorporated into the gradual constitution of identitarian thinking in Eurocentric thought, a paradox which resulted from two antithetical versions of the idea of culture in the West. On the one hand, the formation of national (English, French, German, etc.) literatures and other cultural achievements was largely coextensive with – and essential to – the construction of national identities and institutions in the years between 1745 and 1945. This same process was also crucial to the *idea* of nationalism as such, now and in the past. On the other hand, the same period also witnessed the birth of a more universalist, more pluralist counter-tradition: the humanistic ideals of secular anthropology and philological hermeneutics whose point of departure was "the belief that mankind formed a marvelous, almost symphonic whole whose progress and formation, again as a whole, could be studied exclusively as a concerted and secular historical experience, not as an exemplification of the divine."[39] Said tells us that this latter tradition is found in its pristine form in the works of Vico, Rousseau, Herder, and the brothers Schlegel. Clearly the allusion – at least partially – is to the idea, discussed in my earlier chapters, that humanity forms an autodidactic fraternity of cultures affiliated together by means of adjacent, complementary, and parallel links. The paradox, at one level, is that this egalitarian, pluralist intellectual current itself in time succumbed to a form of exclusionary hierarchism and hence betrayed its inaugural ideals. According to Said, this hierarchical impulse led to what came to be known as "comparative literature," a notion that, though at times broadly inclusive (for example in "Goethe's idea of Weltliteratur"),[40] eventually consolidated itself – as it was elaborated by De Sanctis, Curtius, Spitzer, and Auerbach, among others – in the form of an exclusively European canon, that is, a continually refined Greco-Roman and Christian heritage. This is the heritage that Arnold – in opposition to what he perceived to be English "philistinism" (or parochialism, complacency, and ignorance) – elevated as "the best that is thought and done" in Europe.

The deeper and more insidious paradox of elite culture emerges at this level: the historical synthesis, in the nineteenth and twentieth centuries, between autonomous national cultures and a common European culture – a synthesis whose *idealistic* emblem Said identifies as comparative literature itself – not only coincided with the *material* consolidation of European imperialism in the non-Western world but was ultimately wedded to it. Rather than arguing for a direct base–

superstructure equivalence between imperialism and comparative literature (or for that matter imperialism and any *single* intellectual field), Said, I think, is pointing to what could be described as an analogous – and ultimately hegemonic – relationship between versions of *centrality* and *peripherality* which are in his estimation best exemplified by comparative literature and imperialism as two forms of socio-cultural practice. To the extent that the idea of comparative literature came to be understood as a *hierarchy* of canons some of which were vigorously promoted while others (i.e., non-European canons) were either seriously faulted or completely excised, to that extent the field acted as the *idealistic* analogue of the geopolitical realities that prevailed during the period of the field's full emergence in the late nineteenth century and early twentieth. European imperial nations like Britain, France, Belgium, and the Netherlands held sway over vast swathes of Africa, Asia, and elsewhere. Moreover, although often in competition with one another, the political and intellectual elites of these nations almost never wavered in their commitment to the doctrine that there was a hierarchy of peoples – namely, the superior Europeans who *ought* to rule and the inferior races who ought to submit to that rule.

The broader point to emerge out of all this is that the idea of having an empire – which in the case of Britain and to a lesser extent France acquired the status of an ontological imperative – came into being as an almost inevitable consequence of the conjunction of a whole ensemble of closely related attitudes, predispositions, and commitments – all of which converged on defining oneself and otherness in terms of valorizations and demotions. For the Englishness of the "Englishman" to be constituted, it was necessary that there be not only Frenchness and Germanness but also an essential Europe, an essential Orient, and an essential Africa – all of them laden with (collaborative and contrastive) meanings and values. It is this set of cultural coordinates, which the United States has inherited from Europe under the rubric of a shared Western destiny, that helped fashion the two affiliated ideas of European supremacism and high European imperialism. As I noted in my first chapter, Said considers Conrad's writing as both inscribing these ideas in their starkest forms and registering an extreme suspicion of them.

Structure of Attitudes and References

What Said detects behind these twin ideas – and this brings us to the first of the specialized metaphors – is "a structure of attitudes and references." This notion in some respects echoes – and refines – the idea of "intentional structure" that I discussed in preceding parts of my study, both in its literary-philosophical sense (i.e., in *Beginnings*) and in the more overtly wordly or political recasting of the term in *Orientalism* and *The World, the Text, and the Critic*. But whereas "intention" or "intentional structure" was thematized in (or at least recovered from) phenomenological and poststructuralist contexts in *Beginnings* and *Orientalism* for example, "structure of attitudes and references" has been appropriated from the more friendly context of cultural Marxism. Said suggests that he has adapted Williams's phrase "structures of feeling." The latter term is at once suggestive and elusive, in part because Williams seems to have subtly expanded – and fine-tuned – its meaning as he repeatedly deployed it in different studies over the years, but it appears that Williams coined the phrase in order to describe a form of practical social consciousness similar to hegemony but less burdened with negative associations and more sensitive to historical change. In other words, it cannot be reduced either to the dominant socio-political power or to a set of explicit doctrines (that is, an ideology), but it is nevertheless capable of incorporating, modifying, or cooperating with these privileged forms of authority – precisely because it constitutes the very process of everyday experience in any given period:

> It is not only that we must go beyond formally held belief [in describing "structures of feeling"] ... It is that we are concerned with meanings and values as they are actively lived and felt, and the relations between these and formal or systematic beliefs are in practice variable (including historically variable), over a range from formal assent with private dissent to the more nuanced interaction between selected and interpreted beliefs and justified experiences.[41]

What should be stressed is that, even though it is "emergent or pre-emergent," this kind of practical consciousness can "exert palpable pressures and effective limits"[42] because it is present, according to Williams, as an active, complex, homogenizing substance in what is *analytically* often dichotomized as opposing pairs – i.e., the personal and the social, the subjective and the objective, the present and the

EDWARD SAID

past, that which is felt and that which is thought, and so on. Rather than being a fixed formation or a finished product, "a structure of feeling" is a lived process, a sort of experiential solution in motion which has *immediate* (as opposed to "sublimated" or "unconscious") implications for what transpires in spheres of cultural life as far apart as the political and the artistic. Williams suggests that the interpretive value of this "hypothesis" lies in the fact that, without collapsing all socio-cultural processes into the political or economic, the radical critic can use it to counteract formalized bourgeois techniques of organization and analysis (the imagination, aesthetic taste, the arts, etc.) which tend to evacuate – or vastly reduce – the affective, social content of literature, thereby transforming it into a privately recoverable, valorized distillation largely unconcerned with – and uncontaminated by – the material processes of everyday socio-political life. Hence its enormous usefulness for discussions of literary production and reception: "structure of feeling" opens up literature (and indeed elite culture in general) both into the broad domain of culture as "a way of life" and into the operations of socio-political institutions – without, however, insisting on a strict equivalence among these interrelated areas. Williams maintains that the same structure of feeling does not continue to operate in society indefinitely; rather specific periods or generations have their own generalizable, distinct styles or milieux; by stressing the historical specificity of the hypothesis, he holds out the possibility that – with the realization of radical, progressive changes in society – more humane structures of feeling may eventually come into being.

Said's adaptation of the term is meant to capture all these nuances, but he hones it further to describe – and interrogate – the imperial ideology (an area to which, in Said's view, Williams did not pay enough attention). The imperial mindset, in other words, can be characterized as a gradually emerging, continually processed experiential field: a network of intentional acts and objects – a hegemonic affiliation – emanating out of Europe, with a global agenda of outward expansion and recovery, an agenda whose historical formation since the eighteenth century (and in some respects even earlier) largely coextends with the gradual constitution of middle-class subjectivity, the trajectory of the Enlightenment master narrative, and the attending explosion of knowledge systems and technologies. "Structure of attitudes and references" designates this constellation at a broad level, but it is at the more localized level of differentiated articulations, and their implicit or explicit relationships with the global constellation, that its cogency becomes evident.

In other words, "structure of attitudes and references" is a meta-device that describes and dissolves the reified, analytically conceived interpretations of Western culture and its relationship with the rest of the world since the mid-eighteenth century. Thereby it uncovers the lived, substantive experiences of individuals and collectivities evolving in that culture, as well as the effective (because felt, thought, acted upon) connections, imbrications, and interactions between, and within, several orders of social reality – the aesthetic, the ethical, the political, the economic, etc. – at various points over the past two to three centuries as this whole cultural drama initiated, then variously rationalized, imperialism as an idea *and* as a program of action, in the process building and fortifying its institutions (both at home and in the imperium) against the none-too-frequent criticism of it in Europe and especially against the gradually intensifying resistance of the colonized. It should be clear at this point that, in its interpretive operations, this device is not a straightforward, descriptive heuristic but rather has some of the features of deconstructive unbalancing, genealogical recovery, and phenomenological (re)construction. It is also emphatically dialectical. That is, it can be conceived horizontally, vertically, or obliquely – or all at once – in the process cutting through received conceptual frames of knowledge and reinterpreting the uses to which that knowledge has been (and continues to be) put in various spheres of Western cultural life.

What does all this mean with respect to specific, identifiable structures that Said believes he has uncovered? Here is a short list of structures of attitudes and references which, though itemized here, could be (and were experientially) combined in a variety of ways, all of them converging on empire – or at least Eurocentric experience – *as a way of life* warranted by the nature of things. One identifiable structure would constitute certain hierarchist/comparatist conceptions (about races and civilizations, about order and rationality, about morality and beauty, etc.) in which European or Western cultural forms were – and still are – invariably seen as *the* norm, while all others (and the gradient would decline in proportion to an imagined cultural distance from Europe) became deviations from it. The reverse side of this normative structure of attitudes and references would be exposed if one were to trace the gradual formation of, say, the presumed inferiority of this or that non-European race as that idea, having gradually worked its way and matured in the culture at large, eventually crystallized in the writings of various Eurocentric ideolo-

gues – the likes of Carlyle, Renan, Charles Temple, and Benjamin
Kidd. Said also uses this device to uncover a large number of other
enactments executed in the course of high European imperialism. In
short, "structure of attitudes and references" disposes the interpretive
and explanatory functions of the notion of hegemony and affiliation
that Said utilized in earlier studies – but with an important difference:
it is more nuanced, more subtle, more responsive to the micro-
arrangements of material culture and to the various historical sedimentations of meaning and value in separate but overlapping spheres
while also solidly retaining the broad meaning of hegemonic domination.

As I pointed out earlier, the form is particularly useful in the
analysis of literary works, as well as their relationship to other
intellectual fields and to the larger cultural formations and processes
at work at strategically chosen historical moments or during long
stretches of time. Intellectual and artistic representations of the
"centre" and "periphery" have a way of colluding with the will to
mastery precisely through the intentional web created by a common
cultural currency – that is a common "structure of attitudes of
references." Understanding the multiple levels, sites, agencies, and
directions of this structure is therefore essential for the critic whose
aim is to show how literature in general, specific genres (say, the
novel), specific authors (for example, Conrad), or specific works (e.g.
Heart of Darkness) maintain their "particularity" or "particular genius"
and yet disguise, modify, and when all is said and done confirm the
explicit formulations of imperial dogma, the moral/theoretical justification of that dogma, and the practical, politico-military enactments
it authorizes.

It should be pointed out that Said makes an *implied* distinction
between comparative literature as described earlier and national literatures in their modulated commitment to imperialism, but that
distinction is only one of degree rather than kind. Whereas the idea of
comparative literature largely coincides with a supremacist idea of
Europe, national literatures – particularly that of Britain – have
tended to elaborate and refine the *idea of imperialism* and its growing
importance as it gradually becomes an all-enveloping cultural and
political practice. That is to say, for example, a specific set of
imperialist attitudes and references – i.e., governing or controlling
distant lands, judging their indigenous inhabitants as less than fully
human, deriving wealth and comfort from their resources, etc. –
which an early nineteenth-century writer like Jane Austen would have

treated both briefly and nonchalantly (Antigua is "vaguely out there"; it is not described in any great detail, but its slave-run plantations must, in the nature of things, generate wealth and distinction for Mansfield Park) becomes, for a late Victorian or early twentieth-century writer (say, a Conrad or a Kipling), a dominant – indeed *the* determinant – socio-cultural theme, precisely because England's stature as an imperialist power unparalleled in history has, by the later date, grown to such an extent that it assumes metaphysical proportions. Britannia is *destined* to rule the waves, and British literature is not in the business of contradicting that destiny.

Expressed in the Foucauldian terminology of *Orientalism*, this means that literary discourse is caught up, along with those of other intellectual fields, in the gradual emergence of a broad new discursive field, which is ultimately none other than the episteme of modernity described by Foucault as being responsible for the disciplinary invention of man. In Gramscian terms, the same socio-historical phenomenon can be seen as the formation of a new hegemonic authority in which Europe – through a process of admonitions, interdictions, preferences, and suppressions – is constituted as the geographical, aesthetic, moral, intellectual, and political center of the entire globe while the rest of humanity becomes its vassals. According to Said, both comparative literature as a field and specific national literatures – especially in their narrative versions – have participated in that process. In short, literature and literary intellectuals do not cause the urge to grab land in any direct mechanical sense, but they often make available subtle justifications or mediations and are, therefore, subject to critical investigations into the operations of imperialist ideology. Conducting such an investigation, believes Said, does not constitute an impoverishment of literature. On the contrary, it is an enhancement of it.

It is with this critical agenda in mind that Said focuses attention on a relatively small number of texts – most of them nineteenth- and early twentieth-century English novels – whose close readings lend support to the thesis that literature has been structured into Euro-centrism and imperialism. Said's extensive analysis of Austen's *Mansfield Park*, Verdi's *Aida*, Kipling's *Kim*, Forster's *A Passage to India*, and Camus' novels and short stories illustrates a thesis that he broached as early as *Beginnings*: the inherent conservatism and collusiveness of modern narrative literature in Europe, a genre which – in the process of institutionalizing itself as the repository of bourgeois subjectivity – opened up into, gave imaginable density to, discursively elaborated, and ultimately ratified Europe's narrativization and historicization of itself in the form of the continuously unfolding master trope of the Enlightenment, as well as Europe's self-empowerment through the normative authorization of its socio-cultural will:

> The crucial aspect of what I have been calling the novel's consolidation of authority is not simply connected to the functioning of social power and governance, but made to appear both normative and sovereign, that is self-validating in the course of the narrative. This is paradoxical only if one forgets that the constitution of narrative subject, however abnormal or unusual, is still a social act *par excellence*, and as such has behind or inside it the authority of history and society. There is first the authority of the author – someone writing the processes of society in an acceptable institutionalized manner, observing conventions, following patterns, and so forth. Then there is the authority of the narrator, whose discourse anchors the narrative in recognizable, and hence existentially referential, circumstances. Last, there is what might be called the authority of the community, whose representative most often is the family but also is the nation, the specific locality, and the concrete historical moment. [By extension, the authority of "essential Europe" is implicated in all this.] Together these functioned most energetically, most noticeably, during the early nineteenth century as the novel opened up to history in an unprecedented way. Conrad's Marlow [as well as all European novels and narrators of this period] inherits all this directly.[43]

It is the English novel that – in its covert (and in Kipling's case overt) commitment to what Said calls (after the historian D. C. M. Platt) a "departmental view" of global imperialism[44] – manifests this codification of social authority in its most pronounced form: "the nineteenth-century English novels stress the continuing existence (as opposed to revolutionary overturning) of England. Moreover, they *never* advocate giving up colonies but take the long-range view that since they fall within the orbit of British dominance, *that* dominance is a sort of norm, and thus conserved along with the colonies."[45] Said suggests that this novelistic consensus for the conservation and continuation of imperialism holds fast – even for novels, such as *A Passage to India* or *Nostromo*, which expose the ideology of political and cultural imperialism and provide a reasonably accurate estimation of the enormous cost that ideology entails. It is in this context – both cultural and historical – that Said's discussion of "structures of attitudes and references," as well as the emphasis that he places on land, should be understood. The metaphor designates this vast, saturated intentional web which is rarely ever acknowledged by mainstream interpreters of culture.

The Geography of Imperialism: Activating the Historical Stage

Said's utilization of the spatial metaphor, and more specifically the cartographical inflection, is designed to delineate the parameters of the discussion further and to introduce a more explicitly materialist dimension into it; but more importantly, it sets the argument up as a *historical stage*. Said repeatedly reminds us that an important objective of the study is to draw the contours of the interfaced intellectual and geopolitical terrains on which current contests are being fought, to describe, in his words, the "intertwined and overlapping histories"[46] of the metropolitan West and those cultures that were paradoxically at once integrated into and excluded from Western society by the omnipresent legislative power of imperialism. This strategic fore-grounding of geography-in-history accentuates motifs that formed part of the background of earlier studies. In preceding chapters, I discussed the way in which materiality, concrete positivity (of the body, the natural environment, cultural objects, etc.), and exteriority interacted with human subjectivity as this whole constellation determined the dynamic configuration of human history in spatio-temporal fields, or experiential gestalts, constructing in the process what we know as society in the context of modernity: one cannot conceive of mind, language, or action – the hallmarks of secular human agency – without locating them, without *placing* them in cultural space and in the drama of praxis. I also argued that one way in which Said has tried to undermine linearity and foundationalism – unsullied origins, essentialized identities, teleological horizons, etc. – has been to insist on the patterns of human interrelatedness – what he has called (in *Beginnings*) the multiplicity, correlation, and com-plementarity of socio-cultural forms from different times and climes. It is this *sensus communis* that is further crystallized by the notion of affiliation in *The World, the Text, and the Critic*. Said suggests that these patterns of development and organization are discernible in modern intellectual history in general but are especially pronounced in the historico-philosophical constructions of Vico and Foucault and in the layered, lateral imbrications of high modernism.

Finally, one of his indictments of Orientalists is that they helped structure a historico-geographical Orient of the mind, a discursive tableau vivant on which "Orientals" could be manufactured, observed, manipulated, preserved, dissected, judged – an intentionally struc-tured place that serves as museum, laboratory, storehouse, and theater in equal measure. What all of these aspects of the earlier studies have in common is that they suggest, and at times insist on, notions of dynamic spatiality: a historical conception of geography or (what is the same thing) a geographical conception of history. Whether accented positively (as in *Beginnings*), negatively (as in *Orientalism*), or ambiguously (as in *The World*), these complementary ways of under-standing time, circumstance, culture, and society underlie what Said has summed up in the idea worldliness. This combination of archaeological excavation and genealogical retrieval – techniques which, thanks to Foucault, Said himself, the new historicists and cultural materialists, as well as the postmodernist dramatization of the social space, have become common currency in recent critical theory debates – is greatly emphasized in *Culture and Imperialism*.

Said's aim, in other words, is interpretively to *activate* and *articulate* (his phrasing) the vast socio-cultural space – in the West and non-West – on which imperialism first expanded, then consolidated itself, and later suffered heavy losses. It is on this same stage that con-temporary intellectual and geopolitical contests are taking place. The following passage gives us an idea of the weight he attaches to land in the contest between the forces of imperialism and those resisting it.

> Underlying social space are territories, lands, geographical domains, the actual geographical underpinnings of the imperial, and also the cultural context. To think about distant places, to colonize them, to populate or depopulate them: all of this occurs on, about, or because of land. The actual geographical possession of land is what empire in the final analysis is all about. At the moment when a coincidence occurs between real control and power, the idea of what a given place was (could be, might become), and an actual place – at that moment the struggle for empire is launched. This coincidence is the logic both for Westerners taking possession of land and, during decolonization, for resisting natives reclaiming it. Imperialism and the culture associated with it affirm both the primacy of geography and an ideology about control of ter-ritory. The geographical sense makes projections – imaginative, cartographic, military, economic, historical, or in a general sense cultural. It also makes possible the construction of various kinds of knowledge, all of them in one way or another dependent upon the perceived character and destiny of a particular geography.[47]

But precisely because this historical theater is global in its dimensions and hence manifests varieties of localized shades, inflec-tions, and intersections, it is almost impossible to provide an ency-clopedic re-presentation of its components. Instead, Said opts for a multi-purpose principle of selection. That principle allows him to identify those imperial nations which (he believes) accumulated so much political, economic, and military power as to enable them to acquire a large number of colonial possessions or (what amounts to the same thing) to exercise the most far-reaching influence over far-flung regions of the globe. Hence his concentration on nineteenth- and early twentieth-century France and (especially) Britain, as well as postwar America. This same principle also enables him to examine what could be called the rhetoric of imperialism – the idioms and tropes in various intellectual fields that advocated the acquisition of land, justified the exploitation of natural resources, rationalized the use of force against rebellious natives, or otherwise dehumanized them (among the large number of influential thinkers Said associates with this kind of rhetoric are Fourier, Ruskin, Tocqueville, and John Stuart Mill). He also isolates literary forms that gave premium to social space and, at least indirectly, afforded sustenance to the imperial project. (As I pointed out in the context of structures of attitudes and references, the novel – and the narrative form in general – occupies this position. According to Said, all the texts alluded to above give priority to social space at home or abroad in a manner that illustrates imperial trans-actions. *Aida*, of course, is not a novel, but as an operatic work staged in an imperialized "Oriental" setting and dramatizing the "exotic" lives of "Oriental" beings, it illustrates what Said characterizes as the coincidence of the will to power and imperial control). And finally he reconstructs carefully selected sites in the West and in the colonies (England, Algeria, Egypt, and India are among them) that, as they were represented in literature, instantiate either the hegemonic pre-servation and consolidation of empire as an achieved enactment of governance over distant peoples, lands, and resources, or the gradual mapping out of spaces *at home* with the help of wealth generated through the imperial venture. All these aspects of territoriality or spatiality strategically work together to light up the historical stage at carefully mapped-out moments of concert, moments that together make up a sedimented series of deployments, ruptures, and transfor-mations rather than a continuous, comprehensive narrative.

Contrapuntality Versus Hierarchy: An Atonal Conception of Community

But if *Culture and Imperialism* in one sense constitutes a theatrically activated genealogy of imperialism, it is in a slightly different sense a diagnostic–therapeutic exercise. In Said's view any attempt to draw

the affective and cognitive map of modern imperialism as a worldwide
phenomenon must account not just for the convergences, alignments,
and overlappings but also for the misrecognized or disavowed faul-
tlines, pressure points, tensions, reversals, and mutations. Clearing a
space for critical consciousness – with all the disjunctions it harbors –
this multi-vectored intervention is essential in order for the symptoms
or "discrepancies" of imperial culture to be unmasked and for the
multiple connections of human communities to emerge into full view.
To phrase the point differently, an interpretive reversal is necessary.
To effect this reversal – or more precisely to suggest a way of effecting
it: this is one of the primary objectives of Said's study. Using the
Gramscian notion of "fissure" as an important illustrative point, he
argues that such an approach would create a new, "contrapuntal"
knowledge which, he suggests, would be far more insightful than the
facilely universalizing, ultimately totalitarian knowledge systems
encouraged by Eurocentrism:

> An example of the new knowledge would be the study of Orientalism or
> Africanism and, to take a related set, the study of Englishness and Frenchness.
> These identities are today analyzed not as god-given essences, but as results of
> collaboration between African history and the study of Africa in England, for
> instance, or between the study of French history and the reorganization of
> knowledge during the First Empire. In an important sense, we are dealing
> with the formation of cultural identities understood not as essentializations
> (although part of their enduring appeal is that they seem and are considered to
> be like essentializations) but as contrapuntal ensembles, for it is the case that
> no identity can ever exist by itself and without an array of opposites, nega-
> tives, oppositions: Greeks always require barbarians, and Europeans Africans,
> Orientals, etc. The opposite is certainly true as well. Even the mammoth
> engagements in our own time over such essentializations as "Islam," the
> "West," and "Orient," "Japan," or "Europe" admit to a particular knowledge
> and structures of attitude and reference, and those require careful research and
> analysis.[48]

It is in that revisionary spirit that he alludes to a large number of non-
Western thinkers critical of the West and, more importantly, focuses
on a carefully selected set of texts each one of which deconstructs
Eurocentric knowledge and the imperial mindset from a historically
and culturally specific locus: C. L. R. James's *The Black Jacobins*,
George Antonius's *The Arab Awakening*, Ranjit Guha's *A Rule of
Property for Bengal*, and S. H. Alatas's *The Myth of the Lazy Native*. Each
of these books examines a localized topic and either contests an
institutionally normalized history, overturns an interpretively con-

secrated judgement, uncovers a duplicitous strategy, or restores a suppressed memory.

That is to say, *Culture and Imperialism* is ultimately a strategic activation and articulation of the *affiliations* that form the constitutive structures of imperial culture, an ensemble of analogous, parallel, collaborative, contrastive, disjunctive, and/or asymmetrical experiences, forces, histories, and orientations: "we must be able to think through and interpret together experiences that are discrepant, each with its particular agenda and pace of development, its own internal formations, its internal coherence and system of external relationships, all of them coexisting and interacting with others."[49] All these elements bring the stage of modern imperial history as Said sees it back to life for a late twentieth- (and early twenty-first-) century audience that is no longer purely Western, as the case would have been for Austen or Conrad, but includes a substantial number of postcolonial intellectuals who, by virtue of their knowledge of the Western tradition as well as their own, have the capacity – and the will – to initiate a productive dialogue between, and within, them.

To set side by side the valorized narrative of "Western civilization" and that other history – Arab nationalism, for instance – which the Western reader more often than not has been taught to hate, despise, demonize; to insist that what to Marlow and Kurtz (and ultimately Conrad himself) was the malign darkness of Africa is in fact none other than an African culture's resistance to imperial intrusion; to demonstrate that the genial innocence claimed for America can be easily translated into a sordid history of rapacity, megalomania, and genocide that continues to the present day in one form or another: this strategic collaging of the familiar, the alien, and the scandalous is probably the most disturbing aspect of the study from the perspective of the vast majority of Western readers who have internalized the mythology of Eurocentrism. Involving the immanent deployment of evidence as technique, it is designed to confront modern Western agency with its Dark Other in the starkest fashion. Said characterizes this method as a comparative literature of imperialism, a dialogue of cultures that, though already massively knotted together, have hitherto been treated by the reigning interpretive consensus as though they were almost ontologically exclusive to one another. It is an attempt to blur the distinction between the so-called center and periphery bandied around in current debates, to show that institutionalizing marginality – the tiny space cleared for, and by, the subaltern in Western academia – is nothing more than a polite (i.e.

"politically correct") way of reinscribing old hierarchies and exclusions, hence reinforcing old essentializations and misrepresentations. In short, Said is arguing for a convocation of multiple cultures and canons.

Said's evocation of a radicalized musical conception is particularly suggestive in this regard; what he calls the "contrapuntal method" is intended to convey the Adornian idea of atonality, hence going beyond symphonic assimilation or harmony and insisting on the contrastive, juxtapositional activation of a negative dialectic:

> [T]his global contrapuntal analysis should be modeled not (as earlier notions of comparative literature were) on a symphony but rather on an atonal ensemble; we must take into account all sorts of spatial or geographical and rhetorical practices – inflections, limits, constraints, intrusions, inclusions, prohibitions – all of them tending to elucidate a complex and uneven topography. A gifted critic's intuitive synthesis, of the type volunteered by hermeneutic or philological interpretation (whose prototype is Dilthey), is still of value, but strikes me as the poignant reminder of a serener time than ours.[50]

The idea of contrapuntality is meant both to warrant multiple thematizations or renditions of the same note and to dramatize the project of imperialism and its interlocution as an ongoing process that links the present with the past and the future:

> As we look back at the cultural archive, we begin to reread it not univocally but *contrapuntally*, with a simultaneous awareness both of the metropolitan history that is narrated and of those other histories against which (and together with which) the dominating discourse acts. In the counterpoint of the Western classical music, various themes play off one another, with only a provisional privilege being given to any particular one; yet in the resulting polyphony there is concert and order, an organized interplay that derives from the themes, not from a rigorous melodic or formal principle outside the work. In the same way, I believe, we can read and interpret English novels, for example, whose engagement (usually suppressed for the most part) with the West Indies or India, say, is shaped and perhaps even determined by the specific history of colonization, resistance, and finally native nationalism. At this point alternative or new narratives emerge, and they become institutionalized or discursively stable entities.[51]

All of this means that, methodologically, the combination of intentionality, structuration, spatiality, polyvocality, and (proactive/retroactive) temporality into an ensemble ensures that what might normally be called the form and content of the argument are structured together immanently at every point rather than being deployed along the lines of the traditional, Aristotelian triad of introduction, middle, and conclusion. The "total" effect of the repetitions, distanciations, doublings, dissonances, and juxtapositions is cumulative rather than narrowly logical. It is also for that same reason open-ended.

Ahabian Megalomania: Imperialism in the American Century

An important strand in Said's argument is that imperialism, like its Orientalist cousin, is alive and well in the contemporary world – though modulated somewhat for purposes of camouflage. On the face of it, this is a bold, potentially risky proposition. How can anyone make such a claim – it might be argued – in a putatively *post*colonial era? After all, successful anti-colonial wars have been fought all over the globe in the past several decades; the unabashedly racist, triumphalist rhetoric of earlier times – the rhetoric of conquest, savage natives, civilizing missions, and other associated humbug – seems laughable to most people in the world today; the visions of such great anti-imperialist leaders as Gandhi and Mandela have been openly embraced worldwide, and not least in the West; there are multiple, internationally sanctioned institutions and legislations – foremost among which are the United Nations and its charter – that unambiguously outlaw any form of domination, imperial or otherwise; and such principles as self-determination, human rights, and democratic governance have been adopted (even enshrined) by most nations of the world as the threshold of acceptable political behavior – even though, to the chagrin of all decent people, many third world governments often flout these principles. These are undeniable realities that all of us should welcome. At worst, they reflect the ambiguities of globalization, but they also emphatically deflate extravagant claims about imperialism in the contemporary world. Obviously Said is talking through his hat!

The response to this challenge can be presented in the form of questions. If imperialism is well and truly dead, then how does one explain the grand Euro-American gestures and projections of power to distant lands in Africa, Asia, and Latin America over the past several decades? How does one account for the large number of American (or American-led) interventions – including assassinations, coups d'état, and massively destructive wars, together with more subtle but no less effective forms of pressure? Why is it that the descendants of yesterday's "natives" have been slaughtered in their millions (for example, in

places like Korea, Vietnam, and Iraq)? How does one get a handle on
the slew of chameleonic rationalizations offered by various American
administrations, sages, "experts," and media operatives for these
projections of power? What common denominator can be found for
such claims as containing the spread of communism, fighting for
freedom and democracy, protecting our vital national interests, com-
bating terrorism, enforcing the will of the international community,
and creating a New World Order? How is it that these stale bromides
are continually circulated, separately or in conjunction with one
another, despite the fact that every single one of them can be shown to
have created (and skirted) logical, epistemological, and moral mine-
fields – begged questions, doctored "solutions," dodged issues – and
hence leaves the emperor unclothed, so to speak? How does one
account for the remarkable consistency with which "third world"
governments (and by extension their peoples) are divided into two
politically and morally antithetical camps, one designated as good and
the other as demonic – while in reality the two camps (both of which
contain a large proportion of highly unpopular kings, dictators, oli-
garchs, and minority regimes) are amazingly similar to each other? Is
there any qualitative difference between those governments embraced
as "pro-Western," "friendly," or "moderate," on the one hand, and on
the other the excommunicated "rogue states" – the realm of the
Saddams, the Castros, the Khomeinis, and all those other dark hydras
of the world: is there any difference between them except that the
approved group are (to use Christopher Hitchens's apt description)
willing to "listen to raison d'état,"[52] whereas the condemned group,
who are by no means more culpable than their favored counterparts,
have had the temerity to defy "the Stern White Man"[53] (Said's
phrase)? In Said's view, all these enactments lead to an unmistakable
conclusion: whereas colonialism, or "the implanting of settlers on
distant territory," is largely a thing of the past, imperialism as a
supremacist, self-promoting structure of attitudes and references
"lingers where it has always been, in a kind of cultural sphere as well
as in specific political, ideological, economic, and social practices."[54]
Said suggests that this constellation of socio-cultural coordinates is
utilizable by all major Western powers. The immediate target of his
critique, however, is what he describes as the intellectual–political
synthesis in the United States since the end of the Second World War,
a synthesis which has institutionalized a mindset of ascendancy.

The close examination of this "institutionalized ideological rhetoric,"[55] in the service of which various ideologues have "employed

idioms of gigantism and apocalypse"[56] in the United States, exposes
the vectors of what could be called (though not by Said) a self-validating *double* dialectic: bipolar interactions between cultural authority
and power, on the one hand, and between Eurocentrism and American
exceptionalism, on the other. The result is the most self-occulting and
the most single-mindedly self-projecting ideology the world has ever
seen – an ideology whose epic proportions are matched only by its
Ahabian propensities. Citing such scholars as Perry Miller and Sacvan
Bercovitch, Said points out that this ideology, whose doctrinal core is
that there is such a thing as a uniquely privileged "American consciousness, identity, destiny, and role,"[57] has been long in the making,
with its roots stretching back all the way to the founding fathers and
the Puritan pilgrims. Though in part fashioned to absorb the diversity
of an immigrant community in order "to re-form it in a uniquely
American way," the gradual, saturating repetition of this kind of
rhetoric generation after generation led to "the illusion, if not the
actuality, of consensus."[58]

An important legacy of that consensus is that the creation of
America was an essentially pre-lapsarian enactment – an Edenic
experience unsullied by the corruptions of the Old World. (Memorialized by Lewis's book *The American Adam*, this mythology has been
articulated in different ways over the years.) It almost automatically
followed that, no matter how destructive it might be, the triumph of
American power was equivalent to the triumph of innocence and
goodness. "Thus [even today] the notion that American military
power might be used for malevolent purposes is relatively impossible
within the consensus, just as the idea that America is a force for good
in the world is routine and normal."[59] Equally important, Americans
have little sympathy for traditional cultures, instinctively siding with
pioneering nations (like Israel) "who are wresting the land from ill use
or from savages."[60] The implication is that – despite a general climate
nurturing unthinking belief in American supremacism, a belief which
is remarkably similar to European self-adulation but is nevertheless far
more cosmic in its symbolism; despite the repeated impositions of
America's will on small, generally non-European nations, just as the
European imperialists had done – with disastrous consequences;
despite the direct or indirect absorption, in the manner of classical
imperialism, of vast, far-flung resources into the American sphere of
influence; despite the hectoring, posturing, and bragging that pass for
American dialogue with "lesser" nations: despite all this, Americans
have almost never seen their "mission" in the world as being in any

way similar to that of European imperialists. Rather, American
political and cultural elites, now as in past centuries, have tended to
wrap themselves in the rhetoric of righteousness – "global responsibilities," "leadership," "peace and freedom," and the like. This, even
if millions have to perish in the process:

> [S]o influential has been the discourse insisting on American specialness,
> altruism, and opportunity, that "imperialism" as a word or ideology has
> turned up only recently and rarely in accounts of US culture, politics and
> history. But the connection between imperial politics and culture is aston-
> ishingly direct. American attitudes to American "greatness," to hierarchies of
> race, to the perils of *other* revolutions (the American revolution being con-
> sidered unique and somehow unrepeatable anywhere else in the world) ...
> have remained constant, have dictated, have obscured, the realities of empire,
> while apologists for overseas American interests have insisted on American
> innocence, doing good, fighting for freedom.[61]

According to Said, these and similar promptings, some of which
(e.g. Manifest Destiny and the Monroe Doctrine) were unambiguously
imperialist, eventually led to the postwar synthesis, a species of
"grandiose self-endowment"[62] contributed to by a large number of
policy-makers, mainstream political theorists and historians, media
pundits, and "experts" of various hues – prominent among whom are
Walter Lippmann, George Kennan, Henry Kissinger, Robert Tucker,
and various presidents. Effectively marginalizing dissent (which has
included both isolationism and anti-colonialism), this consensus has
largely determined the parameters of public discourse in the Cold
War years and beyond – leading in turn to militarism, inter-
ventionism, and various other forms of megalomaniacal self-expan-
sion.

Said suggests that this American synthesis has spawned a new
harvest of grand illusions about what America stands for, illusions
that both recover and refine in specific ways nineteenth-century
European self-deception: the illusion that America is militarily
invincible (a sense of omnipotence which has become part of the
almost unconsciously manufactured paraphernalia of superpowerism);
that "the American way of life" – sweepingly identified with freedom,
equality, prosperity, the "American dream," etc. and carefully purified
of any contaminations by genocide, slavery, and racism – is the best
conceived by man; that the so-called liberation movements in the
"third world" are either unthinking pawns of the communist bloc or
pathological terrorists whose envy and hatred of the West drive them
to mindless (and ultimately self-defeating) violence; that the salvation

of the "underdeveloped" nations (notice how this much-used term gently conjoins Spencerianism with the more commonly approved version of "progress") lies in "modernization" – that is to say, the adoption of "modern lifestyles," the creation of "metropolitan" social spaces and infrastructures, the "liberalization" and commodification of the economy, etc., together with the unquestioned belief in the innate superiority of Western, especially American, civilization. This colossal ruse of self-persuasion, which has determined America's relationship with the countries of Africa, Asia, the Caribbean, and Latin America, is in Said's view perfectly allegorized by Melville's Captain Ahab: "obsessed, compelling, unstoppable, completely wrapped in his rhetorical justification and his sense of cosmic symbolism."[63]

Said particularly stresses the extent to which, unlike its European predecessor, the American consensus is both empowered and concealed by the pervasive presence of the contemporary media:

> [The] twinning of power and legitimacy, one force obtaining in the world of direct domination, the other in the cultural sphere, is a characteristic of classical imperial hegemony. Where it differs in the American century is the quantum leap in the reach of cultural authority, thanks to the unprecedented growth in the apparatus for the diffusion and control of the information ... [T]he media are central to the domestic culture. Whereas a century ago European culture was associated with a white man's presence, indeed with his directly domineering (and hence resistible) physical presence, we now have in addition an international media presence that insinuates itself, frequently at a level below conscious awareness, over a fantastically wide range.[64]

The implications of all this are almost as predictable as they are disheartening. These typical American "attitudes and the policies they gave rise to were [and still are] based on almost petulant misrepresentations and ignorance, unrelieved except by a desire for mastery and domination, itself stamped by ideas of American exceptionalism."[65] Much of the anger that Said directs against American literary and other intellectuals is animated by his conviction that this consensus would not have been possible without the acquiescence of the vast majority of leftist and liberal intellectuals. As we shall see presently, he believes that this is most particularly true where Israel is concerned.

Zionism, Orientalism, and Euro-American Imperialism

Our discussion has been brought to a point where we can lay bare the

historical–cultural sites on which Zionist political philosophy and
practice have evolved since the 1860s. The twisted doings of Zionism
are nothing short of remarkable: its multiple contradictions, its
spectacular successes, its hardiness and perdurability, its capacity to
conceal its true striations – these and similar Zionist enactments
together exemplify one of the most fascinating ideologies to come out
of modern socio-political culture. Let us look at these enactments a bit
more closely. First, Zionism involves an astounding irony. It has
helped transform the Jewish people, the victims of Europe's most
heinous crime – the Holocaust – into willing participants in Europe's
greatest misadventure, that is, high imperialism. Second, Zionism has
helped execute the hand-and-foot ideological capture of America for
Israel – the gradually intensifying mobilization of the vast economic,
cultural, and military resources of a superpower in behalf of a tiny
state half a world away. Third, it is a historical oddity: at a time when
implanting colonizing settlers on distant lands is deemed either
morally too indefensible or economically and militarily too expensive,
Zionists persist precisely in this kind of colonialist activity – without,
however, calling it by its proper name. Finally, Zionism has presented
itself in terms of what it emphatically is not: despite the fact that it
has, in both doctrine and practice, been theocentric, discriminatory,
and colonialist, Zionism has consistently wrapped itself in the mantle
of democracy – a claim in turn invested with moral exclusivity and
redemption.

The question that now arises is this: what accounts for the unique
survivability and appeal of Zionism, both as an ideal horizon and as a
set of institutionalized practices in the state of Israel? This is the
question that Said grapples with in a large number of texts, some of
which I have already alluded to. They include academic monographs
whose main argument is designed, in both detail and scope, to retrieve
contested historical materials genealogically (e.g. *The Question of
Palestine*); collections of "occasional" essays (like *The Politics of Dispossession, Peace and Its Discontents*, and *Oslo and After: the End of the
Peace Process*) written over stretches of time and later reissued in book
form; and a cluster of meditative, almost lyrical, running commentaries that, in the manner of extended captions, bring still photos back
to life (*After the Last Sky*). And of course Said's own personal story
(presented most fully in *Out of Place*) is caught up in all of this. What
emerges out of this disparate cluster of texts is that the unique
achievements and symptoms of Zionism will not be appreciated fully
without the close examination of its strategic interaction with classical

European imperialism, with the worst elements of Orientalist discourse, and with contemporary American hegemonism. Let us start
with Zionism's relationship with high European imperialism:

> Every idea or system of ideas exists *somewhere*, is mixed in with historical
> circumstances, is part of what one may very simply call "reality." One of the
> enduring attributes of self-serving idealism, however, is the notion that ideas
> are just ideas, and that they exist only in the realm of ideas. The tendency to
> view ideas as pertaining only to a world of abstractions increases among people
> for whom an idea is essentially perfect, good, uncontaminated by human desire
> or will. Such a view also applies when the ideas are considered to be evil,
> absolutely perfect in their evil and so forth. When an idea has become effective
> – that is, when its value has been proved in reality by its widespread acceptance
> – some revision of it will of course seem to be necessary, since the idea must be
> viewed as having taken on some of the characteristics of brute reality. Thus it is
> frequently argued that such an idea as Zionism, for all its political tribulations
> and the struggles on its behalf, is at bottom an *unchanging* idea that expresses
> the yearning for Jewish political and religious self-determination – for Jewish
> national selfhood – to be exercised on the promised land. Because Zionism
> seems to have culminated in the creation of the state of Israel, it is also argued
> that the historical realization of the idea confirms its unchanging essence and,
> no less important, the means used for its realization. Very little is said about
> what Zionism entailed for non-Jews who happened to have encountered it; for
> that matter, nothing is said about where (outside Jewish history) it took place,
> and from what in the historical context of nineteenth-century Europe Zionism
> drew its force. To the Palestinian, for whom Zionism was somebody else's idea
> imported into Palestine and for which in a very concrete way he or she was
> made to pay and suffer, these forgotten things about Zionism are the very
> things that are centrally important.
>
> In short, effective political ideas like Zionism need to be examined
> historically in two ways: (1) *genealogically* in order that their provenance, their
> kinship and descent, their affiliation both with other ideas and with political
> institutions may be demonstrated; (2) as practical systems for *accumulation* (of
> power, land, ideological legitimacy) and *displacement* (of people, other ideas,
> prior legitimacy). Present political and cultural actualities make such an
> examination extraordinarily difficult, as much because Zionism in the post-
> industrial West has acquired for itself an almost unchallenged hegemony in
> liberal "establishment" discourse, as because in keeping with one of its central
> ideological characteristics, Zionism has hidden, or caused to disappear, the
> literal historical ground of its growth, its political cost to the native inha-
> bitants of Palestine, and its militantly oppressive discriminations between
> Jews and non-Jews.[66]

All ideas exist "somewhere," are "mixed in with historical circumstances"; yet "self-serving idealism" pretends otherwise, insisting
that ideas – be they good or evil – are perfectly self-subsistent in their
"uncontaminated" abstractness. Even when, through a great deal of

hard work, ideas (that is ideas of the "noble," privileged type) have become successful *inside* history; even when they have been translated into an established political system sustained with the apparatus of material institutions, a process of upward revision ensures that they retain their elevated status. History does not ensnare them in its quotidian messiness; nor does it leave any compromising traces in them. Rather, it is *made* to preserve their essential purity; more important, it confirms their *real* worth, their compelling *rightness*. Vouching for their fundamentally timeless validity, history also paradoxically imparts practical meaning and value to them, "proving" – by virtue of its capacity to stand witness, to occasion, or to propitiate – that the realization of these ideas was warranted *in advance* by a transcendent necessity. History, that is to say, has in a manner of speaking caught up with prophecy. All this, therefore, calls for the activation of a counter-memory, the need to awaken – and give voice to – an interpretive agency from an oppositional perspective. Critical engagement illuminates the historical tracks covered (and deliberately covered over) in the long process of institutionalizing these ideas, to determine their disavowed "kinship and descent." Critical interrogation will shed light on the carefully planned strategies that have allowed these ideas to accumulate both political power and ideological capital. It will also retrieve the concealed forensic evidence, the injuries that bespeak culpability: the enormous price they have exacted from those unfortunate enough to have been in the way can finally be put on display.

If these words sound familiar, the reason is that they echo – and add a substantial new inflection to – a contention which, though phrased in different ways, Said has never wavered from since the beginning of his career: that ideas are self-ratifying, imperialistic, and worldly. And a corollary to this thesis: complete totalization, essentialization, and conformity are never possible because there is always resistance in the form of ruptures, distanciations, dispersions, and excess. Criticism is always not only possible but also desirable. The passage, then, is at one level a reiteration and a summation.

But at another, more circumscribed level, it introduces a particular ideology, one which has had a profound impact on modern socio-political experience in the West and in the Arab-Islamic world, an ideology which – more specifically – has helped entangle the destinies of two peoples, Jews and Palestinians, in the most unfortunate political circumstances one can conceive of: Zionism, "the yearning for Jewish political and religious self-determination . . . to be exercised on the promised land," has been experienced by its victims as a peculiarly nightmarish form of punishment from whose Kafkaesque logic it has been almost impossible to escape. It is this intractable problem, this almost total incommensurability, that Said repeatedly struggles with, a struggle which assumes several different guises all at once. Existentially, it takes the form of a complaint against (and a debate with) the most formidable of foes. Inaugurated in the name of the greatest victims of European racism and religious bigotry in history – a people with a long tradition of moral and intellectual grandeur behind them – Zionism was from the outset (and in its institutionalized, Israeli version continues to be) able to accomplish two seemingly incompatible goals at once: on the one hand, it has created political facts on the ground by any means available (including military force); on the other hand, its advocates have been able to denounce any criticism of its program of action as out-and-out anti-Semitism. Intellectually, Said's struggle is an attempt to illuminate interrogatively a vastly complex tissue of contested historical and cultural phenomena whose dramatic enactments have shaped – and continue to shape – modern consciousness in a powerfully emotional way. Finally, the struggle constitutes a radical humanist's leap of faith, an attempt to envision an alternative conception of human community. According to Said, this struggle has been "extraordinarily difficult" to conduct – now and in the past – precisely because of the positional superiority of the socio-cultural space from which modern Zionism was first launched in the 1880s, a site from which the political and intellectual leaders of Israel – as well as various apologists of Israeli policy – have continued to wage their ideological war to this day.

The fundamental, "totally intractable" paradox – "something that totally resists any theory, any one-plus-one explanation, any display of feelings or attitudes"[67] – that, in Said's view, needs to be addressed can be formulated in this way: why was it possible early last century for a European power to make a decision – in the form of Balfour's well-known promise – which eventually enabled European Jews to take control of a territory *outside* the borders of Europe, namely Palestine, a land that had "as a huge majority for hundreds of years a largely pastoral, a nevertheless socially, culturally, politically, economically identifiable people, whose language and religion were (for a huge majority) Arabic and Islam, respectively"?[68] Said's confrontation with this paradox and its consequences takes him to the historical and cultural site where Eurocentrism emerged, the site where European self-invention, self-idealization, and self-fortification – interacting with scientific knowledge and technological progress – empowered European political and intellectual elites to deliver a grand judgement: Europe (its peoples, history, civilization, etc.) constituted the moral, political, and aesthetic center of the world; the rest of humanity, the natives, in the nature of things occupied a lower position. The idea of having an empire – that is, establishing colonial settlements in distant lands forcibly cleared of their original inhabitants; appropriating their natural resources; taking effective control (through diplomatic, economic, political, or military means) of the destinies of lesser peoples; "civilizing" the natives – or where that had failed or appeared undesirable – simply destroying them: this powerfully self-justifying idea was, in Said's view, an almost inevitable product of that collective European structure of attitudes and references. Imperialism itself (as distinct from European supremacism) constituted, Said maintains, the dominant ideology of nineteenth- and early twentieth-century France and especially Britain. Orientalism, as an intention and as a discourse, constituted an important component of this ensemble – a component fashioned for the Orient in general and for the Arab-Islamic world in particular.

According to Said, this ideological project was appropriated – and refined for Palestine – by the fathers of modern Zionism, who (with the active encouragement and support of Western intellectual and political elites) applied it as a highly organized program of action with particularly chilling efficiency and ferocity. In other words, where "natives" and plans for their land were concerned, there was total unanimity of views – epistemologically, morally, politically – between European colonial officials like Balfour, on the one hand, and such Zionists as Herzl, Lord Rothschild, Weizmann, and Jabotinsky, on the other:

> There is no separating Balfour's ideology from that of Zionism, even though Zionist Jews perforce had a different feeling for, a different history and historical experience of, ideas about Palestine. For all their differences (and they *were* numerous), both the British imperialist and the Zionist vision are united in playing down and even canceling out the Arabs in Palestine as somehow secondary and negligible. Both raise the moral importance of the visions very far above the mere presence of natives on a piece of immensely significant territory. And both visions ... belong fundamentally to the ethos of a European *mission civilisatrice* – nineteenth-century, colonialist, racist even – built on notions about the inequality of men, races, and civilizations, an inequality allowing the most extreme forms of self-aggrandizing projections, and the most extreme forms of punitive discipline toward the unfortunate natives whose existence, paradoxically, was denied.[69]

Said's insistence on this thesis – that modern Zionism from the outset allied itself with the most pernicious versions of European exclusionism, supremacism, and self-projectionism – runs through the entire corpus of writing under consideration in this section, from the articles he wrote in the early Seventies, through major texts like *The Question of Palestine* (1979; the above passages come from that text), to the latest reflections on the current impasse. He illustrates with a vast wealth of documentation the various striations and transformations of this project – and the potent, collective energies mobilized in its behalf: from the earliest, purely imaginative emergence (in the 1860s) of the possibility of reconquest, to the creation of an exclusively Jewish state in 1948, and beyond.

In terminology that brings to mind Gramsci and Foucault, Said shows the extent to which the Zionist-colonialist enterprise, both in its inaugural drive and in its gradual execution, constituted a discipline of detail – "the slow accumulation of land by a policy of detail as well as the painstaking drama of the [Israeli] state taking shape before the world's eyes" with the full knowledge that "there *were* other people already in Palestine."[70] This firm-footed, highly organized, piecemeal growth or "thickening" of the colonizing process – by acquiring "another acre, another goat," as Weizmann once put it – was meant eventually to lead to the total "reconstitution" of Palestine as a Jewish state that had no room for non-Jews whatsoever. "Thus," Said tells us in *The Question of Palestine*, "I have in mind the whole dialectic between theory and actual day-to-day effectiveness" which transformed Zionist ideology into the reality of the Israeli state. He adds:

> My premise is that Israel developed as a social polity out of the Zionist thesis that Palestine's colonization was to be accomplished simultaneously for and by Jews *and* by the displacement of the Palestinians; moreover, that in its conscious and declared ideas about Palestine, Zionism attempted first to minimize, then to eliminate, and then, all else failing, finally to subjugate the natives as a way of guaranteeing that Israel would not be simply the state of its citizens (which included Arabs, of course) but the state of "the whole Jewish People," having a kind of sovereignty over land and peoples that no other state possessed or possesses. It is this anomaly that the Arab Palestinians have since been trying both to resist and [to] provide an alternative for.[71]

Here is the summary of that historical evidence in itemized form: (1) the articulation, romanticization, and diffusion in European high culture – including literature – of Zionist claims (in the form of an inherent, exclusive ownership right) on Palestine, claims rationalized on historical, religious, and moral grounds (Said cites Moses Hess's *Rome and Jerusalem* and George Eliot's *Daniel Deronda* as two of the earliest works embodying this kind of propagation); (2) the formation in the late nineteenth and early twentieth centuries of politically active organizations and funds (the Jewish Colonial Trust Limited, the Anglo-Palestine Company, and the Jewish National Fund were among them) whose express purpose was to encourage and expedite Jewish immigration to Palestine, to purchase land in Palestine and hold it *in perpetuity* "for the Jewish people," and to implant – and gradually expand – colonial settlements. In order to guarantee the moral purity of these enactments, the Zionists, according to Said, deployed a positive ideological mechanism: only Jewish labor, it was argued, should be utilized in order to bring into being economically self-sufficient Jewish communities on Jewish land. That is to say, if you don't exploit Arab labor, then you will not be obligated to the Arab – this, of course, while the land was all the time being cut from under the Arab's feet! (3) Strengthening these two strategies was the coordination of important political maneuvers and decisions between Zionist leaders and colonial governments (notably the British, who took control of Palestine after the engineered collapse of the Ottoman Empire, but also the French). This concerted effort took the form of lobbies and solicitations on the part of Herzl, Rothschild, and Weizmann, on the one hand; and, on the other, gradual accommodation and eventual identification on the part of colonial officials. It is this collective effort that paved the way for Balfour's 1917 declaration, a momentous political event which officially legitimized Jewish conquest of Palestine.

Likewise, the denial of Arabs and their rights assumed several different forms: (a) in justifying conquest, both Zionists and Britons often described the land in a manner that emphasized its dereliction or misuse by the natives – the implication being that European Jews somehow deserved to own the land because they would use it efficiently; (b) both Britons and Zionists delivered themselves of characterizations of Islam (as a religion and as a culture) in terms that invariably equated it with backwardness, fatalism, irrationality, or xenophobia; (c) the Palestinians were almost invariably described – again by Zionists and Britons alike – in such a way that they were either made to disappear politically and morally or – more commonly – transformed into subhuman creatures; (d) the most symptomatically disturbing manifestation of this supremacist ideology was the cold, deliberate, calculated use of enormous violence against Arab civilians both before the creation of Israel and since – as a "pre-emptive" measure, as an instrument of punishment, or as a means of dislodging them from desired land. According to Said, the consolidation of the Zionist vision was premised not only on wresting control of Palestine from the natives but also on the total extirpation of any evidence that might link them historically to the land. During and after the 1948 war hundreds of Palestinian villages that fell into the hands of the Zionist forces were literally razed to the ground.

Said's genealogical activation of the intellectual and political force-field that empowered Zionism is not restricted to the (arguably) bygone era of high European imperialism. For, in Said's view, the twin projects of the Zionist vision – namely, the gradual realization of an ideologically positive (in the sense of visible, viable, legitimate) Jewish nationhood in Palestine and the total (or near-total) negation of Palestinians and their rights – are still powerfully operative. Despite the passage of more than one hundred years since the inception of politically active Zionism; the eruption of countless crises as a consequence of that colonial mission; the grudging realization that Palestinians cannot be made simply to go away – despite all this, the doctrinal core of Zionism, enshrined in the very structure of Israeli law, political discourse, and institutionalized practice, remains fundamentally unrevised: that is to say, some cosmetic touching-up (mostly in the form of apologetics), and tactical maneuvering (such as the unending talk about something called "the peace process") have been undertaken in the last several decades; however, in Said's view the exclusionary, hierarchist, and imperialist policies of Zionism are as strategically in place in the early twenty-first century as they were in the late nineteenth. And to understand the effectiveness of Zionism in a postcolonial context, we need to examine its fortunes in contemporary America.

As I suggested earlier, the "special relationship" between America and Israel (and hence Zionism) is premised on a unique logic all its own, one which has no equivalence anywhere else in the world. It is a logic written in the vocabulary of a truly strange political tongue. It is not just that internationally sanctioned norms that govern (or are expected to govern) political behavior *within* and *between* nations – norms breached on pain of excommunication or worse (witness Iraq, for example) – are changed or defied; they are simply rendered meaningless and inoperative *in advance*, as if by divine necessity. More precisely, the enactments effected in the name of that "special relationship," both in America and in the Middle East, entail the near-

total erasure of certain boundary lines which are normally considered
crucial to modern political culture – crucial because the very idea of
political accountability would be almost impossible to conceive
without them: the line between domestic and foreign policy, between
leftist and rightist political conceptions, between justice and injustice
(and hence between law and illegality), between war and peace,
between justifiable self-defense and self-aggrandizing aggression,
between secular and religious prerogatives, between civil and political
institutions, and so on and on. Another way of phrasing (and sum-
ming up) these enactments is to say that a climate of extreme crisis – a
sense of perpetual emergency which in turn authorizes the extremest
of measures – has been not only tolerated but actually encouraged and
normalized. The following passage from *The Question of Palestine* gives
us an idea of the extent to which this normalization has succeeded:

> The concealment by Zionism of its own history has by now ... become
> institutionalized [in the United States], and not only in Israel ... In no other
> country, except Israel, is Zionism enshrined as an unquestioned good, and in
> no other country is there so strong a conjuncture of powerful institutions and
> interests – the press, the liberal intelligentsia, the military-industrial com-
> plex, the academic community, labor unions – for whom ... uncritical sup-
> port of Israel and Zionism enhances their domestic as well as international
> standing.[72]

Consider the different forms that this unique privileging of
Zionism and Israel has assumed over the past several decades: (1) the
yearly outlay of billions of dollars in US aid to Israel; this almost
unlimited flow of funds, hardware, and know-how, which "includes
assistance to the Israeli defense industry, proceeds from the sale of tax-
free bonds, forgiven loans, all at the rate of about $7.4 million per
day" and adds up to "about $1,000 per Israeli man, woman, and child
every year," has made Israel "almost wholly dependent on the United
States for military and economic support";[73] (2) the ritualized avowals
and declarations of total support for Israel – "the only democracy in
the Middle East" – by every presidential candidate and any number of
politician-wannabes, a collective attitude whose logical consequence is
the chorus of praise sung habitually to this day in the US Congress, to
take just one pre-eminent institution; (3) the active, often abusive
muzzling of any serious criticism of Israel and its policies in American
public discourse – even in the Eighties and Nineties when the atrocities committed by the Israeli military and security forces could no
longer be hidden from public view; (4) the protection afforded almost
exclusively to Israel by the US government in the world body – this

usually assumes the form of vetoes against (or dilutions of) UN resolutions which criticize Israel for various failings, including human rights abuses, violations of various internationally warranted laws, and defiance of the will of the world community.

The atrocities and violations that Israel has habitually committed could bear further scrutiny. Said's extensive analyses of these practices can only be summarized here: the imprisonment – often without being officially charged with any wrongdoing – and torture of Palestinians and other Arabs; deportations and kidnappings of Arab political activists; collective punishment of entire communities (including extended curfews, demolition of houses, destruction of crops, massive round-ups, etc.) for actions carried out by an isolated individual or a small band of guerrillas; the continuing, decades-long occupation of Arab land – despite United Nations resolutions calling for its end; confiscations and annexations of Arab land (including East Jerusalem) on which illegal settlements have been built; the illegal exploitation of resources (like water, for example) on occupied Arab land; assassinations of Palestinian leaders in various parts of the globe; repeated invasions and other cross-border raids which deliberately target Palestinian refugee camps and other urban centers with large concentrations of civilians – actions which have led to the killing and maiming of literally tens of thousands as well as the forced dislocation of hundreds of thousands of Palestinians, Lebanese, and other Arabs, most of them non-combatants. The extent of Israeli brutality is conveyed in this passage (one of many on this subject) in which Said summarizes the Sean MacBride commission report on Israel's 1982 invasion of Lebanon:

> The findings [of the six-member commission] are horrifying – and almost as much because they are forgotten or routinely denied in press reports as because they occurred. The commission says that Israel was indeed guilty of acts of aggression contrary to international law; it made use of forbidden weapons and methods; it deliberately, indiscriminately, and recklessly bombed civilian targets – "for example, schools, hospitals, and other nonmilitary targets"; it systematically bombed towns, cities, villages, and refugee camps; it deported, dispersed, and ill-treated civilian populations; it had no really valid reasons "under international law for its invasion of Lebanon, for the manner in which it conducted hostilities, or for its actions as an occupying force"; it was directly responsible for the Sabra and Shatila massacres.[74]

That Israel has for a long time engaged in acts like these, which Said says can arguably be called genocidal, is no secret in the United States. Various American administrations have known very well that such atrocities – as well as countless other practices which may be less violent but certainly no less humiliating or dehumanizing – have been visited by Israel on its Arab neighbors. They are acknowledged even by some Israelis – including government officials who never tire of using old hand-me-downs (fighting against "terrorism," maintaining "our national security," etc.) and a tiny, disparate minority (composed of human rights activists, conscientious journalists, and the occasional odd critic of Israel from the inside). Yet Israel has never been the worse for any of this. If anything, the rewards – financial, military, moral – have increased exponentially. How does one account for any of this strange set of political practices?

One obvious, and perhaps tempting, way of responding to this question is to claim that the rise of Nazism and the consequent destruction of European Jewry somehow necessitated actions like these. The postwar discovery of the extermination camps in Poland, Germany, and elsewhere in Europe – camps in which millions of innocent men, women, and children had lost their lives in the most agonizing fashion imaginable – brought home to a dazed Western world the realization that the Nazi monstrosity was an incarnation of absolute evil. That this evil, in its most virulent form, had targeted the Jews was also beyond any doubt, even though millions of others had also perished in the death camps. It is the poignant resonance of these horrifying events within the context of the Palestine conflict over the past half-century – namely, the Palestinians as a doubly handicapped people, the victims of victims, as Said often puts it – that needs special emphasis at this point.

I think it is important, however, that the Nazi phenomenon be placed in the broader intellectual–cultural context that gave sustenance to it. What is often obscured in discussions related to Palestine and the modern experience of the Jewish people is the extent to which Nazi doctrine (Aryan supremacism, the Lebensraum concept, the resurrection of Teutonic gods and myths, the veneration of raw strength, the dehumanization of the Jews, etc.), although in an obvious sense peculiar to Hitler's dictatorship, is in its fundamentals a version (albeit a particularly single-minded one) of a common European ideology which we have already discussed in detail: that is, the collective designation of European peoples, cultures and/or civilizations as constituting the center of the world, intellectually, morally, and racially. Seen in this light, neither the racism of the Nazis nor their territorial ambitions (like the Kaiser's two decades earlier) were an ontologically new species of ideological madness – after all, as we have already noted in an earlier section, Britain, France, and other European powers (as well as descendants of European settlers in Australia and the Americas) had been doing exactly the same thing for centuries: conquer new lands; subordinate, enslave, or destroy their original inhabitants; exploit their resources; and manufacture a reasonably satisfactory ruse to justify these actions. In material terms, the main difference between German imperialism and racism, on the one hand, and those practiced by other European powers, on the other, is that the former were turned inward. That is, Germany's primary targets were European peoples and lands.

One way of accounting for this internal imperialism is to say that, because its unification did not take place until well after the middle of the nineteenth century, Germany lacked the competitive wherewithal necessary for imperial practice outside Europe. Britain, France, and Holland (as well as the Iberian powers before them) had long imperial traditions behind them and, by the end of the nineteenth century, were in a position to take the lion's share in the scramble for Africa – the last continent to fall into the hands of Europeans (Germany did take possession of a few territories in southern and eastern Africa, but lost all of them after the First World War). The point to be stressed is that the powerful post-Bismarckian Germany (whether Kaiserian or Nazi) had imperial ambitions similar to those of its European sister states, but the most feasible way to display its imperial credentials was to flex its muscles against its immediate neighbors, most of whom already had huge possessions in distant lands. That is to say Kaiser Wilhelm and Adolf Hitler both breached, like Napoleon Bonaparte before them, a (perhaps unwritten) European code: let the status quo be *in Europe*. There is a sense, then, in which the twentieth century's two so-called world wars were specifically European implosions – implosions which, as a direct or indirect consequence of European imperial outreach, reverberated to the rest of the world (Japanese imperialism being both a direct response to Western intrusion into Japan and a duplication of European imperialism).

A further point has to be made – about Nazism. Nazism in and of itself can arguably be characterized as a unique, exceptionally loathsome breed of political consciousness whose appearance in the heart of modern Europe cannot be explained historically or rationally. I think, however, it is more plausible to describe it as a particularly unapologetic caricature of European supremacism and expansionism. Whereas other European powers were often able to justify their imperial designs by deploying relatively attractive ideologies (for example, enlightening the natives or spreading European civilization) – ideologies which at times even included the idea of a common humanity – the Nazi doctrine concealed neither its narrow identity base nor its barbarism: the Nazis' exclusively Nordic tribalism; their crudely offensive defamations of Slavs, Jews, Gipsies, and others judged below par; and above all their indulgence in sadism for its own sake should ultimately be seen as manifestations of European supremacism taken to its logical conclusion.

The catastrophe that befell European Jewry in the middle decades of the last century should be seen in this wider context. When Said characterizes the Jewish people's position in Western discourse as "special" – that is, special "sometimes for its horrendous tragedy and suffering, at other times for its uniquely impressive intellectual and moral triumphs"[75] – he is, I think, referring to the dual status that Ashkenazi Jews have had in Europe (and the West in general) for centuries. They were – and are – clearly a European (in the sense of privileged) people who, in the hierarchy of races and cultures constructed in the course of modern imperialism, could not simply be deposited in the site reserved for the "natives" – the site to be occupied by the black, brown, and yellow masses who had been brought under Europe's imperial sway. Even more important, it is extremely difficult to imagine what shape "Western" civilization would assume without the enormous contribution of (Ashkenazi and other) Jews – Moses, Marx, and Freud being among the large number of luminaries whose ideas have permanently shaped the self-understanding of Europeans and Americans from antiquity to the present.

And yet Jews were also, in the course of that same European history, subjected to a uniquely Western form of hatred which, though not strictly coextensive with modern Western racism, nevertheless substantially opens up to it. The peculiar malignancy of that hatred is captured by the term anti-Semitism and all that it implies beyond racism as such: an originary form of scapegoating; segregation from the majority (that is, "normal" or Christian) community; official confiscations of property and all manner of dispossession whenever such robbery was deemed necessary; various forms of persecution – including baiting and psychological abuse, desecration of synagogues, gratuitous violence, and massively destructive pogroms tolerated (or even encouraged) by those in power. It was this long process of negative accumulation – which in the course of nearly two millennia had saturated the collective psyche of Christian Europe – that had prepared the way for (and culminated in) Hitler's program of "final solution." In short, the Holocaust – the specific form taken by Nazi depravity – is *also* undeniably the end-product of a long history of European culpability against the only significant religious minority to be found in Europe until very recently, when Muslims arrived in Europe in substantial numbers. That this horrific event took place *after* (and not before) the much-vaunted Enlightenment makes it all the more baffling – although it certainly comes as no surprise to those familiar with the massive genocides conducted against the natives of North America or Australia, for example.

To sum up: to "make sense" of Jewish suffering in European hands, in the twentieth century and throughout the ages, is to point out what should be obvious by now; to the extent that they were perceived as racially or doctrinally unassimilable into an approved idea of Europe, to the extent that their Semiteness, their "crime" against the Savior, and their resistance to Christian proselytization together placed them beyond the boundaries of redemption, to that extent Jews were seen as a manifestation of the irreducible Other, the ultimate negative entity deemed necessary for Europeans' self-definition. But unlike the Arabs and Sephardic Jews – their fellow Semites – who had their home in the Middle East and North Africa, European Jews happened to be a small, vulnerable minority at home – an easy prey for the powers that be. The implications of this point (for example in the discourse of Orientalism) are often forgotten in discussions related to the contemporary Middle East in general and to the question of Palestine in particular – although in recent years Sephardic writers, like Ella Shohat, who have been alarmed by the Eurocentric assumptions of Zionism and Israeli political life, have drawn attention to these largely forgotten historical phenomena.[76]

A series of important questions propose themselves at this point: to what extent is this selective amnesia a function of Zionism's deliberate presentational strategy? Is it possible to identify a triadic interaction between Zionism, American neo-imperialism, and Orientalist discourse – an enactment designed to maintain Israeli supremacism? If so, how does one account for such a strange marriage? Granted that each of them has its own internal symptoms – rifts, contradictions, and oppositions to be smoothed over, dodged, denied, dismissed, or otherwise simply ignored in order to forge a working consensus for it – how is it that the three-way transaction (a daunting task indeed) was achieved at all? If the postwar American ascendancy is largely hegemonic (that is, at least in principle surreptitious and non-coercive) in character, how is it *made* to cohere with Zionism – a doctrine whose ideological tenets are far more explicitly stated? To phrase the point differently, if neo-imperialism (principally an American enterprise) is a *post*colonial affair that cannot be legitimized (domestically or internationally) by simply deploying the frankly supremacist, often explicitly racist rhetoric of high European imperialism – and has therefore to be modulated by the use of one or more of the rhetorical somersaults I referred to earlier – then how is it refined to dovetail neatly with the project of Zionism, a project inaugurated a century ago as, and in its fundamentals continues to be, an unabashedly *colonialist* venture? What specific interdictions have been put in place, by whom, and in whose favor, at the strategic intersection of the global hegemonism and the local colonialism? What kinds of punitive measures are threatened – and often taken – to enforce these inter-dictions?

To complete the three-way arrangement of this ideological colla-boration, what role has Orientalism played in America? If one agrees with Said that contemporary (largely American) Orientalism lacks the high-powered erudition, ambitious range, and broad coherence that authorized European Orientalists of yesteryear both to deliver the Orient for political and cultural control by Europe and to confer on their intellectual labors a great deal of prestige (and even a dash of romantic mystique), then what specific function does it have now in its attenuated postcolonial form, particularly in its transplanted American version? What peculiar relationship obtains, for example, between Zionism on the one hand and the vulgarized, popular version of Orientalism discussed in an earlier section? To what extent are the crude representations of Islam deliberately meant to create a foil for Israel and Zionism? In what way does the adversarial animus reduc-tively ascribed to Islam as a religion (including the hysteria over Islamic fundamentalism, which is no more widespread in the Muslim world than is Jewish or Christian fundamentalism in the West and in Israel) and to Arab-Islamic culture and history at large serve as a malicious diversion from the considerable shortcomings of Israel, "the only democracy in the Middle East"?

Apropos of this last bit of rhetorical redemption, which is recited like a mantra in American public discourse, just exactly what *does* "democracy" mean as it is practiced in Israel anyway? How has Zionism succeeded – if only in the United States and nowhere else – in convincing a vast number of intelligent men and women that the *idea* of democracy perfectly corresponds with the *reality* of a Jewish state? That is to say, how has it been possible to claim – and actually persuade others to *believe* – that a theologically conceived political system, whose very institutions are premised on an inherent inequality between Jews and non-Jews, is also at the same time a fundamentally secular, liberal, and pluralistic polity? Granted that the horrors to which the Jews have been subjected can in no way be compared to the experience of the Afrikaners, how does one nevertheless account for the uncomfortable resemblance between apartheid, the system which for decades rightly earned a pariah status for South Africa, and Zionism? Can the mere use of the word "democracy" somehow alchemically transform an exclusivist minority polity – which from the outset systematically displaced a *more* pluralistic and *more* tolerant society – into something that it has never been, except in the extremely limited domain of that minority's internal political arrangements? Finally, and perhaps most unconscionably, how has the long suffering of the Jewish people *in European hands* been employed as a license for the continuing suffering of the Palestinian people? In what ways have anti-Semitism in general and the Holocaust in particular been transmuted into a mechanism of moral blackmail – a powerful weapon which retroactively and proactively legislates a large number of injunctions, both legitimate and illegitimate? These questions, which go directly to the heart of the perpetual crisis that has haunted the Middle East for the past five decades, are addressed in most of the large number of political texts Said has written since the Seventies.

What emerges out of this cluster of questions is that the "special relationship" between Israel and the US – another name for which is the normalization of extreme political eccentricity – is a function of a particularly ferocious version of the ideological dialectic that I have examined in various contexts: the camouflaging of power in all its forms and effects (its specific instrumentalities, its victims, the historical ground it has covered and covered over, the agency that exercises it, etc.) by virtue of strategic maneuvers aimed at intellectual and moral laundering. The point of convergence here is this: the necessity of Israel's well-being at any cost, whereby "well-being" is decidedly overdetermined; it is to be understood in the most extensional and most intensional manner – the ontotheological unification of sense and reference – which in turn translates into the almost absolute valorization of everything that Zionism (and hence Israel) claims as its own and the unadulterated demonization (and hence punishment) of everything that resists its will. The strident, institutionalized rhetoric that has saturated Israeli and American public discourse over the past several decades – that America is merely

coming to the rescue of a tiny but heroic nation of survivors about to
be overrun by hordes of Arab terrorists and Muslim fundamentalists
who are determined to finish Hitler's project; that America and Israel
share humane values based on democratic principles; that the alliance
between the two countries helps maintain the stability of the Middle
East, a region which holds vast reserves of oil necessary for the economic health of the Western World, and is therefore justifiable on
pragmatic grounds of enlightened mutual interest – this rhetoric is an
important part of the multi-vectored strategy which has been necessitated to buy legitimacy for Israel and to justify the enormous moral
and material price it has exacted.

Once again, I would like to re-cite two passages quoted by Said,
passages that reveal more about their authors than about the subject
they are claiming to offer enlightenment about. (As in the earlier recited passages, I have left the excerpts intact as they were originally
presented in Said's text.) The first passage – by an Israeli doctor, a
"distinguished citizen and not a crude demagogue" (Said's ironic
description) called A. Carlebach – was published in *Ma'ariv* in 1955;
the second was written by Martin Peretz, the owner of *The New
Republic*, in 1984 (Peretz's article is a review of a play):

> These Arab Islamic countries do not suffer from poverty, or disease, or illit-
> eracy, or exploitation; they only suffer from the worst of all plagues: Islam.
> Wherever Islamic psychology rules, there is the inevitable rule of despotism
> and criminal aggression. The danger lies in Islamic psychology, which cannot
> integrate itself into the world of efficiency and progress, that lives in a world
> of illusion, perturbed by attacks of inferiority complexes and megalomania,
> lost in dreams of the holy sword. The danger stems from the totalitarian
> conception of the world, the passion for murder deeply rooted in their blood,
> from the lack of logic, the easily inflamed brains, the boasting, and above all:
> the blasphemous disregard for all that is sacred to the civilized world ... their
> reactions – to anything – have nothing to do with good sense. They are all
> emotional, unbalanced, instantaneous, senseless. It is always the lunatic that
> speaks from their throat. You can talk "business" with everyone, and even
> with the devil. But not with Allah ... This is what every grain in this country
> shouts. There were many great cultures here, and invaders of all kinds. All of
> them – even the Crusaders – left signs of culture and blossoming. But on the
> path of Islam, even the trees have died. [This dovetails perfectly with
> Weizmann's observations about neglect in Palestine; one assumes that had
> Weizmann been writing later he would have said similar things to Carlebach.]
> We pile sin upon crime when we distort the picture and reduce the discussion
> to a conflict of border between Israel and her neighbors. First of all, it is not
> the truth. The heart of the conflict is not the question of the borders; it is the
> question of Muslim psychology ... Moreover, to present the problem as a
> conflict between two similar parts is to provide the Arabs with the weapon of

a claim that is not theirs. If the discussion with them is truly a political one, then it can be seen from both sides. Then we appear as those who came to a country that was entirely Arab, and we conquered and implanted ourselves as an alien body among them, and we loaded them with refugees and constitute a military danger for them, etc., etc. ... one can justify this or that side and such a presentation, sophisticated and political, of the problem is under-standable for European minds – at our expense. The Arabs raise claims that make sense to the Western understanding of the simple legal dispute. But in reality, who knows better than us that such is not the source of their hostile stand? All those political and social concepts are never theirs. Occupation by force of arms, in their own eyes, in the eyes of Islam, is not all associated with injustice. To the contrary, it constitutes a certificate and demonstration of authentic ownership. The sorrow for the refugees, for the expropriated brothers, has no room in their thinking. Allah expelled, Allah will care. Never has a Muslim politician been moved by such things (unless, indeed, the catastrophe endangered his personal status). If there were no refugees and no conquest, they would oppose us just the same. By discussing with them on the basis of Western concepts, we dress savages in a European robe of justice.[77]

[A] visiting German businessman, an American Jewess come as an immigrant, and an Arab Palestinian find themselves taking refuge in a bomb shelter in Jerusalem under Arab siege. If there is something a bit startling about the emerging empathy between the play's German and its Jew, even less have the universalist prejudices of our culture prepared us for its Arab – a crazed Arab, to be sure, but crazed in the distinctive ways of his culture. He is intoxicated by language, cannot discern between fantasy and reality, abhors compromise, always blames others for his predicament, and in the end lances the painful boil of his frustration in a pointless, though momentarily gratifying, act of bloodlust. This is a political play and what makes it compelling is its pes-simism, which is to say its truthfulness. We have seen this play's Arab in Tripoli and in Damascus, and in recent weeks hijacking a bus to Gaza and shooting up a street of innocents in Jerusalem. On the Rep. stage he is a fictional character, of course, but in the real world it is not he but his "moderate" brother who is a figment of the imagination.[78]

That defamations like these could have been made at all is aston-ishing in itself. That they are routinely made in the Israeli and American press – and in public discourse in general – should be manifestly clear by now. That they are made by individuals claiming to be speaking on behalf of the Jewish people is extremely unfortu-nate. Yet none of this remarkable convergence of debased discourse and vested interest seems to have in the least troubled the likes of Robert Griffin, the Boyarin brothers, William Phillips, and Mark Krupnick – critics who have over the years complained about what they consider to be Said's distorted and unjust characterization of Israeli political practice. Nor has it troubled the famous Edward Alexander – the author of "Professor of Terror" – or the army of

Zionists and fellow travelers who, coming to his defense, heaped more
abuse on Said.[79]

What I would like to draw specific attention to, however, is the
extent to which the American consensus that I discussed earlier is
caught up in all this. In its most tellingly conformist (and most
politically effective) form, the large liberal–conservative consensus
that Said has denounced repeatedly converges on this point of intersection between two self-fortifying cultural dogmas. American and
Zionist versions of supremacism cross-fertilize each other, interacting
in the process with the most malignant streak of Orientalist discourse.
And the primary socio-political instrument for enforcing this consensus is of course the aggressive phalange known as the Jewish
Lobby. This is what Nicholas Thomas says about it:

> What must still be considered one of the most effective public relations
> operations of modern politics created [in the second half of the twentieth
> century] a climate in which any advocacy of an Arab perspective, and even
> merely scholarly interests in more balanced accounts of events that had been
> profoundly distorted, was stigmatized and identified with anti-Semitism.
> Even though Israel is now more widely perceived as a colonial-settler state –
> unique in its genesis and strategic location, but not in the political contra-
> dictions its existence engenders – and as a racist society that presents problems
> not wholly alien to those belatedly being addressed in South Africa, the
> climate of opinion is still such that Said can be described as a "Professor of
> Terror".[80]

It is at this most strategic – and yet most symptomatic (and hence
potentially most vulnerable) – fulcrum that the ideological usefulness
of the "intellectual flacks" (Said's characterization) whose "scholarly"
ruminations were examined earlier becomes fully intelligible:

> What matters to "experts" like [Judith] Miller, Samuel Huntington, Martin
> Kramer, Bernard Lewis, Daniel Pipes and Barry Rubin, plus a whole battery
> of Israeli academics, is to make sure that the "threat" [of Islamic funda-
> mentalism and Arab terrorism] is kept before our eyes, the better to excoriate
> Islam for terror, despotism and violence, while assuring themselves profitable
> consultancies, frequent TV appearances and book contracts. The Islamic threat
> is made to seem disproportionately fearsome, lending support to the thesis
> (which is an interesting parallel to anti-Semitic paranoia) that there is a
> worldwide conspiracy behind every explosion."[81]

Phrased differently, this means that – for this carefully engineered
consensus to hold forth and for Israel to hold its privileged place in
the hearts and minds of Americans – public discourse (and hence the
collective cultural consciousness that it shapes) must be saturated with

bad news (in both senses of the phrase): Islam, in an unholy alliance with anti-Semitism, is about to attack not only democratic Israel but also the whole of Western civilization. The consensus has a long history: from the late Forties and early Fifties, when distinguished theologians like Reinhold Niebuhr and humanists like Edmund Wilson – men whose views were very different otherwise – were united either in publicly expressing their support for the Zionist cause, or in acknowledging their antipathy toward Arabs; through the late Fifties and early Sixties when it was fashionable to describe Egypt's Jamal Abdel-Nasser as a clone of Hitler whose ultimate aim was to drive Jews into the Mediterranean Sea; to the 1967 war and its aftermath, when the tiny victim was suddenly transformed by the Western – especially American – media into a David vanquishing a hulking Goliath; through the crises of the Seventies, Eighties, and beyond. The deeply symptomatic strains of the anti-Islamic rhetoric that we have witnessed in the last three decades should be viewed in this context: unable to account morally or rationally for what Zionism, and later Israel, had done to the Palestinians; anxious to somehow rationalize what Israel was *now* doing as an occupying power abusing *its* victims right under the glare of the television camera; worried that Palestinian military and political resistance was becoming more effective against Israel; unwilling or unable to envision (as Palestinians had) a possible future political horizon beyond Zionist exclusionism and hierarchism: beset by all these problems, Zionists and other friends of Israel had one desperate tactic to resort to: demonize Arab-Islamic religion and culture at large and dissolve the specific headache caused by the Palestinian challenge into the discourse of that broader demonization. And if this discourse itself was ready to hand in the form of Orientalism, so much the better! This is the disheartening conclusion that Said has arrived at – a conclusion that his Zionist critics have shown little inclination to refute or otherwise seriously come to terms with.

Zionism and God: Divine Self-legitimation

The following question now arises. By implicating the Zionist movement and Israeli policies so closely with the worst of Orientalism and Euro-American imperialism, isn't Said running the risk of reductiveness and essentialism, which he so often accuses others of committing? Aren't there, after all, legitimate Jewish claims on his-

torical Palestine? How can he be so dismissive of the fact that there
was once an independent Jewish state in the Holy Land? Above all,
isn't Palestine the very land God promised His Chosen People when
He made the Covenant with them? An adequate response to these and
similar questions could start with this passage:

> The idea of the Orient, very much like the idea of the West that is its polar
> opposite, has functioned as an inhibition on what I have been calling secular
> criticism. Orientalism is the discourse derived from and dependent on "the
> Orient." To say of such grand ideas and their discourse that they have
> something in common with religious discourse is to say that each serves as an
> agent of closure, shutting off human investigation, criticism, and effort, in
> deference to the authority of the more-than-human, the supernatural, the
> other-worldly. Like culture, religion therefore furnishes us with systems of
> authority and with canons of order whose regular effect is either to compel
> subservience or to gain adherents. This in turn gives rise to organized col-
> lective passions whose social and intellectual results are often disastrous. The
> persistence of these and other religious-cultural effects testifies amply to what
> seem to be necessary features of human life, the need for certainty, group
> solidarity, and a sense of communal belonging. Sometimes, of course, these
> things are beneficial. Still it is also true that what a secular attitude enables – a
> sense of history and of human production, along with a healthy skepticism
> about the various official idols venerated by culture and by system – is
> diminished, if not eliminated, by appeals to what cannot be thought through
> and explained, except by consensus and appeals to authority.[82]

This is the opening paragraph of "Religious Criticism," the concluding article of *The World, the Text, and the Critic*. At one level, the
article is meant to illustrate – if only in a perfunctory manner – one
way in which the efficient dialectic of ideology which I discussed in
various contexts is transacted in what might initially appear to be
unrelated spheres of Western cultural life. On the one hand,
Orientalism quite comfortably – even ostentatiously – wears its
worldliness (its "radical realism" delivers and vouches for the West's
idea of the Orient and Orientals) while all the time emphatically
disavowing its ideological stripes. On the other hand, the new forms
of "critical" system-building – ahistorical, self-restricting, formalistic,
elaborative – bracket off the material, everyday realities of ordinary
people while also becoming available (by virtue of their Arnoldian
capacity to elevate and consecrate knowledge as "culture") as a protective, cocoon-like sanctuary for a privileged class of traditional
intellectuals whose specialized productions in turn bestow legitimacy
on an imperialized power structure with a global outreach.

But the article is not just a gloss on Orientalist discourse and on

garden variety criticism. In fact its main purpose is to draw attention
to what Said considers to be a creeping process of theologization in
modern criticism. He specifically alludes to a number of studies
undertaken in recent decades by major scholars (among them Frye's
The Great Code, Bloom's *Kabbalah and Criticism*, and Altizer's *Deconstruction and Theology*) all of which in Said's view transmute the
secular, potentially demystifying power of literary-critical insights
and methodologies into exegetical elaborations of a religious orthodoxy whose overall effect is, paradoxically, one of profound alienation.
In Said's opinion, these and similar works, which add up to "a significant trend" in modern literary theory and practice, cultivate religious sensibility as a "result of exhaustion, consolation, and
disappointment."[83] This kind of critical labor ponders "varieties of
unthinkability, undecidability, and paradox together with a remarkable consistency of appeals to magic, divine ordinance, or sacred
texts."[84] Said's immediate point is that this form of religious criticism
fundamentally coheres with the more overtly secular variety of critical
writing that, as I tried to show in an earlier chapter, constitutes the
major topic of most of the essays in *The World, the Text, and the Critic*:
deploying various specialized idioms; obsessed with aporias, cul-de-
sacs, and other obfuscations; restricted to a tiny audience of clubby
initiates, modern criticism – whether religious or secular – is afflicted
with the most crippling sort of hermeticism. In short, religious and
secular versions of modern criticism are alike in that they both tend to
be opaque, otherworldly, and conservative.

Beyond this establishment of affinities, Said also presents an
explicit challenge to an aspect of ostentatiously otherworldly
authority which, as a consequence of its capacity to rouse powerful
"collective passions," can – and often does – visit enormous violence
on *this* world: that is, organized religion as an arational (if not anti-
rational) mechanism of socio-political regimentation and mobilization. It should be pointed out immediately that Said's treatment of
this most explosive of subjects is rarely ever as direct as it is here. In
none of his major texts do religious themes form a central concern, his
direct confrontation with religious dogma and (especially) what he
considers to be the unhealthy uses made of it occurring in a relatively
small number of shorter pieces. It should also be added that Said
doesn't seem to be averse to religion as such; nor does he denounce the
mere presence of religious feeling in human cultural life. In the
passage quoted above, he notes – perhaps with a touch of resignation –
that religious belief, like such other broad designations as the West

and the East, may indeed be "beneficial" in some ways; it is, at any
rate, a necessary feature of all societies, expressing "the need for certainty, group solidarity, and a sense of communal belonging." Conceived in these terms, religion is that which fills the gigantic void of
the unknown – a measure of "certainty" that there is some larger
purpose beyond (and behind) human facticity; it also functions as a
social glue that binds individuals to larger wholes. Elsewhere, Said
makes an explicit distinction between politically motivated religious
dogma (like Muslim fundamentalism, which he condemns outright)
and religious ethos in general – understood as a broad, enveloping,
life-enhancing socio-cultural environment, capable of nurturing
internal differentiation, variety, and tolerance.[85]

Despite all of this, in Said's view, of all the "official idols venerated
by culture and system," organized religion – political or otherwise –
constitutes the most potentially insidious. Why? Because as the
ultimate "more-than-human" authority – an authority equipped with
"canons of order whose regular effect is either to compel subservience
or to gain adherents" – it is capable of imposing the most formidable
injunctions on human thought and action. Religious dogma of this
sort – atavistic, intolerant, pontifical, imperialist – tends to ossify into
a set of unchanging, essentialized prescriptions and prohibitions that
severely inhibit any exercise of the "secular attitude" – that is "a sense
of history and human production, along with a healthy skepticism" of
received wisdom. This, I maintain, is the ultimate target of Said's
entire critical career. To him, organized religious belief, whether
Muslim, Christian, Jewish, or whatever, is the antithesis of secular
humanism, which – though in his opinion disastrously aborted by
imperialism, Orientalism, and any number of other self-projecting
tribalisms – remains as the best hope for a massively interconnected
global culture. This is the argument most forcefully presented in
Beginnings (where the idea of Origins has, as I noted in an earlier
chapter, a theological dimension to it) and *The World, the Text, and the
Critic*, but it constitutes a major (perhaps the most important) presupposition of all of his studies.

He is, in effect, saying: if the project of modernity was inaugurated
on the reluctant but nevertheless inevitable (and ultimately salu-
brious) acknowledgement that originary mythologies, both religious
and philosophic, are no longer utilizable as viable horizons of socio-
political organization; if the constellation of human mind-in-language-and-history always enacts its operations *in medias res*; if, that is,
the very constitution of self, society, history, meaning, and value takes

place in secular, worldly circumstances where unmediated Truth is – in the almost unanimous estimation of major modern thinkers – decidedly unavailable, if all this, then it is unconscionable for public intellectuals in any society to invoke sacred texts and other forms of divine ordinance as a source of moral, epistemological, and (especially) political self-authorization. In short, slumbering Silent Origins had best be left alone. Any attempt to wake them up – any attempt to make their oracular voices heard above that of mere humans – will almost certainly "give rise to organized collective passions whose social and intellectual results are often disastrous."

What does all this have to do with Zionist ideology or its institutionally realized application in Israel? Said's response to this question directly concerns the religious epistemology and normative authority that sustain the Zionist claims on Palestine, the uniquely privileged "difference" that bestows exclusive ownership rights of the land on Jews. Said counters that claim with honest agnosticism: "As applied to 'The Jewish People' on 'The Land of Israel,' difference [between Jews and non-Jews] takes various forms. Theologically, of course, difference here means 'the chosen people' who have a different relationship to God from that enjoyed by any other group. But this sort of 'difference' is, I confess, impossible for me to understand."[86] Apropos of this self-endowment, the only thing that can be understood from a secular perspective is that historically "Palestine," as both land and idea, was (and still is) an immensely significant territory: an overdetermined palimpsest, a place holy to three world religions, a site saturated with the "mysterious entanglement" and symbolism of "monotheistic religion at its most profound" – that is, "the Christian Resurrection and Incarnation, the Ascension to heaven of Prophet Mohammed, [and] the Covenant of Yahweh with his people."[87] Palestine is a closed universal center, the seat of Silent Origins par excellence: its self-subsistent, transcendent meaning is antithetical to the earthbound, skeptical attitude of modernity. Seen in this light, the ideological and historical consolidation of political Zionism instantiates the triumph of one theological interpretation over all other interpretations, religious or secular.

Said's denunciation of religious fundamentalism in general and Zionist exclusivism in particular is perhaps best captured in his withering review of Michael Walzer's *Exodus and Revolution*. He expresses bafflement at Walzer's major thesis (namely, that the biblical narrative of Jewish exodus from Pharaonic Egypt to the "Promised Land" embodies a revolutionary spirit that coheres with twentieth-century radical politics) in this passage which is bound to rouse the wrath of many a cleric – Jewish, Christian, and Muslim alike:

> [N]ot only does Exodus seem to blind its intellectuals to the rights of others, it permits them to believe that history – the world of societies and nations, made by men and women – vouchsafes certain peoples the extremely problematic gift of "Redemption." Another of the many endowments Walzer bestows on Exodus insiders, Redemption, alas, elevates human beings in their own judgment to the status of divinely inspired moral agents. And this status in turn minimizes, if it does not completely obliterate, a sense of responsibility for what a people undergoing Redemption does to other less fortunate people, unredeemed, strange, displaced and outside moral concern. For this small deficiency Walzer has a reassuring answer too: "to be a moral agent," he says, "is not to act rightly but to be capable of acting rightly." While it is not blindingly clear to me how national righteousness – a highly dubious idea to begin with – derives from such precepts, I can certainly see its value as a mechanism for self-excuse and self-affirmation. Little of such writing derives from "radicalism" or from "righteousness." Walzer's Exodus book is written from the perspective of victory, which it consolidates and authorizes after the fact. As a result, the book is shot through with a confidence that comes from an easy commerce between successful enterprise in the secular world and similar (if only anticipated) triumphs in the extra-historical world. As to how radicalism and realism square with Walzer's astonishing reliance upon God, I cannot at all understand. I have no way – and Walzer proposes none – for distinguishing between the claims put forth by competing monotheistic clerics in today's Middle East, all of whom – Ayatollah Khomeini, Ayatollah Begin, Ayatollah Gemayel (and there are others) – say that God is indisputably on their side. That the Falwells, the Swaggerts, the Farrakhans in America say much the same thing piles Pelion on Ossa, and leaves Walzer unperturbed, urging a remarkable amalgam of God and realism upon us, as we try to muddle through.[88]

Said's alternative to Zionism is intimately tied to his vision of a reconciliation between Jews and Palestinians – a vision which he has articulated over the years with remarkable consistency: a binational, secular, democratic polity in which *all* the citizens of the state, regardless of their ethnic or religious background, enjoy equal rights under the law. Implied in ideas, such as affiliation and contrapuntality, which I have already discussed, such a position is broadly premised on the interrelatedness of human cultures in general, but it acquires greater, more poignant resonance in the tragic context of what Said sometimes calls Palestine/Israel. It is a recognition that, despite more than a century of mutual demonization and hatred, Palestinians and Israelis are destined to live together willy-nilly; that neither side can make the other go away; that apartheid-like exclusionism and hierarchism will only exacerbate an already explosive situation. "There can be no reconciliation," Said wrote recently, "unless both peoples, two communities of suffering, resolve that their existence is a secular fact, and that it has to be dealt with as such." He adds, "Reading Palestinian and Jewish history together not only gives the tragedies of the Holocaust and of what subsequently happened to the Palestinians their full force but also reveals how in the course of interrelated Israeli and Palestinian life since 1948, one people, the Palestinians, has borne a disproportional share of the pain and loss."[89] In Said's view, the Oslo Agreement only perpetuates that pain and loss.

Conclusion

Normativity, Critique, and Philosophical Method

It should be clear by now that, both as historical reconstructions and as critical interventions, Said's various writings are premised on a prolonged, dramatic confrontation between two opposing attitudes: a deep-seated commitment to the secular principles of humanism and an equally deep-seated disillusionment with the profound disparities created in the name of those same principles. It is also equally clear that, instead of dodging, denying, or smoothing over the contradictions entailed in his critical position, he has opted to confront them and radicalize them. There is no celebration of grand cultural achievements here, just as there is no wholesale condemnation of culture. Culture (or history, or civilization, or tradition) is not being characterized as the source of redemption or as the object of elevation; nor is it being reductively denounced as oppressive, duplicitous, self-serving.

Rather Said's oppositional writings are intended to effect maximum estrangement and reflection: they reverse, subvert, and up-end received wisdom; they are counter-histories written against the grain of self-contained traditions, of founding fathers and originary centers, of restorative interpretations and exclusive canons. As post-narrative accounts articulated in various registers of human cultural life, they leave little room for apologias, embellishments, mystifications, or valorizations; they are oblique reconstructions of an anxiety-laden modernity – left-handed descriptions of the sites where the orphaned but ambitious subject of modernity was first incubated, the twisted roads it has since traveled, the hubristic yet vulnerable forms it has assumed, the ideological boundaries it has crossed or fortified, the enormous perils it has caused or confronted. In short, Said's studies, from *The Fiction of Autobiography* to *Culture and Imperialism*, and beyond, function as depictions of human agency, both individually and collectively, under conditions of extremity; they are stories not just about what is euphemistically called progress but also about the patently unconscionable price exacted in the course of that progress. It is probably this unflinching attention to what Said calls (in *Beginnings*) the scandalous underside of reason that accounts for the unnerving feeling that one often gets from reading his works – a feeling of intense, almost searing, alternation between hope and despair. Aptly described by Christopher Hitchens as a form of "pessoptimism" (an evocation of the Pessoptimist – or *Almutasha'il* – the main character of Emil Habibi's novel),[1] this heightened awareness of history's nightmare as much as of its promise distinguishes Said's criticism from that of most contemporary theorists on the left, including Jameson, Eagleton, and Habermas. Jim Merod's elegantly phrased recent assessment offers an accurate characterization of Said's career:

> If Said's lifelong intellectual work has been a labor of love, excruciation, delicacy, deliberation, ascesis, pride, worry, commitment, and hope – and I think it exhibits such pressures all across its verbal landscape – it also has achieved tangible results in the world that few university intellectuals aspire to or accomplish. Its permanent value cannot be assessed yet, but it will surely carry among its attributes, and for an indeterminate time, the inextinguishable example of Said's principled refusal of certainties: dogmas, doctrines, and received premises that torment any mind aiming to approach Michel de Montaigne's vulnerable self-conscious dereliction. Or to embody its own. Such a mind, in that instance, rejects and, ultimately, refutes the seductive persuasion of certainties that impede its own meandering path.[2]

One of the potential weaknesses of Said's "technique of trouble" is that – despite (or perhaps because of) its almost unparalleled diagnostic cogency – it leaves him with almost no viable theoretical space for normativity as such to emerge. Apropos of this problematic one could, for example, raise questions similar to these: How can Said make strongly prescriptive (and not value-neutral, descriptive) statements about epistemological, ethical, and political matters without at the same time offering us a strong theory of validity – i.e., a set of objectively determinable standards or criteria which could be used as a final court of appeal? Given that he privileges a species of (arguably) perspectivalist valuation – with its vast potential for arbitrariness, decisionism, even disharmony – over philosophically or scientifically

knowable truth, how does one distinguish sound judgement from
error? If in his view all consensus inevitably leads to self-idealization
and self-fortification, how does he conceive of civil society – indeed of
the very idea of polity itself? How can he insist on justice, equality,
and freedom for all human beings and at the same time fail to provide
an exemplary vision of these ideals – a vision which, whether interpreted minimally or maximally, would have the capacity to oper-
ationalize these imperatives in the institutional history of society?
Given that other contemporary thinkers, among them noted leftists
and liberal democrats, are acutely aware of the same ethico-political
problems that he has struggled with – and have each been obliged to
propose what they consider to be cogently theorized hypotheses of
adjudication and justification – why is he unable or unwilling to
present a similarly nuanced teleological conception of human community? Why can't he work out a program of political action,
institute a set of procedural rules, or describe an already established
socio-political order (something analogous to, say, Rawls's neo-con-
tractarian theory of justice, Habermas's pragmatist/neo-Marxist ideal
of communicative ethics, or Taylor's communitarian core of strong
values) which would give us an adequate understanding of his utopian
goals? To formulate the question in terms of a specific tributary of
modern thought, does it make sense to deploy – as Said consistently
does – the crucial Marxian concept of ideology critique while at the
same time resisting the ultimate utopian horizon of that tradition:
namely, the transformation of society as a totality? With respect to his
trenchant assaults on Eurocentrism and imperialism, how can Said at
once critique the West and appeal to conceptions of human community, such as freedom and equality, which were historically realized
(and conceptually forged) in the Western cultural tradition?

As I have noted at various points in the study, questions like these
have actually been addressed to Said. They are directly or indirectly
germane to the large number of objections raised specifically about
Orientalism, but given Said's deliberately intransigent metacritical
infrastructure, the scope of these questions can be extended to cover
almost his entire career.

I happen to believe that these questions do have some merit, which
is not to say that all of Said's many critics have demonstrated the high
caliber of integrity, care, and rigor which the debates about his views
warrant: after all, no one in his or her right mind would equate the
judicious critiques of such conscientious scholars as James Clifford and
Bart Moore-Gilbert – both of them fair-minded, liberal scholars –

with, for example, the soupy apologetics of a neo-conservative like John MacKenzie,[3] or with the scurrilities of morally embattled Zionists (one of whom is Edward Alexander), or with the intemperate rhetorical blasts of a Marxist-nativist like Aijaz Ahmad. Still, however, to the extent that the objections raised against Said have claims to any logical cogency, they imply an ultimately *philosophical* (in the sense of analytically exhaustive) common denominator – a plane where insight into difficult epistemological, ethical, and political problems rests, not *primarily* on the corrosive power of critical acid or on an alternative historical reconstruction, but on the architectonics and persuasive force of the argument as a rigorous, airtight, rationally compelling inquiry. Hence one could argue that, for the conceptual landscape of normativity to take shape, Said needs to address these questions more systematically. That is to say, he must give them a more focused, more clearly differentiated, more analytically accented treatment – a treatment in which the empirical realities of history, politics, and society are bracketed off tactically so that generic ideas of freedom, justice, truth, and equality can come into sharp relief as a constellation of carefully delimited topics capable of being unpacked propositionally and examined on their own metaleptic ground.

Of course this kind of intellectual labor belongs to the ahistorical formalism that Said has denounced as disembodied, abstract system-building. It is my considered judgement, however, that an enactment like this on Said's part would be a worthwhile exercise – if only because it would serve as an effective response to his critics in a manner more directly consonant with mainstream Anglo-American styles of theorizing, if only because it would help sweep away a massive cloud of misinterpretation and misrepresentation that has accumulated around his writings over the years. It would also, I believe, go a long way toward disclosing the conceptual nexus between norm and critique, a nexus which he has alluded to (and often directly asserted) repeatedly throughout his career.

It should be clear by now, however, that Said's almost total disregard for the professed techniques of analytic philosophy and related fields (such as, for example, Anglo-American "political science") is a matter of strategic choice; moreover (as we shall see shortly), the specifically historical and theoretical challenges that he indirectly poses for that tradition are quite formidable. For, despite its impressive record over the past one hundred years, mainstream Anglo-American philosophy has been a spectacular failure in vast areas of human cultural life. Consider the following judgement delivered by a noted contemporary thinker on the strengths and shortcomings of analytic philosophy:

> On the side of analytic philosophy, perhaps no other movement in the history of philosophy has placed such a high priority on clarity, rigor, and subtlety. It has made us self-conscious of intellectual standards that must be placed on any legitimate intellectual position, including Marxism. It places upon Marxism the challenge to seriously encounter the insights, distinctions, and claims that have been made the fruit of analytic investigations ... But analytic philosophy has paid a heavy price for this clarity and rigor. It is itself guilty of harboring suppressed premises and convictions. To a greater extent than is warranted, analytic philosophy has isolated itself from the practical concerns of men, from what Dewey called the "problems of men." Its contribution to political and social philosophy has been virtually nonexistent, and analytic ethics has tended to become an arid, scholastic jungle. Analytic philosophers, and especially younger students of analytic philosophy, are growing restless with the artificial, self-imposed limitations of the movement ... There has been virtually no attempt among analytic philosophers ... to ask critical questions about the origin and development of [the] social institutions and practices which shape what we are.[4]

This assessment was made in 1971 by Richard Bernstein, a scholar who can hardly be accused of polemicism. In a series of books written with judicious rigor and tact, he has tried over the past three decades to help effect a productive dialogue between the Continental and Anglo-American branches of philosophy by explicating and evaluating the central claims of, on the one hand, pragmatism, logical atomism and positivism, and various post-positivist trends and, on the other, Marxism, existentialism, hermeneutics, critical theory, and poststructuralism. The above critique, which comes from his first major text, *Praxis and Action: Contemporary Philosophies of Human Activity*, was delivered in that spirit of hoped-for synthesis and mutual enrichment.[5] He is careful to highlight the considerable achievements of the analytic tradition, specifically defending it against the charge habitually leveled at it by Marxists – that "the whole movement is nothing but a faulty outcropping of an idealistic bourgeois superstructure." That reductive talk, argues Bernstein, makes Marxists "guilty of the worst sort of intellectual provincialism. It is to betray what was so fundamental to Marx himself, the willingness and ability to carry on *a careful critique* of alternative intellectual orientations" (emphasis added). Yet Bernstein is uncompromising in his verdict on analytic philosophers' inability to grapple with important questions about socio-historical formations and practices; about the genesis and power of institutions; about the short-term and long-term consequences of human action; and about a whole host of other matters all of which lie within the purview of philosophy properly understood. These "questions concerning the origin and nature of social institutions ... cannot be conveniently assigned to some other approach or discipline; they are questions that must be confronted in pursuing the very issues central to analytic philosophy."[6] Thirty years on, there is little convincing evidence that this confrontation has taken place. On the contrary, most contemporary analytic philosophers are, to all intents and purposes, as oblivious to these questions as their mentors were.

What I think is implied in Bernstein's criticism is that an unacknowledged combination of naive scientism and restrictive specialization has severely limited the scope and relevance of analytic philosophy. Bernstein doesn't quite put the matter in these terms, but it is fair to say that the tradition's provincialism and antihistoricist bias; its embrace of semantic "clarity" and "precision" at the expense of critical bite; its addiction to a dreary, "technical" terminology, endlessly elaborated syllogisms, and mind-numbing computations — all in the absence of useful theoretical insight; its enormous capacity for minuscule pseudo-problems and "solutions" while Rome burns; its inability to reflect on its hidden assumptions, moment in history, or ideological freight: these perdurable failings have considerably narrowed the horizons of analytic philosophy — even at the same time that its practitioners continue to make pretentious epistemic claims for it. Considering the vast amounts of energy poured by "professional" philosophers — from Moore, Wittgenstein, and Ayer down to Searle and Dennett — into the "problems" of language and logic, of meaning and intention, of sense-data, qualia, and causation, of truth, reality, and possible worlds; considering the ferocious repertoire of formulas, definitions, suppositions, reductions, and deductions, of categorial schemes, close analysis, minute details, and hair-splitting distinctions; and considering the almost endless polemical battles between realists, quasi-realists, and anti-realists; between internalists, externalists, and beyondists; considering all of this tremendous exertion, one might be tempted to think that something at once profound and pertinent is at stake here. One might be justified in believing that at one point philosophers would step back from the teacup storm and begin to examine the gigantic wreckage of the past century, for example that they might ask serious philosophic questions about the motivations that lay behind two world wars which between them consumed sixty million lives; that someone somewhere might wonder about the possibility of a compelling ideological connection between a philosophical classic of the Seventies (say, *A Theory of Justice*) and the Vietnam adventure (which was, after all, *justified* in the name of "freedom and democracy"); or that philosophers might want to take seriously the fact that they do not operate in a socio-historical vacuum where objective knowledge is delivered from an Archimedean vantage point but rather "are always enmeshed in circumstance, time, place, and society"[7] – just like the rest of us.

With the exception of such indefatigable activists as Bertrand Russell and (more recently) Noam Chomsky, Anglo-American philosophers have shown little recognition that these matters are worth bothering with, philosophically or otherwise. This lack of concern with the scandalous dimension of reason and its often catastrophic historical consequences is, I believe, as true of such broad-minded thinkers as Richard Rorty and Charles Taylor – both of whom are at heart exuberant and celebratory rather than diagnostic and critical – as it is of the more narrowly focused, technically inclined philosophers.

The point to be made about all of this is that, whatever merit the objections raised against Said from the *analytic* viewpoint might have, the implications of his critical practice for analytic philosophy are far more damaging to the field. Said has not written about Anglo-American philosophy as extensively as some other critical theorists (Christopher Norris, for example) have,[8] but there is little doubt that analytic philosophy constitutes the *principal* component of what he has, in a Bachelardian frame of mind, described as "a rationalism based on dry-as-dust traditionalism, memory, and scholastic rigidity."[9] In other words, there is a sense in which his entire career can be characterized as an attempt to combat the kind of naiveté, mystification, and self-limitation that he ascribes to mimetic representation, in both its idealist and empiricist guises. At a more specific level, his critique of literary-critical formalism can be extended to philosophical formalism – with even greater justification. In both cases, what could be called a narrow ethic of professionalism covers up the absence of any really engaged ethics of worldliness. With the exception of a tiny minority, the members of both interpretive communities have undoubtedly succumbed to the same fastidious dodginess that hamstrings the typical academic humanist – the self-inflicted amnesia about serious socio-political issues; the studied, carefully nursed, quasi-religious quietism; the stuffy self-importance and pettifoggery; the spurious myth that weightless "theoria" effortlessly wafts over the quotidian realm of "praxis." In short, most of what transpires under the grandiloquent rubrics of "philosophy," "literary studies," and "critical theory" in the United States and Britain constitutes a substantial part of the cloying, immunizing minutiae of hegemonic culture – that vast, multi-dimensional process of elaboration, saturation, and fine-tuning which cocoons individuals and collectivities in civil society while at the same time camouflaging projections of political, industrial, and military power.

To conclude: the most powerful challenge Said presents not only to analytic philosophy but to the humanistic fields in general resides in his insistence that there is a direct, non-negotiable, ethically binding relationship between, on the one hand, a radically historicized, interdisciplinary, activist conception of criticism and, on the other, the very idea (and practice) of what it means to be a secular intellectual. This, I think, is the import of the distinction that he has made (explicitly or implicitly) over the years between what he considers as oppressively coercive ideologies, together with the collusive intellectuals who sustain them by commission or by omission, and the critical knowledge deployed by oppositional intellectuals. In my view, that historical–theoretical matrix – and not a vacant, miraculously created space of transcendence – should be seen as the proper arena of any debates about normative standards for human knowledge or for ethico-political responsibility. In other words, what emerges out of Said's critical practice is *not* that epistemic insight and moral evaluation are impossible or can somehow be waived (in fact the exact opposite is true) but that they have to be sought after – actively, one might add – in the *socio-historical* horizons of space-time, with all the constraints and opportunities this materialist–phenomenological idea implies.

I have argued that, at a broad level, the trajectory of Said's career unfolds as a protracted demythologization of the practical and theoretical rationality whose spectacular successes and disastrous failures have been woven into the very structure and texture of what has come to be known as modernity. It is of course in this respect that Said's writings make available precisely the element that has been missing from the analytic tradition – what Bernstein has called "the practical concerns of men" (and, we must add, of women too): if it is the case that ideas and ideals do not subsist on their own as pure essences but are, as Vico recognized, made by human beings in concrete socio-historical situations; if it is also inevitably the case that – as *applied* institutional agencies caught up in contests over power, authority, and privilege – these ideas and ideals have had profound consequences (psychological, social, political, economic, cultural); and if it is emphatically the case that, far from being always life-enhancing, these consequences have, more often than not, assumed the form of almost unimaginable destruction and suffering: if all this, then it is nothing short of "reprehensible" and "corrupting" (Said's phrasing) for philosophers, literary interpreters, social theorists, historians, journalists, and other humanistic intellectuals to anesthetize the critical sense in the name of professionalism, moderation, objectivity, self-interest, and the like:

> Nothing in my view is more reprehensible than those habits of mind in the intellectual that induce avoidance, that characteristic turning away from a difficult and principled position which you know to be the right one, but which you decide not to take. You do not want to appear too political; you are afraid of seeming controversial; you need the approval of a boss or an authority figure; you want to keep a reputation for being balanced, objective, moderate; your hope is to be asked back, to consult, to be on a board or prestigious committee, and so to remain within the responsible mainstream; someday you hope to get an honorary degree, a big prize, perhaps even an ambassadorship. For an intellectual these habits of mind are corrupting *par excellence*. If anything can denature, neutralize, and finally kill a passionate intellectual life it is the internalization of such habits.[10]

As I have tried to demonstrate in various contexts, Said believes that the "knowledge" produced by intellectuals of this kind is responsible for the creation of (or is otherwise implicated in) two complementary myths – the cult of the expert and the doctrine of essentialized identities: the "professional" philosopher dispenses specialized (hence "expert") knowledge about the "weightiest" issues at an appropriately rarefied level of abstraction; the Orientalist delivers "expert" wisdom about the Orient – its peoples, cultures, histories; the reporter relays fresh, objective news about the world; and so on and on. This positivistic "expertise," which is somehow miraculously assumed to rise above mere "opinion" or "doxa," gradually but effectively helps construct (and is in turn further motivated by) identitarian ideas: the West, Afrocentrism, Jews, "our" race, Islam, the Arab nation, "our" national interest, Zionism, the American way of life, the Oriental mind, "Western" philosophy, Americans, Iranians, the natives, etc. Alternately idealized and demonized, every single one of these and similar ideological illusions can – and very often does – ossify into a harsh, exclusionary, hierarchist dogma in the name of (or in opposition to) which horrific acts of injustice can be (and have been) repeatedly committed.

What alternative "habits of mind" does Said propose for intellectuals to counteract these instruments of power and victimization? The following passage from *Representations of the Intellectual* (one of a large number of such passages) gives us a brief but cogent answer:

> [The oppositional] intellectual is an individual with a specific public role in society that cannot be reduced to being a faceless professional, a competent member of a class just going about her/his business. The central fact for me is, I think, that the intellectual is an individual endowed with a faculty for representing, embodying, articulating a message, a view, an attitude, philosophy, or opinion to, as well as for, a public. And this role has an edge to it, and cannot be played without a sense of being someone whose place it is publicly to raise embarrassing questions, to confront orthodoxy and dogma (rather than to produce them), to be someone who cannot easily be co-opted by governments or corporations, and whose *raison d'être* is to represent all those people and issues that are routinely forgotten or swept under the rug. The intellectual does so on the basis of universal principles that all human beings are entitled to expect decent standards of behavior concerning freedom and justice from worldly powers or nations, and that deliberate or inadvertent violations of these standards need to be testified and fought against courageously.[11]

To buttress this exacting view of intellectual responsibility, Said carefully picks his way between Gramsci and Benda. Drawing upon Gramsci's distinction between traditional and organic intellectuals (the former broadly to be understood as guardians and transmitters of established socio-cultural authority, the latter as thinkers directly engaged in the struggle for emergent or alternative counter-authorities and movements), he suggests that the modern intellectual can (and ought to) play the activist role implied by the idea of organicity – without, however, surrendering his or her independence, withholding judicious criticism, or forgetting that there are universal values which cannot be disregarded for the sake of loyalty to one's immediate class or enterprise.

It is, I think, apposite at this point to stress the extent to which Said values the capacity and willingness of intellectuals to resist what he has on occasion called the collective passions of group identity. That kind of resistance, he insists, "does not mean opposition for opposition's sake. But it does mean asking questions, making distinctions, restoring to memory all those things that tend to be overlooked or walked past in the rush to collective judgment and action. With respect to the consensus on group or national identity it is the intellectual's task to show how the group is not a natural or god-given entity but is a constructed, manufactured, even in some cases invented object, with a history of struggle and conquest behind it, that it is sometimes important to represent."[12] In other words, organicity is a double-edged sword, one edge of which has to be blunted. Hence Benda's usefulness for Said. He criticizes Benda's inherent conservatism and finds untenable the latter's unrealistic, even otherworldly demands of intellectuals – that they be "a clerisy [of] very rare creatures" upholding platonic ideals, "a tiny band of super-gifted and morally endowed philosopher-kings who [in the manner of Socrates and Jesus] constitute the conscience of mankind."[13] To excoriate intellectuals, as Benda does, for having departed from this ideal – argues Said – is to insist on an "impossible absolutism."[14] But, he adds, Benda's conception of the intellectual on the whole "remains an attractive and compelling one."[15] Why? Because "Real intellectuals are never more themselves than when, moved by metaphysical passion and disinterested principles of justice and truth, they denounce corruption, defend the weak, defy imperfect or oppressive authority."[16]

It is with this broad imperative in mind that Said draws a multifaceted portrait of the modern critical intellectual as he or she has appeared both in socio-cultural history and in fictional writing. The features of this portrait partake of the dogged, highly publicized activism of major philosophers (Russell and Sartre, for example); the explosive anarchism and willful alienation of precocious fictional characters (Turgenev's Bazarov and Joyce's Dedalus); and the high-minded, mandarin elitism of tragic figures like Adorno. The true intellectual vocation in Said's view embodies and dramatizes the contradictions of modernity to the highest degree in that it "involves both commitment and risk, boldness and vulnerability."[17] The modern critical intellectual has a "peculiar, even abrasive style of life and social performance that is uniquely" personal;[18] he or she can be "embarrassing, contrary, even unpleasant."[19] Often "anarchic and yet highly concentrated,"[20] the intellectual is a curmudgeon who will not win "official honors" or "friends in high places."[21] For all these reasons, being an intellectual is an extraordinarily self-disciplined, even ascetic habit of mind – "a state of constant alertness" and equilibration, "an almost athletic rational energy"[22] which combines rigor, resolve, resilience, and self-irony in equal measure. Above all – and this brings us to the heart of the matter – the intellectual's primary purpose "is to advance human freedom and knowledge":[23]

The intellectual's representations, his or her articulations of a cause or idea to society, are not meant primarily to fortify ego or celebrate status. Nor are they principally intended for service within powerful bureaucracies and generous employers. Intellectual representations are the *activity itself*, dependent on a kind of consciousness that is skeptical, engaged, unremittingly devoted to rational investigation and moral judgment; and this puts the individual on record and on the line.[24]

This activity and this consciousness together constitute what Said has called criticism – that is, critical consciousness allied with radical theory. Described at the beginning of my study as a readiness to debate with knowledge and to wrestle with history, it could also be characterized as a retroactive and proactive process of reckoning and stock-taking, a willingness to take an unvarnished view of civilization, to take a negative measure of modernity and not just celebrate its grand achievements. That, according to Said, is the true calling of the intellectual.

The real intellectual is neither an expert nor a consensus-builder, neither the defender of a favorite dogma nor the leader of an idealized tribe: "intellectuals [are] precisely those figures whose public performances can neither be predicted nor compelled into some slogan, orthodox party line, or fixed dogma," for – after all – "standards of truth about human misery and oppression [transcend] the individual intellectual's party affiliation, national origin, and primeval loyalties."[25] Hence the intellectual is best understood as an outsider who is also committed to the defense of the weak against victimization – that is "as exile and marginal, as amateur, and as the author of a language that tries to speak the truth to power."[26] The true intellectual does not pontificate on the wonders of "the Western canon," glorify the monuments of "Islamic civilization," or declaim about the virtues of "the free world." Nor does he or she airily philosophize about "the conversation of mankind" in a world beset with massive inequalities and threatened with destruction through megalomaniacal wars. Rather the true intellectual "raises embarrassing questions" about histories, cultures, policies, practices, institutions. He or she probes texts, minds, events, and agencies so that the knowledge made available by virtue of such an investigation has the capacity to rouse society from multiple states of complacency and arrogance.

It is ultimately in this historically informed sense that critique and norm have engaged each other throughout Said's career, an enactment which I have been describing as part ideology critique, part philosophical reflection, part intellectual history, and part socio-political history – all of them radical in the extreme. This dramatic encounter between critique and norm manifests itself both in the extraordinarily broad range of disciplinary interest found in his oeuvre and in the multi-purpose heuristic (what I have been calling agonistic dialectic and genealogy/archaeology) which he has deployed consistently. Whether it is posited as irreducible dissonance, as corrosive intellectual energy, or as radically demystifying analysis, the Saidian conception of criticism is not a nay-saying exercise signaling cynicism or nihilism; on the contrary, it is saturated with moral indignation: profound suspicion coexists with unlimited utopianism, with both of them (to be) achieved in the open-ended unfolding of historical time. This permanent insurrection is best conveyed by the idea of radical theory and criticism transgressively "traveling" and doing necessary work in various socio-cultural contexts:

> The work of theory, criticism, demystification, deconsecration, and decentralization ... is never finished. The point of [radical] theory [and critical intentionality] therefore is to travel, always to move beyond its confinements, to emigrate, to remain in a sense in exile. Adorno and Fanon exemplify this profound restlessness in the way they refuse the emoluments offered by the Hegelian dialectic as stabilized into resolution by Lukacs – [this same restlessness is also found in] the Lukacs who appeared to speak for class consciousness as something to be gained, possessed, held onto.[27]

Said's utilization of such dynamic and relational terms as meditation, affiliation, contrapuntality, and structure of attitudes and references, all of which (as I have noted in various contexts) suggest adjacency, multiplicity and complementarity, is meant to give an accounting of this interaction between norm and critique. They are also emphatically intended to stress the bond (and the distance) between the individual and the multiple communities in which she or he is embedded. Hence, of course, his insistence on both the particularity of the intellectual and the universality of the values she or he is urged to uphold.

Conceived in this way, normativity is an ideal invoked in partial absentia as a potentiality inherent in humanity's quest for shareable value, a negative determination of utopia (an oxymoronic term which itself, after all, means "a nonplace"). Normativity is the name given to that against which the always imperfect actualities of the present are measured – a moral–intellectual latitude (figural or spatial) which is at once inside and outside social reality, a zone from which history's at best ambiguous achievements can be exposed to the radical light of criticism. In my opinion, very few modern thinkers (Williams, Chomsky, Sartre, Foucault at his best) have ever managed to provide this kind of insight into the meaning of modernity.

Notes

Introduction

1 Bruce Robbins, "Homelessness and Worldliness," *Diacritics*, vol. 13, no. 3, 1983, pp. 69–77. See also Robbins' recent book *Secular Vocations: Intellectuals, Professionalism, Culture*, London: Verso, 1998, pp. 152–60.

2 Daniel O'Hara, "Criticism Worldly and Unworldly: Edward W. Said and the Cult of Theory," *Boundary 2*, vol. 12, no. 3, & vol. 13, no. 1, 1984, pp. 379–403.

3 Abdul R. JanMohamed, "Worldliness-without-World, Homelessness-as-Home: Toward a Definition of the Specular Border Intellectual," in Michael Sprinker, ed., *Edward Said: A Critical Reader*, Oxford: Blackwell Publishers, 1992, pp. 96–120. For details of (and commentary on) JanMohamed's article on Said, see Chapter 2 of my study.

4 James Clifford, "On *Orientalism*," in *The Predicament of Culture: Twentieth-Century Ethnography, Literature, and Art*, Cambridge MA: Harvard University Press, 1988, pp. 255–76; for more details see Chapter 5 below.

5 Aijaz Ahmad, *In Theory: Classes, Nations, Literatures*, London: Verso, 1987, pp. 159–242. Here is a typical passage:

All such *systems* are rejected [by Said], in the characteristic postmodernist way, so that resistance can always only be personal, micro, and shared only by a small, determinate number of individuals who happen, perchance, to come together, outside the so-called "grand narratives" of class, gender, nation ... Ambivalences on this question are already notable in "Travelling Theory", but even more representative in all this is the essay "Opponents, Audiences, Constituencies and Community" ... where Said first speaks derisively of "the self-policing, self-purifying communities erected even by Marxists, as well as other disciplinary discourses", and then goes on to specify what he considers to be a key project that needs to be posed against the "disciplinary" character of Marxism, etc.: "to restore the nonsequential energy of lived historical memory and subjectivity ... to tell other stories than the official sequential or ideological ones produced by institutional power." I am not quite sure what this last formulation actually means, but it would not, I think, be unfair to say that the sense in which Marxism is said to be "self-policing, self-purifying", as well as "disciplinary", "institutional" and "ideological", applies inescapably to particular tendencies – notably the socialist tendencies – within feminism too. Meanwhile, theoretical eclecticism runs increasingly out of control: sweeping, patently post-structuralist denunciations of Marxism can be delivered in the name of Gramsci, using the terminology explicitly drawn from Althusser, and listing the names of communist poets like Aimé Césaire, Pablo Neruda and Mahmoud Darwish to illustrate the sites of resistance (see *In Theory*, p. 200).

6 Mahdi Amil, *Marx fī Istishrāq Edward Said* [Marx in Edward Said's *Orientalism*], Beirut: Dār el-Fārābi, 1985. The subject of Amil's book is what he considers to be multiple distortions and confusions on Said's part in the latter's critique of Marx for colluding with Orientalist thought and with European imperialism.

7 In his interview with Imre Salusinszky from which I have quoted at the top of this introduction, Said responds to a question about his being a refugee in this way: "To describe me as a refugee is probably overstating it a bit"; he then proceeds to provide a broad biographical sketch towards the end of which he says, "It's been a very good life for me, and I haven't regretted it for a moment"; see Edward Said, "Interview," in Imre Salusinszky, ed., *Criticism in Society*, New York: Routledge, 1987, pp. 127–8.

8 *After the Last Sky: Palestinian Lives*, London: Faber and Faber, 1986, p. 20; the book was prepared in collaboration with Jean Mohr, who provided a photographic collage of Palestinian lives and locales collected over a long period of time. Said offers intensely personal, almost lyrical reflections which, in turns hopeful and elegiac, activate the still photos into an almost aleatory experience – the modern experience of the Palestinian people, with all its tragedies and triumphs.

9 Edward Said, "Permission to Narrate," in *The Politics of Dispossession: The Struggle for Palestinian Self-Determination, 1969–1994*, New York: Pantheon Books, 1994, pp. 247–68.

10 See Robbins, "Homelessness and Worldliness," already cited above; Mustapha Ben T. Marrouchi, "The Critic as Dis/placed Intelligence: The Case of Edward Said," *Diacritics*, vol. 2, no. 1, 1991, pp. 63–74; Asha Varadharajan, "Edward W. Said," in *Exotic Parodies: Subjectivity in Adorno, Said, and Spivak*, Minneapolis: University of Minnesota Press, 1995, pp. 113–41 (for my commentary on Varadharajan, see the final chapter below); Ella Shohat, "Antinomies of Exile: Said at the Frontiers of National Narrations," in Michael Sprinker, ed., *Edward Said: A Critical Reader*, pp. 121–43.

11 London: Routledge, 1999.

12 *Beginnings: Intention and Method*, New York: Basic Books, Inc., 1975, p. 283. Also see "The Horizons of R. P. Blackmur," *Raritan*, Fall 1986, pp. 28–50; Said does not overlook Blackmur's limitations, but he gives him credit for courageously confronting the perplexities and paradoxes of the modernist imagination, for recognizing modern "literature as secular incarnation," and for dramatizing the difficult transaction "between *life* and *art*":

Because he saw the relationship between this pair of terms [i.e., life and art] as encompassing every possibility from opposition to absolute correspondence, he read poetry, fiction, and criticism as processes giving provisional resolution to the differences and similarities between art and life. Criticism for him therefore dramatized and reperformed the mediations by which art and the symbolic imagination actualized life, but by its very nature criticism also undermined itself. It did not define ideas, taste, and values so much as it set them back into what he calls the Moha, "the vital, fundamental stupidity of the human race," from which as art or as Numen they then emerged. Criticism is best seen as a provisional act, as perhaps even a temporary deformation of and deflection from literature, which itself is approximate, tentative, irresolute. "Literature," Blackmur writes . . . "is one of our skills of notation of the incarnation of the real into the actual" ("Horizons," p. 32).

13 For a discussion of the "either/or" metaphor and Said's invocation of it in the context of Conrad's life and career, see Chapter 1 below.

14 Said, "Opponents, Audiences, Constituencies, and Community," *Critical Inquiry*, September 1982, p. 24.

15 Said, "Traveling Theory Reconsidered" in Robert M. Polhemus and Roger B. Henkle, eds, *Critical Reconstructions: The Relationship of Fiction and Life*, Stanford: Stanford University Press, 1994, p. 265.

16 Said, "Adorno as Lateness Itself," in Malcolm Bull, ed., *Apocalypse Theory and the Ends of the World*, Oxford: Blackwell Publishers, 1995, pp. 264–81.

17 Said, "The World, the Text, and the Critic," in *The World, the Text, and the Critic*, Cambridge MA: Harvard University Press, 1983, p. 51.

18 Said, "Opponents, Audiences, Constituencies, and Community," pp. 24–5.

19 Said, *Beginnings*, p. 40.

20 Said, "Afterword, to *Orientalism*," *Orientalism*, New York: Vintage Books, 1978, p. 330. (The "Afterword" was included in the 1994 printing of the book.)

21 See Clifford's review article, already cited above (note 4). For a discussion of Bové's various – and sometimes conflicting – commentaries on Said's writing, see Chapter 4 below.

22 In his article, "Places of Mind, Occupied Lands: Edward Said and Philology" (in Sprinker, ed., *Edward Said: A Critical Reader*), pp. 74–95, Brennan provides cogent insights into the connections between *Beginnings* and *Orientalism* in terms of Said's broad interest in philology. In like manner, Bhatnagar frames the issue of Said's idea of origins, as it is treated in *Beginnings* and *Orientalism*, in a comparatist context where Said is played off against Foucault (see "Uses and Limits of Foucault: A Study of the Theme of Origins in Edward Said's 'Orientalism'," *Social Scientist*, vol. 158, 1986, pp. 3–22). Though steps in the right interpretive direction, Brennan's and Bhatnagar's comments are too brief and too localized to help us with the kind of reconception I am suggesting. Clifford's pointed references to *Beginnings*, which are offered as glosses in the review article I have already cited, are largely meant to illustrate the epistemological tensions, ambivalences, and confusions that he detects in *Orientalism*.

23 See, for example, Said's review of *Among the Believers* in *New Statesman*, October 16, 1981; also see Said, "An Intellectual Catastrophe," *Al-Ahram Weekly*, August 12, 1998.

24 Said, "The Politics of Knowledge," in David H. Richter, ed., *Falling into Theory: Conflicting Views of Reading Literature*, Boston: Bedford Books, 1994, pp. 197–8.

Chapter 1

1 Edward Said, *Joseph Conrad and the Fiction of Autobiography*, Cambridge MA: Harvard University Press, 1966. Hereafter *The Fiction*.

2 See, for example, Said, "Conrad and Nietzsche," in Norman Sherry, ed., *Joseph Conrad: A Commemoration; Papers from the 1974 International Conference on Conrad*, London: The MacMillan Press, 1976, pp. 64–74.

3 Said, "Interview," in Imre Salusinszky, ed., *Criticism in Society*, p. 128.

4 On misappropriations of Foucault's and Derrida's thought by American scholars respectively, see, for example, Said, "Traveling Theory," p. 244, and "Criticism Between Culture and System," p. 191, both in *The World, the Text, and the Critic*, Cambridge MA: Harvard University Press, 1983.

5 Said, *The Fiction*, p. 67.

6 The first passage is cited in "Conrad: The Presentation of Narrative," in *The World, the Text, and the Critic*, p. 91. The second passage is quoted in *The Fiction*, p. 137, and again in *Culture and Imperialism*, New York: Alfred A. Knopf, 1993, p. 69.

7 Said writes:

> [I]f it is true that Conrad ironically sees the imperialism of the San Tomé silver mine's British and American owners as doomed by its own pretentious and impossible ambitions, it is also true that he writes as a man whose *Western* view of the non-Western world is as ingrained as to blind him to other histories, other cultures, other aspirations. All Conrad can see is a world totally dominated by the Atlantic West, in which every opposition to the West only confirms the West's wicked power. What Conrad cannot see is an alternative to this cruel tautology. He could neither understand that India, Africa, and South America also had lives and cultures with integrities not totally controlled by the gringo imperialists and reformers of this world, nor allow himself to believe that anti-imperialist independence movements were not all corrupt and in the pay of the puppet masters in London or Washington.

See *Culture and Imperialism*, p. xviii.

8 See Said, "A Standing Civil War," *Hudson Review*, vol. 23, no. 4, 1970–71, pp. 758–66.

9 See, for example, Said, *Culture and Imperialism*, p. 76.

10 Said's book on Conrad has not attracted much attention beyond the initial reviews, most of which were critical. In a piece published in *Review of English Studies*, vol. 19, 1968, pp. 233–5, Douglas Hewitt claims that Said has committed serious errors, distortions, and obfuscations. Hewitt seems to have difficulty making sense of Said's phenomenological approach. A similarly negative judgement is delivered by Frederick P. W. McDowell, who (in "Review Essay: The Most Recent Books on Joseph Conrad," in *Papers on Language and Literature*, vol. 4, no. 2, 1968, pp. 201–23) dismisses

Said's book as "an opportunity missed." At one point he complains that Said "is the most difficult writer of prose I have come upon in a long time. He writes with the same density, opacity, and turgidity found in some of R. P. Blackmur's essays. After one wrestles to grasp Said's meaning, he generally finds the meaning not worth that much effort" (p. 206). Eloise Knapp Hay, though less harsh than Hewitt and McDowell, also finds problems in *The Fiction* (see her review in *Modern Language Quarterly*, vol. 28, no. 2, 1967, pp. 252–4). Samuel Hynes demonstrates a greater understanding of the phenomenological method employed by Said but does not express much sympathy for the method in general or for Said's application of it (see his review in *Novel*, vol. 2, 1969, pp. 179–81).

11 Said, "Conrad: The Presentation of Narrative," *The World*, p. 90.

12 Said, "What is Beyond Formalism," *Modern Language Notes*, vol. 86, 1971, pp. 933–45; Said's critique of Hassan's book is given in "Eclecticism and Orthodoxy in Criticism," *Diacritics 2*, Spring 1972, pp. 2–8; Hassan responds in "Polemic," *Diacritics 2*, Fall 1972, pp. 55–60.

13 Said, *The Fiction*, p. 6.

14 Paul Ricoeur, "Phenomenology and Hermeneutics," in *Hermeneutics and the Human Sciences: Essays on Language, Action, and Interpretation*, ed. & trans. John B. Thompson, Cambridge: Cambridge University Press, 1981, p. 102.

15 See Said, "Labyrinth of Incarnations: The Essays of Maurice Merleau-Ponty," *Kenyon Review*, vol. 29, no. 1, 1967, pp. 54–68.

16 Said cites John Galsworthy on the possibility that Conrad may not only have been familiar with Schopenhauer's will philosophy but may actually have been "deeply impressed" by it; see *The Fiction*, p. 102.

17 Ibid., p. 13.

18 Ibid., p. 19.

19 Ibid., p. 100.

20 Ibid., p. 108.

21 Quoted by Said in *The Fiction*, p. 101; my summary of Sartre's reflections is based on Said's own analysis. See *The Fiction*, p. 100.

22 Ibid., pp. 108–9.

23 Ibid., p. 109.

24 Ibid., pp. 110–11.

25 Ibid., p. 137.

26 Ibid., p. 139.

27 Chinua Achebe, "An Image of Africa: Racism in Conrad's *Heart of Darkness*," in *Hopes and Impediments: Selected Essays*, New York: Doubleday, 1984, pp. 1–20. Achebe argues that Conrad projects an image of "triumphant bestiality" and savagery on to the continent and that this is a good example of the reductive, stereotypical characterization of Africa that Europeans have come to impose on everything African in order to accentuate contrastively Europe's refinement and civilization. Likewise, Homi Bhabha, "Articulating the Archaic: Notes on Colonial Nonsense," in P. Collier and H. Geyer-Ryan, eds, *Literary Theory Today*, Cambridge, UK: Polity Press, 1990, pp. 203–18, implicates Conrad in a conspiracy of silence that colonial writers fashioned in order to further Europe's imperialist aims. See Said, *Culture and Imperialism*, p. 76, for his response to Achebe's criticism of Conrad for racism.

28 Said, *The Fiction*, p. 138.

29 Ibid., p. 139.

30 Quoted by Said in *The Fiction*, p. 139. Here and elsewhere in this chapter, I have summarized Said's analysis of Schopenhauer's philosophical speculations.

31 Said's article on Conrad and Nietzsche, already cited above (note 2), is a discussion of the "affinities" between Conrad and Nietzsche and the possibility that Schopenhauer's views may lie behind both of these two thinkers' common interest in the will to power and to truth as well as in the disjunction between words and intention.

32 Quoted by Said in *The Fiction*, p. 25.

33 Quoted by Said in ibid., p. 35.

34 Quoted by Said in ibid., p. 27.

35 Ibid., p. 32.

36 Ibid., p. 140.

37 Joseph Conrad, *Heart of Darkness*, ed. Robert Kimbrough, New York: W. W. Norton & Company, Inc., 1963, p. 69.

38 Ibid., p. 51.

39 Said, *The Fiction*, p. 79.

40 Ibid., p. 183.

41 Ibid., p. 196.

Chapter 2

1 Paul de Man, "The Literary Self as Origin: The Work of Georges Poulet," in *Blindness and Insight: Essays in the Rhetoric of Contemporary Criticism*, 2nd edn., Minneapolis: University of Minnesota Press, 1983, p. 91.

2 Ibid., p. 97.

3 Edward Said, *Beginnings: Intention and Method*, New York: Basic Books, Inc., 1975, p. 13.

4 Stanley Fish, *Is There a Text in the Class? The Authority of Interpretive Communities*, Cambridge MA: Harvard University Press, 1980.

5 For a detailed discussion of affiliation, see the relevant sections of Chapter 4 below.

6 Hayden White, "Criticism as Cultural Politics," *Diacritics*, vol. 6, Fall 1976, p. 9.

7 J. Hillis Miller, "Beginning with a Text," *Diacritics*, vol. 6, Fall 1976, p. 2.

8 Ibid., p. 4.

9 Joseph Riddel, "Scriptive Fate/Scriptive Hope," *Diacritics*, vol. 6, Fall 1976, p. 14.

10 Abdul R. JanMohamed, "Worldliness-without-World, Homelessness-as-a-Home: Toward a Definition of the Specular Border Intellectual," in Michael Sprinker, ed., *Edward Said: A Critical Reader*, Oxford: Blackwell Publishers, 1992, p. 97.

11 Ibid., p. 103.

12 Ibid., p. 113.

13 Ibid., p. 108.
14 Ibid., p. 107.
15 Ibid., p. 106.
16 Ibid., p. 108.
17 Ibid.
18 Said, *Beginnings*, p. 23.
19 Ibid., p. 6.
20 Ibid., p. 16.
21 Ibid., p. 83.
22 Ibid., pp. 372-3.
23 Ibid., p. 280.
24 Ibid.
25 Ibid., p. 12.
26 Ibid., p. 51.
27 Ibid., pp. 48-9.
28 Ibid., p. 49.
29 Ibid., p. 78.
30 Ibid., p. 50.
31 Ibid., p. 76.
32 Ibid., p. 51.
33 Two examples will suffice here. Linda Hutcheon approvingly cites Said's
    work (in conjunction with that of many other contemporary thinkers) in an
    attempt to theorize what she calls "a 'poetics' of postmodernism." The
    following statement is typical: "When Edward Said calls for theory today to
    have an 'awareness of the differences between situations' ... in its 'critical
    consciousness' of its position in the world, he is going beyond the early
    Foucauldian ... definition of modernity in terms of otherness alone. Dif-
    ference suggests multiplicity, heterogeneity, plurality, rather than binary
    opposition and exclusion." See her book *A Poetics of Postmodernism: History,
    Theory, Fiction*, London: Routledge, 1988, p. 61. On the other hand, John
    McGowan, who in his important book *Postmodernism and Its Critics*, Ithaca:
    Cornell University Press, 1991, tries to unmask what he considers to be the
    contradictions of contemporary "leftist" thinkers (who seem to comprise
    not only neopragmatists and postmodernists – like Rorty and Lyotard – but
    also poststructuralists and traditional Marxists), at one point avers that
    "Said's work presents ... the most extreme form of the literary left's
    postmodernist vicissitudes, but he is hardly unrepresentative." What he
    means by this is that, with the help of highly individualist, often anarchist
    formulations, postmodernists (like Said) declare war on universalist ideals
    on the ground that these ideals are hierarchist, ideological, etc. – but that
    on the other hand these same critics are in the end forced, however reluc-
    tantly or obliquely, to appeal to these same ideals. This kind of contra-
    diction is, according to McGowan, especially true of Said (hence the latter's
    alleged extreme postmodernism). McGowan is a careful and rigorous
    scholar, and his analysis of Said's theoretical and political positions is often
    illuminating. However, to the extent that he disregards what I have been
    describing as the dynamism of Said's criticism – particularly as that
    dynamism assumes a confrontation between an agonistic dialectic and
    archaeo-genealogy – to that extent he misrecognizes Said's work at the

metacritical level. In this respect, his analysis succumbs to the kind of static formalism that hobbles much "theoretical" discussion in Anglo-American circles – a species of interpretation which neatly dovetails McGowan's "tolerant" ideology of liberal humanism and the synthesizing, universalist holism that serves as his final court of appeal. My disagreement with McGowan is not so much that he embraces liberal political ideals as that he almost totally disregards the burdens of history and dismisses the powerful tradition of ideology critique which has historically acted as the main (if not the only) instrument to wage war against oppression. Moreover, his characterization of Said as a postmodernist is certainly misleading in certain respects – note what Said says of Lyotard's and his protégé's dismissal of grand narratives and of critical activism: "I've always thought that Lyotard and his followers are admitting their own lazy incapacities, perhaps even indifference, rather than a correct assessment of what remains for the intellectual a vast array of opportunities despite postmodernism. For in fact governments still manifestly oppress people, grave miscarriages of justice still occur, the co-optation and inclusion of intellectuals by power can still effectively quieten their voices, and the deviation of intellectuals from their vocation is still very often the case." See Edward Said, *Representations of the Intellectual: The 1993 Reith Lectures*, New York: Vintage Books, 1994, p. 14. As I will try to show throughout this study, even though Said's writing cannot be reduced to any easily identifiable version of postmodernism, it is nevertheless more acccurate to say it approximates Hutcheon's characterization than McGowan's.

34 Said, *Beginnings*, pp. 39–40.
35 Ibid., p. 39.
36 Ibid., p. 40.
37 See ibid., pp. 35 ff., for references to Descartes.
38 Ibid., pp. 11–12.
39 Ibid., p. 19.
40 Ibid., p. 11.
41 Ibid., p. 12.
42 Ibid.
43 Ibid., pp. 59–60.
44 Ibid., p. 48.
45 Ibid., p. 60.
46 Ibid., p. 19.
47 Ibid., p. 71.
48 Ibid.
49 Said, "Secular Criticism," in *The World, the Text, and the Critic*, Cambridge MA: Harvard University Press, 1983, p. 28.
50 Said, *Beginnings*, p. 66.
51 Edward Said, *Orientalism*, New York: Vintage Books, 1978, p. 12.
52 Said, "The World, the Text, and the Critic," *The World*, p. 38.
53 Said, *Beginnings*, pp. 65–6.
54 Ibid., p. 20.
55 Ibid., p. 23.
56 Ibid.
57 Ibid., p. 24.

58 Ibid., pp. 217–8.
59 Ibid., pp. 202 ff.

Chapter 3

1 Edward Said, *Beginnings: Intention and Method*, New York: Basic Books, Inc., 1975 pp. 83–8.
2 Ibid., p. 84.
3 Ibid., p. 92.
4 Ibid., p. 94.
5 Ibid., p. 135.
6 Ibid., p. 195.
7 Ibid., p. 226–7.
8 Ibid., p. 225.
9 Ibid., p. 236.
10 Ibid.
11 Said, *Culture and Imperialism*, New York: Alfred A. Knopf, 1993, p. 187.
12 Ibid.
13 Ibid., p. 188.
14 Ibid., p. 189.
15 Ibid.
16 Ibid.
17 Said, "Adorno as Lateness Itself," in Malcolm Bull, ed., *Apocalypse Theory and the Ends of the World*, Oxford: Blackwell Publishers, 1995, pp. 271–2.
18 Ibid., p. 273.
19 Ibid., p. 272.
20 See Said, "On Lost Causes," in Grethe B. Peterson, ed., *The Tanner Lectures on Human Values*, Salt Lake City: University of Utah Press, 1997, pp. 125–54; "Traveling Theory Reconsidered," in Robert M. Polhemus and Roger B. Henkle, eds., *Critical Reconstructions: The Relationship of Fiction and Life*, Stanford: Stanford University Press, 1994, pp. 251–75.
21 Said, "Adorno as Lateness Itself," p. 274.
22 Ibid., pp. 282–3.
23 The phrase is from Foucault's *The Order of Things*; Said cites it in *Beginnings*, p. 281.
24 Ibid., p. 336.
25 Ibid., pp. 336–7.
26 Ibid., p. 337.
27 Ibid., p. 323.
28 Ibid., p. 337.
29 Ibid., p. 331.
30 Ibid., p. 323.
31 Ibid.
32 Ibid., p. 291.
33 Ibid.
34 Ibid., p. 295.
35 Ibid., p. 283.

36 Ibid., p. 284.
37 Ibid., p. 313.
38 Ibid., p. 302.
39 Ibid.
40 Ibid., p. 310.
41 Quoted by Said in ibid., p. 285.
42 Ibid., p. 283.
43 Quoted by Said in ibid., p. 285.
44 Ibid., p. 286.
45 Ibid., p. 287.
46 Ibid., p. 301.
47 Ibid., p. 291.
48 Ibid., p. 292.
49 Ibid., p. 297.
50 Ibid., p. 357.
51 Ibid., p. 348.
52 Ibid., p. 362.
53 Ibid., p. 364.
54 Ibid.
55 Ibid., p. 366.
56 Ibid., p. 365.
57 Quoted by Said in ibid., p. 355.
58 Ibid., p. 352.

Chapter 4

1 Edward Said, "Secular Criticism," in *The World, the Text, and the Critic*, Cambridge MA: Harvard University Press, 1983, pp. 11–12. Titles hereafter abbreviated as "Secular Criticism," and *The World* respectively.
2 Said, "Secular Criticism," p. 6.
3 Ibid., p. 9.
4 Said, 'Swift's Tory Anarchy," in *The World*, p. 58.
5 Said, "On Originality," in *The World*, p. 133.
6 Ibid., p. 132.
7 Said, "The World, the Text, and the Critic," in *The World*, pp. 51–2.
8 Quoted by Said, ibid., p. 52.
9 Said, "Secular Criticism," p. 25.
10 A. R. Louch, "Critical Discussions," *Philosophy and Literature*, vol. 8, no. 2, 1984, p. 275.
11 Gerald Weales, "Books in Review," *Kenyon Review*, Fall 1983, vol. 5, no. 4, pp. 122–5. This is Weales's opening paragraph:

In the vacant lot behind my house groups of boys, a mixture of blacks and Asians, gather from time to time and smash coins with bricks. All of them pound with a kind of relentless deliberation, but there are variations among the pounders. Most of them are simply plodders, but some work with *éclat*, some with a quality very like wit. Their style fascinates me, but their motivation completely baffles me. Why do they want to

flatten coins? Is the process or the product the lure and, if the latter, is the value of the deformed coin aesthetic, mystical, political (anticapitalist gesture), or practical? Something of a pragmatist, I suspect the last of these; they may have found a way to alter a nickel so that it will go into the quarter slots of the Pac-Man machines in the corner supermarket.
Apparently this little tale, whether factual or manufactured (I am almost convinced the latter is the case), is designed to cover up Weales's total lack of insight and his knee-jerk conservatism. The smug dismissiveness manifested here is to be found throughout his review of Said's book.

12 Edward Alexander, "Professor of Terror," *Commentary*, vol. 88, no. 2, 1989, pp. 49–50. Alexander's attack on Said brought forth angry protests from distinguished scholars – many of them Jews (including Israelis). But others sided with Alexander. See "Letters from Readers" in the November and December 1989 issues of *Commentary*.

13 Denis Donoghue, "An Organic Intellectual," *New Republic*, April 18, 1983, p. 30.

14 William E. Cain, "Criticism and Knowledge," *Virginia Quarterly Review*, vol. 60, no. 1, 1984, p. 181.

15 Ibid., p. 185.

16 See Bruce Robbins "Homelessness and Worldliness," *Diacritics*, vol. 13, no. 3, 1983, pp. 69–77, and Abdul R. JanMohamed, "Worldliness-without-world, Homelessness-as-home: Toward a Definition of the Specular Border Intellectual," in Michael Sprinker, ed., *Edward Said: a Critical Reader*, Oxford: Blackwell Publishers, 1992, pp. 96–120.

17 Daniel O'Hara, "Criticism Worldly and Otherworldly: Edward W. Said and The Cult of Theory," *Boundary 2*, vol. 12, no. 3, & vol. 13, no. 1, 1984, p. 403.

18 Paul Bové, "In Defense of Edward Said," *Boundary 2*, vol. 18, no. 1, 1992, pp. 11–12; both here and in a letter to *Commentary*, vol. 88, no. 6, 1989, pp. 4–5, Bové comes to Said's defense against the forces of Zionism. In the *Boundary 2* piece, Bové expresses dismay at threats reportedly made in 1990 on Said's life by "elements of the party Kach." In the letter to *Commentary*, Bové responds to Edward Alexander, the author of the notorious "Professor of Terror." When Said's book *Culture and Imperialism* was published in 1993, Bové wrote a generous review of it in *Boundary 2*; (see "Hope and Reconciliation: A Review of Edward W. Said," vol. 20, no. 2, 1993, pp. 266–82; indeed the journal, which is co-edited by Bové, recently devoted an entire issue to Said (vol. 25, no. 2, 1998); in his introduction there, Bové is expansive in his praise of Said. The articles in that volume, along with an article originally published elsewhere and a recent interview with Said, were later issued as *Edward Said and the Work of the Critic: Speaking Truth to Power* by Duke University Press.

19 Paul Bové, *Intellectuals in Power*, New York: Columbia University Press, 1986.

20 Ibid., pp. 1–2.

21 Quoted by Bruce Robbins in *Secular Vocations: Intellectuals, Professionalism, Culture*, London: Verso, 1993, p. 155.

22 Catherine Gallagher, "Politics, the Profession, and the Critic," *Diacritics*, vol. 15, no. 2, 1985, p. 37.

23 Ibid., pp. 37–8.
24 Ibid., p. 41.
25 Ibid.
26 Bruce Robbins, "Deformed Profession, Empty Politics," *Diacritics*, vol. 16, no. 3, 1986, p. 68.
27 See note 21 above.
28 Russell Jacoby, *The Last Intellectuals: American Culture in the Age of Academe*, New York: Basic Books, Inc., 1987.
29 Said, "Secular Criticism," p. 26.
30 Robbins, "Homelessness and Worldliness," pp. 74–5.
31 Said, "Interview," in Bruce Robbins, ed., *Intellectuals: Aesthetics, Politics, Academics*, Minneapolis: University of Minnesota Press, 1990, p. 145.
32 Donoghue, "An Organic Intellectual," p. 31.
33 Review by Tom Conley, *Sub-Stance*, vol. 46, 1985, pp. 98–103.
34 Said, "Secular Criticism," pp. 2–3.
35 Said, "Linguistics and the Archeology of Mind," *International Philosophical Review*, vol. 11, no. 1, pp. 104–34; see particularly the discussion of Chomsky's critique of the war, pp. 111 ff.
36 Said, "Roads Taken and Not Taken in Contemporary Criticism," in *The World*, p. 15.
37 Said, "Interview," in Bruce Robbins, ed., *Intellectuals: Aesthetics, Politics, Academics*, p. 145.
38 Said, "Secular Criticism," pp. 19–20.
39 Ibid., p. 25.
40 Ibid.
41 Robbins, "Homelessness and Worldliness," p. 75.
42 Said, "On Repetition," in *The World*, p. 118.
43 Ibid., pp. 112–13.
44 Ibid.
45 Said, "American 'Left' Literary Criticism," in *The World*, pp. 174–5.
46 Raymond Williams, *Marxism and Literature*, Oxford: Oxford University Press, 1977, pp. 11–20.
47 Said, "American 'Left' Literary Criticism", pp. 170–1.
48 Ibid., p. 171.
49 Williams, *Marxism and Literature*, p. 110.
50 Said, "Secular Criticism," p. 23.
51 See, for example, Said, *Culture and Imperialism*, New York: Alfred A. Knopf, 1993, p. 14.
52 Said, "Secular Criticism," p. 8.
53 Ibid.
54 Ibid., p. 9.
55 Ibid., p. 10.
56 Ibid., p. 9.
57 Ibid.
58 Ibid., p. 11.
59 Ibid., pp. 13–14.
60 Ibid., p. 15.
61 Said, "Criticism Between Culture and System," in *The World*, p. 216.
62 Said, "The World, the Text, and the Critic," in *The World*, pp. 34–5.

63 M. H. Abrams, *The Mirror and the Lamp: Romantic Theory and the Critical Tradition*, Oxford: Oxford University Press, 1953.

64 Said, "The World, the Text, and the Critic," p. 40.

65 Ibid., p. 41.

66 Ibid., pp. 42–3.

67 Said, "Conrad: The Presentation of Narrative," in *The World*, p. 90.

68 Ibid., p. 93.

69 Ibid., pp. 92–3.

70 Ibid., p. 101.

71 Ibid., pp. 101–2.

72 Ibid., p. 97.

73 Ibid., p. 95.

74 Ibid., p. 103.

75 Ibid., p. 101.

76 Ferial J. Ghazoul, "The Resonance of the Arab-Islamic Heritage in the Work of Edward Said," in Michael Sprinker, ed., *Edward Said: A Critical Reader*, Oxford: Blackwell Publishers, 1992, pp. 160–1.

77 Said, "The World, The Text, and the Critic," p. 37.

78 Ibid.

79 Ibid.

80 Ibid.

81 Ibid.

82 Ibid., pp. 37–8.

83 Said, "Secular Criticism," p. 26.

84 Said, "Criticism Between Culture and System," p. 191.

85 Ibid., p. 184.

86 Ibid., p. 185.

87 Ibid., p. 214.

88 Ibid., p. 207.

89 Ibid., p. 185.

90 Said, "The World, the Text, and the Critic," p. 55.

91 Said, "Criticism Between Culture and System," p. 220.

92 Said, "Traveling Theory," in *The World*, p. 242.

93 Said, "Criticism Between Culture and System," p. 188.

94 Said, "Traveling Theory," p. 245.

95 Said, "Criticism Between Culture and System," p. 221.

96 Said, "Traveling Theory," p. 245.

97 See Paul Bové, *Intellectuals in Power*, pp. 25 ff.

98 Ibid., pp. 223–4.

99 Bové, "Introduction," *Boundary 2*, vol. 25, no. 2, 1998, p. 1.

100 See above, note 18, for details.

101 Bové, "Hope and Reconciliation: A Review of Edward Said," *Boundary 2*, vol. 20, no. 2, p. 266.

102 Said, "Secular Criticism," p. 25.

103 Ibid., p. 28.

104 Said, "American 'Left' Literary Criticism," p. 165.

105 Said, "Roads Taken and Not Taken in Contemporary Criticism," pp. 144–5.

106 Said, "American 'Left' Literary Criticism," p. 165.

107 Ibid.
108 Ibid., pp. 165–6.
109 Said, *Beginnings: Intention and Method*, New York: Basic Books, Inc., 1975, p. 19.
110 Said, "American 'Left' Literary Criticism," p. 173.
111 Ibid., p. 175.
112 Said, "Secular Criticism," p. 22.
113 See, for example, Said, "Opponents, Audiences, Constituencies, and Community," in W. J. T. Mitchell, ed., *The Politics of Interpretation*, Chicago: The University of Chicago Press, 1983, pp. 7–32. In a polemical jab clearly aimed at the theoretically self-conscious New New Critics, Said writes:

> Charges made against the American New Criticism that its ethos was clubby, gentlemanly, or Episcopalian are, I think, correct only if it is added that in practice New Criticism, for all its elitism, was strangely populist in intention. The idea behind the pedagogy, and of course the preaching, of [Cleanth] Brooks and Robert Penn Warren was that everyone properly instructed could feel, perhaps even act, like an educated gentleman. In its sheer projection this was by no means a trivial ambition. No amount of snide mocking at their quaint gentility can conceal the fact that, in order to accomplish the conversion, the New Critics aimed at nothing less than the removal of *all* of what they considered the specialized rubbish – put there, they presumed, by professors of literature – standing between the reader of a poem and the poem. Leaving aside the questionable value of the New Criticism's ultimate social and moral message, we must concede that the school deliberately and perhaps incongruously tried to create a wide community of responsive readers out of a very large, potentially unlimited, constituency of students and teachers of literature (pp. 10–11).

114 Said, "American 'Left' Literary Criticism," p. 167.
115 Ibid., p.159.
116 Said, "Roads Taken and Not Taken in Contemporary Criticism," p. 144.
117 Ibid.
118 Ibid., p. 148.
119 Ibid., p. 147.
120 Ibid., p. 163.
121 Ibid.
122 See, for example, Aamir R. Mufti, "Auerbach in Istanbul: Edward Said, Secular Criticism, and the Question of Minority Culture," in Paul A. Bové, ed., *Edward Said and the Work of the Critic: Speaking Truth to Power*, Durham: Duke University Press, 2000, pp. 229–56. In an attempt to rescue Said's conception of critical practice from widespread misunderstanding, Mufti proposes the thesis that Said's criticism can be described as a form of "Secularism imbued with the experience of minority – a secularism for which *minority* is not simply the name of a crisis" (p. 230). According to Mufti, it is for this reason that Said has been able to appreciate the work of Auerbach: "The German Jewish critic in ('Oriental') exile becomes, for Said, the paradigmatic for modern criticism, an object lesson in what it means to have a critical consciousness" (p. 237). While, as I have noted from time to time, the idea of exile plays a crucial role in Said's criticism, it is – I believe

– somewhat misleading to use it as a general model for his entire thought. Indeed, it has been my contention throughout this study that a more nuanced, comprehensive interpretation reveals that Said is a very complex, highly reflexive critic who has over the years evolved his own methodological consistency.

123 Said, "Conrad: the Presentation of Narrative," p. 92.
124 Said, "Secular Criticism," p. 29.
125 See Aijaz Ahmad, *In Theory: Classics, Nations, Literatures*, London: Verso, 1992, pp. 159–242.
126 Said, "Secular Criticism," p. 28.
127 Ibid., p. 27.
128 Said, "Swift as Intellectual," in *The World*, pp. 74–5.
129 Said, "Swift's Tory Anarchy," in *The World*, pp. 55–6.
130 Ibid., p. 54.
131 Ibid., p. 56.
132 Ibid., pp. 54–5.
133 Said, "Swift as Intellectual," in *The World*, p. 77.
134 Ibid.
135 Ibid., p. 78.
136 Ibid., p. 79.
137 Ibid., p. 78.
138 Ibid., p. 87.
139 Ibid., p. 84.
140 Said, "Secular Criticism," ibid., p. 27.
141 See, for example, James Clifford, "Notes on Travel and Theory," in James Clifford and Vicek Dharshwar, eds, *Traveling Theories, Traveling Theorists*, Santa Cruz: University of California Press, 1989, pp. 177–87.
142 Edward Said, "Traveling Theory Reconsidered," in Robert Polhemus and Roger B. Henkle, eds, *Critical Reconstructions: The Relationship of Fiction and Life*, Stanford: Stanford University Press, 1994.
143 Said, "Traveling Theory," in *The World*, pp. 232–3.
144 Ibid., p. 236.
145 Ibid.
146 Ibid., pp. 236–7.
147 JanMohamed, "Worldliness-without-World, Homelessness-as-Home: Toward a Definition of the Specular Border Intellectual," p. 100.
148 Said, "Traveling Theory," p. 238.
149 Quoted by Said in ibid., p. 239.
150 Ibid., p. 241.
151 Ibid.
152 Ibid., p. 239.
153 Said, "American 'Left' Literary Criticism," p. 174.
154 Said, "Traveling Theory," pp. 241–2.
155 Ibid., p. 242.
156 Said, "Opponents, Audiences, Constituencies, and Community," p. 30.
157 Ibid.
158 Charles Taylor, "Introduction," in *Human Agency and Language: Philosophical Papers I*, Cambridge: Cambridge University Press, 1985, p. 1.

Chapter 5

1 Walter Allen, *The English Novel: A Short Critical History*, London: Phoenix House Ltd., 1954, pp. 291–2.

2 See, for example, Edward Said, "Discrepant Experiences," in *Culture and Imperialism*, New York: Alfred A. Knopf, 1993, pp. 31–43.

3 Quoted by Lata Mani and Ruth Frankenberg, "The Challenge of *Orientalism*," *Economy and Society*, vol. 14, no. 2, 1985, p. 15.

4 Quoted by Nicholas Thomas in *Colonialism's Culture: Anthropology, Travel, and Government*, Cambridge, UK: Polity Press, 1994, p. 22.

5 James Clifford, "On *Orientalism*," in *The Predicament of Culture: Twentieth-Century Ethnography, Literature, and Art*, Cambridge MA: Harvard University Press, 1988, p. 260.

6 Dennis Porter, "*Orientalism* and its Problems," in Francis Barker *et al.*, eds, *The Politics of Theory: Proceedings of the Essex Conference on the Sociology of Literature, July 1982*, Colchester: University of Essex Press, 1983, pp. 179–94; Sadik Jalal al-'Azm, "Orientalism and Orientalism in Reverse," *Khamsin*, vol. 8, 1980, pp. 5–26; see my citations in Chapter 4 of various comments by Bové on Said's writings; also see Bart Moore-Gilbert, *Postcolonial Theory: Contexts, Practices, Politics*, London: Verso, 1997. Although these writers are not all (or always) hostile to Said, all of them aver (in different ways) that *Orientalism* is shot through with contradictions, prevarications, and ambivalences. Almost none of them have much of any significance to say about such important books as *Beginnings*, about the theoretical complexity of *The World, the Text, and the Critic* (a work which some of them cite selectively or in passing), or about what I have been calling Said's technique of trouble.

7 See my citation of Ahmad's assault on Said in the Introduction to his study, especially note 5.

8 Homi Bhabha, "The Other Question: Difference, Discrimination, and the Discourse of Colonialism," in Francis Barker *et al.*, eds, *Literature, Politics, and Society: Papers from the Essex Conference*, 1976–84, London: Methuen, 1988, pp. 148–72; see notes 5 and 7 above for citations of Clifford and Moore-Gilbert. Also see Robert Young, *White Mythologies: Writing, History, and the West*, London: Routledge, 1990, pp. 119–40.

9 Thomas, *Colonialism's Culture*, pp. 26–7; see my citation below in the sections on Orientalist discourse, Zionism, and imperialism.

10 Said's highly appreciative (but not entirely uncritical) commentary on Schwab is offered in an article, devoted exclusively to him, which was included in *The World, the Text, and the Critic*, Cambridge MA: Harvard University Press, 1983. (See "Raymond Schwab and the Romance of Ideas," in *The World*, pp. 248–67.) Another article in *The World* (pp. 268–92), "Islam, Philology, and French Culture: Renan and Massignon," is presented in such a manner that Renan's almost completely hostile representation of Islam and Arabs is contrasted with Massignon's genuine (though eccentric) attempt to understand and commune with Islam. Said also has much to say about Massignon's sympathetic treatment of Islam in *Orientalism*. The same cannot be said about Lewis, who (as Said tries to show in *Orientalism*,

Covering Islam, and elsewhere) has consistently presented Arab-Islamic culture and religion with barely disguised contempt (see, for example, *Orientalism*, pp. 315–21; also see my citation later on in this chapter). Said's sympathetic review of Hourani's *A History of the Arab Peoples* is given in "The Splendid Tapestry of Arab Life," in *The Politics of Dispossession: The Struggle for Palestinian Self-Determination, 1969–1994*, New York: Pantheon Books, 1994, pp. 379–83.

11 In the final chapter of *Covering Islam*, Said says this:

[A]ll interpretations are what might be called *situational*: they always occur in a situation whose bearing on the interpretation is *affiliative* ... It is related to what other interpreters have said, either by confirming them, or by disputing them, or by continuing them. No interpretation is without precedents or without some connection to other interpretations. Thus anyone writing seriously about Islam, or China, or Shakespeare, or Marx must in some way take account of what has been said about these subjects, if only because he or she wishes not to be irrelevant or redundant. No writing is (or can be) so new as to be completely original, for in writing about human society one is not doing mathematics, and therefore one cannot aspire to the radical originality possible in that activity ... Knowledge of other cultures, then, is especially subject to "unscientific" imprecision and to the circumstances of interpretation. Nevertheless, we can say tentatively that knowledge of another culture is possible, and it is important to add, desirable, if two conditions are fulfilled – which, incidentally, are precisely the two conditions that today's Middle East or Islamic studies by and large do not fulfill. One, the student must feel that he or she is answerable to and in uncoercive contact with the culture and the people being studied ... The second condition complements and fulfills the first. Knowledge of the social world, as opposed to knowledge of nature, is at bottom what I have been called interpretation: it acquires the status of knowledge by various means, some of them intellectual, many of them social and even political. Interpretation is first of all a form of making: that is, it depends on the willed intentional activity of the human mind, molding and forming the objects of its attention with care and study. Such an activity takes place perforce in a specific time and place and is engaged in by a specifically located individual, with a specific background, in a specific situation, for a particular series of ends. Therefore the interpretation of texts, which is what the knowledge of other cultures is principally based on, neither takes place in a clinically secure laboratory nor pretends to objective results. It is a social activity and inextricably tied to the situation out of which it arose in the first place, which then either gives it the status of knowledge or rejects it as unsuitable for that status. No interpretation can neglect this situation, and no interpretation is complete without an interpretation of the situation.

(See *Covering Islam: How the Media and the Experts Determine How We See the Rest of the World*, revised edn., New York: Vintage Books, 1997, pp. 154–6.)

12 For a useful discussion of this constellation of topics, see Laurence J. Silberstein, *The Postzionism Debates: Knowledge and Power in Israeli Culture*, London: Routledge, 1999.

13 See, for example, Said, "Traveling Theory Reconsidered," in Robert Polhemus and Roger B. Henkle, eds, *Critical Reconstructions: The Relationship of Fiction and Life*, Stanford: Stanford University Press, 1994, pp. 251–65. Also see Said, *Musical Elaborations*, New York: Columbia University Press, 1991.

14 See my discussion of "contrapuntality" below.

15 Edward Said, *Representations of the Intellectual: The 1993 Reith Lectures*, New York: Vintage Books, 1994, p. 40.

16 Asha Varadharajan, "Edward W. Said," in *Exotic Parodies: Subjectivity in Adorno, Said, and Spivak*, Minneapolis: University of Minnesota Press, 1995, p. 114.

17 Ibid., p. 115.

18 Ibid., p. 123.

19 Ibid., p. 114.

20 Ibid.

21 Ibid., p. xi.

22 Said, *Orientalism*, New York: Vintage Books, 1978, p. 12.

23 Ibid., p. 23.

24 Ibid., pp. 23–4.

25 Said, *Culture and Imperialism*, pp. 260–1.

26 Said, *Covering Islam*, p. 15.

27 Ibid., p. 13.

28 Ibid.

29 Said, "Introduction to the Vintage Edition," *Covering Islam*, pp. xi–xii.

30 Ibid., p. xviii.

31 Ibid., p. xxx.

32 Ibid., p. xx.

33 Quoted by Said in ibid., p. xxxiii.

34 Quoted by Said in ibid., pp. 32–3.

35 Said, *Representations of the Intellectual*, p. 83.

36 Thomas, *Colonialism's Culture*, p. 25.

37 Ibid., pp. 26–7.

38 Said, *Culture and Imperialism*, pp. 131–2.

39 Ibid., p. 44.

40 Ibid., p. 45.

41 Raymond Williams, *Marxism and Literature*, Oxford: Oxford University Press, 1977, p. 132.

42 Ibid.

43 Said, *Culture and Imperialism*, p. 77.

44 Ibid., p. 74.

45 Ibid.

46 Ibid., p. 18.

47 Ibid., p. 78.

48 Ibid., p. 52.

49 Ibid., p. 32.

50 Ibid., p. 318.

51 Ibid., p. 51.

52 Christopher Hitchens, "Preface," in Said, *Peace and Its Discontents: Essays on Palestine in the Middle East Process*, New York: Vintage Books, 1996, p. xiii.

53 Said, *Culture and Imperialism*, p. 295.

54 Ibid., p. 9.

55 Said, "The Formation of American Public Opinion on the Question of Palestine," in *The Politics of Dispossession*, p. 57.

56 Said, *Culture and Imperialism*, p. 283.

57 Said, "The Formation of American Public Opinion on the Question of Palestine," p. 57.

58 Ibid.

59 Ibid.

60 Ibid.

61 Said, *Culture and Imperialism*, pp. 8–9.

62 Ibid., p. 295.

63 Ibid., p. 288.

64 Ibid., p. 291.

65 Ibid., pp. 289–90.

66 Edward Said, *The Question of Palestine*, New York: Vintage Books, 1992, pp. 56–7; originally published in 1979 by Times Books.

67 Ibid., p. 7.

68 Ibid.

69 Ibid., pp. 18–9.

70 Said, "The Acre and the Goat," in *The Politics of Dispossession*, p. 34.

71 Said, *The Question of Palestine*, p. 84.

72 Ibid., p. 58.

73 Said, "An Ideology of Difference," in *The Politics of Dispossession*, p. 90.

74 Said, "Permission to Narrate," in ibid., p. 247.

75 Said, "An Ideology of Difference," in ibid., p. 78.

76 See Ella Shohat, "Sephardim in Israel: Zionism from the Standpoint of Its Jewish Victims," *Social Text*, vols 19 & 20, 1988, pp. 1–35; see also Ella Shohat and Robert Stam, *Unthinking Eurocentrism*, London: Routledge, 1994.

77 Quoted by Said in *The Question of Palestine*, pp. 89–90. Also see pp. 84–6, ibid., with respect to Weizman's pronouncements on the same topic.

78 Quoted by Said in "Introduction to the Vintage Edition," in *Covering Islam*, p. xxiii.

79 Robert Griffin, "Ideology and Misrepresentation: A Response to Edward Said," *Critical Inquiry*, vol. 15, no. 3, 1989, pp. 611–25; Daniel Boyarin and Jonathan Boyarin, "Toward a Dialogue with Edward Said," *Critical Inquiry*, vol. 15, no. 3, 1989, pp. 626–33; William Phillips, "Intellectuals, Academics, and Politics," *Partisan Review*, vol. LVI, no. 3, 1989, pp. 342–7; Mark Krupnick, "Edward Said: Discourse and Palestinian Rage," *Tikkun*, vol. 4, no. 6, 1989, pp. 21–4; Edward Alexander, "Professor of Terror," *Commentary*, vol. 88, no. 2, 1989, pp. 49–50.

80 Thomas, *Colonialism's Culture*, p. 27.

81 Said, "Introduction to the Vintage Edition," in *Covering Islam*, p. xxxiv.

82 "Religious Criticism," in *The World*, p. 290.

83 Ibid., p. 291.

84 Ibid.
85 See, for example, "The Splendid Tapestry of Arab Life" and "The Other Arab Muslims," both in *The Politics of Dispossession*, pp. 379–83 and 384–411 respectively.
86 Said, "An Ideology of Difference," in *The Politics of Dispossession*, pp. 81–2.
87 Said, *After the Last Sky: Palestinian Lives*, London: Faber and Faber, 1986, p. 36.
88 Said, "Michael Walzer's 'Exodus and Revolution' – A Canaanite Reading," in Ben Sonnenberg, ed., *Performance and Reality: Essays from Grand Street*, New Brunswick: Rutgers University Press, 1989, pp. 115–16.
89 "The One-State Solution," *The New York Times Magazine*, January 16, 1999, p. 39.

Conclusion

1 Christopher Hitchens, ed., "Preface," in Edward Said, *Peace and Its Discontents: Essays on Palestine in the Middle East*, New York: Vintage Books, 1996, p. xxi. See Emil Habibi, *The Secret Life of Saeed, the Ill-fated Pessoptimist: A Palestinian Who Became A Citizen of Israel*, translated by Salma Jayyusi and Trevor Le Gassick, New York: Vantage Press, 1982.
2 Jim Merod, "The Sublime Lyrical Abstractions of Edward W. Said," in Paul A. Bové, ed., *Edward Said and the Work of the Critic: Speaking Truth to Power*, Durham: Duke University Press, 2000, pp. 115–16.
3 See John MacKenzie, *Orientalism: History, Theory, and the Arts*, Manchester: Manchester University Press, 1995.
4 Richard Bernstein, *Praxis and Action: Contemporary Philosophies of Human Activity*, Philadelphia: University of Pennsylvania Press, 1971, pp. 81–2.
5 Bernstein's other books include: *The Restructuring of Social and Political Theory*, Philadelphia: University of Pennsylvania Press, 1978; *Beyond Objectivism and Relativism: Science, Hermeneutics, and Praxis*, Philadelphia: University of Pennsylvania Press, 1983 (arguably Bernstein's best book); and *The New Constellation: The Ethical-Political Horizons of Modernity/Postmodernity*, Cambridge, UK: Polity Press, 1991.
6 Bernstein, *Praxis and Action*, pp. 82–3.
7 Said, "The World, the Text, and the Critic," in *The World, the Text, and the Critic*, Cambridge MA: Harvard University Press, 1983, p. 35.
8 See, especially the following: Christopher Norris, *The Contest of the Faculties: Philosophy and Theory after Deconstruction*, London and New York: Routledge, 1985; *The Deconstructive Turn: Essays in the Rhetoric of Philosophy*, London and New York: Routledge, 1983; *Resources of Realism: Prospects for "Post-Analytic" Philosophy*, New York: St Martin's Press, 1997, *Minding the Gap: Epistemology & Philosophy of Science in the Traditions*, Amherst: University of Massachusetts Press, 2000.
9 Said, *Beginnings*: Intention and Method, New York: Basic Books, Inc., 1975, p. 40.
10 Said, *Representations of the Intellectual: The 1993 Reith Lectures*, New York: Vintage Books, 1994, p. 74.

11 Ibid., pp. 8–9.
12 Ibid., p. 25.
13 Ibid., p. 4.
14 Ibid., p. 5.
15 Ibid., p. 6.
16 Ibid., p. 5.
17 Ibid., p. 10.
18 Ibid., p. 11.
19 Ibid., p. 10.
20 Ibid., p. 11.
21 Ibid., p. xv.
22 Ibid., p. 17.
23 Ibid., p. 13.
24 Ibid., p. 15.
25 Ibid., p. xiv.
26 Ibid., p. xi.
27 Said, "Traveling Theory Reconsidered," in Polhemus and Henkle, eds, *Critical Reconstructions: The Relationship of Fiction and Life*, Stanford: Stanford University Press, 1994, p. 264.

Index